PRAISE FOR

Blue

is Just a Word

Anyone who reads this book, even those who have suffered through painful loss and endured the darkest depths of depression, will feel anything but blue. Despite the heart-breaking losses of his brother and wife and his subsequent gut-wrenching battle with depression, Robert Foster overcame these steep emotional challenges through an intense study of the cruelty and injustice of slavery, and the Civil War that brought an end to the inhumane institution. Finding inspiration in the struggle of the enslaved and the leadership of Abraham Lincoln, he broke the bonds of his own private captivity to embrace life with a new sense of purpose.

—Thomas A. Horrocks: historian, former Harvard and Brown University library administrator, and author, editor and co-editor of seven books, including, *The Living Lincoln, Lincoln's Campaign Biographies* and *The Annotated Lincoln.*

W9-BGJ-933

Aeschylus tells us that pain, which we cannot forget, falls drop by drop upon the heart until, in our despair, comes wisdom. This telling of searing loss allows us to be touched by jolts of grief that reminds us of the wisdom we may have lost in looking at the suffering of others from the distance of time. To understand today and the essential truth of the Civil War and its enduring consequences in the continuing suffering of those still denied human dignity, you must read this book.

> —Nadine H. Mironchuk: The Lincoln Group of Boston, The General Lander Civil War Roundtable (Ma.) and The Bull Run Civil War Roundtable (Va.)

Academic historians usually pride themselves on their objectivity and emotional detachment from subjects they study. Robert Foster's semi-autobiographical account of his wife's and brother's deaths, and American slavery reminds us that we are inescapably influenced by the events in our lives. In this fascinating story, his struggle to overcome depression not only provides deeper insights about slavery but a life-long devotion to Abraham Lincoln and the Civil War.

> —Dr. Thomas R. Turner: Professor Emeritus Bridgewater State University and editor of The Lincoln Herald. Author of *Beware the People Weeping* and *The Assassination of Abraham Lincoln*.

Blue
is Just a Word

THE CIVIL WAR WITHIN

Robert A. Foster

For information about this title or to order other books and/or electronic media, contact the publisher:

Book Architecture
One Richmond Square, Suite #112K
Providence, RI 02906
www.bookarchitecture.com
blueisjustaword@gmail.com

ISBNs: 978-0-9864204-8-1 (Softcover)
        978-0-9864204-9-8 (eBook)

Printed in the United States of America
Cover and Interior design: 1106 Design

Dedicated to one, who despite learning young what men are, loved them anyway. The greatest history teacher and lover of truth I've ever known. My mother, my friend, my guiding light.

And to my father, who later in life, received his master's degree in psychology for the pure joy of knowledge.

TABLE OF CONTENTS

AN OFFERING

If every life has a grain of truth to offer this tired old world, which
Abraham Lincoln once said needs all the help it can get in order
that we "disenthrall ourselves . . . from ancient dogmas . . .
that only make us squabble," then this is mine.

THE LADY
IN THE CASKET

Her mother, sister, stepfather and I arrived by limousine to enter St. Mary's Church in Lynn, Massachusetts. The magnificent choir organ whispered a sad, one-note-at-a-time melody of longing, remiss and farewell. Tone-wise, it sounded a little like the heavenly Hammond John Paul Jones played on the song "Your Time Is Gonna Come" from Led Zeppelin's first album which had been released eleven years earlier in 1968. No other organ ever sounded that good to me, except perhaps Steve Winwood's of Traffic, but still, the church's was beautiful in its own right. We were met by ushers who would escort us to the first pew as soon as they placed the casket in front of the altar. Being dignitaries for the day, we had prime, front row seats reserved for the funeral mass festivities. Many of the pews were partially filled and people were still arriving.

Each note of the music extended a little into the next with few pauses in between. Bach composed it that way so mourners wouldn't have time to feel abandoned. When the briefest of pauses did come, because every musician's hand has to breathe sometime, it reminded me that some of the most beautiful music ever written is found in the silence between notes, and in that silence

I was not alone. But when the sad procession of sound stopped, I was lost until the organ resumed its motherly coo, giving my heart something to hold on to. It was the sound of God weeping, telling us we were not crying alone, and it connected us to the millions who've been comforted by it through the centuries. Music has always been my lifeline, so I closed my eyes and meditated into it as we waited for the guest of honor to arrive.

I could make those organ sound comparisons because I'd graduated from St. Mary's High School ten years earlier and I was familiar with the way theirs sounded. Also, my brother David had introduced me to Jones's when he interrupted my eleventh-grade mechanical drawing homework to play Zeppelin's album for me. By the time the opening song, "Good Times Bad Times," was a third of the way in, my mechanical drawing went out the window, and long before the song with Jones's organ came on, the rest of my homework—except history—was gone too. We were in a contest, of sorts, that nobody could win. We'd introduce each other to the newest music to come out in the '60s. The week before, I had introduced him to Jethro Tull so we were pretty much even for that week. He seemed to be working at it a little harder than I was because I'd presented him with Jimi Hendrix a few months before and he knew he could never catch up after that. But he never stopped trying. Every time one of us made a new discovery, our homework became insignificant because this education was alive. Dave knew what I would like and vice versa. The only other person who ever understood me like that was now entering the Church. She was the Lady in the casket.

After she was wheeled between us, I embraced the Lady's mother, who was a stronger woman than anyone in the church realized, but I wondered how in God's name she was able to stand it. When the ushers finished putting the casket in its proper place, they turned to take us to our seats. As we waited, I took the mother's hand in mine and whispered, "She was a very unusual girl!" She whispered back, "Very!" This had been an ongoing thing between us the past eight years. The first time the Lady introduced me to her mother I noticed the mother look at her daughter with something of a laughing, surprised, almost disbelieving light in her eyes. It was as if it was a constant entertainment for her to observe and wonder what kind of new organic nuance or circumstance her third and youngest child would reveal to her next. I got the impression this had been going on since the daughter was born and the mother still hadn't figured out what this life force that had come out of her was all about. The fact that the Lady was her daughter and they loved each other and got along extremely well was beside the point.

Shortly after meeting the mother, I became her fellow Confederate; I too was trying to figure out the nature of her daughter while rebelling against every instinct that told me she couldn't be real. I simply couldn't believe she was true or genuine or whatever word one can use to describe the inconceivable. It wasn't love, infatuation, physical attraction, or anything like that at first but more of a *nah . . . this ain't right* feeling. But I couldn't stay away; the atmosphere surrounding her made me feel a freedom I'd never felt before. With her, you became like she was, even if it was against your will. And it never was, because she made you be yourself, even if you didn't know who you were. The only difference between me and the mother was that she'd made an agreement with herself years before to accept this person, this phenomenon, this enigma, or whatever she was and go along for the ride. She knew that, with or without her understanding it, it was going to take place anyhow. But I was new to this, and it never changed, only multiplied as the years rolled by. Now, holding the mother's hand at her daughter's funeral, there wasn't any earthly form of multiplication that could describe this kind of *nah . . . this ain't right* feeling of despair.

As we waited to be ushered I thought of the first time the Lady brought me to her home in the early fall of 1971. I followed as she floated through her front door. She never ever entered anywhere walking, she only floated. The shades were drawn as if to hide a secret and, though it was a sunny, beautiful New England morning, it was dark, dank, and cold inside. Wallpaper peeled off the hallway leading to the living room in an old house that'd once been a small chapel in the Cliftondale section of Saugus, Massachusetts. If we looked down from a nearby hill, the house was shaped like a cross and the hallway was the top part of a crucifix. Her mother was out shopping but the Lady wanted me to meet her father, whom she'd told me nothing about except that he was a good guy and had been in World War II. He was awake this late morning and I thought it might've been because of me. I also got the feeling it took great effort for him to get out of bed in a room located halfway down the hall, which would be the right horizontal arm of the cross. He was sitting in the living room where the boards of the crucifix intersected. The Lady said, "This is my dad," in the way a girl says it of a father she's proud of, but his appearance pulled the rug out from under me. By luck or instinct I told him not to get up as he attempted to do so. He said, "Okay, thank you." I shook a hand as cold and clammy as the hallway, then sat down while his daughter brought us glasses of water from the kitchen in the bottom part of the crucifix. Then she left us.

I watched him look at the clear, annoying liquid in front of him with childlike disappointment, trying to remember the last time he drank it. As he contemplated, I *somehow* thought of Abraham Lincoln stating water was his favorite drink and calling it "Adam's Ale," saying he didn't drink alcohol because he "didn't like feeling seasick on dry land." Lincoln certainly had a point, but as young as I was I knew it wasn't that simple.

Then, without warning, I found myself incapable of being fair in my assessment of this father. Out of nowhere, a sudden eruption of emotion ruined any semblance of rational thought. An unbeknownst instinct to protect—a protection the Lady didn't ask for or likely need, and that I had no right to offer—came from deep within me. It was tangled with my desire to make a good impression on her dad and it confused the hell out of me. And because confusion and I are a bad mix, I didn't know what to say or how to act while saying it. I was in over my head, and any chance of my knowing him objectively was gone. But then he picked up his water and I picked up mine. And as we drank, I realized that *this* father would make *this* most difficult sacrifice for *this daughter.* She was worth drinking this glass of "Adam's Ale." And so, we had something in common and that was a start.

My confusion was compounded by powerful guilt because ten months prior I'd come within an inch of losing my life in a horrendous car accident. I had been coming home from a music gig's after-party with my best friend when he passed out at the wheel. The crash was just as much my fault because, had I been driving, the outcome would've most likely been the same. We hit a telephone pole, sheared it in two, and then slammed into a rock ledge in Salem, Massachusetts at 3:30 in the morning. We'd been drinking like inexperienced, irresponsible, idiotic teenage boys sometimes do and came as close as possible to paying the ultimate price. All I remembered was the car swerved, I looked at my friend leaning forward, and before I could grab the wheel the pole was there. I woke the next morning in Salem Hospital in the most excruciating pain I've ever known. My friend was in the bed next to mine with a broken arm, cracked chest, and facial cuts. I had a dislocated hip, facial cuts, and *somehow* had lost a back tooth. The doctor told me my injury was one of the most painful injuries one could experience. I was in the kind of agony that changes a person. With my strange way of always thinking in musical and historical terms, I briefly realized the pain a Civil War kid in Blue or Gray must've felt trying to get back to his lines dragging twenty feet of his intestines behind him.

My friend was the kind of person who wouldn't hurt a fly. When the doctor slid my hip back into place in the emergency room, my friend could hear my screams and I knew it brought him unbearable misery. We'd had so much alcohol in us they couldn't give us the pain medication we desperately needed. I remember thinking, *This sucks!* followed by, *Never again, it's not worth it!* In the afternoon, we finally received medication and I was able to lay back to look at a hospital ceiling telling me what a nitwit I was. The next day, the police officers who had responded to the accident came to the hospital. They were only a few years older than we were and actually knew us because our band was quite popular in the area. They said they'd found us unconscious twenty to thirty feet away from the car. They surmised I went flying through the windshield when we hit the pole and that, because the driver's side door snapped off, my friend ejected that way. Neither of them had ever seen anything like it. One officer placed my shoes on my bed and said he'd found them on the car floor, perfectly side by side and still tied as if attending church. Before he left he said God must have a purpose for me because he couldn't see how I had survived.

When my parents brought me home a couple of days later they didn't read me the riot act in their usual, civilized, sophisticated way. Instead, they gave me a picture of the wreck from the local newspaper. It looked like a smashed-up accordion. My youthful stupidity had aged my kind and gentle parents by ten years. My friend and I were lucky we didn't kill anyone. The late hour meant the roads were empty and for some reason—our parents may have intervened somehow—we didn't get into trouble with the law even though we absolutely should've. Also, it was 1970 and things *were* a little different back then. The worst part of the whole ordeal was the look of concern and disappointment, in that order, on my parents' faces when they came to the hospital. Their first born had the ability to behave like a madman. No parent deserved that!

In light of the accident, not to mention the guilt and trauma that accompanied it, I felt very uncomfortable drinking "Adam's Ale" with the Lady's father. And although it was nice remembering the policeman say God must have a purpose for me, it brought little comfort because that could be said of anyone. But I wondered, if every life has a purpose, living the way this father was couldn't have been his. And God forgive me, I didn't want to, but couldn't help noticing his bluish/gray face, hands, arms and legs looked like water balloons about to explode. His purple feet were so swollen from being seasick on dry land that his slippers only covered three quarters of his soles. It perplexed, unnerved, and repulsed me. I was ashamed for feeling that way because I thought I was better than that but, in actuality, I wasn't even close. My shame increased as I realized that in no way did I feel threatened. I felt gentleness in him and a desire for him to say, "Look kid, it wasn't always like this, but it is what it is, and it ain't changing no matter what. I was in the war and saw things you can't imagine, not that that's my excuse." But he couldn't say that because he was in a trap of his own making. Saying that feels grossly unfair, but damn, when I'm honest with myself, which is rare, I can't think of a single trap I've been in that I haven't somehow created.

He and I were in a foxhole circumstance, with his daughter in the bottom part of a crucifix making lunch, and that dictated everything. I tried not to have the negative feelings I had no right to have in the first place, but as any nineteen-year-old might've felt in that situation for the first time, I was stunned. It's hard enough as it is meeting a girl's dad, and I didn't want to make a fool of myself just because I was thinking like one. It entered my mind that he most likely was the same age I was when he decided he'd earned the right to drink like that, but I had no desire to say anything about it even if I had known what to say. Still, I couldn't help wondering at what point it was that someone decided to up the ante to drink themselves to death. Was it a choice at all? If it was, how does someone make that choice?

As we made small talk—something I've never been good at or comfortable with—I wondered how alcohol could even be legal if it could do this to a person. It seemed every family I knew, including my own, was plagued by it to one degree or another. But I knew Abraham Lincoln was right when he said outlawing the substance would do more harm than good, even with the Temperance Society urging him to ban it. They said that the reason the Union Army was losing so many battles early in the war was because it drank too much. He replied to their well meaning yet unenforceable suggestion that that couldn't possibly be so because the Rebels "drank more and worse whiskey than we do." Of course he was making a joke about something he knew was a very serious matter, but he was right.

A century and a decade after Lincoln said that, the Lady and I were listening to a Kinks record with Ray Davies singing a song called "Demon Alcohol." A week later we saw him fall down, half lit, at a concert in Boston after he walked across the stage to punch his lead guitarist brother Dave in the face because Dave wouldn't turn down his amp. So maybe Ray and Lincoln were right, alcohol was a demon but trying to outlaw it would do more harm than good because people would fight over it. And maybe it wasn't the father's fault at all, maybe a demon snuck up on him when he wasn't looking. I just didn't know and still don't. For most people it's not a problem, but for those who are enslaved by it, it's so very sad. That much I knew. This was the first time in my young life that I was up close to a form of slavery and recognized it. It shook me to my core . . . . The father was a slave to alcohol—either by choice, inherited genes, a demon, the war, or God knows what. If I'd known then what being a slave would soon to do to him, and that in a few short years I'd learn of far worse forms of slavery, I would've grabbed the Lady and never stopped running from the cross in Saugus, but it was beyond my awareness. Somehow though, even then, I knew the only way to not become a slave to anything was to be true to myself. And if I didn't know how to do that, the Lady was already in the process of teaching me.

Just as I was about to wish a missile would blow up the foxhole we were in, the mother walked in with grocery bags. She looked at me and her husband with water in front of us and let out a loud, falsetto, ear-piercing laugh that sounded like a cat escaping a bag. Even the father laughed, so the jig was up. Their laughter indicated the father wasn't a physically mean alcoholic; a wife wouldn't have the freedom to laugh like that if he had been, and this lightened the atmosphere to a degree. His closed-mouth laugh showed there was love between them and also that they had an unspoken, sacred (to him anyway) understanding that she was his partner and accomplice in all this. He needed her and maybe she needed him to need her. It was a fate neither could escape. For the mother, though, it must've been against her will and this was *her* form of slavery. Her laugh brought their daughter into the stagnant room. Her entrance was a cool breeze that allowed me to breathe as if she'd brought me up from somewhere deep underwater. For the first time I realized I could depend on her to rescue me. That would *never* change.

I saw the groceries as a way to get the hell out of there for a moment because I was long past claustrophobic, and I volunteered to bring in the rest. This provided an opportunity to show my good manners, but really I was full of crap. When I got up, the mother insisted on following me to the car, saying we could get everything in one trip. As soon as we were outside she said, "So you're the new beau she's been talking about."

I said, "I'm nobody's beau, I just like hanging out with your daughter."

"Oh, everyone who knows her says that, but let me give you a heads up. There's a boy down the street who's been chasing her for years, and you wouldn't want to lose her to him," she said.

"Well no, I wouldn't want to lose her *friendship* to anyone."

Then I heard that laugh again. "You don't have to worry about losing that. Once she's your friend, she's your friend for life. She's very unusual that way."

"She's a very unusual girl in other ways too." I said.

"Yes she is, and you don't know the half of it!"

When we got to the car she opened the trunk and quickly got in front of me so I wouldn't lift the bag that contained four large bottles of cheap wine. This must've been an ongoing bi-or tri-weekly covert operation and she said, "If you could get the other two we'll be all set."

Just before I reached for them I said, "You said I wouldn't want to lose her to the boy down the street. Is that because he's a jerk or mean to her in some way?"

Another cat escaped the bag as she said, "Oh God no, he's a wonderful boy and his parents go to our church." Then, even though we were the only ones around, she looked up and down the street and got very close and whispered something no one was supposed to hear. "It's just that he's a Greek boy."

"He's what?" I asked.

"You know, he's Greek, like an Eye-tale-eon." (how she pronounced Italian).

I replied, "I don't know what you mean," because I didn't.

Then she got even closer and whispered from the side of her mouth, "You know, he's the dark-skinned type!"

This floored me. I couldn't for the life of me put together what was happening. Who talks this way? My parents raised me and my two younger brothers to walk away from racial comments and jokes. They taught us that people who said these things were ignorant and some were even dangerous. Yet here was a woman who appeared to be very nice, although maybe a little flaky, with what appeared to be the sweetest daughter in creation and a husband thirty feet away drinking himself to death inside a crucifix. This was different from what my mom taught us; this mother wasn't joking or commenting. She was warning me—a young hazel-eyed blond boy, whose appearance Hitler would've loved—that her blond, jewel green-eyed daughter needed protection because she didn't realize the scandal in being chased by—*hush now*— "a Greek boy."

As we carried the bags she expertly ignored the clinking bottles and I wondered how many other things she had to ignore to survive. A pillar of slavery is the ability to turn a blind eye. When we got back inside I inhaled my sandwich so the Lady and I could leave. As we did, I noticed a picture of her parents on their wedding day. Her mom was beautiful, like one of the singing Andrews Sisters of the 1940s and her dad was so handsome in his World War II army uniform. He looked like a young Burt Lancaster just before Lancaster left the circus to seek his fortune in Hollywood. I couldn't help thinking how happy they looked, and how slavery had changed that. Rod Stewart was right: *Every picture tells a story . . .*

The freedom outside was bright and sunny and I hid behind sunglasses, feeling like I'd escaped a nightmare. The Lady's disposition was brighter than the day and she said, "My father likes you."

She was not ashamed of her dad or house in any way and I saw how willingly she accepted the always shaky, unpredictable ground she must've grown up on, in a way totally without malice or envy of any other way anyone else had grown up. But damn, she knew the difference and it made me angry with that new, powerful, unexpected desire to protect her that would *never* go away. Her acceptance of her world was trusting and pure. I was humbled, awe-inspired, and a little frightened in a way completely foreign to me.

"Can I ask you a personal question?" I said.

She replied, "Of course."

"How often does your dad drink?"

"Well, he never drinks on Sundays because he's very religious."

"Is that why you brought me here today, because it's a Sunday?" I asked.

She made a melancholy face of resignation so damn cute that if you were driving down the street and saw someone make it, even a stranger, male or female, you'd stop your car, jump out, run up, hug them, never let go, and probably get arrested.

She said, "No, I brought you today because it's not a Saturday."

"How long has he been drinking like that?"

"I don't know, but you can ask my older sister when you meet her; she'll know. How come?"

"No reason," I said.

I never asked but years later, when her sister and I were sharing family history, she said she didn't know a time her father didn't drink. As an afterthought, with a far-off expression as if remembering something painful, she quietly said that, long before she was old enough to drive, when her father couldn't, he'd toss her the keys so she could drive him to The Crystal, a dive down by the Saugus River where he'd go in to drink while she did her homework in the car parked along the mucky riverbank where rats ran between tires. She had been twelve! Hearing this, it dawned on me that this father-child bonding ritual must've happened with the Lady and her brother too, when their mother was working, because she told me they learned to drive when they were ten. This history helped me understand the slavery dynamics that determined how her family lived, and it made me so sad. To this day, I feel a deep bitterness I'm only partly able to control by substituting anguish.

It's another pillar of slavery. It has direct parallels to American history; the way rich, slave owning politicians of the South risked the lives of kids from dirt-poor, non-slave owning families to do their dirty work in order to satisfy and

11

protect their addiction to their opulent, aristocratic lifestyle, which was created and sustained by their peculiar institution, slavery. Though 44 percent of Rebel officers came from slave owning families and their fighting for The Cause was arguably admirable, as sick as it all was, owners too cowardly to saddle up used religion and propaganda as car keys to throw at innocent, brainwashed white kids. All the risk was theirs and hundreds of thousands had their brains blown out for nothing. Slavery in any form is a lie, and saying "it ain't so, Joe" reveals the addiction that puts everyone connected to it in danger. It makes the master believe that every sun that rises and every one that sets is for his benefit because his society and religion have convinced him he's entitled. Slave-owning is *All about me!*

Lincoln put it best by questioning slave-owners who proclaimed slavery a good and sacred thing for slaves; he asked if that was so, why they never tried it for themselves or better yet, encouraged their children to become slaves. Also, why they never asked a slave if she liked being one. He answered the question they wouldn't and considered an insult to their honor, that their answer was an incredulous *No!* He added the historical and social facts that although "the Southern system is designed to keep the slave ignorant . . . the most ignorant slave that ever toiled knows he is being wronged." He knew a slave felt in every fiber that she was being wronged. His reasoning made those addicted to slavery want to kill him. One eventually did, and I was left to wonder if the Lady's father ever asked if she liked living as she did, but slavery made it impossible for him to ask, let alone ponder the question. My immaturity and growing affection for her made me see things the way I did, and I couldn't understand.

I didn't remember a single thing the father and I talked about that first meeting except that he knew and respected my grandfather, who was the Catholic Grand Knight of the Knights of Columbus in the town of Saugus. Being his grandson made me look good, not because he was well-known but because everybody loved him, especially me. Later when I told my grandfather of the father I'd met, he said he knew him long ago and that the daughter was right, her father was a good man, but my grandfather looked troubled and concerned saying it. When he met the Lady his troubled look vanished, but his concern still remained until she made it go away. She and my grandfather grew to love each other very much.

For the next few days I felt disoriented in my little world because of my visit to the cross in Saugus, though not because of the Lady who lived in it. Soon we found ourselves walking on a beautiful beach at Lynch Park in Beverly, where she picked up a stick and drew a heart in the sand. Inside she wrote T. L. F. E.

"Forever is just F, not F. E.," I said.

"I know silly," she replied, "but the T has the L and I don't want the F to feel lonely."

Then she asked what was wrong. She knew something bothered me so I blurted out what her mother said about the "dark-skinned" boy chasing her.

"I'm so sorry, that's terrible," she said. "It's because of the way she was raised out in Ohio. She was taught that if you weren't Protestant, Scandinavian, German, English, or Northern Irish, then you were to be feared. Her sisters are worse than she is about it."

"Well, what about your father, he's French Catholic, isn't he?" I asked.

"Yes. My mother's family almost disowned her when she married him."

"What are you, Protestant or Catholic?"

"I never thought much about it. My mother brought me to Catholic mass when I was little, so I must be Catholic."

"Why'd she bring you there, if she's Protestant?" I asked.

"Because my father's sisters are as uptight about religion as my mother's and we live nearer them," she said. This made us laugh to tears.

Then I said something I shouldn't have. "It must be so messed up having your mother think like that." I then quickly added, "I'm sorry, I didn't mean it the way it sounds."

"Yes you do, and don't apologize. I'm sorry you had to go through that after meeting my father." Then, with the wisdom of a historian, she said, "It seems messed up if you don't understand why she thinks that way. You'll never give her a chance if you don't understand. I hope you can, but I'll understand if you can't." Then she sighed. "It's the only thing about her I don't like. If you could ignore this, I know you'd grow to love her."

"I don't dislike her, but it's not right." I said.

"Of course it's not right, and you can tell her any time she says an ignorant thing like that and I'll back you up. I *never* put up with it," she said.

"How do you deal with it then?" I asked.

"Well for one thing, she won't talk that way around me because she knows I'll leave and not come home for a few days and that freaks her out."

"Do you go to the house of the guy from down the street?" I asked.

She laughed. "No, I go to my girlfriend's but I could go to his house if I wanted to because his parents love me and I love them."

"Well, what about him?"

She gave me the sympathetic smile one might give a naughty kid and said, "Didn't you see what I just wrote in the sand?"

"Yeah but . . ." I said.

"Well, that should spell it out for you, shouldn't it? Do you need a diagram too?" she laughed.

"As a matter of fact I do," I said.

Then I asked, "Hey Jude, can I ask one more question?"

"Ask all you want. It tells me who you are and lets me know you care," she said.

"Okay, I know the things your mom says are wrong because my parents taught me they're wrong, but how do you know they're wrong?"

"Well, let me ask you a question," she firmly replied. This was the first serious question she had ever asked me and I began to sweat. "How could they *not* be wrong?"

Then I asked, "Yes, I know that, but how do *you* know?"

It's impossible to describe her expression except to say it didn't include irritation or disappointment, which would've been well justified by my clumsy, arrogant question. Instead her face had more of a deep concern, as if for a sheep that had been lost for a long time and then just found.

She said, "When something is wrong, you can feel it in your whole body, and if you ignore those feelings you'll never understand what's going on. I can feel when things are wrong." Then she laughed. "Everybody can, even you."

Those last two words coming from anyone else would've wounded my fragile ego, but from her I felt an embarrassed sense of relief that I'd never felt before.

She said, "Good, you didn't get puffy, not that I thought you would. Now pay attention to how that makes you feel." She had me dead center, and from somewhere deep inside came the feeling that I could trust her with my every fear, hope, and dream, good or bad, and she would be able to sort it out.

"Can you feel when things are *right?*" I asked.

She laughed. "I'm here aren't I?"

I had no more questions. We spent the rest of that magical day at Lynch Park by the ocean. I had my acoustic guitar to strum and later we strolled through the beautiful Greco-Roman flower garden where I kissed her for the first time. It was October 4, 1971 and all was right with the world.

Continued Education
In Slavery

We began seeing each other every day we could. She'd been a gymnast in high school and was quite athletic so we did a lot of outdoor activities. I loved bike riding (still do) and she said she also did, so one day I showed up with a new ten-speed bike for her. She refused to accept it but somehow I convinced her to go for a ride. Well, she took off like a bat out of hell and I had to work hard to keep up. We did about twenty miles in and around Saugus and it seemed like every person we passed called her name.

With our adrenaline pumping, I yelled up to her, "Hey, how come everyone knows you?"

"They're my friends!" she yelled back.

On the way back to her house we stopped to get a drink in a little mom-and-pop variety store, the kind you don't see nowadays. As we were leaving, an older couple came in. It was the "dark-skinned" boy's parents. When they saw my riding partner the mother hugged her and they whispered something to each other and then both laughed. Then the father hugged her. You could tell they loved her and they were friendly to me too. As we were leaving, the mother gave me a look of approval one might give when one unknowingly arrives at the perfect moment to buy a warm loaf of bread just out of the oven. We got outside just in time to see a crook put her bike in a pickup truck, intending to drive away with it.

"That blankety blank stole your blanken bike!" I yelled.

"You mean, *your* bike!" she said.

We reported it to the police but never got it back.

Later that week we climbed the hill near her house as the "dark-skinned" boy was coming down. They hugged and I felt right away he was a good, kind, and intelligent person who was in love with my climbing partner. When she introduced us it was obvious it pained him seeing her with me, but also that it was important to him that she was happy. He seemed like a person who didn't have a selfish bone in his body.

"Are you going away to college next semester or attending locally?" she asked him.

"I'm going away," he said, and I got the feeling he'd made that decision at that very moment.

"Is he as nice as he seemed?" I asked her when we got to the top of the hill.

"He's nicer!" she said.

"Hey Jude, does he know your mom doesn't like him?" I asked.

"No way, I wouldn't let him know! And besides she doesn't really dislike him. It's weird," she said.

"Yeah, it *is* and it's even weirder because he's not any darker than me," I said.

"That's why my mother's way of looking at things is so bizarre. Even if it made sense in some freaky way, who cares how dark anyone is; what difference does it make?"

"Do you know that he loves you?" I asked her.

"I know," she replied.

"Do you love him?"

"I do, but he deserves someone who loves him like he loves me and he won't find her around here."

I was beginning to think I was with the most rational person I'd ever met. Her rationale had elements of intellect and large shades of experience to be sure, but it was solely based on a foundation of compassion and the kind of organic, innate virtue that couldn't be acquired by choice. If there's such a thing as grace, maybe that's what it was. I just didn't know and still don't. I was falling in love with this long before I fell in love with her because it would take awhile for her to teach me what true love really was. When I learned what it was, there was nothing separating her from her grace.

I couldn't help my growing frustration when I went to her house because I saw clearly it was her father's slavery that allowed him to let his house fall apart, causing his kids to literally have to scrape for food and clothing, to go without regular medical and dental care. It made me so angry! They were living like animals with absolutely no supervision because the mother had to do everything just to pay the bills, all the while keeping her husband from setting the house on fire if he fell asleep with a butt in his mouth. If not for her, he would've been homeless, there's no doubt! It's why, for the rest of her life, she'd look like she wasn't completely present when I'd introduce her to someone.

Women like her, married to husbands like hers, are never where they appear to be because their minds are always thinking of the next catastrophe waiting at home. Every ringing phone or distant siren puts them on edge because it could mean their house is burning down with their drunken husband in it. They can *never* relax. They'll breathe a sigh of relief and consider themselves lucky when all they come home to is something broken or the discovery of the occasional bloody tooth, found by accidentally stepping on it in a dark, dank house in which a husband is passed out in a pile of puke.

That god-awful blank look never dies even when the reason for it does. I wanted to tell people not to judge her by it, to be gentle with her, that it wasn't her fault. Because who can know the hell wives, husbands, and children live in when they or those they love are slaves. I told myself the next time I saw the father I'd give him a piece of my mind and tell him to put the cork back in the bottle and never take it out again. But then I'd sit with him and see he was oblivious to it all, or maybe that he'd decided somewhere along the line the quicker he drank himself to death the quicker his family could escape the slavery he'd put them in. If that were the case, he deserved some credit, but thinking that felt so very wrong, even while my overpowering desire to protect his daughter was too strong to stop the thought. I was learning slavery was a disease of the mind, body, and spirit, and it affected all connected. That they don't teach that in school is part of the sickness. Was I seeing the last stages of what slavery can do? Was slavery some kind of perpetual self-sustaining monster that fed on itself and the innocent around it?

Guys like Lincoln, Christ, Buddha, Gandhi, Fredrick Douglass, Lloyd Garrison, Mandela, Martin Luther King, Jr., and a thousand others who rubbed elbows with slavery said it was. But somewhere deep inside I was convinced this father was a kind, decent man, and my youthful perception was incomplete and thereby made it ugly. Would this someday be a window to help me understand that being a slave-owner and a slave were two forms of the same disease, like Thomas Jefferson said it was?

I'd seen the effects of alcohol in my family and others but never like this, and I couldn't reconcile how he wouldn't drink on the Lord's Day. It really got to me. Didn't it prove he could go along with the "one day at a time" and "higher power" philosophies that had helped so many? Maybe some people can't help themselves and those who think they can, can't help themselves either. Maybe we're all addicted to something. Was being a believer right and healthy for some, while being a nonbeliever right and healthy for others? Did the phrase "There but for the grace of God go I." have something to it or not?

The Civil War inside me didn't allow me to buy into the higher power philosophy, but that didn't mean I was right. And not having to be right was a freedom the Lady was teaching me. The first step was to be kind and non-judgmental, "lest ye be judged." That's how she was to every living creature and somehow her grace helped me keep my feelings about her dad to myself. Not having to be right was my first lesson in understanding what true love really was. It would help me see that wherever slavery's cruelty was, it must be faced with compassion that would unchain the chained, never with malice but instead "with charity for all." If there's malice, then you become the cruelty you're trying to destroy. Still, my desire to protect her was becoming too strong to contain.

Gradually, I learned that neighbors on both sides of the street cared deeply about her and her family. I'd see them looking at me as I entered and exited the house so I started to wave hello and they'd wave back. They were curious about what was going on inside because the youngest daughter was the light of the neighborhood. None knew to what depths the spirits had deteriorated for four of the five people who lived in the cross. The neighbors told me how very special the daughter was and how every person and house pet in the neighborhood loved her. I also learned I was not the only one who noticed she floated because she'd been floating around the neighborhood her whole life.

One kind and concerned neighbor, an official in the Saugus chapter of AA and a longtime friend of the father, told me, "For years I tried to help when I should've walked away for my own health, but I couldn't because of the kids. The little one"—referring to the Lady—"seems unaffected but I don't know how that can be. They've all suffered. The booze has the father by the balls worse than I've ever seen. Thank God it can't go on much longer. Before his disease made him do crazy things, like letting a ten-year-old drive, and before it was impossible for him to work as a custodian in the Saugus school system, he was a loved soldier who came home from 'The War.'"

Ignorantly, I said, "Maybe so, but his kids will suffer for the rest of their lives and that's not right!"

This wise neighbor knew far better than I if what I'd said was true. It made him look so sad.

One of the Lady's closest girlfriends and classmates, who to this day is my good friend, told me that for the longest time she could tolerate going into the house—the "House of Horrors" she called it—despite the smell and condition of the place.

"But eventually I could no longer visit because I couldn't stand how her father yelled at her, telling her to clean up his messes and make food that he'd pass out on while eating," she said.

"How does she respond?" I asked.

"She just takes it like she's taken it her whole life," she replied.

I had never suspected this, and the girlfriend said it was because the father was on his best behavior when I was around. She told me of gut-wrenching, embarrassing incidents his drinking had caused for her at various schools she attended, the worst in high school when some mean kids wrote graffiti on the walls about her being "Trailer Trash" because of her tattered and torn clothes, and how that cruelty became further exacerbated when she befriended a black male student and terrible racial slurs were added to the walls. They were simply friends, but she insisted on letting people think what they would because who should care if they were more? The violent, bigoted graffiti brought the police to the school to address the situation and, after it was removed, the Lady walked with her head high, just as she had while the graffiti had been there, during this time of tolerance, love, and flower power of the late 1960s.

I was about ready to explode because I thought, just when she needed a strong father the most to stand up and protect her, he was in the stinking bottle, and God help me I wanted to wring his neck, but when I came the next night to pick her up she met me at the door and fell into my arms crying, "My daddy's dead!" She cried as if he'd been the greatest father in the world. Maybe because he was the only one she had, or maybe because she understood love far beyond what most people can. It was the latter. Twice before he'd been given the Last Rites of the Catholic Church, but this time it stuck. The day before when I had come by he had been smashed, sitting in his chair with half its upholstery and springs hanging out, watching a show about the Red Sox while listening to Petula Clark music. He loved the song "Downtown" but "Don't Sleep In The Subway Darling" was playing while the irony surrounded us. History and songs somehow forever connect themselves to events in my life and always have. Right before his daughter floated into the room, he turned to me with far away eyes and struggled to say, "Always remember, my baby's an angel from heaven." I never spoke to him again. The memory haunts me still.

His death made me feel guilty and cruel, because maybe he truly was controlled by a master too strong to overcome. Did the system the family lived under share similarities to the system Abraham Lincoln said could only be justified by first deciding a slave was not a human being? Did an "angel from heaven" fit that bill? If you could justify that, Lincoln said, it's smooth sailing from there. But what I saw foremost were helpless kids and a mother lost in a sea of confusion, and I knew Lincoln was right when he said, "We can do better than this" while slavery said, "No, we can't!" When we can't, fathers of baby angels, like the old South, die long, terrible, avoidable deaths. It made me think of how a very young Lincoln first came to understand the attitude of slave-masters by asking a friend catching eels if it was cruel to skin them while they were alive. His friend replied, "No," that it'd been done like that for so long the eels were "used to it by now."

With God being my judge, if I am wrong—and I very well may be in saying the things I've said about the father—I am so sorry. My slant was one of youthful emotion because I was falling in love with his daughter. Even now I'm not capable of being rational about it, but I've told the truth as I know it. If something good can come from acknowledging the suffering these beautiful children went through by putting it on the table for those with a family member enslaved by booze, money, bigotry, violence, religion, or even worse, their own thoughts and ambitions, then this is what history does. These kids had no voice so I had to try. If God finds me wrong (and I feel I am), I'll live and die with that. But, I've found some comfort in the wisdom of Lincoln, that *the voice of the slave is the only one that matters.* And when that voice is not heard, another child pays because, as an ex-Confederate soldier named Mark Twain taught me, "In the end, it is not the loudness of our enemies we will remember, but the silence of our friends."

History teaches that when the strong remain silent out of convenience, indifference, or to avoid some personal unpleasantness, the innocent suffer. Harriet Beecher Stowe borrowed a phrase from the Bible to give voice to the oppressed, "O, ye who take freedom from man, with what words shall ye answer it to God?" It's that question that inspired me to ask one of my own in my youthful, clumsy way. *What do we say of those who take innocence from a child?*

When the war was winding down, Lincoln also borrowed phrases from the Bible to illustrate points to the nation and to warn future generations, "Woe unto the world because of offenses! For it must needs be that offenses come; but woe to that man by whom the offenses cometh!" Yet he cautioned it could only be understood by practicing, "Let us judge not that we be not judged." He understood far better than my miserable self that, "What you do for the least of my brethren you do for me."

In trying not to judge the father, I know I have failed woefully. If he were here, I'd tell him I'm sorry. Yet if his spirit is hovering somewhere slavery can't exist, if love is as blind as the poet says, and if he's able to see into my heart, he'll see that I loved and love still his daughter. If that's the case, loving her was my choice, and she took away some of my blindness by the way she loved her dad while Lincoln's words rang in my soul, *"Somehow* slavery caused the war."

I'm Always Meditating

Within a few weeks, the mother and daughter were back to their old selves. There was deep sadness, but it appeared that a burden had been lifted, particularly from the mother. I continued entertaining lingering doubts about her daughter that irritated the hell out of me. I still couldn't believe anyone could be as nice as she was, and I determined to get to the bottom of it once and for all by interrogating her with every trick question I could think of that would reveal some hidden part that just *had* to be there. The fact that she took no offense to my Perry Mason-ish inquisition and didn't tell me to get lost, didn't help. She actually took delight in my disbelief, and her mother thought the whole thing was hilarious. Every question provided her with great entertainment. If I got what I thought was a little too personal, I would preface with, "Now you don't have to answer this but . . ." Then she'd say, "No problem Shakespeare, bring it" and give me an answer with a look that asked, "You poor bastard, why are you torturing yourself?" She thought this was so funny it brought tears to her eyes. Finally I confessed, threw myself on the mercy of the court and flat-out told her what I was up to; that she just had to have a dark side, and that made her laugh all the harder, saying, "Keep looking, but don't hold your breath."

The last time I had her on the witness stand she reached for a cigarette. A lot of kids smoked back then. "Please don't light it until after I kiss you," I said.

"Okay, why not?" she asked.

"I don't like the smell," I replied.

"Why didn't you tell me before?"

"I didn't want to be a pain."

She then took the three-quarters-full pack of Marlboros over to a trash barrel and threw them away. She never had another cigarette.

"Why the hell did you do that?" I asked her.

"Didn't you just say you didn't like the smell?"

"Yeah, but I didn't ask you to quit."

"Well, I just did, and besides, they're not good for me anyway."

"Please don't do that for me," I said.

"I'm not, I'm doing it for *us,* and you don't have to like it. You've got to get with the program here."

Then she said something that ticked me off.

"You should stop your silliness and consider the fact that I'm really as nice as your good instincts are telling you. So do us a favor and *relax!*"

Now I was really irritated because I was usually the one telling people to relax. And I know quitting cigarettes is not as simple as I'm describing but that's exactly how she did it. She may have wanted to anyway, and was looking for an excuse, but saying that doesn't feel right because she was a person that didn't need an excuse to do anything. I had one last thing to try to get to the bottom of what in the name of God was going on with this "very unusual girl." And to do it, I needed to get her mother alone.

Like a secret agent, I showed up a little early the next day, knowing her mother would be there by herself. I asked her, "Do you remember when I met you a few months ago, and you told me your daughter was a very unusual girl?"

"I remember," she said.

"Well, I'm discovering that the more I get to know her, the more that description is exactly right. Can you shed any light on this? I mean, has she always been unusual in the way she is now?"

She laughed very hard and it was probably the first really good laugh she'd had since her husband died. She was a person who loved to laugh, and for the rest of her life I could somehow make her. "Well she's always been unusual, and I can't shed any more light on it than you can. I was hoping you'd figure her out and tell me," she said.

"Has she always been a good daughter? It seems she never does or says anything wrong to anyone," I said.

"Yes, she's always been good, but she's scared the life out me more than once."

"Like how?" I asked.

"Have you ever noticed the four small scars that look like puncture wounds above her left cheek?"

"Yes, but I thought they were birthmarks."

"Ooohhh nooo, that's not what they are."

Then she told me a story as unbelievable to tell as to hear.

"When Judi was five years old a vicious dog lived next door. It was always chained and kept behind a fence. Seeing the dog like that upset her because she said he was trapped and it made *him* sad. One day she was outside playing while I was making dinner when suddenly there was a pounding on the door. When I opened it our neighbor was carrying Judi and her face and head were covered in blood. The neighbor said he just happened to look out his window to see her climbing over the fence to approach the sleeping dog from behind. When she went to pat him it startled him and in an instant he snapped on her face, shook her for a second, and then let go. My neighbor saw this and brought her to me. I rushed her to the hospital and brought her home with bandages covering half her face. The next day I was in the kitchen and she was watching television. When I went to check on her she wasn't there. She'd snuck out the front door, and when I found her she'd climbed the fence again and was patting the dog. My heart sank and I called to her that it was time to eat and she got up like it was any old day and said 'okay, momma' and 'bye-bye, doggie.' When I got her home I asked why she'd done that and she said she wanted the dog to know she was sorry for scaring him. I made her promise she'd never do it again and she said she wouldn't. It was one of many times I realized she was 'a very unusual girl.' She never sees the bad, viciousness, or meanness in any animal or person. If she does, she says it's because someone must've been mean to them."

From that day on the mother and I used the term "a very unusual girl" every time her daughter preformed an act of kindness, generosity, or understanding beyond the scope of what would be considered typical of the most virtuous person. To witness her was to witness her spirit of giving *all the time* because it was an engine that never slept. She was indeed very unusual and was the only person I ever knew that wasn't a slave to her environment, culture, family, circumstance, or religion in any way whatsoever. The words "free spirit" are too understated. There wasn't a molecule of jealousy or meanness in her being.

When I think of history and why I really love it, I remember Abraham Lincoln saying slavery comes from "the meanness of man's heart," and it makes sense, because Judi could never enslave anyone for any reason. And maybe it's why it wasn't she who was unusual, but rather the rest of us. Now, eight years later, the ushers at St. Mary's Church had returned from putting her casket next to the altar to escort me, her mother, sister, and new step-father to our seats.

The first group of mourners we passed was kids from the neighborhood, representing every ethnicity the city of Lynn had to offer. They knew Judi from when she worked as a park counselor for a couple of summers. They were a little older now, and for some this might've been their first funeral. The girl crying the hardest was a tough city kid who could kick the crap out of any boy at the park. Seeing her made me think of the time I visited Judi at the park and arrived just as this girl was beating up a boy. As Judi was trying to break it up, the girl punched her in the face. I jumped in and helped the boy escape while Judi, trying to restrain the girl, was knocked down. The girl then turned on her and challenged her to fight. Judi replied, "I don't fight!"

Somehow that disarmed the girl and she walked away.

I said, "Jude, when that stuff happens, you have to defend yourself." It was the only time *ever* that she looked at me like I'd lost my marbles, even though I deserved that look a thousand times after that.

A few days later I visited her at the park again and not only was the boy there but the girl who beat him was as well. They were helping Judi with an arts-and-crafts project. Now, years later, this girl's weeping echoed above the others and the boy she'd fought had his arm around her.

If someone said the next set of mourners were real, live Confederate soldiers reincarnated from the American Civil War, along with their wives, mistresses and girlfriends, that claim couldn't be disproved by their appearance. Some weighed more than real Rebs of course, but their long hair, leather, and "self-evident" rebellious demeanor said more than words. The women had their tattoos covered and even though Judi was not the type to ever get one, she would have had no problem if Mick Jagger's tongue was sticking out somewhere in the church. Most of these "Rebs" looked like biker types in clothes they weren't used to wearing, but in reality they were musicians, poets, and road crews from various bands that worked in and around the Boston music scene. Not a single one had a mean disposition. The slightly more formally dressed were club owners who knew and loved Judi very much. The aromas of cigarettes and marijuana clung to this group, and it wasn't something they'd ever considered hiding. Everyone's entitled to a crutch at a time like this. Even the Church burns herbs on certain days of its calendar, and that's a crutch too.

The smell of pot, tobacco, leather and rock n roll made me smile a bit because I knew if you were a couple miles downwind from the real Rebs during the war, you could have smelled them too, as if they were standing next to you, not that the Yankees smelled much better. Hemp had been used for everything during the war, and the smoke-able kind sometimes wafted through the air.

What a strange thing it is that so many modern-day people don't want to think of Civil War soldiers on either side sitting down to smoke marijuana or read pornography, but at the same time have no problem imagining them getting drunk, reading the Bible, and getting into fistfights. The truth is that for some, all those things were true and, like now, could destroy a person when they became addictive. In other words, the book of Ecclesiastes is right when it says there's really nothing new under the sun. Those magnificent American armies in Gray and Blue were made up of ordinary kids far away from home for the first time, and some did things just like kids today. And who could blame them, going through the hell they did? It's why Lincoln knew the lessons of his time were for *all* time. It's a truth worth knowing, because it helps us honor *all* who die in war—Blue or Gray.

It's very strange that I knew of these things. For some reason, I've always loved reading about the American Civil War; what caused it and who the characters were. If someone at the funeral had told me that in twenty years' time I'd become the vice president of a Civil War Roundtable in Massachusetts and lifetime member of two of the most prestigious history organizations in America—The Lincoln Group of Boston and Lincoln Forum of Gettysburg—I'd have thought that person crazy. All I was really good at in school was daydreaming, thinking about music and girls (in that order), but I loved to read about the war from my earliest age as if it was somehow nectar to my being. And if someone also told me I'd one day be speaking to historical societies, museums, colleges and high schools, sometimes to standing-room-only audiences and other times to twelve crusty old white guys (nincompoops) waving little Confederate flags, wearing Rebel flag underwear and T-shirts with "Hurrah For Jeff Davis," "The South Shall Rise Again," "Long Live The South," "Hang Abe Lincoln From A Sour Apple Tree," and other such nonsense printed on them, after I drove two hours through a storm to get there, I wouldn't have believed that either.

And if someone had told me I'd be rubbing elbows with America's greatest historians, those on the other end of the spectrum from the lunatic fringe because they're rational lovers of truth, who *know* facts matter; that I'd hold my own with them in discussion groups; and that I'd have the honor of walking the battlefield of Antietam with Pulitzer Prize–winning Civil War historian/author James McPherson and later have the further honor to spill gravy on his shoe in a buffet line at Gettysburg, I'd have thought that was crazy too. More than a few prominent historian/authors have told me I see things others don't and that I should write about it. Only I know it's because I had the privilege of witnessing Judi combined with *knowing* Lincoln was right when he said the Declaration of Independence is meant for everyone. And only she would've believed it all because she told me long ago that people had an instinctive way of understanding me, even if at first they didn't agree, because I used historical facts and the human heartstring to explain my rationale, especially in regard to how racial stereotyping and bigotry were and are *always* wrong.

But it would've upset her deeply had she lived to see that on rare occasions friendly warnings have come my way. One such instance occurred during a break at a marvelous Civil War symposium at the Massachusetts School of Law. A professor from Mississippi, who wrote a tremendous book about Ulysses S. Grant, approached me during a break and told me that if I said the things I had earlier that day in certain parts of the South, I'd have to watch my back in the parking lot. I asked if it was because I wasn't telling the truth and he replied, "No, it's because *you are!* God bless you for doing it, just be careful!"

As bizarre as it is, even today, there are more people than can be imagined that hate Lincoln for saying the Declaration of Independence was meant to be true for all races. As children of the 1960s, both Judi and I would've been gravely disappointed knowing that, in solving the issue of race, we aren't further along than we are today, and in some areas, appear to be regressing. But again, back then, she would've been the only one in the church not surprised by the scenario my life ended up taking, while I wouldn't have believed it for a second.

The next group of mourners had brothers who were band roadies of mine. These Confederates were two of my dearest friends and as sad as could be. Never would I have dreamed that one of them would dissolve our friendship, unbeknownst to himself, when thirty years later, with his drinking and drug consumption out of control, just before the election of President Obama, he would, with all sincerity, put his drunken arm around me at our annual reunion and say, "Beau, I know you're into all that history shit. Can you tell me what's happening to our country where people would actually consider voting for a nigger for president?"

But at the time of the funeral, the thought of electing a black man was a far off dream that would've made Judi and I overjoyed. The other brother had already begun to dissolve our friendship by repeatedly saying he was proud there were no Jews on our road crew, even though I told him my first cousins on both sides of my family married Jews and that many Jews in Europe shared my mother's maiden name and furthermore that his own mother, who was a good friend of mine, had a maiden name that most likely indicated she had Russian Jewish blood running through her veins. When I told him these things he said, "Well, at least you ain't no Jew!"

These things bring clarity to who your friends are, that is, if you're into "all that history shit." The sad irony is that they worshiped Bob (Dylan) Zimmerman and were huge connoisseurs of the Three Stooges and Marx Brothers. And if they're not examples of indispensable, iconic, Jewish Americana running the gamut of genius to silly to genius, then there aren't any. And to add further insult, these brothers had a deep love and profound appreciation for the blues of black American musicians from the 1930s, '40s, and '50s up to the present day, and they could tell their history too. Missing was the respect these American giants deserved as human beings. Still, I'll always love these two misguided Confederates. I just can't hang around with them anymore.

Next came the Lady's neighbors and classmates from high school. The "dark-skinned" boy was crushed and looking like he'd aged twenty-five years. He wore the saddest face you could imagine. When our eyes met I wanted to reach out to hug him but there were too many people between us. His parents were next to him, shriveled and shaking. The family of our landlord, who lived directly above Judi and I, were next. They adopted us as their own; to this day I love them as if they were family. They were so sad. Here too, Judi's three closest lifelong girlfriends (and my friends too) crying, sadder than sad. We embraced because we had to. Then there was Charles with the longest hair of anyone in the church. He'd once been a roadie of mine and was one of the sweetest people in the world. He learned the practice of transcendental meditation at the time Judi and I met, and he was so enthralled by it he went away and came back a full fledged teacher and guru of this form of meditation. Judi and I became his students; if I ever had a crutch, then meditation was it. It's perhaps the most beautiful thing in life that I experience to this very day. Charles said Judi was the only one of all the hundreds he taught that he knew could say "I think I'm always meditating" and have it be true. We always laughed hysterically when she said it after a group meditation. And then she'd add, "No really, I'm serious," and the laughing would begin again. Charles would eventually cut his hair and become an outstanding compassionate teacher of special-ed students in the Saugus school system. He's a beautiful person and maybe he was right: Judi was one of the few that really did spend their entire lives in the moment.

It must be an extremely rare thing, but because I've seen it up close I can unequivocally say it's not the defect that makes most of us look to the past with regret and future with trepidation, but rather her lack of one. Lincoln used to tell the story of two preachers: one, a Northerner, pointing out a word in the Bible to the other, a Southerner. The Northerner asked if the Southerner could see it and was told "yes." Then he took out a coin and put it over the word and asked, "Can you see it now?" The reply was "no." The word was *slavery* and what Lincoln implied was that slavery couldn't be seen for what it was if it was looked at through the greed of man's heart. The only way to see it for what it was was to remove the coin. Judi never saw things through coins and seemed to remove them from those around her by simply being herself. So maybe she was right, she was meditating all the time because one of the most beautiful things meditation does—if you let it—is get rid of coins that make you blind.

Finally we got to Judi's family; the vast majority from her father's side of the family with every make, model and age of French Canadian Catholic you could imagine mixed in with my family in the second and third rows. The greatest role model a kid could have, my grandfather, was there with my grandmother. For me, he was the best example of anyone in the church of what a good Catholic was supposed to be. I could tell that this was killing him! He loved Judi like he loved his grandchildren. My grandmother's grief was just as unbearable because, not only did she share her husband's love for Judi, but she became one of Judi's best girlfriends.

The four of us double-dated often and, as I looked at them, I thought of the time we were in a crowded line waiting to get into a restaurant and I tried to sneak an affectionate pinch on Judi's behind but it was my grandmother who made a cute little squeak of appreciation. When I realized my mistake I got all red-faced and said, "I'm sorry, Nan, I thought you were Judi."

"That's all right, I thought you were your grandfather," she replied.

My parents had the look of people who'd recently lost a son in the same nightmarish way we lost Judi. They loved her very much and now were worried about me, their oldest son. My mother once told me Judi was good for me because we were so much alike. It made me realize that mothers are burdened with coins when they look at their sons, because I could only wish to be like Judi. It's sort of like Jeffrey Dahmer's mother saying he really was a good boy except he liked to kill and eat people every once in awhile. But other than that, he was every mother's dream.

As soon as we were seated the music stopped and I looked at the huge cross above the altar with a dead, bloodied Jesus hanging from it. In the silence I could tell by the way my grandfather was breathing in the pew behind me that this was too much for him. The cross made me think this kind of breathing must have occurred two thousand years ago when people found *that* scene too much to handle. This particular statue of a crucified Jesus was very familiar to my dad and grandmother. She attended St. Mary's grammar and high schools and received all her religious instructions within the parish. Her son, my dad, also attended St. Mary's for twelve years and got his religious instructions there too. I'd have twelve of my own with the first eight at St. Michael's down the street and then four at St. Mary's. So when I looked at the cross I looked at it from a personal family history perspective. This was a cross my grandmother looked at as a little girl and then my dad and then me, so it was in my blood. And because it was *about* blood, the suffering depicted had a particular significance this day because of the mind-numbing suffering I saw Judi endure. If there was ever a time to justify my pondering the meaning of life, this might've been it, but Catholics are taught that too much pondering can lead to sin; that we must "take things on faith."

The cross made me flash back to my earliest recollections, as vague as they were but still very real. I thought of seeing a dead, bloodied man above my crib. He was on the wall of my bedroom, hanging from a small, sky blue plastic cross. As soon as I was old enough to ask who it was I was told, "It's God and he died for you." At five and six, I began to wonder why anyone had to die for me at all. It gave me an uncomfortable feeling, as if I'd been assaulted, that got worse as my little kid instincts wanted to know more. When I learned in the first grade that it was more important to know Jesus' death was not only the fault of all of us kids, but my very own personal fault, it frightened me to the depths of my innocent being because I couldn't for the life of me figure out what I'd done to cause such suffering. Maybe it's how the concept of doing something unforgivable was first implanted in me. And maybe the eternal struggle created in me with the insistence that only someone else could atone for my sins by getting nailed to slabs of wood was how I became an official member of the neurotic human race.

Sitting there I thought of the books my dad exposed me to in recent years, suggesting there were many ways to know God besides this one of suffering, murder, and sacrifice. The image of Buddha sitting as if in the lap of God with a smile on his face made me wonder if blood and suffering were really necessary to know God. I was under no illusion life could be lived without suffering but it seemed most suffering was manmade and I wanted to know if *that* kind was necessary. It made me think of Abraham Lincoln at twenty-nine years of age, only two years older than I was, explaining in his first great (Lyceum) speech in 1838 that the problems within The United States were caused by a Civil War between religion and reason, and if reason didn't win out we'd end up in a heap of heartache. Now, this same war was inside me as I sat in a church named after the holy virgin mother of God. I had my doubts which were creating more guilt and it made me miserable; telling me I was a fool while I remembered young Lincoln saying religious passion may have given us a nation but in the future it would destroy us if it replaces "unimpassioned cold calculating reason." Reason, he warned, must become our, "political religion" or we were headed for disaster and a whole lot of unnecessary manmade suffering. Then the beautiful organ exhaled a somber note and I stopped thinking these things. And as the priest stepped onto the altar I got the feeling one gets right before an umpire says, "play ball." It was showtime!

Father Tom had grown to deeply love Judi over the last few months because he'd drop by to give her counseling and comfort. But the truth was, it was she who ended up comforting him and he'd graciously speak of it this day. For us in the front rows it was easy to see his eyes overflowing and for those not so close, you could hear his voice shaking over the speaker system reciting the words of the mass. I never saw a priest blow his nose so much. When it came time to say something about her he stepped to the lectern and it became unbearably uncomfortable because it took so long for him to compose himself, making us all the sadder but we were with him every step of the way, feeling his emotions as if we'd been in his shoes. (Lincoln's most charitable sentiment).

Then, out of the blue, for the briefest moment, a peace came over me. Looking at Father Tom with the giant statue of Jesus over his shoulder somehow made me think of Martin Luther King, Jr. giving his "Free At Last" speech with a giant statue of Lincoln over his shoulder. "Free at last, free at last, thank God almighty we are free at last." Judi was free from the most hellish suffering anyone could endure.

"Hallelujah," I whispered. She was no longer a slave! I felt an overwhelming feeling of gratitude and desire to thank God for revealing to me that maybe having *both* faith and reason on the same team was the best way to understand suffering in this world because it was embodied by the statues and people standing in front of them. But the moment of peace passed when my always imperfect perception of reality rebounded.

Not for a moment was I comparing the men those statues depicted, although a few philosophers and historians still do, but the logistics of where Father Tom and Martin Luther King stood in relation to them were too obvious for the strange mind that sometimes belongs to me to miss. Jesus, I was taught, said, "I am God" and did everything humanly possible to prove he meant what he said. Regardless of one's faith, that determination can only be admired. Lincoln, on the other hand, only claimed to be a mere mortal and not a very good one; even in Richmond when he walked through the fallen city and hundreds of people who were slaves just hours before and now were free praised him as their *savior.* It can be argued he was the savior of our nation (if anyone was) and he would've been satisfied in that as long as people understood his soldiers (his saviors) made it possible. But he never claimed to have saved a soul and once told a friend, "Imagine a blockhead like me being president of the United States." So I'm not comparing the two, but what they did have in common was that *they were not spectators!* Neither sat on the sidelines and both were murdered because of it.

After a couple starts and stops Father Tom said, "Sometimes saints really do enter this world and sometimes God waits till All Saints' Day to take them home, as he did with Judi three days ago. God wants to make sure *we get it.* Years from now, if you meet someone who didn't know her and you tried to describe her, they won't believe you. And how could they? I can't believe her myself and I'm supposed to believe these things. She was the most kind, thoughtful, humble, and virtuous person I've ever known. Those who haven't known her can't know what we in this church have felt in her presence." Then he stopped and looked like he couldn't go on. He wiped his eyes, blew his nose and for some reason God only knows, looked at me. All I could do was to give him a thumbs-up for encouragement. Somehow it acted as a lifeline to him and he said something that surprised everyone because we never thought of Judi that way but it was true. "What Judi taught me to know more than anything is that when the going gets tough, the tough get going, and she never gave up."

Ohhh Father, I thought, *you're so right in many respects but there's so much more to it than that.* For some reason I'll never know, despite being the closest witness to her life, suffering, and death and the way she accepted it with never a thought for herself but only for those around her, it would always be impossible to believe. Still, the words of Father Tom were perfect.

He then motioned for me to say a few words and, though I knew this might be a possibility because he mentioned it the day before, I had nothing prepared. For years I'd made a living of sorts playing music in front of people but the thought of speaking in front of anyone paralyzed me with fear. But the circumstances somehow minimized that fear. I knew how petty and selfish it'd be to succumb to it, so shame also motivated me to get up. Judi though, as always, supplied the courage. Standing at the lectern my heart was pounding and then the strangest thing happened. I became calm— something I never would've expected in a million years. I can't remember all I said but I confessed I had nothing prepared and wasn't going to say anything about Judi anyway. Instead I said:

"Here, *all know* Father Tom is right; sometimes saints walk among us. But I want to share what's in my heart. If someone had told me ahead of time that my relationship with Judi would end this way, I'd still have taken the path I did to be with her. But there'd be two things I'd change: One, she wouldn't have suffered the way she did, and two, it would be me in the casket because I don't see how we can suffer a loss like this. We need saints in this world and it doesn't appear there's many left. For me, being with her wasn't a choice, it was a privilege." Then I looked at Judi's mother and said, "She truly was a very unusual girl." I never planned to, but somehow I asked everyone to join me to give Judi a standing ovation because if anyone deserved it, she did. And that's what we did. When I got back to my seat I took her mother's hand in mine and Father Tom finished the mass with words that were a blur.

"What does it all mean?" was a question Judi never asked even in her darkest hour. She knew life was to be lived because she felt it. It was that simple. If some of the living and half living that day needed her helping hand to understand that, because that's what she'd been doing for all of us, where would it come from now? But a bigger truth I was unaware of was that nobody needed her hand more than me, and God, I need it still. Like a Robert of the previous century who wept at the death of his brave red-shirted general A. P. Hill toward the end of a war that decided what it means to be human in this nation, I was like Lee when he said Hill's suffering was over and it was left for him and his fellow Americans "to suffer."

But on this day, I couldn't spare any more strength of mind, body, or spirit to make another foolish analogy like that because later that night I'd need all the strength I could muster to perform the most important task of my life. Judi just so happened to have a "very unusual" daughter who had turned three years and nine months old on the day her momma died. My task was to tuck her into bed.

DAUGHTER & BROTHER

How does a father look at his little girl, much less know what to say, after putting her momma's body in the ground forever? And how does he answer questions that surely must come, unless there were none because she truly was the daughter of a very unusual girl? I'd lived a day that was all too real but knew I hadn't fully experienced it and wouldn't until I felt it, and I wouldn't feel it till I saw the face of Judi's daughter. The thought frightened me to the depths of my being. I wanted my expression to tell her everything was going to be okay, while knowing it was a lie, and I'd never lied to her before about anything. Truth, honesty, and openness were the foundations of our relationship from the moment the doctor put her into my arms. Of all the horrible, regretful, selfish things I've done in life, and I'm probably not done doing them, being truthful with her is one thing I've done well. It's something we *know* together.

But, being honest with her is not something I deserve credit for, morally or otherwise. It's a decision I made long before I had her. Partly because there's nothing to lie about and partly because it made sense to me when Mark Twain said life was easier when you told the truth because you didn't have to remember everything. My memory is so full of holes as it is and lies only make them bigger. This, coupled with the knowledge that Abraham Lincoln was "monomaniacal" about honesty, made me resolve to be truthful. It might be the only thing I've ever been practical about. My daughter could trust in it and I could too and now I was about to shatter it all by telling her everything was going to be okay. But when I peeked into my old bedroom, she, with the golden hair of her mother, was sitting in a curled-up kneeling position on a rug my mother had braided, quietly singing to herself in the off-key voice of her mother and combing the hair of her doll. Like an angel radiating on a cloud, she was waiting for me.

I didn't want to disturb her and could've watched for the rest of my days. But somehow I approached her and when she turned to me it was her expression that talked and mine that listened. She was the teacher and I the student, and although I'd never been a bright student, and despite being deaf, dumb, and blind with grief, I saw trust in her expression, like that of her mother who told me who I was so no lie need be told. She had no questions but only a smile, as if I'd just come in from planting something beautiful in the garden, an expression that said, "Hi Daddy. I missed you and everything *is* okay!" She didn't run or walk but floated to me in the way only a daughter of a woman who floated the earth could float. When she put her arms around me it was the first time in three years I felt safe and from somewhere deep I felt her mother whisper, *"It is finished! Into your hands . . ."*

I was half-dead with fatigue and the feeling of safety she wrapped me in was drink to a dying man in a desert. It was long past bedtime but my sweet little savior wasn't ready for sleep, so we played a game or two of the Parker Brothers game Sorry and then I read her a story. When I told her it was time for bed she asked if I would play one of her favorite songs before she slept so I grabbed an old acoustic and sang one about green beans. She loved the chorus that sings, *"I love you more than green beans."* Finally she became sleepy like most kids not yet four do and I tucked her into bed. I brushed her hair back and asked if there was anything she wanted to talk about. She said, "No Daddy, do you?" Dear Lord, "do you?" coming from someone so small penetrated my soul and I heard the word "no" escape my throat in the softest way it'd ever come out. She was rescuing me like her mother did. When her eyes became heavy I stared in wonder and heard the music of Paul McCartney: *"Maybe I'm amazed at the way I really need you."*

It seemed like yesterday that I was singing, *"Someone's knocking at the door, somebody's ringing a bell"* from another McCartney tune when she was tiny while I was bathing or changing her diapers, and now she was asking me on the day of her momma's funeral if I needed to talk before she went to sleep. Did she really understand Momma wasn't coming home this time? I was too tired to think it. When I bent down to give her a kiss she gave me a look that made me wonder how someone could so trust the wretch kissing them. Was that what innocence does and why I no longer had a clue what it was, if ever I even did? Her mother looked at me that way and I so often wondered if I deserved it. Now all I was sure of was that I wasn't sure of anything. In every living situation and now with death, even *this* death, in *this* life, I felt like the square peg.

I turned out the light and my little friend yawned "I love you Daddy."

"I love you too sweetheart."

She was my lifeline to sanity (Still is!). She looked like an angel in my old bed; she got it all from her mother. It's easy stating a truth like that when, as Lincoln had said, it's done "with malice toward none."

My other lifeline to sanity, same as in my youth, was my parents who were waiting downstairs. "In my youth" might be the wrong phrase to use because when I turned twenty I thought ten was my youth and if I make it to sixty, fifty might seem young. Maybe in our parents' eyes we're always in our youth. The logistics of the funeral and gathering afterward, meant it was easier for their granddaughter and me to spend the night with them. We'd slept there three nights earlier when her momma died because I had to pick out a casket the next morning and bringing the little one on that happy chore wasn't an option.

Now I descended the soft, carpeted stairs of my childhood home in the empty shell of a twenty-seven-year-old wifeless husband and father of a motherless little girl. The sadness in the eyes greeting me matched the concern for their eldest son. I'd always admired my father, and when I became one myself I admired him even more, but it was the compassion and understanding in the eyes of my mother and the little girl upstairs that made me think of Lincoln's sentiment that everything of value in this world he had learned from a woman.

"Are you okay?" my mom asked.

"I think so." I told a lie, or rather an untruth that was unintentional.

"Are you hungry, would you like to talk?"

"No Ma. I'm okay. I just want to go down to Dave's room to get some sleep."

"Okay, try to get a good one, and don't worry about getting up too early. I'm taking Anna shopping so you can sleep late."

"All right Ma, I'll try."

This time the stairs I descended weren't so soft and I didn't know I was a Confederate soldier retreating from Gettysburg but I was because somehow my physical self came through the last three days after surviving three years of hell, which led to my heart shattering in ways it would *never* recover from. If someone took a picture of my shadow as it walked that day it would show it "dripped with melancholy"—this was how someone once described the way Lincoln looked—and from that day on it always would. I descended those stairs in deep psychological post traumatic stress but didn't know it.

When I reached the bottom it felt like the first solid footing I'd been on all day; not because it was a basement floor but because it was the floor of my brother David's room and everything about him was solid, organized, and in place. He was someone who never appeared to be confused like me, a deer in the headlights. He didn't agonize over mundane decisions of daily life and never got caught in the minutia of it. He came, he saw, he conquered, but never destroyed or looked back, making sure to take stock and admire because he experienced each day so fully there was no need for him to reminisce or waste time on yesterdays. He *knew* things by instinct and could feel the way Judi did when things were right or wrong, but his perspective and approach in relying on that instinct was different in how he tested, trusted, and learned from it. Whereas Judi gently floated to it, Dave never floated toward anything but instead walked with both feet on the ground as if he were metal and the earth a magnet; he walked with a deliberation that was both scary and beautiful. Nothing could deter him from the clarity he sought and when he found it, it was done, and he'd smile an *"Is that all there is?"* smile. I was like neither of them in that respect, even if they'd differ in that opinion because understanding has always been sporadic with me until I think of them and somehow get a jolt or loving nudge from beyond to make me pay attention. I'm a hopeless dreamer and they never were. Between them I was safe.

When I introduced Judi to Dave he had none of the silly doubts I had about her because he saw instantly there were none to be had. Their first words seemed like they'd known each other a long time. In many ways he knew her better than I did. Later when I asked him what he thought of her he simply said, "She's great!" as if my question was a waste of air. His approval somehow gave me freedom to let go and allow myself to love her the way my heart had been telling me all along. Unlike the approval of a parent, *this* kind of freedom is what the bond of *this* kind of brother can give when it's founded not only on love, but respect. I loved my brother beyond words but my admiration went beyond that. Now, at the bottom of his stairs after tucking his niece into bed after I'd just buried his sister; his spirit was bonded with this room. When I was here with him and Judi and they believed I could accomplish something, no matter what it was, it was as good as done even if I didn't believe I could do it.

The first thing I saw when I turned on the light was the old board from the floor to the ceiling where our dad marked the height of his three boys on their birthdays. Behind me on a closet door was a poster of The Who's Pete Townshend doing his trademark windmill at London's famous Marquee Club, which would've done the nation of Holland proud had Pete been Dutch.

The walls of Dave's room, which had also been the music room for all three brothers, were a retrospective history of the mid 1960s to mid '70s with nothing added since May of '75 because Dave didn't live there anymore, or anywhere for that matter. He'd left the building four years earlier in the same horrific way Judi had. And now, in his room, I was in the only place on earth where my mind could drift freely between them without feeling as if I were betraying Judi because they were together. She'd scold me for stating it like that because *never* would she think like that. She loved it when I was with my brother because she knew he loved me like she did. Dave saw in me what Judi saw in me; what I've never seen but what their little daughter and niece sleeping upstairs needed me to. Maybe that's why I felt ashamed for the first time in this long day or maybe it was for simply being alive. Here, where they officially met, with their journey over, if my mind's eye saw or felt anything or was hallucinating, it was that both of them were "free at last."

Music bonded me and my brother as much as blood, and music brought Judi into my life. Out of the blue she began appearing wherever I was playing. Dave bumped into her a couple of times before I brought her home because he worked the equipment for the band and she'd ask him where we were playing next. She told him she liked the music but as soon as the last song was over she'd vanish into the night. One night though, after the last song, I saw her leaving and asked if she wanted to go for a walk on Lynn Beach. I was really shy and clumsy about it and she laughed and said, "Just because I like your music doesn't mean I want to go for a walk with you!" and she left. But she kept coming and somehow eventually we ended up going for that walk.

Now she and Dave were gone and I was alone, surrounded by the walls of this holy shrine covered with posters of The Beatles, The Stones, Brian Jones, Hendrix, Cream, The Who, Zeppelin, The Kinks, Jethro Tull, Traffic, Dylan, Buffalo Springfield, Crosby Stills Nash and Young, The Jeff Beck Group (with Rod Stewart, Ronnie Wood and Cozy Powell), Santana, Janis Joplin, Jefferson Airplane, The Doors, Spirit, Chicago, Creedence Clearwater, Quick Silver (with

Nicky Hopkins), Donovan, Van Morrison, Emerson Lake and Palmer, Pink Floyd, The Byrds, The Beach Boys, The Yardbirds, The Animals, Ten Years After, Blue Cheer, Yes, Genesis (with Peter Gabriel), Fleetwood Mac (the Peter Green version), Mountain (Dave did roadie work for them when they played in New England), Steely Dan (which a lot of people didn't know was the brand name of a dildo company), The Faces, Humble Pie, John Mayall, Lee Michaels, Grand Funk, The MC5, The Mothers of Invention (because of Frank Zappa), Joe Cocker (because of Joe), The Velvet Underground, Leon Russell, The Kings Of Leon (only kidding, KOL weren't born yet; some great songs though, so far. The Stone Temple Pilots, Foo Fighters, and many others would've been there too, using that rule), Jean-Luc Ponty, John McLaughlin, Chick Chorea, Stanley Clarke, Jan Hammer, and many more. There were posters of old blues masters too, like Robert Johnson, James Cotton, Howlin' Wolf, Muddy Waters, and Koko Taylor as well as early rock n' roll trailblazers like Little Richard, Johnnie Johnson, Chuck Berry, and Jerry Lee Lewis, because they inspired and influenced our heroes more than anyone.

There would've been more posters of Motown artists besides Stevie Wonder if the walls had been bigger. He just had to be there with songs as good, catchy, and clever as anyone's, including The Beatles; not that we compared them because, to us, music was art, not a contest. Not only did we love and appreciate the music coming out of Motown because it was as good as any by the bands we had on the walls and far superior to a lot of it, but it had the extra bonus of showcasing to the world that we had a wide variety of musical geniuses living and breathing in the USA; a lot of them recording in a little studio in Detroit. The truth was, it didn't get any better than Motown; a fact that stands today as it did then. It's a pure American, brilliant celebration of life and we knew it.

Scattered through the room were boxes of broken sticks, strings, and guitar picks Dave kept as souvenirs from his roadie work with Mountain. They were a great American band that did much more than just their big hit, "Mississippi Queen." Their second album, Nantucket Sleighride, is considered a classic. There were also kick, tom tom, and snare drum skins from the likes of Led Zeppelin, Jethro Tull, and Grand Funk Railroad, along with cracked cymbals. There were personal items too, like a drinking cup belonging to The Who's Roger Daltrey, along with handwritten set lists by various bands that passed through The Boston Garden, Music Hall, Orpheum, and the greatest venue of all, the old Boston Tea Party. Dave was in it up to his eyeballs because he was in love with the music. He was comfortable in the culture too, but never got caught up or addicted to it. Everything revolved around the music and he met the culture halfway, on his terms, because it allowed him to maneuver closer to the music. He never grew his hair too long, just long enough to say, "I get it!" He wasn't against the hippie flower power philosophy of the times but saw through it. He thought that those who wanted to turn it into a religion were only slightly more practical than those who didn't. To him, like it was to the musicians—the great ones anyway—it was all about the music. Everything else was incidental.

If I wasn't with him on a particular night, the next day he might mention some kid got his head smashed in outside The Tea Party by a policeman's nightstick. This would happen because the kid was either smoking a joint along with others as they waited in line and the policeman felt the urge. Or he got his head cracked for protesting a little too enthusiastically against the Vietnam War. That could be good for a nice whack from an ultraconservative crew-cut kind of policeman who believed America never made a mistake because he didn't know *his* history. Dave would tell me these things because he knew I was interested (always) in the social happenings of our generation or of any for that matter. Then he'd focus on what really mattered, the music.

He seemed to be at The Tea Party as much as those who owned the place. Once he mentioned a new band called Ten Years After that he'd seen the night before. They had a guitarist I "had to see" who was faster than Beck, Clapton, and Hendrix. They were doing a two-night stand and Dave handed me a ticket so I could go with him because he was going back for a second look. He said he never heard of the opening act but they were powerful and predicted correctly,

"They'll be headlining next time." They were the original Fleetwood Mac (with Peter Greene), a much heavier, bluesier group than the more recent incarnation.

Seeing them play a song called Rattle Snake Shake ten feet away through a thick cloud of smoke with volume so ferocious it rattled teeth and genitals while it shook flecks of paint from the low ceiling, was one of the most sacred spiritual experiences one could have. After, at the beach, Dave asked what I thought of the Ten Years After guy and I told him he was right, the guy was fast as hell and entertaining too but that didn't make him better than the other guitarists he mentioned. Actually, the other guys, I told him, were in another league altogether than Alvin Lee but Lee was a pro nonetheless. Then Dave smiled his wicked Dave smile that only our younger brother John and I were privy to, and said, "I thought that's how it was; that's why I wanted you to check him out. Tomorrow, when the store opens, I'll pick up Fleetwood Mac's album."

He relied on me to occasionally tell him things about musicianship but *never* if a song was good or not. His instincts and tastes in that regard were superb. We were the kind of brothers that songs meant everything to. If in its rawest form it wasn't catchy and emotionally stimulating, no amount of musical speed, flash, or dexterity could make it so. That's why he liked what he liked. His taste ran from the yearning beauty and simplicity of Dave Mason's "Sad And Deep As You" to the urgency and power of Jimi Hendrix's "Spanish Castle Magic," which, like a Tyrannosaurus on the hunt, took no prisoners. He was funny in his analogies too, as when he was a little younger than his Tea Party days and I observed him listening to The Rolling Stones for the first time. Mick's voice made his face cringe as if he wasn't sure if he was smelling something good or not. He asked, "Does that guy sing on every song?" I told him he did, and he said Mick was hard to listen to but he loved the raw power of the songs.

The next day I went down to his room and the great Stones version of "Mercy Mercy" was blasting from the speakers. He said he was getting used to Mick's voice because he "didn't have a choice" and that listening to it was like sipping beer for the first time—you didn't really like it but wanted another anyway. I laughed hard because he nailed my feelings too. He became a huge Stones fan, and when I thought of his analogy I smiled because it reminded me that of all the kids we hung out with, he was the one who liked beer or any alcohol the least. He said, "Why make yourself stupider than you have to be?" He never got much into pot either; he thought it was boring.

I picked up a percussion instrument, a shaker I still have, that Chris Wood of Traffic gave Dave at The Tea Party, and I looked at miscellaneous posters of the times. There was one of Black Panther Huey Newton and the so-called flower power representative Timothy Leary and The Beatles one-time meditation guru Maharishi Mahesh Yogi. We had Leary on the wall not for the philosophy he espoused or because he was an icon of the '60s but because The Beatles wrote two songs about him. And although our parents would've been gravely concerned had they known the extent to which we experimented with psychedelics, Dave and I did "tune out and turn on" more than a few times in the manner Leary suggested. I'm not for a minute saying this was good or bad; it was simply part of the dangerous Vietnam times we lived in. Danger then, like now, was all around.

For me, in the deepest, most beautiful ways, when I began practicing meditation I found what I needed, and Leary's suggested way to enlightenment went out the window with no regrets for having tried it because I *did* learn things. I'm an extremely curious person and my curiosity was satisfied. Meditation doesn't solve everything but can be a key tool to finding genuineness. The more you find the more satisfying meditation can be and vice versa, and that's pretty cool. In a nutshell, it's the opposite of slavery!

I had quite a laugh reading that the great author and philosopher Aldous Huxley, a friend of Leary's, once said Leary could be brilliant but most of the time acted like a pompous twit. Dave always said Leary seemed phony and I thought so too, but I was a kid so what did I know? But I *did* know from experience that meditation *could* allow for the purest form of consciousness, even though I felt Maharishi was a strange little dude in so many ways. I was feeling that even before The Beatles came back from India and John Lennon said they felt "duped" because Maharishi was not the selfless benefactor of mankind he portrayed himself to be. But I felt a "God bless you, John" in my heart toward Lennon for saying the practice of meditation was a beautiful and powerful thing and you didn't have to rely on anyone, particularly a Maharishi, for that. Lennon, like the Dalai Lama, whom I love and admire deeply, told the truth that one must become one's own guru and teacher. I became even more "turned off" when Maharishi allowed his followers to practically worship him because one of meditation's best tools is gaining the insight to see that if you blindly follow anyone for any reason, you're lost because you've allowed yourself to become a slave. For me, meditation was and always will be *freedom* and in my case, freedom from the biggest oppressor of my happiness I've ever known, *me!*

I fell in love with the effect it had on my overall outlook and maintenance of my existence while the increasingly hard sell sales pitch to bring it to the masses grew more disturbing. As the price tag of taking a course in meditation went up, so did the flakiness. It was distressing when Maharishi began telling his followers they could actually levitate off the ground when they reached the deepest state of meditation. If he had said that deep meditation could bring one to a lightness of being where one finds inner peace so profound it feels like one's spirit could float with joy, I'd concur completely—but he wasn't saying that. Instead he was saying you could literally, physically levitate. I made doubly sure by asking meditation instructors if that's what he meant and it was the only time these kind, well-meaning instructors couldn't look me in the eye. It was a fraudulent, cruel hoax; equivalent to saying eating Fruit Loops during a solar eclipse could cure cancer making some innocent, gullible souls discontinue life-saving chemo. It made me sad for wonderful, duped, instructors; my friends, who had to profess this nonsense. It turned off many thousands if not millions to the idea of meditation. I became suspicious of Maharishi's intentions because his discomforting ideas were getting in the way of his one good one, which wasn't actually his but a very ancient and beautiful one, which was simply to meditate to experience clarity of thought, thereby creating wisdom to reason clearly which then induces compassionate activity that is healthy to all.

Lincoln once said the only thing necessary to solve the troubles of the world was for "right thinking men" to come to the fore, and now a little more than a hundred years later, in the confusing times of Vietnam and flower power, when everyone was searching for ways to make sense of it all, I decided Maharishi was not a "right thinking man." As for flying meditators, I was quite certain guys like Isaac Newton, Copernicus, Galileo, Da Vinci, Carl Sagan, Einstein, Hubble, Hawkins, and many others had already explained how gravity worked. And people ranging from Thaddeus Lowe, the great Union Civil War balloon-ist, to the Wright Brothers to Chuck Yeager simply proved that these "right thinking" scientists were correct. I always felt that if people claimed they could write beautiful music they should at least let someone hear a song they wrote, so Maharishi should have someone see him fly, but he never showed himself or anyone flying. Hopping is not flying. I never saw any flying meditators in "my end of the vineyard," as Lincoln would say, and there certainly were plenty of meditators around. But maybe I'm wrong and they're flying somewhere, keeping air traffic controllers busy.

My other concern was how Maharishi preached that one could change the world by simply meditating. This reminded me of being taught that Christian monks could live a cloistered life of silence, obedience, and prayer, while also making great jam, and by doing so could change the world. I saw nothing wrong then, or now, in living that lifestyle, but when the dam up the road from the monastery is about to break, no amount of meditation and prayer is going to plug the leak. Someone has to get up off their knees and cushions to go down and stick their finger in the hole, or it's kaput for everyone. Meditation *does* change our internal world yet it isn't (only) about that. And although in some ways it is, knowing the extent is an individual thing. Mostly and hopefully, meditation can give one strength to turn the insight and wisdom one may discover into action to change the world using the physical laws of nature Newton, Einstein,

Hawkins, and company identified. And if that's not one's cup of tea, then to know the difference and do no harm. But again, I was a kid so what did I know?

Dave, on the other hand, *did know* and wasn't a spectator! He understood the value of meditation and would be the first one down the road to plug the leak and not just because he liked the jam the monks made. He dismissed Maharishi's silly pronouncements out of hand, and though he learned transcendental meditation the same time I did, he was one of those rare people you felt didn't need it as much as a more confused, insecure person like his older brother did and still does. But what I did know, despite my naivety, was the 1960s, like the 1860s, were both "the best and worst of times" because "right thinking men" like Dave knew "all men are created equal" while others didn't believe it.

In some unexplainable way, Dave lived as if he sensed his lifespan would be short. When we indulged in the late '60s and early '70s, he didn't go gently but went with a reckless abandon to let the chips fall where they would. Leary's method of opening "Doors of Perception" was perhaps the most reckless indulgence, but we were a generation of Confederates rebelling against things we instinctively knew were a lie. That Vietnam was a good and just war was the most serious lie, and that if you smoked a single joint of pot your children would be born with two heads was one of the more ridiculous. Lied to in the gamut of these extremes, mistrust and rebellion were inevitable. No one knew how powerful LSD was unless they tried it, and the promise or illusion of mind expansion was too enticing for many of the curious-minded to resist. It seemed almost everyone deep into the music scene in our neck of the woods was experimenting with it or had friends who were. Somehow it hovered over our generation.

When others were crying, rolling on the floor, begging for mercy after popping half of what Dave popped, he'd look at me (completely scared out of my wits) with a look that said *"isn't this interesting, let's make sure nobody gets hurt."* And when more of the lysergic acid, the key ingredient in LSD that produces effects similar to chemicals found in fungi used by various cultures for thousands of years as a right of passage and in religious ceremonies, began infiltrating sections of our young brains that'd never been infiltrated by anything, some of our friends would moan and make promises to God that if they ever got out of this alive, they'd never do it again. Then Dave, true to his nature, would ratchet it up by putting on Jimi Hendrix's first album so we could hear Jimi sing the question *"Have you ever been experienced?"* because not only did Hendrix put the question starkly, nakedly before us, but the sheer magnificence and audacity of his music made it impossible to hide or run no matter how fast or clever you thought you were. Some of his songs were beautiful, majestic, and gentle, capturing how peaceful things could be, but others told how frightening things actually were by capturing the violence of bombs, napalm, machine guns, and Agent Orange killing needlessly in Vietnam while bigotry killed the innocent at home.

Jimi said the reason people fought was because they struggled with an internal Civil War within themselves caused by what they'd been taught to believe. And because they didn't know how to deal with it, they ended up turning on each other. His message was that of Buddha, Jesus, Mohammed, and all the great sages throughout history. He knew truth because, as a young black man with a guitar who'd served in the 21st Army Airborne, he'd *experienced* the backhand slap of life in America. If 6 wasn't 9 but it *"turned out"* that for him it had to be in order to walk his path, *"I don't mind, I don't mind!"* He held a mirror up to ultra right wing conservatives shouting, "Kill the commie bastards and while you're at it, kill the hippies too!" And in that same mirror were ultra left wing, hippie-dippie liberals, putting down, with some spitting and throwing rocks at the poor kids coming home from the war in mangled physical and spiritual pieces, so there were two sides to the coin, like there always are. But he loved his country and showed how much by honoring it at Woodstock, playing the national anthem in the way only he could. And if he'd had to choose sides he'd have sided with the kids coming home from war who put flowers in their hair to let their *"freak flags fly,"* because no one can know what war is unless they've been in it. All he wanted was to make music and spread the message that if we surrendered to love, we'd find a better way. And even then, as young as we were, Dave and I chose Jimi's side because we could feel the hypocrisy of both sides. And, because of the way our mother raised us, we saw Jimi for the beautiful human he was, flaws and all, and not the spectacle he felt he had to portray, for a while anyway. When the chips were down, as they were for this misguided generation, we wore the uniform of flowers and peace just like Jimi, and in my heart I always will.

Like Jimi's music, Dave didn't pussyfoot around. This was his music because it had the urgency of now, which it had to have because taking it slowly meant more kids would die for nothing. The intensity was too hard for some to take, even the most flowery of the flower power generation who went the Grateful Dead route that would've bored us to death. When Dave put the needle in the groove for the opening notes you could feel people thinking, "Oh no, not this," because a part of you felt that way too. And when someone got up saying, "I can't take this," Dave would gently reply, "Stay awhile, it'll be all right!" and they would until they were all right. But someone might slip away in the confusion to run down the street and later be taken into protective custody for trying and succeeding at having sexual relations with a Volkswagen Beetle. After all, they were cute little cars and the medicine man preached correctly, that everything—rocks, water, rubber and steel—came alive and brewed together with plants, animals, spirits, and people to become "the soup of the universe." Separation between physical and nonphysical concepts, the past, present, future, and every conceivable religious and scientific perception were obliterated. *Everything* became one and even dust to dust was okay as long as someone wasn't in the car getting its hood humped. That way you wouldn't get into too much trouble, but still you didn't want to get caught because you'd never hear the end of it, especially if it got in the papers.

Then again, if someone was inside the "Bug" that wasn't necessarily a bad thing either, if it wasn't a family coming home from church that is, because the psychedelically induced desire to sexually melt into inanimate objects sometimes brought husbands, wives, boyfriends and girlfriends together that would've never met otherwise. And at the very least, they'd always have a story to tell their grandchildren of how Nana and Pa met. Marriages actually came about that way at Woodstock and other festivals and that didn't surprise anyone who was "experienced" in the second half of the 1960s.

But I was too paralyzed with fear to move, let alone run down the street to have sex with a Beetle. When I was sure I was going to die; swallowed up by the earth with every conceivable color, shape, and concept swirling around me, I'd look at my brother and he'd be looking directly at me with his wild, glorious, wide open, frightening, dilated, brown eyes that said everything was going to be okay but just between us, if it's not, who gives a sweet fuck? Then he'd crack that wicked Dave smile of his just as Jimi sang the answer, *"Well . . . I have!"* And you'd have to look away for a millisecond because his gaze was too powerful to hold or stand or because it penetrated so deep into you, you thought he saw what you thought you were and when you looked back at him, Jimi would be singing, *"Not necessarily stoned . . . but . . . beautiful!"* Then, using the language of God to make sure you got it, he added an exclamation point with the greatest four-second guitar passage of all time while Dave sat, cool as a cucumber, his eyes closed with the assenting smile of a Buddha in nirvana, as beautiful as any guru on a mountain ever was. He, unlike me and the others, was not reborn but baptized, performing the ceremony himself. He was now "experienced!"

When we "came down" I'd feel for the first time that everything in the universe was in its proper place and I'd survived the fire run rapids of Dante's Inferno, while holding so tightly to a blow-up toy for dear life my hands hurt. Up to this point, I believed my religion and perception of existence had some solid basis of validity but now, I had to let that toy float away. I'd been perceiving life falsely, but being partly "experienced" I hadn't only entered *into* a state of awareness, I *became* awareness, with the me part of me having been put aside somewhere. Words to describe it do not exist; the language of music comes close but it too is insufficient and comparisons like these have no meaning. I had the kind of clarity ancient mystics spoke of and I knew it. And if it was all a hallucination, that was of equal value because I accepted I'd never be believed if I told anyone and knew I shouldn't be. But I was alive and knew life was not a dream unless it was a dream of someone or something real that opened my eyes and all I wanted was for the world to love itself.

Then Dave said, sounding like Spock or Sherlock Holmes, "From a psychological standpoint, I can see how people go crazy on this shit if they don't know themselves. It holds up your dirty laundry and makes you look even if you don't want to. And when you see others looking at theirs and they see you can see theirs and they yours and they're going nuts because it's too much to handle, that can definitely send you off the deep end. It makes you confront yourself and everything you and the ones you're with believe, and doesn't give anyone time to ease into it. It's complete chaos like atoms and stars smashing into each other. You're in a frickin' *Fleetoscram.'*"—a word he invented—"And if you get through that part in one piece, it takes you on a trip out of yourself so you can look at yourself honestly for the first time and choose whether you want to exist that way or exist at all. And if the answer is yes, that you like seeing things the way you have *so far,* as incredibly incomplete as that view is, and like being who you are, despite being half alive, then, you hang tight so the beast can take you where you need to go. It can be the most awesome, peaceful ride ever even if it's through the gates of hell because you *know* it's one big fucking joke and if not, you're screwed big time." Then he laughed and said, "At least that's how it is for me, how 'bout you?"

As I digested his words like nourishment from the Gods, because they might've been, I thought, *You suck, you crazy bastard, but I love so much that you're my brother and we come from the same place.* But I only had the courage to say, "It's that way for me too, Dave. One of the things I've learned *this time* is I'm not as brave as I thought I was and when people like you think I am, because you think I do brave things, you don't know how scared shitless I am but I do them anyway."

He said, "Hmmm," while nodding his red-haired head, and this was where we parted ways because *his* laundry didn't scare him like mine did me. Then he said, "Well, scared shitless isn't such a bad thing. I mean, people pay to go on roller-coaster rides and see monster movies, right? They just make me laugh. I wonder sometimes what it's like to be scared shitless."

Confronting himself, he was in his element. It was inspiring and sometimes scary to see. He would've been an awesome soldier or brave knight in the ancient court of King Arthur. Instead, he was the greatest brother a person like me could ever have.

He realized even the most stable of people could suffer LSD hallucinations with devastating effects so he said, "This is not for everyone!" It was his way of saying Timothy Leary was incredibly irresponsible to make the claims he did because this really was a dangerous business to be involved in. But we believed this door opening could have benefits because The Beatles said it could and Jimi did too. But we also knew from "experience" it could open doors to insanity because we knew a real nice kid (Timmy A.) who jumped out a window to his death while on his first trip because a door told him he could fly, and this wasn't an isolated thing. You'd see it on the news happening in other cities too.

So somewhere between people jumping out of windows and the possibility of getting drafted to fight in one of the most pigheaded, arrogant, and unnecessary of wars, there was the promise of meditation and flower power telling us if one simply loved, the horrors of bad thought leading to war could be seen for the mistakes they were. As a nation, we never really tried that kind of love and I don't know why. Maybe we never had the courage that Dave had. He knew "the better angels of *his* nature." And to people like Abraham Lincoln, nothing more was required of anyone.

WHERE ANCIENT DOGMAS
WEREN'T ADEQUATE

Dave's room was where young epiphanies felt safe. It was where I wondered for the first time, why in my twelve years of Catholic education, we weren't taught to meditate even though we were taught that Christ went to the desert to fast and meditate for forty days before going on his mission. Did church dogma not want us to know we could find God or inner peace or whatever one is supposed to look for without being in a fraternity of believers that followed articles of faith that only a chosen few could be entrusted to understand? Did everything not making sense have to remain a mystery we *had to* accept without question? I felt that through no fault of their own, the nuns taught us to read but not to understand, to hear music but not how to feel it, to memorize history but not the truth it reveals. I wanted to know things, like why the church imprisoned people like Da Vinci, who got off easy compared to others that lost their heads or were boiled in oil, for simply seeking the truth of how nature worked and how fascinatingly beautiful it is. What was my ancient faith so afraid of?

Somehow Dave saw right through it and we'd discuss it after gigs as we waited for that most beautiful, living, golden orb to rise from a breathing ocean after we walked through a "door of perception." The beach, ocean, and stars became our church, our discussions and experiences our holy communion, and music our sacraments making sense of it all. When it was just the two of us, nothing scared me because everything was sacred. And maybe because some deep organic instinct told him he didn't have the luxury of time that meditation sometimes needs to open doors for the heart and mind in the natural way it does, was why he did things with such frightening intensity. Or maybe it was simply who he was, curious with absolutely no time for triviality, the mundane or ridiculous. When he'd opened all the doors he could with psychedelic ritual as old as time, his curiosity was satisfied. Now it was time to once again climb mountains as we had as kids with our parents in New Hampshire, and that opened even more doors. So many remnants and souvenirs from our "trips" through doors and peaks of the White Mountains were in his room and they were holding me up.

I looked at eclectic posters, like one of a local children's television show astronaut, Major Mudd; he was pointing to a picture of Tricky Dick suggesting Nixon was really the one "out in space." Then a famous obligatory poster of a young, beautiful Farrah Fawcett before hard living enslaved her. If we had been a generation older, Marilyn Monroe would've been there instead. There was the old dart board with thousands of holes made by my two dead friends. Each hole told a story. It was next to a poster of Moe, Larry, and Curly looking eerily like recent politicians who've led us to war and not told us why. Maybe Shemp knows? Looking at Hendrix's poster, it seemed to me that his death, nine years earlier in 1970, was just another one that happened too soon. My God, like Brian Jones, Janis Joplin, and Jim Morrison, Jimi was only twenty-seven when he died, and now Judi too. And if blues historians are correct, one of the most influential of all, Robert Johnson, was only twenty-seven when he died in 1938. More recently, Kurt Cobain and Amy Winehouse have joined the list of twenty-sevens that have left the building.

Looking at Jimi I could hear "Little Wing," a song from his second album that conveyed more than any other song on earth the relationship I had and will always have with Judi. Next to him was a poster of Keith Richards, and I snickered to myself sarcastically but with strong affection for the first time in months, because The Stones have always entertained me and made me smile. They taught me more than anyone what you could musically get away with. So often they sounded on the brink of disaster, but from them I learned that you could both butcher and make love to a song at the same time and if done in the proper balance, the soul of the song would shine through more than if you worried about getting each note just right. Sometimes you have to get them right of course, but if they don't *feel* right, they won't move anyone to sway, dance, or do something inappropriate or sacred and that's what rock is all about. It's an art form both brutal and beautiful but unlike other forms, it's a contact sport where people can get hurt. It ain't always pretty and there's danger to be had but God, can it inspire.

In the early days and forever after, we, like most everyone, were totally hooked on The Beatles. No one who didn't live through that era could possibly understand the impact they had. The silly comparisons—even then—that people made between them and The Stones, to us, were a non issue. We were in the camps of both and totally aware of the distinction. The Beatles never sounded on the brink of disaster, even if at times they felt that way. Their guitars were in tune, vocals on key, timing tight, with songs that will live forever. The Stones, on the other hand, had guitars not always in tune, vocals often not on key, timing at times wobbly, but songs that made you aware primitive man still had something important to say. You first had to give them the benefit of doubt if you were able to, but it wasn't easy, and then, if you were lucky enough to get past the way they sounded, you might discover that when they weren't lazy and were paying attention, they, like a wounded, cornered animal, could rock like no one else and that liberation was a visit from the Gods. A good example would be them on their song with the crude yet somehow appropriate and almost forgivable title "Bitch," from their Sticky Fingers album. It's primal, catchy, perfect, and complete with every note just right! And my God, Charlie just a hair behind the beat (in the pocket) on purpose is spiritual decadence at its best. Everyone thinks it's Mick and Keith riding the beast but it's Charlie, and you can hear it plain as day if you listen with your gut instead of your ears.

When you got past the obstacles The Stones put in front of you, you could fall in love if you wanted to, just like you were with The Beatles, and be part of a club that would always have your funny bone tickled because you'd listen to what each individual was doing and wonder how in the hell they'd pulled it off. And if you were very, very lucky you'd discover that the soul and inspiration of it all came from the music of blacks from the American South. The eventual results of the American Civil War allowed that soul and inspiration to burst upon the world. The Stones, probably more than anyone, were influenced by it, celebrated it, paid homage to it, and reaped the benefits. But the truth was that all the bands on my brother's walls were influenced by it too.

It has to be said though, The Stones could betray you by not caring or just going through the motions because maybe they were lazy, uninspired, or too blitzed to do otherwise and to some that was unforgivable; especially our friends who had formal Berklee College of Music educations and wondered why in the hell we put up with them in the first place. People like that only took The Stones' "screw you" attitude one time and then it was good-bye, and who could blame them. While we, without that precise musical education but with ears to hear as well as anyone, we who had worked so hard in the first place to fall in love with them, while knowing it shouldn't have to be like that, were willing to forgive if we sensed an inkling of effort towards redemption. It wouldn't have been so bad if The Stones felt bad or even faked that they did, but they didn't. Being a Stones fan was not always easy. When they were bad, they were very bad and it made you realize that when it's that hard to fall in love but you do it anyway, it can be even harder to fall out, even though it might be healthier. But we never wanted that!

If you had to, you could make an analogy that The Beatles were like the mighty Yankee Army and The Stones like the ill-equipped, underfed, profane, dirty, foul smelling, yet glorious underdog, "ragamuffin" Rebel Army that with grit, luck, and determination could pull off a victory or two or four against the mighty Yankee juggernaut like at Second Manassas (2nd Bull Run), Fredericksburg, Chancellorsville, or Chickamauga when they had the strength to receive or go on the attack. But no one would make that strange analogy if they didn't understand it couldn't be made without the historical retrospect of the Yankees winning the war. As a kid, I thought of things that way and thank God, still do. The clean cut Beatles were my Yankees, my healthy fruit, my wholesome All-American Superman, where insults and bullets bounced off and the means justified the end. The shoeless, tattered, and "shattered" Stones were my Rebels, my forbidden fruit, my mysterious, brooding, freakish Batman, where bullets and insults tore through flesh only to strengthen spirit, determination, and rage, where the end was all and the means required no justification. But I couldn't have one without the other, and unlike The Beatles and The Stones, where each didn't need the other for their existence, despite the silly hype of the times that said they did, the real Yankees and Rebels existed *because* of each other and the results were devastating.

One Rebel, Keith Richards, was and still is *the* patron saint for much of the debauchery that went with the times. Even then he was said to have died and been resurrected more times than a cat, and rumored to have had more blood transfused into him in Switzerland than Bela Lugosi (the Hollywood actor who did the great portrayal of Dracula in the 1930s) in order to flush out the heroin in his veins. And God bless him, he's still with us. But back then I always felt a little sad every time he came back from the dead because I'd hear him in interviews and it seemed like another piece of his mind was missing, and I wondered if that was a nightmare for those who loved and worked with him. But that assessment was coming from a fan who was only a kid and what did I know? No one could deny, though, Keith did and may still come up with some of the greatest, catchiest guitar riffs God and the Devil must surely envy. Maybe God and the Devil collaborated and sent those riffs to the world through him as a sort of wicked and holy wink to all of us, but who knows?

I was taught that thinking like that was a serious sin I'd have to pay for, and to make doubly sure we understood, we were quizzed and given written tests about it. It's how we learned God and Satan hadn't been on speaking terms since before the world was created but before that had gotten along just fine, at least until Satan began asking God pesky questions about the political hierarchy and makeup of heaven, which in turn made God tell St. Michael to kick Satan out of heaven. That was *exactly* how it was explained to us in catechism class in the first grade in 1956 at Saint Michael The Archangel's Grammar School in Lynn, Massachusetts, and it terrified me.

Satan wanted heaven to be more egalitarian instead of what he saw as a dictatorship, but his ideas for improving the place were overruled by God. Kind of like Thomas Jefferson having a similar wish for the early United States, that as time passed it would progress closer to a more egalitarian society than it was in his day. But whereas Jefferson's wish was good, the nuns did an excellent job making us understand that Satan's view of politics was evil at a time when we were young and too scared to ask pesky questions about it. Questions could land us in hell, which was a place God created so he'd have someplace to send pesky questioners. Having this knowledge injected into me felt like a root canal to my young psyche because I wrongly had the naive impression my teeth were coming in just fine, and that curiosity was a good thing. But *that* curiosity could send one to purgatory for a few months or to everlasting damnation if we didn't get rid of it. Still, a part of me (the innocent part) couldn't accept that at one time in heaven, God and the angels *he created* had knock-down, drag-out fights over politics. I wished I could've been a fly on a cloud so I could've eavesdropped on their arguments. In the end I learned the most important thing for us kids to know was the political structure of heaven was not and had never been a democracy. The sooner we understood that the better for our earthly good and the eternal salvation of our souls. God made the rules and that was that!

Admittedly though, it was interesting, fascinating, frightening, and somehow a little sad to be taught that the reason you wanted to ask pesky questions was because you were born a sinner and became a bigger one when you doubted, all the while being too young to know what a sin actually was. This was the first time I learned if curiosity was a sin; I was in big trouble because I wanted to know how the nuns knew all this stuff. It's why I'm still in trouble because I want to know all I can in this short life. It might reveal if the innocent girls who grew up to become nuns teaching us those "ancient dogmas of faith" had root canals deeper than mine, but I'll never know. At the very least, by their rules, they'll get into heaven and in all probability, I won't! The reason: I just can't seem to "take it on faith" by ignoring my favorite ex-Confederate soldier Mark Twain's critique that "faith is believing what deep, deep down inside . . . we know . . . just ain't so!" And I can't seem to push away from my funny bone what he said were the three most important things he learned in his childhood Christian religious classes out in Missouri: the existence of the human soul, that slavery was sacred, and that the world was flat. The truth is, my flip attitude, for which I must apologize, can't be blamed on my schooling or on anyone but me. I'm just comfortable *here* and not too comfortable anywhere else. My early education was just part of being a good Catholic. You took things on faith in order to get to heaven. It was inconsequential whether they made sense or, God forbid, felt right. You accepted it and if you ever wondered if it was true or not, that could get you in deep trouble because *someone* was always watching.

So maybe, my young kid mind thought, the guitar riffs really were sent through Keith and were written a long, long time ago when God and Satan were on speaking terms. If it wasn't Keith, it had to be that collaboration I speculated. I was no teenage expert of course, but I wished someone (I was forbidden to) would ask the pesky question of how many riffs never got through to Keith because he was nodding off and didn't receive them. I felt bad wondering that because maybe this was too harsh on old Keith, but it was only because I was wishing he'd take better care of himself so The Stones could roll on forever. Without him, Charlie or Mick (sorry Ronnie), they couldn't roll on. It was awful for us kids when The Stones lost Brian Jones to drugs. No doubt, Mick Taylor was cool and fit in fine for a while, but even he could only take so much and left. That's what was happening back then and we felt rotten about it.

Maybe I'm being mean-spirited here, but years later when I was becoming a Rebel (with the reluctant blessing of my parents) by rebelling against the religious education they'd paid for that made me see things the way I did, my friend Craig (an all-around great musician) and I were watching Keith on a solo tour at the Orpheum Theatre in Boston, and he was so hammered he made us feel straight. During the song "Happy," that he must've played a thousand times with his regular band, we heard the most god-awful sound because he played the guitar solo in the wrong key. The other guitarist, Waddy Wachtel I think it was, walked across the stage and we read his lips yelling at Keith, "You're in the wrong fucking key," and Keith just gave him a stupid grin and shrugged his shoulders as if to say, "Who cares?" But now, putting all this youthful, sarcastic facetiousness aside, I don't need to know if God, Satan, or both sent riffs to Keith like they did to Mozart, Beethoven, and John Lennon. Keith's riffs sure sound like they did, but who knows? All I know as a "Forever Rebel" is I'll always have a little "Sympathy For The Devil" in me, and that's a lot more comfortable than ancient dogmas that made me too frightened to think, let alone ask, a pesky question.

By no means was I an angel during these years, but things affected me deeply, like when Dave and I were at The Boston Garden and saw The Who's Keith Moon pass out and fall into his drums halfway through their first song. We saw Townshend yelling at him as two roadies put him back on his seat only to see him crawl away before the song started again. The next thing we knew the lights came on, the show's been canceled and there's smoke all over the place because some disgruntled fan or fans lit seats on fire in protest. Luckily the twelve thousand in attendance got out alive, but it made a major impression on me that there should be a sacred rule that musicians, especially of that stature, should wait until after the show to get blitzed. Some kids had driven many miles to be there and one, a close friend who was a huge Who fan and who'd been paralyzed in a football accident the year before, was in a wheelchair on his first big venture out. It was a major undertaking, not to mention things weren't as accessible for the handicapped back then. Things weren't all roses in those days of love and flowers. And sometimes, like during The Stones' show at Altamont, people got killed, so I'm not exaggerating the danger.

The poster of Keith was the last poster I looked at that sad night. Looking at them gave me a brief modicum of peace because they epitomized the times Dave, Judi, and I had lived together. They knew the world the way I did because we discovered it together, and the posters represented something important, sacred, and profound. I'll hold fast for the rest of my days that the music of the icons, including the exasperating ones on Dave's walls, defined the twentieth century just as much as did Gershwin, Porter, Berlin, Hammerstein, Copeland, and Bernstein to name a few from previous generations. As proud as I am of the '60s and early '70s generation of musicians, perhaps the thing I love most is that not a single one, including The Beatles, would tell you they wrote anything as good or powerful as, say, Gershwin's "Rhapsody In Blue" or the blues of Robert Johnson. They knew apples weren't oranges and realized music of that nature was not a contest to be judged against but a sound to be learned from, because music, when it's honest, is the truest language of God as history proves every generation has something to say. No one knew that better than my brother.

We used to say that if there was only one art form allowed into heaven, it had to be music. We'd discuss to all hours of the night waiting for that orb to rise from the ocean that maybe this time was different, because even though music of previous generations was profound, much of it was a way to escape the troubles of the times by "singing in the rain" about "how happy and gay" life was, when the reality of war and oppression here and around the world was another thing altogether. The uniqueness of our generation's music was that it didn't offer escapism from our troubled times and, thank God, it never tried to. It *identified* the true cause of war and held it high for all to see. And when it was whacked down like a Civil War battle flag by a young schmuck wielding a National Guard or policeman's stick, it was picked up again and again. The music told it like it was because that was the only hope for seeing things for what they were. There truly were "four dead in Ohio" and fifty thousand more in Vietnam. And every hundred years or so a generation comes along with the courage to tell it like it is about its war because God help us, every generation demands its war. This generation told the truth with its music, and for that it deserves thanks and the benefit of doubt.

All these things came at me as I stood in the middle of Dave's room on the night after Judi's funeral. I was in the loneliest "fleetoscram" of heart, mind, and spirit I'd ever known. And because the feelings attached to these things had always been shared with the only two who got it, I'd been able to believe our generation was closer to picking up the truth that "all men (and women) are created equal." But now, a soldier who chose to be a soldier instead of a saint because he saw more nobility in it, and a saint who could be nothing else, people with whom I could believe these things with, were gone. And I, the weakest link, couldn't do without them! Then it hit me. As much as *they* died, *we* had died! David was gone, and Goliath, the cause of war, still roamed the earth, and the person who inspired me to keep an eye on him was now gone too.

BILLY YANK & JOHNNIE REB

I sat on my dead brother's bed in a weird, hazy feeling of aloneness, about to enter an unfamiliar yet recognizable déjà vu universe. But how could that be? Everything was quiet except for the usual house noises from the old oil furnace and the rustling of wind outside on this Yankee New England November 4th night of 1979. I was in a strange, new "peculiar institution" of emotion where I didn't feel sad or happy. I felt nothing, no contentment and, for the first time in years, no frustration. If a giant meteor was heading towards the earth that would destroy it, it was okay. If it missed that was okay too. Nothing mattered! I was the incarnation of indifference with no phone calls to make or to answer from people asking how Judi was and if there was anything they could do. There were no doctors or nurses to consult with, no appointments to keep, no food to prepare, no clothes or sheets to wash, no bed pans to clean, and no prescriptions to fill. I had no place to go and all the time in the world to get there. Everything was calm, not peaceful, just calm; two very different things. Maybe this was a good time to cry but I didn't feel like crying, and that gave me a pang of guilt that lasted a tenth of a second or lifetime. I was so damn tired of crying anyway and couldn't have summoned tears if I had wanted to. With me, grief and tears come when they will and I can't hold them back when they do. And God, I knew they'd come soon enough. I felt like I'd been through an earthly and cosmic meat-grinder battle and had come out with soul raped and body tossed like a rag doll in a nightmare tornado, with the taste of war and slavery forever in my mouth. My spirit was dead or, at best, in a coma.

Somehow my bloodshot eyes began to scan the rest of my brother's room and I felt a brief moment of comfort knowing I was one of the lucky ones, because the knowledge that every generation has something valuable to say was a gift given to me by my parents. And, when a generation has nothing to say, that, in itself, is saying a lot too. Sitting on Dave's bed brought me to eye level with this "self-evident truth" that I'll hold dear for the rest of my days. It was displayed by row after row of history and philosophy books that helped shape the minds of my mother and father, and those books could help shape and save anyone, even me, but I was too blind with sorrow to know it. Maybe that's a weak excuse because, in almost everything, I usually learn things the hard way. Judi pointed that out to me one time but said that, because I had no agenda to deceive, learning things the hard way might be my natural way. To this day I've always wished I had an additional thirty to forty points of IQ but never knew where to get them. If I'm honest about it, I could use a lot more.

I wasn't lucky enough to inherit the intelligence genes of my parents. My brothers and daughter did but I've always had to struggle and hold concepts awhile before I get them. My mother, a great history teacher and musician, became a teacher not just because she loved to teach or we needed the income, though we did, but because she loved to learn and the history books were hers. She, like all historians, was forever curious and would remain a great student for the rest of her life. Curiosity is what makes a great history teacher. The philosophy books were my father's; written by Western and, more often, Eastern philosophers of the last hundred years. Stacks of *National Geographic, Life,* and *Look* magazines with several volumes of encyclopedias were next to every comic book known to kid-dom. Hidden among the comics were *Playboy* magazines from the late '60s that were used by my brothers and me to assist in an adolescent ritual boys perform when they have to. Who the biggest culprit was, I'm not saying, but I know! If our mom knew about the *Playboys* she never said anything. She was too cool to worry anyway, much less care because, as a historian, she knew human nature and consequence were a constant.

There were shelves of vinyl music albums from the likes of Beethoven to The Beatles, and all of it was covered by the thinnest layer of dust, reminding one of the old Irish saying that although dust is not welcomed "it's the natural covering of things domestic." Families with a passion for reading and music accumulate books and records in rooms like these. And if 99 percent of the authors were dead, it would somehow become their ideas that would mean more to me than whether their spirits lived on or not. After all, the dust was a sign that everything in the universe returns to dust, but how do you kill an idea? History explains the birth and evolution of ideas and how, when a certain idea's time has come, it will tell us if *we know how to listen.* And when we do, it willingly gives up the ghost while we give thanks. Then it points us toward a better idea, one that inspires men like Lincoln to say with confidence, "The dogmas of the past are no longer adequate for the present." When history does this, it's art and it's beautiful. Historians rightly teach that Lincoln was a political genius but a bigger truth is that he was a political artist! Perhaps the best we've ever had, and it was ideas in books that showed him how to become who he was. He had no real education; his teachers were the words he read.

Books, in all their forms, are the delivery systems for ideas, and when they're suppressed by the despot who believes he must burn six million books before he can burn six million Jews, it's the suppression of ideas that make it possible. As the holocaust of America happened in the American South, the aristocracy (slaveocracy) burned books that suggested the Declaration of Independence was more than just an idea, that it was a reality, a "standard maxim" to be continually striven for. Burning books that spoke in favor of that maxim and outlawing the right to read for people held in bondage allowed our holocaust to flourish. Suppression of knowledge was the only way it could. But where knowledge couldn't be suppressed it somehow seeped into the farthest reaches of the American wilderness; into the soul of someone who grew out of the American psyche and soil, and the roots became too strong for the Hitlerites (which is not too harsh a term if you were a mother whose child was sold away right in front of you) of the American South who said slavery was a sacred blessing from God.

Lincoln said the written word was mankind's greatest invention because it allowed the past to speak to the present and the present to speak to those not yet born. It reminds us, as it did him, that all the fancy ideas we think we've had are not our own, but have been built on the ideas of others. They belong to history so we can know and recognize, as Lincoln said, "the eternal struggle between right and wrong since the beginning of time." Knowing that is freedom, which is the spirit of history. Facts and dates help get good grades and win trivia contests, but knowing ideas because you know how to listen makes one a better person because it fosters truth and understanding and that's *the foundation of compassion.* Then, without seeking to do so, learning things, even when they disturb, have the added benefit of keeping one forever young. My history teacher mother taught me these things! And when one gets it, along with it comes a responsibility to help promote and share that foundation. It's why she loved historians like Arthur M. Schlesinger, Jr. who taught that great history (real history) is not only about the movers and shakers of the world but about those who were moved and shaken and why they were.

But even with that truth as part of one's foundation, it's not always easy because you *know*—which is different from *believing*—that God didn't "shed (all) his grace on thee," like politicians holding fast to ancient dogmas want us to believe. For what kind of nation could allow for a "trail of tears" out of Georgia and the loss of so many innocent lives, mostly woman and children, because of something none of us can deny—human greed; not American greed, human greed! Andrew Jackson and his minions committed American genocide on thousands of innocent people, and if that's not the case, then what in God's name is the explanation? Only a people who can admit they're not perfect can understand, and might even have the right to say this greed is universal, because they started out on the right foot by declaring, "All men are created equal." Still, while declaring this hope for the world, countless massacres of Native Americans were taking place when it was no longer convenient to simply break a supposed legal treaty; all while mothers, fathers, sons, and daughters were being unpacked like sardines from slave ships the Devil himself would find difficult to visit for their putridness and misery.

We, with God's grace shed on us, had to enslave and wipe out races of people in order to establish "The Land of the Free and Home of the Brave." And this is not to say that the people living here long before Columbus discovered Columbus (he didn't discover anything, let alone America) weren't wiping out and enslaving people too. Humans of every race and color can be vicious; there's no monopoly on that. And it's not easy either, but indispensably necessary if one resolves to be true to oneself, to say that America can at times fight for the right thing and wrong thing at the same time, with the right side not being perfect and never claiming to be and the wrong side completely wrong because it claimed to be the perfection of human social order. The Confederacy taught children their slave society was perfect while Lincoln said American society, North and South, was far from perfect. Only human compassion and understanding allowed him to call these stewards of perfection "our wayward brethren" while they painted him with horns, tail, and pitchfork and told their children to beware. If the American Civil War was not the epitome of the contradictory ideas of what freedom and liberty really are, then *nothing* is right. If we can't face what caused the war we had with ourselves, then how can we understand anything? But if we can, then hope springs eternal for the Earth. All the courage and wisdom to know these things were in my brother's room, and I needed them in me because I had nothing to sustain me.

Surrounded and partially protected by this sea of books in shelves underneath The Beatles and The Stones; I sought refuge. These 'Gimme Shelter' breastworks gave the illusion of safety, like those dug outside Petersburg in 1864 and 1865, which gave a starving, louse-infested Rebel twenty-seven years of age a false sense of security; knowing any minute his brains could splatter on his younger brother next to him if a Yankee Berdan sharpshooter two hundred yards away happened to be precise with a Minie ball. He kept his head down for whatever good that would do. The day before he had handed his fourteen-year-old cousin a letter from Richmond and as he opened it the kid had the top part of his head blown off. The letter was from his mother, a reply to his letter where he had said he prayed to God the war wouldn't end before he "got hisself a chance to shoot a nigger." She wrote back for him to come home alive, that she loved and was proud of her "sweet Christian boy" and that "Paw would've been proud too. And as for shooting a nigger, don't come home if you don't!" His cousin knew this because after he wiped bone shards, brain matter, and blood sharing half his DNA off the letter, he read his aunt's soothing words.

And God forgive me, not for using the N word but for worrying it might make someone uncomfortable, because no words can describe how I hate it with all my heart and soul. I can say, because it's true, that I've never heard that word spoken in my home growing up and have never used it myself; not because of any decency of character I may profess because I have none, or because my mother would've washed my mouth out with soap if I had, or because she loved me; but more because she was a history teacher who raised me to know the damage that word has done to all mankind. It has its history and history has to be accurate so I reluctantly use it in a historical way *only*. Otherwise, history is just a theory or supposition, instead of a gift that sometimes has no choice but to give birth painfully to clarity to understand why things are still so damn screwed up in the world. The word is not just the worst word in the English language because if that's all it was, it would be less assaulting to the senses than it is. It's the worst word in the history of the world because more than any it was invented to denigrate and degenerate a life in the first nation claiming to be founded on human equality, based on reason, a nation Lincoln called "The Last Best Hope of Earth." I know, wherever the word is used, even here, hope suffers if it's used for sensation or to wound.

Some publishers today are offering sanitized versions of *Huck Finn* without the word and I suppose they'll declaw *The Cat In The Hat* someday too but what good will that do for a kid when she's confronted with the slur or a clinging kitten for the first time? *Huck Finn* is not meant to be elevator music or a feel-good Thomas Kincaid painting where poison ivy never stings. *Huck Finn* is meant to tell the truth of the American dilemma in all its ugliness so it can take the world to a higher place. History needs all its claws to climb through ignorance.

Above the breastworks of books was a mantelpiece over the old fireplace. On it were swimming, baseball, hockey, football, and weightlifting trophies along with ribbons won in races on land and water. I couldn't hear it, but everything was whispering that a reason to live was hidden in this room. Not that there wasn't enough sleeping in my old bed two flights above me. But a reason and maybe a way to continue to be myself while *believing* it was no longer possible, because everything was, as an old Rebel soldier said, "a world turned upside down." I needed to be reborn or die and if it was to be the former it somehow had to involve this room. But if it held the secret to my rebirth, I hadn't the slightest notion. I was like the "fighting general" Lincoln had (not Joe Hooker but William Rosecrans) who finally became so confused and shell-shocked from repeated battle that Lincoln said he "was like a duck hit on the head." I was desperate, swimming in circles with no shore in sight, totally lost.

Somehow I thought of Thomas Jefferson asking, "If there is a just God ruling the universe," and felt that maybe for the first time in my life I'd done enough thinking for one day and earned the right to sleep, but something happened. As if on cue someone was calling me, faintly at first but gradually louder with increasing persistence. They didn't want me to sleep just yet. I recognized their voices instantly. I knew them well, two of my oldest childhood friends; toy soldiers, one Gray that I'd always hold in my left hand, the other Blue I'd hold in my right. Their generation had more to say than any generation in American history. Lincoln said every generation to come should study theirs because theirs made every mistake in the book, bigger and bloodier than any future or past generation ever could. Only these old comrades could make me move so I got up, walked over, picked them up and a feeling of coming home entered my being in some strange, soothing way. There *are* people in this world who know what I mean but I didn't know they existed. I knew these Civil War soldiers intimately because I'd spent entire seasons and campaigns with them as a kid. It'd been years since I held them but the need for us to reacquaint wasn't necessary. The Yankee said, "We been watchin' ya, Robby. We know ya seen the elephant!" (This was a term soldiers used for being in battle.)

As I held them I thought of all the fights they'd had in my backyard and in the giant sandbox our dad built for us. The Rebel always won because for some reason I can't explain I liked him better than the Yankee. There's always been something in my nature that makes me root for the underdog, even when, as in the case of this particular dog, he was so wrong. Maybe because of the little history I knew, in the big fight I never let them have, the Yankee would win in the end and that's what made the fun possible. I never took notice that they came from the same plastic mold because my history teacher mom already taught me Americans were supposed to be equal. But for my childhood fantasy they had to be different so they could shoot, stab, and kill each other while my mom made supper. But now that I was a man and had seen the elephant, I couldn't ignore their sameness. It was a powerful thing. Realizing this, they said, "Welcome home," and the Yank said, "It's about time you saw the real us, Robby, now spread the word!"

The irony was that Lincoln *always* saw them that way. He understood the flesh-and-blood brothers in Blue and Gray were cut from the same American cloth, despite the nonsense that led to war. But he also knew the fabric of their

American minds was dipped in the differently colored dyes of Northern and Southern culture, and that it was saturated in their respective social and religious beliefs, which went hand in hand, and nobody could be blamed for that. He was in the middle of it his whole life, having been born in Kentucky, and carried that influence to the very end. Kentucky supplied soldiers like the soldiers I held to both sides, more than any other state. And near the war's end, when Lincoln was preaching forgiveness instead of blame, many thousands from all the states North and South said they needed to blame someone anyway in order to heal. In that case, Lincoln said the blame must be assigned "to all of us."

He knew the dye of culture was not something one was born with and only became deadly when it leaked from the uniform through the skin, into the bloodstream, and then the heart. That's why he said a hundred times that the issue that caused the war was "the meanness of man's heart." He knew his side was not without fault, and plenty of it, but he knew too that for the nation to have a chance, "that it might live," the side he was leading had to win if there was to be justice in the world. And when a mean-spirited critic who didn't understand these things told him there were some Gray soldiers buried alongside the Blue, that his "little speech" in Gettysburg was supposed to honor, Lincoln reminded him that the speech was meant to honor the Rebs too. It's the only way his speech could fully make sense, especially "the new birth of freedom" part. But that part means so much more because *it's a meditation* we must give to ourselves or perish by, ending up a lunatic talking to toy soldiers in a dusty old cellar.

It's the only way he could step aside on March 4, 1865 to let God make a speech of forgiveness if God was so inclined. When a woman who lost her husband and sons in the war confronted him after the speech, she said she did not have it in her heart to forgive the enemies that killed everything she held dear; she only wanted to destroy them. Lincoln understood her sentiment but told her, "When we make our enemies our friends, we destroy our enemies." It's the only way to truly heal, then, now, always. But for me on the saddest night of my life, holding little toy soldiers, I had no strength of mind, body, or spirit to make any more foolish analogies. My wife, my soul mate, the mother of my child, my best friend was dead! And like the speech Lincoln let God give to the American people, even though he knew they wouldn't like or accept it but needed to hear it anyway, this death was a truth I've never been able to come to grips with no matter how many years slip by. Her death, like the deaths that made the mother seek revenge, was of someone too young to die; a death too horrifying and sad for my mind to comprehend.

Accepting her death then, like accepting it now, was out of the question and God only knows how quickly I'd welcome that commodity if offered. But it's never been offered and I could never ask. But because of the gift of her and Dave's wisdom as well as Lincoln's words, revenge and bitterness were not something I shared with the woman who lost everything. Still, I was left with the truth, that death is serious business and nobody but nobody comes back from it. The only thing sadder than the unavoidable deaths of my two heroes were the *avoidable* deaths of the woman's husband and sons brought on by the "meanness of man's heart," so I had no right to think her wrong.

"For Christ's sake Robby, go to bed!" my little soldiers cried in unison.

"Ya'll mopin', cow-eyed like we did surrendering at Appomattox," said my Gray friend.

My Blue friend added, "You're about as sad as we Yanks were glad on that day, which if you think on it, some future history writer might say Lee signing those papers was the real signing of The Declaration of Independence. I changed my birthday and been celebrating on April 9 ever since because, when I thought on it, it's when we was all born. But could you please bivouac for the night, you look sick?"

I said, "Okay," but before I put them back on the mantelpiece I asked, "Would you guys mind much if I started hanging out with you again like I did in my youth?"

"O' course ya'll can, but it ain't nohow, noway, gonna be the same as when you was a kid 'cause ya'll seen the God-damned elephant, and ya'll know it's a real live livin' creature and not some plastic, glorifyin' lie like many o' y'alls gineration tells about the war. And what's plastic anyhow? We had rubber ya'll know! Hell, old Stonewall was shot by one of our men because he had on that God-damned black rubber coat we got off a dead Yankee that looked blue in the dark. And ya'll know if we hadn't lost 'Old Jack,' we'd a taken the high ground at Gettysburg 'stead of Ewell falling asleep and we woulda swept the field of all those stinking Blue-bellies with our artillery and won the God-damned war and blah, blah, *oh blah dee, o blah da,* we'd a won blah, blah, blah . . ."

The Yank rolled his eyes in the way one rolls them when he's heard this rant a thousand times and knows once it gets rolling there ain't no stopping it. He winked at me and said under his breath, *"Our* Johnnie is like so many of the diehards, you cain't convince him of nuthin'. He might be a crazy a son of a bitch, but he's honest and he don't lie about why his side was fighting like a lot of modern-day people who have clubs that talk about us. I don't mean you, Robby. You never lied about us; that's why *we both* like talkin' to ya! And don't be upset by what he's saying. It makes him feel important because historic facts and politics confuse and mystify him. Facts don't help his argument none so he barks at the moon for shinin' a light on what is. As the moon gets brighter the barkin' gets louder. Hell, a blind man can tell when the moon's full just by how loud Johnnie howls. He jus cain't help hisself. He's so balled up with hate 'n' anger he cain't see straight. The poor prick lost his wife, kids, and everything else 'cause o' the infernal war. But underneath his wind, he's a soft pile of hay that'd do jus about anything for ya, 'cept make sense. Once you know that, he ain't so bad to live with and that's good for me cause I'm stuck with him for eternity; we all are! And it's a good thing to remind those clubs that talk about us, Robby, 'cause without the two of us there'd be no ball for them to attend and no dance partner to do the do-si-do. And damn it, that was Old Abe's take on it from the git go. He said we belonged together and needed each other despite our differences. He said if we relied on the ballot instead of the bullet there ain't nothin we cain't solve. Ain't that what The Declaration of Independence,

The Revolution, The Constitution, and The Bill of Rights is supposed to be about? Ain't voting at the ballot American democracy at work? Hell, Johnnie's side chose the bullet because the ballot chose Old Abe fair 'n' square and they didn't like the result one bit nohow. So what's that say about their cause? And o' course there's the black thing that caused the whole mess, and I cain't even mention that to him cause we'll start fist fightin' and you'll never get any sleep."

"And no offense, Robby, you look like horseshit. And for fuck's sake"—plastic Civil War soldiers swear as much as real ones did, using the same swear words we use today—"old Reb General Joe Johnson was right when he told Uncle Billy (Sherman), after he surrendered and found out a maniac shot 'n' killed Old Abe, that 'The South's lost the best friend it ever had.' I mean, some in our government wanted to hang the Rebs but Old Abe had been sayin' they should be forgiven, that enough blood had been spilt and the whole shebang was a family affair anyhow, and the Rebs couldn't help themselves. And we woulda acted like them had we grown up in the South. O' course Johnnie don't want to hear none of that. It's why he makes so much noise, 'cause common sense and reasoning give him a headache 'cause he's too pigheaded. I tell 'em *ya only gotta face it once* and it ain't so painful there on out, but Robby, you know how some Johnnies are. I jus wish the stubborn bastard would shut up now and then so we could all find some peace. Robby, didn't Old Abe say when he was young that if we just used 'right thinking, common sense, and courtesy instead of 'hateful passion' that everything would turn out all right?"

I said, "Yeah Billy, it's something Old Abe would say."

Johnnie was still yapping in lunatic land but when he stopped for a breath I jumped in and said it was the highest honor to see them again even under these saddest of circumstances. I didn't ask what they meant by modern clubs that discussed the war but told them how much I missed them and they said they'd missed me too. Then I put them back on the mantelpiece and turned away as Johnnie revved up again. "And another thing, if Longstreet let Pickett charge when he was supposed to . . ." You had to have the patience of Job not to put a sock in his mouth or melt him and apparently Billy did. But I loved them equally because Billy and Lincoln were right, "Johnnie couldn't help hisself."

When you get innocent people like Johnnie frothing at the mouth by using religious chicanery and political falsehoods to threaten the safety of their wives and children, it's not so hard to get them to charge Yankee cannons, but it's near impossible to get them to reason. With reason gone, a man can justify his ten-year-old daughter driving him to the joint so he can have a drink or twelve. With reason gone people can enslave one another, buy and sell each other, and put people into concentration camps to incinerate them. You can even get some who'd been educated in America frothing so much they'll fly jet planes into buildings in New York City. And get uneducated Americans to burn orphanages in that same city in July of 1863 and hang innocent children from lampposts for having the wrong color skin. With reason gone, education is as "useless" as John Wilkes Booth said his hands were as he lay paralyzed taking his last breath. Without reason, the struggle between "hateful passion" and "cold unimpassioned reason" is as Lincoln said it was, "eternal." Ex-Confederate soldier Mark Twain said that nothing muddies the water of that struggle like human passion stirred up by religion.

It is reason then, not education as we've been repeatedly told, that's the key to understanding. There's no doubt education fertilizes reason and helps it grow, but when reason takes root a miracle happens; the desire for education never ceases. The egg of reason laid by the hen of education hatches an eagle of wisdom and Lincoln said the hen was the wisest of animals for she never cackles until the egg is hatched. The struggle between reason, passion, religious belief, and my own superficial, self-serving superstitions were tearing me apart because reason was the thing I lacked more than education, and the two people who provided all the reasoning a flake like me needed were dead. And because I always pick the scab, despite the events of *even this day,* there was one more thing I needed to see before I'd try to sleep, even though I needed sleep more than air. To get to it, I had to sit in an old dilapidated chair because that's how it was done in a room where ancient dogmas weren't adequate.

CHAIR IN
JONAH'S WHALE

The chair was in the corner next to the shelf of old encyclopedias, comics, and *National Geographics*. It'd clearly seen better days and was long past the point when someone desperate might rescue it from a curb. It was a family member we couldn't put down because the old dog *never* let us down, so it could stay as long as it could breathe. The more decrepit it got the more glorious it became. You couldn't simply sit in it, and it never invited you, it dared you! If you accepted the challenge, you had to do a backward type of butt first bungee jump and trust fate you wouldn't sink to Australia, China, Sri Lanka, or some other faraway land. And, with me being embarrassingly afraid of heights, this was always an adventure. Most of the time you eventually stopped but you had to be very careful not to sink through the wormhole to another dimension. That might've been good in my case, but I stopped nonetheless after going extra deep. I knew by instinct, not consciously, exactly where the picture I needed to see was, as if I'd put it there an hour ago as opposed to eight, ten, or sixteen years ago. If the Bible said Jonah was swallowed further by a chair in the belly of the whale, I would've known how that felt because as soon as I sank into the chair, I reached out past the leviathan's teeth and without looking, found the book. As he began to close his mouth I pulled it in and as books that've been opened to a specific page a thousand times sometimes do, it opened itself and that made the whale regurgitate the chair with me in it, and there it was!

The scene I had looked at countless times as a boy was exactly how I'd left it. I was visiting an old friend. I can't explain why I felt compelled to see it so I won't try. Some things just are. Maybe the historical image of people long dead was a way for me to connect to the idea of mortality. But then, why did I look at it so often when I was young and convinced I was going to live forever? It had to be something else. It wasn't a bucolic or friendly picture like that of a feel-good Disney tale. It was somehow, no, not somehow, it was a scene of absolute horror and desperate determination mixed with futile resignation that once again became my comfort. It was the famous painting by John Elder of Confederate General William (Little Billy) Mahone's Rebel troops on the attack just after the crater explosion at 4:45 on the morning of July 30, 1864, that blew a several-hundred-yard gap in Lee's Petersburg lines. Little Billy, as his soldiers affectionately called him, was only as tall as his beard was long. Here, he rallied his troops to plug the breach by attending to what some called "the turkey shoot," because the Yankees unwittingly marched into the pit they created and couldn't get out, and the starving, angry Rebs said it was like "shooting fish in a barrel."

I knew the faces of these Confederates intimately. My childhood eyes had studied each for hours with a magnifying glass. I'd look at one face one day and imagine his life before the war, then look at another the next day until I imagined them all. It gave me something to look forward to in the private world of my mind. When I finished the Rebs I studied the Yanks but felt I already knew their story, which didn't interest me as much. Now the deaths of Dave and Judi somehow changed that because I knew what it was like to witness fish dying in a barrel. I'd seen them die that way. Instinctively I'd always known, but never verbalized at that young age because there was no one to tell, that the artist was telling me directly that these ragged soldiers in

Gray were fathers, husbands, brothers, sons, cousins, neighbors, and not a single one a bad or evil person. He wanted me to get that and I did. I *always* saw the humanity of these brave Confederates and now, because of Dave and Judi, I saw the humanity of everyone.

In the center of the painting was the Confederate flag, held high in the right hand of a good man who appeared to be in a captured Federal coat. His flag says to the world, "All men are *not* created equal," and he believes this not only because his government says it but because his religion taught him, his parents, and his grandparents that from the moment they'd been born. He's a southerner fighting as anyone would fight had they been born into his culture. If there's another reason, no one *ever* has identified it. With his left hand he's attempting to prevent a comrade from falling after being hit by a Yankee bullet. The Rebel hit is looking straight to heaven with a gaze that says he knows the shot is fatal but that he's given his life to a noble cause and is about to enter the kingdom of heaven. To his left, on the ground, is someone who's already gone to meet his maker. A little closer is a soldier running swiftly towards the melee, his bayonet leading the charge. He's done this before, killed many a Yankee! You can see it in his careful, hawkish eyes. He's willing to die, but not before his bullet has found a Yankee heart or his bayonet a Yankee artery. Behind him on the ground is a wounded Rebel in a red shirt calling to the rear, "I'm shot." To this man's left is a soldier who looks like the soldier with hawk eyes, maybe his older brother, eyes also looking forward. Between them is an officer with his sword in the air, urging his men forward. I know these men well and I respect and love every one of them. Some are too young to die, some too old to fight, but all are willing.

To the right of the soldier with the flag is a Rebel whose foot is on rubble from the explosion, or maybe on a corpse. He's firing a Minie ball missile at a coagulated clump of Yankee fish trying to climb out the barrel in a desperate attempt to have a fair fight. "Everything is fair in love and war," says the poet, but the poet has it wrong; it should be amended to, "Everything is fair in war," because this war had nothing to do with love. The Minie ball appears to be heading for a black Union soldier who may have glasses on. It is hard to tell in this old encyclopedia. The original painting, wherever it hangs, must show that detail in a more satisfactory way. The soldier reminds one of the well-educated black soldier portrayed in the movie *Glory* who worked for the Shaw family of Massachusetts. He'll eventually become a good soldier and be killed at Fort Wagner making a charge more glorious than any of the war. The Rebels will *try* to disgrace the body of his white colonel, Robert Shaw, by burying him "with his niggers," yet Robert's parents will consider this the highest honor from their "wayward brethren" and fellow countrymen.

Could this be, a faint line drawn by pencil with a ruler laid on the Rebel's rifle in order to trace the trajectory of the bullet, with my little boy hand many years before? It appeared, as it did then, to be aimed at the black soldier's jugular. I didn't have an issue as a kid with black Union soldiers being shot at by Confederates because they knew the risk better than anyone, especially those who were once enslaved. It wasn't until I grew up to become the vice president of a Civil War Roundtable and lifetime member of the Lincoln Forum of Gettysburg and Lincoln Group of Boston that I discovered to my astonishment that some (even one is too many) people still didn't understand the reality of the war, and it was usually because they didn't want to understand. They might say the war was strictly an issue of *state rights,* and when you asked them for an example (just one) of a state right the Lincoln administration was taking away or even threatening to take away from the South they'd have none to give. And as Lincoln so eloquently reminded everyone in his first inaugural, there was not a single state right the United States was taking away from anyone, so the argument *is false.* And before he ended his address, he said the only real difference between the North and the South was the South thought slavery was *right* and ought to be extended while the North thought it was *wrong* and ought not to be.

History clarifies, but I was astonished that some grown up people, and even a small number of professional historians, pick and choose their history instead of taking it whole, because taking it whole would free them and their students from "ancient dogmas," and this minute number of historians don't want anyone free from the hypocrisy the Confederacy truly was. My astonishment, though, was far in the future of this sad night.

To the black soldier's left was a white Yankee about to bayonet a Reb as the Reb was about to use the butt end of his rifle to club another Yank who was drawing a bead on an unseen Reb. The question: Did the Yank's bayonet get there in time? Would the bayonet even be necessary because of the bead drawn by yet another Yank trying to send a bullet through the Reb raising the butt end of his gun? Will the bullet of this bead pass through the upper arm into the skull of the Reb? I wondered this and then noticed another small faintly visible pencil line, so the boy had wondered the same as the man. Was the Rebel raising the butt end of his gun because he'd just sent a bullet into the other black soldier on the ground raising his eyes to heaven? And of heaven, my little boy mind wondered, what happened when a black Yankee and white Rebel met in heaven? Would one say, "I'm sorry," and the other, "Okay?" If they were in heaven, it might go like that and if it didn't, then they didn't go to heaven but the other place. That much I knew and still know!

And who was this in the bottom left hand corner of the painting? Is that a woman crawling out of the crater, reaching for a fallen, almost upside down Union soldier? Could that be her husband or brother? Was she a nurse or soldier? Was she even a she? Her shirt was the same color red as the fallen Confederate a few yards away, was there a connection? Time and again my little boy hand would use a magnifying glass to discern if this was a man or woman. Was that an earring hanging from her right ear or was it a shadow? As God is my witness, without looking I reached up from my chair of truth and found my old magnifying glass. It was right where I left it and somehow another feeling of homecoming entered my stomach. This was passion and it didn't matter or enter the equation that I might be good at it, and that's never mattered anyway because passion doesn't require that realization or any other.

It settled me a little, like sitting at a piano settles a pianist or running settles a runner. Her eyebrows certainly looked like a woman's, just as I thought they had years ago. The shape of her right hip had the shape of a woman's and I remembered innocently being drawn to it as a little boy and now as a man I was drawn again. Judi has, I mean had, a hip like that.

There can be something so pure in the way a little boy looks at a woman long before he knows about the birds and bees, before his hormones kick in and make him curious to know many things. He'll believe a mother and father simply pray to God for a baby to come into their midst. And when the miracle happens he'll believe it's because the father looked at the mother like a little boy who believes prayers are answered looks at a woman crawling out of a crater at Petersburg. And if later he's embarrassed by some kid on his little league team who informs the others that he still believes in this nonsense because he doesn't yet know the gory details and gaudy forensics of the baby-making process, even those facts won't necessarily chase away the image he has because he *knows* that all good parents who want a child, *do* pray to God and that supersedes everything. Forever he'll look at this woman as he would a sunset, flower, earthquake, volcano, mountain stream, or ocean because she is Mother Nature, his mother, his sister, his daughter, his friend, and *always* his wife.

When women, through no fault of their own, aren't taught to see boys with that innocence in them, they'll raise boys who can be hoodwinked, and many of them lose the ability to see women the way I saw Judi and the woman at the crater. But when a woman sees men and boys *for what they are,* and when she's a musician who understands music is the truest language of God and later becomes a history teacher, well, her sons are the luckiest people in the world. And when they become fathers of daughters, they'll want their daughters to be looked at the way I looked at this woman at the rim of a crater, with dignity and respect. But I only had this faded eight-by-four inch photo in an old, worn, and torn encyclopedia, so my interpretation of what I could see may be way off.

The image, even if my interpretation is not exactly right, is something I'll have deep inside me for the rest of my days, and it called out to me on the night after the day I buried my wife and my world. Perhaps my childhood imagination created things in the image that weren't there because I needed something I couldn't find anywhere else. And now, my shattered spirit needed something to help me understand why God had the urge to let Dave, Judi, me, or any of us be at all. But even if that's not what was happening, I had these Confederates with good faces and that was enough in this tired old world to remind me the reason we should seek truth is so faces like these don't have to suffer as they did; fighting against what for them was "a world turned upside down." And maybe miraculously, I found camaraderie with them again as I confronted a world without Dave and Judi, that would forever be my "world turned upside down."

It was time to put the book back on the shelf because the sun would soon be up and without Dave and Judi there was no stopping it—*this time.* But one last look, just to be sure, before I closed it for perhaps another decade, told me I was different from these desperate Rebs. For I had no desire to fight, destroy, or secede from anything. All I had was just a wish to tell them it was all for naught and they should've tried harder to get along with their fellow man. But that would've been cruel and I couldn't talk to the dead anyway, not like they could talk to me with the written word, so it was simply my place to listen. I was alone with my future sleeping upstairs and she needed stability, but the elephant had me so messed up that nothing about me was stable. But damn, I knew one thing: These Rebs and Yanks were ripping each other's throats out over what they believed, not over what they knew, and that's been the case of warring people forever. My God, how did I know, *the truth of war is we fight over what we believe and not over what we know.* If that's not the case, then there's no hope. Dave and Judi's suffering somehow made me know this.

Then, thanks to exhaustion, fate, or just me, my insidious, personal demons started to wake from their slumber. They'd been at bay the last few days while my mind was busy with a wake and funeral. Now they began to manifest themselves in their usual forms of panic, anxiety, desperation, and gloom, slowly turning my indifference of an hour ago on me with a vengeance, the likes of which I'd never known. I'd always been haunted by stifling depression from time to time; it brought a sense of dread, doom, and guilt but this time it was indescribable and overwhelming. I suddenly knew what it was like to look over the edge and, God help me, *know* what it was like to want to go over. But the thought of my daughter brought me back to where I found myself on the rim of the "fish barrel" with the Yankees trying to climb out and the Rebels I loved, with good faces, having turned on me, despising me and rightly so, for I despised me too. For what right did I have to interpret their faces, their cause, their religion? I had none so it was right that I should suffer. It's what I deserved!

I began to shake uncontrollably like the coward I truly am but managed to put the book back where it came from. I couldn't help but wonder what Godly purpose any of this misery served? Did my life or anyone's have purpose, or was it assigned by others along the way, or by ourselves as we lost our innocence by surrendering to "ancient dogmas" that allowed our egos to overrule rationality? Did ego really stand for "easing God out," as some famous philosopher once said, demanding things like immortality? Whatever happened to being good for goodness' sake, without the need for reward or eternal blessings in an afterlife? Even cloistered monks want to gain heaven or nirvana by surrendering their desires, but isn't that the biggest contradiction of all? Isn't wanting heaven the ultimate desire? Like saying I'll be good by depriving myself these temporary things, and then I'll get everything later and, to boot, it'll be forever? Isn't that the ultimate form of reward seeking? So screw it then, maybe the Rebs were right; enslave everyone you can and be done with it. What the hell did any of this mean? I wanted to know, but would that wanting to know be the root of my downfall or my salvation?

Were the deaths of Dave and Judi, with their indescribable suffering, somehow in some way my fault because I had the most arrogant ego to wonder about *the nature of things* against the advice of my once and now abandoned ancient faith, which had warned me to keep quiet, accept it all, and ask no pesky questions? And if it wasn't my fault, why did it feel like it was? Was this what therapists call "survivor's guilt?" Or was it left over Catholic guilt that no one can totally get away from (at least not me anyway?) Was I losing my mind? Did I have one to lose? Dear Lord, what was happening and why was my confusion so physical? Was this punishment for not fearing God because I had the gall to think that fearing God was the last thing one should fear, with slavery being the first? Didn't fear imply alarm, painful emotion, dread, danger, anxious anticipation, and panic? Wasn't God love, truth, compassion, generosity, forgiveness, and peace, which were supposedly, or so I thought, the opposite of fear?

In a desperate, defensive grasp, I asked myself, who among us can rise above their circumstances and time in history? "I'm only human for God's sake," I told myself. But the truth of the Civil War within me told me I could've and should've done so much more in helping Dave and Judi deal with their suffering, and would've if I hadn't been such a selfish, egotistical, blowhard coward, but now it was too late to face that reality to do any good. But wasn't that what therapists tell their patients they must do; that in order to have a stable life—because maybe an innocent little girl sleeping upstairs deserves that from a father, because, God, she's growing up without a mother—the least I could do was to be honest with myself for the first time by facing it. That I must put it, warts and all, on the table to see things for what they were because the only way to possibly forgive myself was to understand what I was forgiving myself for? What kind of self-pitying narcissist was I?

My anguish and internal war had suffering on a numerical scale I could count on one hand compared to the kind Lincoln, the Yanks, and Rebs went through, which needed a million hands to count. But my elephant had nothing to do with numbers and everything to do with intensity and at least I knew that. For the suffering I witnessed was no less a horror than the most brutal kind they went through and God help me, the suffering of Dave and Judi far surpassed that of many soldiers but was equal to that of men, women, and children held in bondage and that, to be *totally honest,* and nothing more was the whole cause of the bloody mess.

Lincoln's witnessing of these events of suffering allowed him to *know,* not just *believe,* because here believing didn't count, that when all was said and done, if he lost every friend he had, there was one he hadn't lost who lived deep inside —himself. He said that to a friend not long before someone consumed with hate killed him. He knew he'd done the best he could for the nation he loved and those who made it and especially for the "wayward brethren" who would destroy it. But on this weary night, if I thought that about myself, it would've been a colossal lie.

Lincoln confessed events controlled him so maybe it was the events of my life that brought me to this dusty old chair, in a dusty old room, in a dusty old city, in a dusty old world. And maybe it's true when psychiatrists say our reaction to events is all we can control and it's influenced by our culture, environment, mothers, and fathers, and theirs from theirs and further still. But the responsibility to live true lies with us, with me; it's where the buck stops. And that meant the blame lay with me too so I couldn't blame events, even if delivered by an elephant that crushed everything in its path. My suffering *was* my fault because I'd lost the friend that lived deep inside me and did it by *not paying attention* to him like Dave and Judi did theirs. There was only one way to get him back with no guarantees. The little girl upstairs had a father who'd at least try, and if I failed I was enough of a bullshit artist to fake the role of a father who knew himself, because that's what children, especially girls, deserve if they can't have the real deal. My daughter, Judi's daughter, needed me to try!

I had to face the history of how I reacted to the suffering and death of my two friends and I had to do it now because it would never again be so fresh. It was before me in plain sight; not "a wen" or "cancer," hidden away like Lincoln said the Constitution hid slavery. And I had to do it alone because unlike Mathew Brady I had no Alexander Gardner and Tim O'Sullivan to help set up tripods to take pictures of dead Blue and Gray kids rotting on battlefields and I had to move quickly because my daughter would be rising with the sun. Brady showed the nation the suffering of war and I needed to show myself what caused the war in me. And even though there wasn't time to make the smallest dent in what I had to do, I took a giant step by getting out of the old decrepit, eclectic chair of truth because Lincoln taught me in order to do the impossible I had to take a step that was possible. It's how he dealt with slavery because all the other ways created a suffering we as a nation have yet to face. Getting out of the chair, still wet with the bile of Jonah's whale, was the first of a lifetime of steps and I felt release in moving.

On the way back to Dave's bed one of my dad's philosophy books caught my eye and I picked it up. It was written by a teacher of Eastern philosophy named Alan Watts. I'd read it a few years earlier when he gave me several of Watts's books when I was nineteen and twenty because he knew I was searching for something. They suggested I had a choice to believe or not believe in things and that action or inaction could lead to my true self: a compassionate human. They suggested that when a truth was undeniable, to accept and never betray it, to *know* love is the only undeniable truth! From there the best path was no path or one without boundaries, with freedom to go in any direction that would bring peace and love into my life. Having glimpses of that freedom through meditation and seeing it whole in Judi was how I learned at an early age that *knowing* is not the same as *believing*. Believing requires faith whereas love—true love, the only kind there is, the kind Judi lived—allows one to know so faith is not required, which is not to say faith is a bad thing. It's only bad when one becomes addicted to it, then it enslaves which makes it possible to enslave someone weaker. Addiction is one or the other! It's hard to explain but I fell so deeply in love with the concept of not having to believe that calling it a concept instead of a precious gift feels inappropriate. Maybe it's why I fell so in love with Judi, because she embodied that freedom and maybe knowing that little bit about myself was what made her take a chance on me. She didn't live long enough for us to know it together but she knew.

On Dave's bed with Watts's book in my hand I decided my daughter, meditation, and the beautiful teachings of history within these breastworks of books and music could be the three-legged stool to show me where I was so I could find a way forward because I *knew* I was out of my mind. I had to do something Lincoln said the nation had to do; he said in order to understand where it should go, it first had to understand where it was, and it couldn't do that until it understood where it had been. I could understand my present by knowing my past and though that couldn't predict the future it would give me a truer foundation from which to start. So I opened the book and found a passage that'd given me peace in the past. "There is no teacher until a student arrives; no problem until a question is raised. Now nobody has a question, but the game of life is to pretend that you do . . ."

What it meant for me then and in many ways now, is the answer to every question is within the question itself. It reminded me of Christ saying every honest prayer is answered, which implies that when prayers are not answered they're not honest. Honest prayers and meditation have that in common, which in many ways is the only thing they *totally* have in common because meditation can't be dishonest but prayers sometimes can be. Like history, if it's dishonest, it's not meditation or history but something else. With honesty, *questions evaporate!* When that happens it's easy to *know* Lincoln was right when he said, "God cannot be for and against the same thing at the same time." It's why he knew "if slavery is not wrong, nothing is!"

Honesty reveals being a slave to any dogma, be it dangerous, silly, ancient, or modern, is seeing the millstone of life for what it is. And when it's seen with no coins covering it, it flies away like a leaf in a windstorm. It doesn't matter if life has purpose. Giving it purpose by embracing it with everything you have that makes you, you, is the only way to find out if it does, and no one, nowhere, no how can teach another person that. If I just *believed* it, I'd end up faking it and would live the life of a slave but if I could somehow *know* it, I might actually live as a free human being, and with the love of a little girl, the moral lessons of the American Civil War, and the meditation of life, I might discover where my guilt came from. Facing the suffering of Dave and Judi the way they faced it was my one chance to live as a *knower* and not a *believer*.

A knower embraces that he doesn't know everything yet knows something is real and true when it makes him a more compassionate human being. *It's the most beautiful, reliable law of life.* When he finds he's wrong, he admits it because he knows being wrong is an invitation from the universe to learn something new and perhaps sacred. Lincoln was a knower who knew this intimately and admitted without embarrassment to people like Grant, "You were right and I was wrong!"

Ironically and sadly, the stronger a believer is attached to his beliefs the more he believes he knows everything and the fear of being wrong can terrify him, making him believe in mysteries and superstitions. Once that happens he can easily slip into becoming an aristocrat by believing the biggest crock of crap in the universe; that slavery is right and he's entitled to have a slave of his own. The Confederacy was born, lived, and died on that premise. Every slave-owner who was proud to be one was addicted to a sense of entitlement, and my daughter didn't deserve that kind of father! If I didn't have the guts to face the slavery of Dave and Judi, I'd do it this one time anyway because a little girl deserved me trying and I owed it to her mother and uncle. It could only work if I was honest with myself in a world without them to help. Maybe *that* would reveal the purpose of my life.

Lying back on Dave's bed was a step possible so I took it. It was my *journey begun.* When my head hit his pillow enough light from the rising sun showed that he'd written something on the ceiling. It was the oracle that ancient Greek philosophers inscribed over the entrance to the Temple of Delphi: *Know Thyself.* He and Judi did; could I?

A DIRT ROAD

David Joseph Foster was born, the second of three sons, to Albert Joseph, Jr. and Marilyn Lucille (Appel) Foster on September 28, 1953, in Lynn, Massachusetts. He arrived to an already smooth running, well-oiled machine that had been revolving around his older brother for twenty-one months. Before he destroyed the peaceful tranquility, I'd been the apple of my parents and both sets of grandparents' eyes because I was the firstborn son and grandson. Every noise I made and every diaper I filled brought applause and words of how special I was. Now, I wasn't so special but being a ham sandwich, I would continue (to this day) to seek applause by adding things to my repertoire, even at the expense of my little brother's health and well-being.

When Dave came home from the hospital there was an earthquake shift to the tectonic plates of my family, my world, and myself. Suddenly I had to share the spotlight with another person and I hadn't even been consulted. Ironically, he'd never care a fig about the spotlight but the powerful feeling of him entering my life was planted forever. If I'm generous about anything it's because I had to learn to share everything with him whether I liked it or not.

He knocked me off my high horse and thank God he did! Against my will, I became a better person by his simply being alive. Like most firstborns, I'd been a self-centered little aristocrat with a strong sense of entitlement, but the water was now out of that tub and I resented it!

He was named after his great-grandfather, whose parents emigrated from Scotland to Canada sometime during the 1800s. There has always been a David Joseph in our family, going all the way back to before Scotland was swallowed by England and, in clan lore, before Rome tried to swallow it too. My youngest brother, John, and his wife, Mary, would name the first of their two sons David and that brings great comfort to us because the sound of that beautiful name binds us as a family. The desire to hear it is in our blood. Since biblical times, it has been a name found in all the great religions of the West. It's cherished by my family and today I'm the proud uncle and godfather of my brother's namesake, David Joseph, who just became the father of his own little Dave.

A number of old-world nationalities found representation in the genes my brothers and I inherited, but we were too young to care about that. We weren't interested anyway, because we were part of that young, first generation after World War II, taught that all that mattered was that we were Americans, swimming in a melting pot called the United States of America. (Whatever happened to that philosophy? Isn't that what made us great?) Being the older brother, I remember hearing that our paternal grandfather was of Scottish and French descent and couldn't speak a word of English when he came to the U.S. from New Brunswick, Canada, at the age of nine. Our grandmother, born here, was of Scottish and Irish descent. And on the maternal side of the ledger, our grandfather, whose great grandfather, Conrad Appel, fought for the Union with the 10th Vermont Regiment during the Civil War, was born here and of German and Irish descent; our grandmother, born here, of Yugoslavic and Irish descent. My maternal grandmother said we had a good dose of "Patty's Pig" (an old Irish saying) in us along with a healthy mix of other garnishes to stew the pot but again, it was more important that we were Americans. Thankfully our socially minded mother subtlety let us know, for reasons she didn't go into, that the American melting pot was tilting tremendous advantages our way while for many others, it was tilting away. I felt very lucky being in this innocent *Leave It To Beaver*-ish world but, around the age of six, I began feeling that somewhere out there someone was getting the shaft.

Because of our mostly northern European ancestry we were brothers of the blond, red-haired, fair-skinned, and freckled persuasion; the type Norman Rockwell often used as models for his paintings. Because of the social policies and programs instituted by Franklin Roosevelt before and during World War II, and because he knew a strong middle class was the key to the future safety and stability of the U.S., ours was a nation on the rise; riding higher than any on the winds of victory over tyranny. Some historians call that war "the good war," which makes me cringe, calling any war a good one, but they're absolutely right; if ever there was a good war that was one, because it was against cruel and irrational mindsets that harmed all humanity. Likewise, although it was a deeply personal struggle within our American family, the Civil War was a war ultimately against a similar kind of unfair and deadly mindset that was entrenched within our borders and even deeper in our souls. These two wars illustrate that when Americans are told the truth about why they're fighting, they attain victory and when they're lied to, disaster follows. These wars also teach what we can do when the majority pulls together. That was the most difficult task for Lincoln and Roosevelt: to make sure people with different political and social persuasions pulled together. It's somehow in the nature of our democracy that telling the truth to the American people brings success. Sadly, at our peril, we sometimes forget that.

Our parents, especially our mom, understood this and recognized our position in the world meant opportunities to advance with the nation were there for the taking for *almost* everyone in the middle class who was willing to work hard, and my young parents (my dad was twenty-two and my mom nineteen when I was born) were willing. And though they couldn't afford precious metals, it felt like they gave us life on a silver platter. The reality was they struggled, but it brought results. They didn't spoil us and wouldn't have if they could've but our grandparents tried. Our parents made us feel safe, protected, and loved, and that's the best any kid could hope for. We were the epitome of the American dream with the best family health insurance our dad's company (General Electric in Lynn, Massachusetts) offered in the 1950s. And even though there were occasional labor strikes that kept both sides on their toes, our modest lifestyle was the crème de la crème of what American democracy provided to the middle class. We were never hungry, warm in winter, went camping in New Hampshire on vacation; what more could we ask for?

Being born into this ultramodern postwar world, in the most powerful and "greatest" nation on earth, we had all the advantages of polio and other vaccines, penicillin, plastic, private telephone lines (although we shared one for awhile) with dial yourself rotary phones, central heating, and the most earth-shaking invention of all besides radio—black-and-white television. Doctors, hand in hand with milk formula companies, discovered human breast milk was inadequate for the modern child and, to boot, that breastfeeding was unhealthy for the mother, so we were a generation raised entirely on formula. Cigarettes, Schlitz malt liquor (beer), Aqua Velva, and Brillcream *("A little dab'll do ya. She'll love to get her fingers in your hair.")* were keys to getting that fancy convertible with a bleached blond beach babe in the passenger seat. Greased DAs (duck's ass) haircuts were so cool for guys, but our mom never let us get one. We were too young anyway, and later when The Beatles came along looking like Moe from *The Three Stooges,* DAs disappeared. Thankfully, The Stones fixed that nightmare.

In those early years, Elvis was king while black artists that inspired him down in Mississippi were hidden away and never heard from. Without question, he was incredibly talented but wasn't as original as he was portrayed to be, and to his everlasting credit, he was the first to admit it. Somehow our mom knew all this so we weren't as brainwashed as most kids were by the goofiness of the 1950s and early 1960s. But just to be on the safe side I had my tonsils ripped out because doctors discovered we didn't need them and that they actually *caused* colds. I got to eat lots of Jell-o and ice cream so there were benefits, and you could bring your tonsils home in a jar if you wanted. My brothers got to keep theirs because doctors then discovered removing them did more harm than good. Still, there were advantages in being the first child in this time of rapid change and experimentation, and I think the only drawback was that sometimes I was subjected to things my parents soon learned weren't so good. But our mom was a quick learner and wasn't prey to popular opinion she knew to be fickle and often wrong.

Our dad had joined the U.S. Army at the tail end of the war. He was always good at reading, writing, math, and mechanical drawing. With live combat drastically winding down, the Army kept him stateside at Fort Dix and later Camp Elmer in New Jersey. He was assigned a desk job going over paperwork with soldiers coming home directly from the front. Within minutes of getting off the plane they'd be sitting with our dad. What a contrast that must've been for kids on both sides of the desk. He'd explain the benefits these young heroes were entitled to and when his time of service was up he too took advantage of the GI Bill, making it possible for him to get a great education at Boston College. How I wish we believed in helping vets today the same as we did then. He'd always been interested in flight so, with his engineering degree in aeronautics, he became a technical writer at General Electric (GE), which meant he could tell how to put a jet engine together starting with the first screw. To put it bluntly, he was one smart guy and still is. Never too much on the athletic side, he loved and appreciated sports growing up because his father, Abe, was a great baseball and football player in the old city of Lynn. So when we, especially me, were not interested in academics, he read books about hockey, baseball, and swimming so he could coach us. He was awesome, fair to everyone, never favoring us over teammates. His attitude was and still is a precious gift!

He grew up in a quiet neighborhood next to Lynn Woods, a 2200 acre forest, and one of the jewels of the city. "The Woods" are enchanting, like having a piece of Maine, Vermont, or New Hampshire inside our old industrial city, which the shoe industry, more than anything else, put on the map. Lynn's been known for its forward, open-minded, liberal thinking through the centuries. Countless reformers felt welcomed to give speeches exposing everything from the evils of slavery to the outright ridiculous notion that the more intelligent half of the human race wasn't wise enough to vote. Fredrick Douglass, the ex-slave, abolitionist, and later friend of Abraham Lincoln, gave speeches on Lynn Common on a spot now commemorated by the Frederick Douglass Bandstand. One hundred years later, GE designed the first jet engine manufactured in the United States. The city has contributed too many important things to America to give it justice here.

Given all the time I spent in "The Woods" with Dave and Judi, and the fact that I still run, hike, mountain bike, and meditate there, the place has become my sanctuary. Our parents met there so it's in my blood. Our dad was home from college, sitting against a tree on a wooded ridge and studying when our mom stumbled upon him while walking her dog. They were sixteen and nineteen, respectively, and our mom was mature enough to recognize a good thing. Surrounded by nature and books, the only thing missing, as corny as it sounds, was music, and our mom remedied that on their first date. They went to Boston to see Georges Bizet's opera *Carmen*. The music is too beautiful and majestic to describe and the story line covers eternal elements of human nature. That our young mother wanted to go to the opera might sound implausible until you knew the passion for music running deep in her family of musicians.

Her entire life music was *the* thing making life precious. It always played in the background in our home while she performed the mundane but critical tasks of running a home with four domestically incompetent males. By osmosis my brothers and I were educated by the old mono record player in the same way she'd been; by hearing the music of Beethoven, Mozart, Strauss, Handel, Schubert, Liszt, Brahms, Bach, Tchaikovsky, Schumann, Wagner, Stravinsky, Prokofiev, Berlin, Gershwin, Porter, Copeland, Leonard Bernstein, and too many others to mention. And it wasn't all classical; she loved the big band sounds of Count Basie, Benny Goodman, and Louie Armstrong. The first time I heard Armstrong I told her he sounded like he was in pain and she said he was but didn't tell me why. She said if I listened with my heart instead of my ears I'd hear how beautiful he sounded. I somehow understood this, and Dave was beside me understanding it too. She'd always tell us who composed the music we heard on Looney Tunes cartoons, *The Lone Ranger, The Three Stooges, The Bugs Bunny Show, The Road Runner Show* (I always wanted the coyote to catch that little bastard), and other shows as we ate oatmeal or cream of wheat on Saturday mornings in our Roy Rogers and Hop-a-long Cassidy pajamas.

Today it makes me smile that as kids, Dave, John, and I were privileged with musical knowledge whereas Ulysses S. Grant as a general in the United States Army was once asked what his favorite songs were and replied, "One is 'Yankee Doodle' and the other isn't!" That's not to disparage Grant's taste in music, but it is to say how lucky we were to grow up in a house of music, a house my parents bought in 1953 shortly before David was born.

It was an old fixer-upper on quiet, unpaved Riverbank Road in Saugus, Massachusetts. The Saugus River ran through our backyard. The housing boom of the 1950s soon brought lots of new homes to the neighborhood and with it, modernity, people, and paving to the ancient rutted dirt road. Until then Dave, John, and I lived an almost shoeless type of summertime lifestyle. Relatives may have thought we lived like hillbillies, but we loved it and our socially aware parents knew it wouldn't last. The boom brought bulldozers, tractors, cranes, and trucks to dig foundations for the new homes and this was terribly exciting because we wanted to see everything this virgin (or so we thought) soil had to reveal. The huge machines were giant, sharp-toothed dinosaurs that clawed through earth, rocks, and tree roots, and what kid in the 1950s wouldn't love that? When the workmen went home for the day we'd crawl or slide deep into the freshly dug pits, and the earth revealed we were living on ground once inhabited by people who had lived along the riverbank and nearby. This had an incredible impact on me; knowing we were not the first to live here and were only borrowing the land. With our dad we combed the dirt and found hundreds of arrowheads, pieces of pottery, and even the stem of a smoking pipe and an axe made of stone. Soon archaeologists and anthropologists from around the country descended on our neighborhood and I peppered them with questions they were only too kind to answer. One told me I was a curious little bugger and that curiosity may kill a cat but could lead to a cool career.

Our father made an incredible find near our garden: a 1652 English shilling, the first coin minted in the New World. It may have belonged to a worker at the Saugus Iron Works, the first producer of iron in America, with all of it shipped to England. The Iron Works were a quarter mile upstream from our house and still functions as a museum today. It's incredible! Scottish convicts originally worked there to pay their debts and our half-Scottish grandfather joked that we were probably related. Our dad put the coin in a protective case and glued dozens of intact arrowheads to display boards that became teaching tools for our mom when she became a history teacher. He was extremely industrious, fixing up the house and yard and making intricate drainage systems that still work today. I know because I drive by the old place when I need to satisfy my nostalgia and because most of the memories are sweet. We always had to help him and when we whined he'd say that one day we'd appreciate the things we learned. For me, he was halfway right but truthfully he never worked us too hard, just hard. It reminds me of Abraham Lincoln saying his father taught him to work hard but not how to like it. Our mother sometimes called us for supper a half hour earlier than she had to, to rescue us, and we'd be off in a flash. It wouldn't surprise me if Lincoln's conscientious mother did the same. But if our dad worked hard around the house and at GE, our mom brought it to another level altogether. And again, she had four boys to take care of, and did everything! Not only the cooking, cleaning, laundry, wiping of noses, etc., but for the longest time she was physically stronger than any of us so she also helped our dad with his "projects."

As the neighborhood grew, young mothers who had moved into the new houses fell in love with our mom. She was younger than most but was the old lady matriarch of the neighborhood for having lived there the longest. Someone was always making our old black rotary phone ring on the wall next to the kitchen stove. All Dave and I ever heard her say was, "Ya, uh ha, I see, is that right, you don't say, oh jeez," and things of that nature. We'd ask why she never said anything back to her friends and she'd just laugh and say, "Oh they're not interested in things I'm interested in." Then we'd ask why she talked to them at all and she'd say they were good people who just needed someone to listen and she didn't mind doing it.

Once, she was on the phone for a half hour (Dave and I timed her) with a neighbor who had plastic covering the couch and chairs of her living room. It never came off, not even at Christmas, and God forbid if you ever trekked a speck of dirt on her floors. Her son was our play friend who tragically died a few years later from a vicious brain tumor. She called our mom several times a day to complain about earth-shattering things like dirt, rain, clouds, the sun, snow, or the next-door neighbor's flea-bitten, mangy, one-eyed, tailless tomcat who tried to sneak into her yard to make mad, passionate, disgusting love to her precious, longhaired, spoiled rotten Persian, Yum Yum. Well, we counted our mom saying, "Uh ha, is that right" fifty-four times. When we told her later, she laughed and told us it was funny but mean-spirited and not to listen anymore. Dave asked, "Listen to what?" but we got the message.

Later I asked her what she'd like to talk about.

"Oh I don't know, maybe something important for a change," she said.

"You can talk to me about important things," I said.

"I already do!" she said.

It made me so happy. I loved talking to her and Dave did too. Somehow we knew we had a good thing with her but it all came close to being lost forever by something that still gives me a chill.

Living next to the river was dangerous, but we were excellent little swimmers thanks to lessons at the Lynn YMCA. We were allowed near the river in the summer to catch minnows, baby herrings (alewifes), and snapping turtles, but were never allowed to swim because it was so filthy. Often we'd find fish, turtles, and eels washed up dead with eyes bulging or barely alive and struggling for oxygen through foamy mouths. There was a German-owned chemical plant a hundred yards upstream from the Iron Works where every couple of days they'd dump hundreds of gallons of foul-smelling sludge containing weirdly colored chemicals into the river. We didn't know how dangerous the stuff was but the colors were gross and we loved that. It sank when thick and sometimes bubbling fumes smoked off the water, burning our eyes and throats so we'd shift upwind. When the current was strong it got swept away, going right past our yard downstream on its way to the ocean. It smelled horrible, especially in summer, and made you dizzy when you got too close. Nobody gave a hoot about the environment like we do today, not because they weren't smart and concerned but because companies were expert at lying and keeping secrets in a time when OSHA and the Freedom of Information Act were only pipe dreams. Winter wasn't as bad because the river froze and chemicals floated unseen under the ice.

If we had an adult with us we could go on the ice to play hockey. Saugus was and still is a hockey town. I was in an indoor pee-wee league, so games on the wild river were a treat. Neighborhood fathers (like ours who wore skates two sizes too big and couldn't skate too well), sons, and brothers played. When spring approached you'd know because you'd hear ice cracking across the marshes before it floated away.

Well one year, when Dave was five, some kids were hopping onto large chunks of ice to float down the river for a hundred yards and then hopping off where a bend brought the ice back to shore. A family that lived in the neighborhood as long as we had, in a house as old as ours, had five boys and one girl, and several of the boys were playing this deadly game while kids watched. One of the boys later died of cancer but before that tragic event the family made for great entertainment. If somehow the Hatfields and McCoys miraculously made peace and their descendants married into the Ma and Pa Kettle family and then combined with Jed Clampett's (a family I love), these would've been their descendants, and they'd all look up to Uncle Jethro for his supreme wisdom. Yet even he wouldn't be so dumb as to jump onto broken ice unless it was in his "ceeement pond." These siblings, including the girl, always fought among themselves if they couldn't find someone in the neighborhood to fight. They were the ones with the one-eyed tomcat that was hot to trot for Yum Yum and sometimes they fought him too.

Our mother knew of this insane ice-hopping activity and forbade us to go anywhere near the river when it was breaking up. I never did but Dave, who *always* did what he was told, as opposed to me, somehow ended up by the river when the youngest Kettle/Clampett boy began screaming for help after a chunk of ice he was on broke in half. Dave *immediately*—we were told—went running along the riverbank to jump on the chunk of ice to help the kid off. Dave pushed him to shore but in doing so slid into the icy river. It was the type of thing he'd do for the rest of his life. The kids on the shore saw him go under and then resurface only to get swept away with the current. I was oblivious to this, playing in our yard thirty feet above the river when the boy's sister ran past to pound on our back door. "Mrs. Foster, Mrs. Foster, David's in the river!" I was seven but remember vividly how everything slowed as my mother, who had just gotten out of our old-fashioned lion-clawed tub to dry off and put on a slip because she was going out with our dad for supper (something they could afford every three months or so), came running out, barefoot through the snow, in her slip only, as if shot from a Porter Alexander cannon prior to Pickett's Charge. As she passed I heard her saying to herself, as a way of processing the situation, "My baby's in the river, my baby's in the river!"

I followed in the approaching twilight to see her slide down the steep, mucky, icy embankment in a single movement and when she got to the bottom, Dave was fifty yards away, halfway to the bend, pulling himself out of the river. Somehow he was a good enough swimmer, wearing winter boots, clothes, and all, to tread water and make it far enough to grab an overhanging tree branch. Our mom ran to him and knelt to hold him and I could see her leg badly cut and bloodied from sliding down the embankment. Her slip was shredded and she was covered in muck that had shiny ice crystals made from river water and chemicals reflecting the descending sun. She held her hatless, shivering, red-haired boy in her arms. I didn't approach because I was simply stunned but in the next second I started to and she got up. The neighborhood kids, some parents arriving on the scene, and I all watched in awed silence as her powerful legs and bare feet dug into the icy riverbank as she carried her baby to our house to strip him down in the tub. I followed up the stairs and noticed each step had a mucky, bloody footprint.

While the tub filled she held him over the toilet because he was frighteningly ill from the *violence* (pollution) he swallowed. When he stopped throwing up she put him in the tub for the first of several baths but had to keep a bucket close by because he kept heaving and the sound was awful. She told me to watch him so she could call our doctor and then our dad who was about to leave work. It was the first time she'd ever asked me to watch one of my brothers and the responsibility felt strange because Dave and I fought like cats and dogs. On occasion, though, we could behave for twelve seconds every few weeks or so. That she trusted me for a half a minute meant this was serious and I felt useful. She also had to check on our two-year-old brother, John, because he'd been alone in the house all this time. Dave looked extra small in the tub with bluish skin and purple lips. He looked at me with a "screw this" expression with the saddest brown eyes you'd ever seen and he shook his head as if to say, "Don't ask me anything," but maybe he was just shaking. I heard our mom telling our dad that Dave had fallen in the river. He must've asked if he was okay because she said, "I hope so but he's blue and the doctor's on his way." When she got off the phone she told me to sit with little John in the living room. He was the most peaceful, sane, and least troublesome of the three of us, and he sensed something bad had happened so I sat on the couch and held his hand.

Our mom scrubbed Dave thoroughly but he was getting a rash anyway. It looked like a bad sunburn. When our doctor arrived—they made house calls in those days—he looked at my mother and was shocked. "My God, what happened?" She waved him off saying, "Don't worry about me," and then told him of Dave's Huck Finnish nightmare. He gave Dave something to drink which made him throw up more than he had already. The doctor said that they probably got out all they could of whatever Dave had ingested, but a night in the hospital might be wise. When Dave heard and somehow understood what the doctor said he shouted his first words since being in the river: "No hospital!" The irony would one day prove powerful beyond description. Dave was the most stubborn of all of us in this stubborn family so when he said it, it had the authority of the god's. The doctor laughed a little and said he could get to our house just as quickly as he could to the hospital so if our mom wanted to keep him home it'd be okay. Then he gave Dave and our mom tetanus shots as well as medicine for Dave to take every few hours.

The doctor then began to examine our mother, who was a bloody mess. She insisted she was okay and just wanted to "clean up" before our dad got home. She didn't know how bad she looked and that would've been the last thing on her mind because even though she was very pretty she was never one to obsess about her looks; she had more important things to worry about at the moment. Most likely she was in a state of shock, still fueled by the powerful adrenaline of a protective mother. But her baby was alive and not being pulled out dead from an icy river. She'd crash later when she was sure he was okay. The doctor gave her gauze wraps, bandages, and salve. Some of our mom's cuts and scrapes, that I saw, looked horrible and needed treatment and possibly stitches. I don't think I saw the worst and the doctor saw less than I did. When he was leaving he told her to call no matter what time just as our dad pulled into our unpaved driveway in our old blue 1954 two-door Plymouth. He had just survived the infamous GE traffic caused by fourteen thousand people getting out of work at the same time.

I looked out the window to see late-winter steam coming out of the mouths of the doctor and my dad as they passed and briefly spoke. When my dad got to the back steps and saw the bloody footprints the size of my mother's feet, I heard him howl in anguish, "Jesus Christ, Marilyn." She was in the bathroom putting lotion on Dave and I think this was the first time she became aware of her appearance because she locked the bathroom door. She didn't want him to see the mess she was. When he opened the backdoor he called for her and she called back that she was in the bathroom with Dave. He said, "Honey"—he always called her that or "Sweetheart"—"the door is locked." She faked a surprised and phony, "Oh, hang on a sec." She bought herself a few seconds and when he walked in and saw what he saw he made a groan of despair like I'd never heard before. It made me cry and I didn't know why. He asked, in the way a father who takes out all his boys' splinters because he's gentler than the mother, "For Christ's sake, hon, why didn't you tell me it was this bad?" I went to the bathroom to see she'd cleaned up a little and had a towel around her legs. She was sitting on the closed toilet seat and holding Dave while drying his hair. Her long, ratty old bathrobe hid her wounds from our dad. She told him what she knew of Dave's mishap in the river and what the doctor had said. Then she told him to take Dave and put his pajamas on while she took a bath.

When she finally came to the living room where our dad, Dave (who was still shaking and didn't feel like talking), John, and I were, she had on long winter pajamas, white socks, and slippers like someone would wear in a drafty old house during a late New England winter. It wouldn't be until summer and bathing suit season—our mom was one of the few female lifeguards around—that we'd see how mangled her legs really were. They canceled their plans for their evening out and when Dave and I went to bed we could hear their murmuring voices through our thin horsehair plaster walls. We shared a bedroom and I asked if he was scared in the river. His shaky voice said, "I was in the water," which inferred an incredulous "No!" Even then, when Dave was in water, even icy, polluted water, he was more at home than on land. Then he said, "I got Joey off the ice but I don't feel good and I smell like the yucky river!" He smelled that way for a few days and his rash developed blisters and bumps that eventually went away but who knows how the crap in the river affected him. My mom had to throw out his clothes. Soon he'd be in the hospital for kidney problems but we never found out if they were related to the river.

Seeing my near naked, bloody mother kneeling, holding my brother next to the icy river was seeing the most powerful form of human instinct that would one day open a window to understand what it's like for a mother to have her baby taken without warning, be it by war, disease, a floating block of ice or slave master. When I had my own baby I understood even more because *only a parent can know*. My mom was lucky *this time* because she got her child back. In a few years, she wouldn't be and none of us would've been able to handle the approaching storm coming Dave's way had we known. It's probably good we can't predict the future but if we could maybe some Scrooge-like aristocrats throwing poisons in rivers when only kids are watching would make a change toward compassion. But then again, the reality is we can't even predict the past!

When Robert E. Lee Made My Mother Groan

The haunting sound of my father's groan at the sight of our mother kept ringing in my ears. It wouldn't go away. I'd hear it when I saw him even though he wasn't making it. Somehow I knew it was a universal sound that I didn't feel ready or old enough to hear because it revealed my all-powerful and wise father was vulnerable. It affected my being much in the way a groan I'd heard from my mother half a year earlier, which had already begun to influence the future course of my life. Hers showed vulnerability too but also more, that all people were vulnerable to things beyond their control, and compassion based on reason was the only way to help anyone enslaved by anything.

It was the summer of 57. I was six and our mom had just given me and Dave baths because we'd been playing in the dirt pits. Little John was in bed and we were between our parents, on the couch in our pajamas watching TV. Our mom was next to me. They weren't particularly big boxing fans but for some reason, maybe the novelty of it, the old *Friday Night Fights* were on and our mom said we could watch a single three-round match before going to bed. The first fighter was introduced; "From the North, in blue trunks, a genuine

Billy Yank." Then the United States flag (I knew what that was) appeared on the screen, followed by a picture of a peculiar-looking guy with a beard, followed by another guy with a rounder head and beard. He was in a dark uniform. They were Abraham Lincoln and Ulysses S. Grant. Then the second fighter was introduced; "And from the South, in gray trunks, a 'jin-you-iieenne' Johnnie Reb." The twangy way the announcer said "genuine" made my mom laugh so I did too. Then the Confederate States flag appeared and I had no clue what it was, followed by a picture of a guy with a beard (Jefferson Davis), who seemed to be clenching his teeth a little more than the first guy, followed by a fourth guy with a gray beard in a lighter colored uniform. I thought he might've been good old St. Nick.

When the fourth man appeared a deeply sympathetic, irrepressible, and conflicted groan came out of the depths of my mother's being. It didn't come from her throat but her soul. It was a groan only a mother could make after she has told her oldest son not to climb a particular tree because it's above a dangerous fence and that if he were to fall, the fall might kill him. But he climbs it anyway when she's not looking, and at the very top a branch breaks, sending him falling through other branches that are cutting him. Finally he hits the ground but not before the fence snaps his leg in a position legs aren't meant to go, ripping his knee apart. She'll rush to his screams. She loves him more than life and, when she sees he's not killed, her love is almost matched by her anguish at his disobeying but this is not the time for that and she lets out a groan only a mother can make. Her son's stubborn stupidity, boyishness, and damn-well persistent, defiant obstinacy caused him to suffer and her more. It was the groan of sorrow, worry, exasperation, disappointment, anger, sympathy, and yet *ever so reluctant* understanding that I felt vibrating from the body housing the spirit of my mother at the sight of Robert Edward Lee.

He represented the finest qualities of a system that at its core epitomized a culture guaranteeing hope and safety for the haves while offering none for the have-nots, nor any future thought, however remote, of them attaining it if there was ever to be justice in the world. He was the best the Confederate States of America had to offer. He was us and we him and our mom knew it. I was about to learn forever that we can't secede from our American brothers and sisters *or ourselves* no matter how much she wanted to divorce the pain and sorrow this brother's fall caused to millions. I'd heard previous groans reserved for our father, for me and my brothers, for neighbors, and for the death of one of our cats. And mild, not so serious groans for the Red Sox, Patriots, Celtics, Bruins, and Floyd Patterson but this was a serious groan. When it seemed the serious ones could be retired for good they'd re-emerge at the assassinations of J. F. K., Martin Luther King, and Bobby Kennedy. But those were groans of pure sadness, not the kind where one brings suffering to himself like the boy falling from the tree or Robert E. Lee.

This groan had pure frustration too, like when a neighbor would say how upset he was that Bill Russell of the Celtics "was such an ungrateful nigger" because he said he didn't feel welcomed in Boston despite bringing home all those championships. She'd gently explain to the neighbor that there were very real reasons why Russell "may appear to be an ungrateful man" and if the offended neighbor did a little homework he'd better understand. But images as black-and-white in Technicolor, as on our black-and-white TV would appear, and groans of pure anguish would emanate. When southern politicians like Lester Maddox, Strom Thurmond, George Wallace, Jesse Helms and others preached their message of racial hatred she'd make the kind of groan she'd make at images of dogs, water cannons, and police with nightsticks attacking people for only asking for a fair chance for their children. At the old Dixiecrat Conventions televised in the 1960s, where thousands waved Confederate flags and speakers shouted from the podium, "We will never let our children go to school with nigger children!" she'd groan and whisper, "Those no good sons of bitches," using language Harry Truman and Lincoln used to describe those who couldn't be described any other way. And when she did, hearing it brought me closer to the love of God than all the Latin "Dominus Vobiscums" I'd hear in the several thousand Catholic Masses I'd attend.

I'm sorry to make references to my once ancient faith like that but it was my mom who picked me up at the Blessed Sacrament Church in Saugus in the 1950s when I was learning my Latin to become an altar boy. She watched us playing basketball one hot summer day with the young, popular priest teaching us the duties of altar boyhood. I felt guilty seeing him all sweaty, shirtless, in tight little black shorts on the court, and guiltier when he hugged us underneath the rectory, the hugs feeling way too long. I thought the guilt was my fault because I was a sinner and, for God's sake, the priest was *the* representative of Christ on earth and every Catholic kid knew that! When I got in the car she told me to "never be alone with 'that man' ever again." Hearing him reduced to "that man" was monumental, because he was supposed to be someone I could trust with my every thought, hope, and dream. That night she told our dad the priest was "way too friendly with the kids" and she didn't want me to be an altar boy anymore. Forty years later I'd see this same priest on television being led away in handcuffs for molesting more than eighty-five kids, four of whom I was playing basketball with that day long ago. He was the infamous Father John Geoghan who the Church protected and lied for, instead of fighting for his victims. His life jaded and affected mine, but because of my mother, didn't ruin it like he did four of my friends who became altar boys while being raped, sodomized, and altered forever below the rectory.

I'd hear her groan at the TV when someone like black heavyweight fighter Floyd Patterson was fighting a guy from Russia, Germany, Sweden, or some-place like that. She'd say, "Come on Floyd, you can do it!" I'd ask why she was rooting for Patterson and she'd reply, "Well, for one thing, he's an American and for another, he's a gentleman!" Her short answer would be the end of it but she knew, as I'd find out later, that thousands, if not millions of white Americans were rooting for the white foreigner, even if he was a communist, to "kick the living shit out of the nigger!" Occasionally there'd be a rare national league baseball game on and she'd get upset if Don Drysdale threw a little too close to Willie Mays. In all fairness to Drysdale though, he'd throw at his own grandmother if she were crowding the plate. When the Celtics were heading for another championship because of a rebound by Russell, who'd pass to Bob Cousy, who'd razzle-dazzle a behind-the-back pass back to Russell, who'd be under the basket and would then dish it to the open man to make the shot, it was a thrill in our home, though it was arrogant as all hell for Red Auerbach to light that cigar before the game was over. Our mom felt the Celtics were truly an American team because blacks and whites worked together and were led by a Jewish coach, and she loved that. When Red lit his cigars I somehow knew she was thinking of the racial makeup of the team and that Red's cigars were exclamation points!

She never set out to teach us about racism and bigotry. It was just how she reacted to the ever-changing, but too slow, gut-wrenching struggle that modern television, radio, books, and newspapers brought to our doorstep. It taught us that many Americans either had blinders on or were too lazy or selfish to look at their doorstep. She somehow knew in an intrinsic way that America was fooling itself and had been since its inception, but still that America was as Lincoln said it was, "The Last Best Hope Of Earth," so she'd *never* give up on it. She knew America wanted to do the right thing but didn't know how, because not all Americans had the correct information about our history or understood that racism was based on the biggest lie in human history: the inferiority and superiority of one race to another. So when she was quite certain our dad had mastered the technique well enough to occasionally pour Rice Krispies into bowls for her three boys, she decided it was time to enroll in what is now Salem State University to get her degree in American history. I was ten and remember well that when she came home from school she still had to care for the four of us or else we'd perish, but she did so with a lighter step, as if the weight of the world was being lifted from her shoulders because of her education and the historical proof that her inclinations of the way things were, were correct. She said to me and Dave, "If you two ever want to know why things are so screwed up in the world, history is the key!"

In this type of home, with a far-seeing, progressive-thinking mother who saw things through the inclinations of an honest, open heart soon to be backed up by historical facts, I heard her groan at the sight of Robert E. Lee. It propelled me to ask who he was. She said it was time for bed and Dave was already on his way, but to my questions came these answers.

"No, he's not Santa Claus!" (I already knew there was no such thing because I asked her when I was five and she said there wasn't but it could be a lot of fun making believe there was.)

"It was Robert E. Lee. He was an American. He fought a war against other Americans."

"Why?"

"Because he was raised to think one way and Northern people were raised to think another."

"Are we Northern?"

"Yes, but all Northerners weren't good and all Southerners weren't bad. Good and bad people fought on both sides, but one side was wrong while the other was 'trying' to be right."

The word "trying" took me by surprise, like she was sharing something important with me on her level.

"The North won, which meant both sides won, but everyone lost so much."

"Like what?" I asked.

"Many hundreds of thousands of innocent kids like you lost their lives."

"Like me?"

"Because too many people didn't like the new president and said he was going to do bad things to the South when all he was trying to do was good things for everyone. But these people lied and ignorant, innocent people believed them."

"Why did they believe them?"

"Because they didn't know any better and that's what ignorance does."

"But why Ma, why didn't they know?"

"It's late and you have to go to bed."

"What would've happened if Lee's side won?"

"It would've been terrible for the whole world if the South won."

"Why?"

"Because they were fighting for a very bad thing! Now go to bed and don't fight with your brother!"

"But Ma, if Robert Lee was fighting for a bad thing why did you make that noise like you liked him?"

"I didn't say I liked him!"

She said "him" with hesitation and a hint of grudging admiration to the question. "But Maaa, you made the noise you make when someone you like does something bad."

I'll never forget the look on my twenty-five-year-old mother's face in that old house up a dirt road in Saugus, Massachusetts. It was as if she didn't want to hurt me or take away a drop of my youthful innocence, all the while being so young herself. I wanted to tell her it was okay to tell me what she wanted to even if I didn't know what it meant.

She said very quietly and gently, "Most everyone will do good things if their parents teach them that all people, no matter what color their skin, are created equal. Lee was not raised to think that way because he lived in a crazy part of the country that made his parents crazy and they taught him that bad things were good." Her voice was mixed with sadness, resignation, compassion, and wisdom but also something new: *conviction*. It excited me and made me want to be on the same team, wearing that conviction jersey.

"What would've happened if Lee's side won?" I asked again.

She said, "Well, for one thing, the big shots on his side didn't want black people to have any fun or rights. They wanted them to be slaves forever, so Jackie Robinson and Willie Mays wouldn't have been able to play baseball. Now go to bed!"

The way she said "go to bed" this time conveyed I'd pushed the questioning to the limit. She gave me answers I could relate to. *Everyone needs that!* But I had a million questions, especially about the word "slave," because the way she said it meant it was the worst thing a person could be. She wanted me to have honest answers while knowing they were incomplete because my innocence was precious to her; this epitomized her character. The picture of Lee was not meant to elicit a groan from anyone in the 1950s. The introductions of the Northern and Southern fighters were all in fun and would've gone on as that if not for her curious son seeking an explanation for her groan. She somehow saw more than anyone I've ever known. Forty-two years later, I was sitting in a room full of history professors (The Lincoln Group of Boston at Bridgewater University) and wondering how the hell I'd gotten there, if things I said were an embarrassment, and whether they'd like me to return. One of the professors (now a good friend) said, "Please join our club. You see things others don't and we need that." I went back and continue to do so to this day but thought, *Oh professor, if you could've only known my mom!*

It would be silly to say that falling out of a tree, ending up on crutches, and suffering the groans of my parents were gifts of any sort. But the physical and mental pain of those things led to my mother's gentle explanations of the American Civil War. They lit a spark under me and made me want to know more. Some historians like to say, and not entirely correctly, that it was the Kansas/Nebraska Act of 1854 that lit a fire under Lincoln and made him jump back into the political arena by speaking out against slavery. But a bigger truth is, it started long before with his mother and step-mother encouraging him to find out how the world worked by reading everything he could get his hands on. That more than anything helped foster his ability to empathize with his fellow man, and that's when his fire was really lit. For sure Kansas/Nebraska was a huge pile of kindling but the pilot light was already on!

Being on crutches for a month, I couldn't play baseball or dig in the pits or run through the fields surrounding our house, but I *could* ask questions. The thought that Americans fought and killed other Americans intrigued me to no end. That good people (Rebs) could fight for bad things because of what they were taught to believe by parents, schools, churches, and political leaders intrigued me further still. To the bombardment of questions I had for our mom; she'd sit and show me pictures in encyclopedias of who was who and what was what and explained that a civil war by definition was a nation at war with itself; meaning a family affair affecting everyone so it was personal. Her answers were as simple as the questions and, although I wasn't able to read that well, the pictures sucked me in. I'd look at them hour after hour, or I'd just have a book open to where I could glance as I hobbled by on crutches. I only had one uneasy feeling about it all and was hesitant to ask about it because I didn't want to disappoint her. When I looked at Yanks and Rebs, I understood the Rebs were usually, but not always, outnumbered and sometimes ill-equipped, and I somehow felt sorry for them. Also, I liked the way they looked more than the Yanks, but still I was glad they lost the war, but not every battle. I was a contradiction without knowing the word. *I was like the country.*

Finally I asked her if it was okay to like the Rebs as much as I did, even though they were fighting for bad things. I was a little afraid to hear her answer but she smiled and said, "Well, it's hard not to like them if you understand they were Americans fighting for what they thought was right. But thank God they lost because they weren't fighting for what America *is* supposed to be. And remember, if they won, people would've been slaves for many more years than they were and the United States would've been destroyed and our lives would be very different than they are now."

"How?" I asked.

"Not as good!" she said.

"How many more years would people have been slaves?" I asked.

"It's hard to say, but a single day would've been too long! But yes, the Rebels look 'way cooler' to me too."

This "permission" to like the Rebs, while disliking their cause, opened the floodgates and they've never been shut. She gave me freedom to investigate and fall in love with the history of our American family in my own way, just like Dave would one day give me freedom to love Judi with all my heart just by saying, "She's great!" My passion for history had begun and to this day is reinforced by every new fact and perspective I learn. I wasn't at it every day of course, because I was into sports and other things, but it was my own private pleasure I could rely on that somehow I felt good at. There's no other way to put it.

No matter what I was doing, whenever anything about the Civil War came on the radio, TV, or at school it'd stop me in my tracks and I'd be drawn to it like a magnet. It comforted me and became my friend. When kids played "cops 'n' robbers" and, "cowboys 'n' Indians" I'd be shooting my Yankee brother. He never minded being one because I told him they won. When he asked why I wanted to be on the losing side I told him they were Americans too but wouldn't tell him that *they're not gonna lose today,* then I'd bayonet him or shoot him with my cap or spud gun, which were popular in the 1950s. But "the damn Yank" never stayed down. I'd fantasize that we were brothers living in the border slave-state of Kentucky (I was learning my Yank and Reb states and Kentucky was "technically" neither or both; caught between because of politics and geography) during the 1850s, amid all the rhetorical hoopla of secession, slavery, and war riding the bluegrass wind that would be drifting in our windows, and Dave would see there was no choice but to be a Yankee. He stuck by me no matter how flaky I got. It helped me learn that if war made brother kill brother and father kill son—and it did—*something* had to be messed up.

Between our mom's groan at the sight of Robert E. Lee and our dad's at his wife and boy up from the terrible river, I saw my first Confederate flag in the flesh waiting under our Christmas tree in 1957. It was inserted into a plastic cannon that shot hollow cannonballs the size of a baseball. The Tredegar Ironworks in Richmond never cast cannons with slots for flags like that during the war but it looked pretty authentic. My first thought was, if it shot, I'd shoot my brothers. My mom read my mind and said, "Don't shoot that thing at anybody." I sensed by the way she said it that the cannon must've been our dad's idea. He knew I'd love it. It was all in fun, as it should've been. He didn't know what the flag meant in the way she did because history and music were mostly her bag and science and philosophy his, but they shared it all, talking about everything. Regrettably my cannon did shoot, so when our mom wasn't looking I shot my brothers, our cat Perry (he'd just bat the balls down like a good Yankee cat), the TV, radio, couch, houseplants, toaster, and anything else within range.

Over the course of the next few years, as our now-paved dirt road neighborhood continued its path into the modern world, I continued my journey to learn more about Yanks and Rebs. Our mom let me know if there was a movie or program on TV about the war. She let me stay up past bedtime to see the 1939 classic *Gone with the Wind* and I got a huge charge seeing aristocratic, future Rebs all excited about secession when they heard about Fort Sumter. Then there was a more modern movie with Bette Davis and Henry Fonda from 1952 called *Jezebel,* which also had excited, aristocratic Rebs. I was too young to know what an aristocrat was but I use the word here because Mark Twain said an aristocrat was a slave-owner by another name. There was 1956's Gary Cooper movie, *Friendly Persuasion,* in which he was a Quaker man of peace who wouldn't fight the Rebs (maybe John Hunt Morgan's cavalry) who were raiding across the river into Indiana. His wife was so pretty! I had no idea wives looked like that during the war. When Cooper's son, portrayed by Anthony Hopkins, went against his father's wishes to fight the Rebs, I hoped he missed when he shot.

Somewhere deep though, it felt eerily creepy when a slave was summoned to the veranda of Vivian Leigh or Bette Davis as they fanned themselves. The slave, who was coming from the fields, had to change his walk because he could only approach these southern belles in a tip-toe tentative gait. He fidgeted with his hat in his hands, and his eyes were opened so wide it looked uncomfortable. It was as if each step was asking permission to come closer so he could hear why he'd been summoned. These women seemed courteous in a dismissive sort of way, and it was obvious they and the slaves weren't on anything resembling equal social footing, even to a little kid watching a movie, but then for the slave to go back to the fields to sing happy songs about his lot in life felt so peculiar, like something out of *The Twilight Zone*. It didn't ring true! The slaves were always portrayed as content and stupid, and no matter how hot the blazing sun was they sang as if slavery was as natural for them as freedom was to those belles sipping mint juleps in the shade of a porch. It made me feel embarrassed without knowing why, for after all, these movies were made by adults and they wouldn't screw with a little kid's head, now would they? Not in America!

There was Cecil B. DeMille's 1956 classic, *Moses,* and later William Wyler's 1959 film, *Ben Hur.* The latter was written by Union Civil War General Lew Wallace. In 1960 Stanley Kubrick's *Spartacus* starred Kirk Douglas as an escaped slave preferring crucifixion as a free man rather than being re-enslaved. There were Victor Mature movies and Steve Reeves's Hercules epics, starting in 1959, in which every time a slave tried to escape he'd be brutally beaten or thrown into a pit of snakes, vipers, and hungry beasts. In *all* of these movies slaves hated being slaves and labor was inspired by the lash, the threat of death or worse: harm or sale of their children. It seemed every single slave parent wanted their children to live free. Slaves everywhere, in every century, were miserable but somehow *not* in movies of the American South where apparently slavery wasn't so bad. What a sad thing for a kid to be taught. If he accepted it because his parents and theirs before were brainwashed to believe this nonsense, what crueler hoax could there be?

It didn't feel right, so maybe the movies with happy American slaves were a lie, but just when my conscience considered it, a television series like 1959's *Johnny Yuma,* which told the adventures of a Rebel veteran roaming the West after the war, rescuing damsels from outlaws and the sort, would come on and my conscience would somehow be tricked into shutting down. There was never a hint of why Johnny's side fought the war except that it was simply a gentle-man's misunderstanding and now it was all settled. The next night *Rawhide,* starring a young Clint Eastwood among others, would appear on the screen with an episode of Civil War veterans from the North and South. They'd be part of a cowboy crew driving cattle up from Texas to market in Chicago and along the way, someone would accidentally say something disparaging about Lee or Grant, and a fistfight would break out just as a band of *always bad* Indians attacked. So they'd have to stop fighting to circle the wagons to kill the Indians, and in the process they'd discover the man next to them "ain't so bad" after all, considering he took an arrow in the back that was meant for his former enemy, and so now they could be friends. And, with his dying breath, the man with the arrow (with no blood on it) would make the guy whom he'd been fighting just a minute earlier swear an oath to look after his "Missus and young'uns" and the music would come on.

These shows were preludes to the biggest of them all, which introduced the Cartwright brothers along with their three-time widowed father to the American television audience in 1959. It ruled the airwaves for over a decade. And what a *Bonanza* it was! I loved it and still enjoy the re-runs. All three boys had different mothers; the oldest, Adam, had a mother who was a Northerner, so a Yankee, and the youngest, Little Joe, had a mother who was Southerner, so a Rebel. I can't recall where the mother of the middle brother, Hoss, came from, most likely a border state, and a Scandinavian country before that. But seeing as how Adam was from good Yankee stock (half of him anyway), it was obvious this was why he hardly ever gave his father trouble, but Little Joe was another matter altogether. It was even more obvious he was from good Rebel stock (half of him anyway), because he had the swagger, the charm, the mischievous smile, the dimples, and the sparkle in his eyes. And, to top it off, the coolest haircut (like James Dean's in *Rebel Without A Cause)* in America until four guys from Liverpool made us look at hair differently. And if that wasn't enough to prove Little Joe was from Rebel stock, he wore his gun low and on the left side, and how cool was that? He couldn't be anything but a Rebel. All the tough scrapes he got into, whether deadly or comical because they varied from week to week, weren't his fault. It was just in his Rebel nature and he couldn't be blamed for that. I never learned what their father was, although I suspected Ben was a Yankee with many friends who fought for the South and they simply resumed their friendly relations as soon as the war ended because that's what real men did in those days.

In one episode, Adam and Joe were out in the courtyard fist-fighting over who started the Civil War (not, of course, what it was actually about—*that* was *never* discussed) while Hop Sing, the embarrassingly stereotyped Chinese cook, looked out the window in horror. Just as the boys looked like they really might hurt each other their father arrived, gracefully hopped off his horse, and grabbed each by the collar, separating them like puppets on a string. As Adam wiped a trickle of blood that always seemed to be in the corner of someone's mouth in fights like these, Joe kept swinging away, while held just out of reach by his father, who was remarkably strong for a man his age.

"Boys, I demand an explanation for this outrageous behavior!" he exploded. Little Joe passionately explained with full confidence that his father would understand that Adam was wrong when he said the South started the war, "because anyone with half a brain knows the North started it." Then Ben asked Adam if Joe's explanation was right and with the same amount of confidence that his father would understand, Adam said in a voice not so controlled by rebellious emotions, "Yeah Pa, that's right!" Angrily, Ben replied, "I don't think the two of you have half a brain between you!" Then he stood back, pulled up his belt, and said in a deep, more understanding tone, "You boys ought to be ashamed of yourselves. The war was a terrible thing for both sides, but we're united now as we should be. Now shake hands and wash up before Hop Sing takes the tar out of both of you. After supper I want you to go up to the northwest corner of the Ponderosa to make sure those cattle rustlers are gone." The boys would shake hands and say, "All right Pa," and that was that.

So, if I wanted to know the truth about the cause of the Civil War I had to go to my mother and to books because those were sources I could trust. But if I wanted to ignore the reason two brothers like Adam and Little Joe would've tried to rip each other's throats out on the battlefield had they been born ten years earlier in the 1840s, television and Hollywood movies were a way to do it. Like all Americans in popular culture, I was taught to ignore a lot of things. Still, I knew I was the luckiest kid to live in the freest nation in the world. And although the U.S. in the '50s and early '60s ignored its dark history more than it does today, at the very least it was more honest than almost every nation on the planet because we had free speech and a free press. Ignoring things is a problem anywhere, but here we had the right *to not* ignore them if we chose. Historians I'd meet and associate with one day were already in the process of doing a sacred job of sorting out the truth. Meeting them, though, was decades away.

But I had my own personal historian: my mother, so I didn't have to wait to have questions answered. She said the reason television and movies ignored the truth was because not enough people were ready for it yet. I said, "But, Ma, it happened a hundred years ago."

She looked at me with a proud, sympathetic expression and said, "Yeah, but the truth won't sell for a few more decades because in too many ways *the mindset* of the war is still alive. The fighting might be over, but the Rebels had kids, grandchildren, and great grandchildren, and they were taught the South was right!"

"But, Ma, it's not true, they weren't right!"

"I know that, but try not to worry too much about it. Historians are sorting it out and some of the best are from the South. They'll educate everyone who wants to know the truth."

"Ma, what if some don't want to know the truth?"

"Then they'll never know how lucky they are to be an American, but they deserve to hear it anyway!"

122

"Ma, what's a historian?"

"Well, a good one is someone always looking for truth to share even if it shows they've been wrong about something they thought they were right about for a long time. History is a living thing; it keeps your mind from getting stuck in the mud, it shows what today *is* by telling what yesterday *was!*"

In A Dolphin's Wake

Dave never really got into the Civil War melodrama that was in my head. No one in our family or neighborhood did, and I can't explain why I did. Some things just are. If I'm interested in something and love it, I'll go to extremes to understand and be part of it. But Dave had equally powerful passions and went to his extremes to *experience* them. If I was into sports, he was into building and understanding how things like motors, radios and televisions worked. He was like our dad in that respect, and I was more like our mom. He tried baseball and hockey, but didn't seem to care about them one way or the other. Team sports seemed to bore him, but something miraculous happened when he entered the water, where the only one he had to rely on was himself. Dave wasn't an average swimmer; he was extraordinary! It's the reason why, in the cold polluted river, where any kid in the neighborhood, including me, would've panicked and drowned, he was in his element even when he slipped under the frozen ice. The only thing that could've taken his life would've been hypothermia or the poisonous chemicals he swallowed that may've affected him later, but that's speculation. He didn't drown because dolphins rarely do!

Our mom came from a swimming family. Around 1888 her maternal grandfather, John Nerich came to the U.S. from Zaton Mali, a town located on the coast of the Adriatic Sea in what was once western Yugoslavia. Legend has it the fastest swimmers in Europe were born there. When John landed on Ellis Island in New York City he couldn't speak a word of English, but somehow found work on the railroad while living with his sister, who had come to America before him. After a couple of years he met and married a girl with a fresh mouth and outrageous sense of humor named Hanorah Delaney, whose parents came from Ireland. They settled in the Bronx and had seven kids. All inherited the swimming gene, but Nicolas, the oldest, and Mary (our grandmother), the second oldest, inherited the most. They swam in the huge "floating pens" submerged in the East River so no one would get swept out to sea by the current.

Every summer the city held races attracting the fastest swimmers from miles around. Uncle Nick easily won every race he entered and was spotted by the prestigious NYC Swimming Club and asked to join. With professional indoor training and natural talent he became more of a swimming sensation than he already was and began to swim national meets, winning several American championships. His best stroke was the freestyle, also known as the crawl. Excelling in sprint events meant he was a speed demon. The Club thought their new prodigy was good enough for the national team that would represent the U.S. in the 1912 Olympics, which was to be held in Stockholm, Sweden, and they sponsored him to try out. He made the team! So, in 1912, Nick was on the greatest athletic stage of all, the Olympics. He swam for the U.S. in the 100- and 200-meter freestyle events and made it to the quarter finals, only to miss the semis by one second. The winner of those events was the fastest swimmer in the world, Hall of Famer Duke Kahanamoku of Hawaii. Nick's times were mere seconds behind the gold medal. If World War I hadn't canceled the 1916 games maybe young Nick would've come back four years later stronger than ever and done even more damage. Still, what a thing to accomplish!

For the rest of their lives he'd correspond by letter and phone with his friend Duke Kahanamoku. What I'd give to have those conversations on tape. He also knew Jim Thorpe, perhaps America's greatest athlete and gold medal winner. Thorpe roomed near him during the games. Nick didn't just rub elbows with greatness, he *was* the essence of American greatness—not for what he did in the water but for the way he loved his country.

I met him a few times when I was little and he'd come up from New York to visit my grandmother or for a family function because a lot of Nerichs eventually settled in Lynn. He was so big my grandmother tacked half of a paper shopping bag above the doorway, on which she'd written "watch your head." He made her laugh the way a young girl laughs at an older brother she adores. He filled the room with good feeling and after tea he'd sit at the piano to play the newest tunes, and then she'd play for him. He'd laugh so hard because she never played a song with sharps or flats. If the Nerichs were great swimmers, it might be more accurate to say they were even better musicians. They could read music but people like them played by ear because of an uncanny ability to hear it by *feeling it*. After the Olympics Nick made a living of sorts playing piano in silent movie theatres of NYC before sound (talkies) came along. Someone always had to be banging an upright in the corner to set the tone while a "Dudley Do-right" rescued a damsel from a villainous "Snidely Whiplash" who had strapped her to train tracks. Above all, the Nerichs were musicians and several married singers and musicians who played in the orchestra pits of NYC Vaudeville. Our dad told me that before I was born, he was introduced to the Nerichs at a wedding and couldn't believe the singing, dancing, and music. He said, "Quite frankly, I was stunned!" The love for music and swimming was passed to my mother, then her sons, who'd have the privilege to not only know how to listen to music but how to *feel it* when hearing it alone would've been enough to love it. It's hard to explain but so wonderfully true.

If a student had to write a paper on the 1912 Olympics, which is forever known as "The Masterpiece" because of the efficient way it was run, they'd find in the library or on the Internet that listed under the swimming events is Nicholas Nerich. Uncle Nick and his racing times are there, but there's nothing about his prowess when playing a musical instrument once it entered his hands.

For us, his family, what we're most proud of is how proud he was to have the American flag next to his name. When Nick's father and his Yugoslav friends played cards on Friday nights in the Nerichs' Bronx home, his dad wouldn't allow them to speak "Yugo." He insisted they speak English because, as he had put it, "We're Americans now!" This family story had been passed down long before it became politically correct and maybe necessary to tell stories like this. It reminds me of George Washington telling his soldiers before battle that they should no longer think of themselves as from Virginia or New Hampshire but from the United States *of* America. And yes, he used the word "of!" Books and the Internet also won't tell how Nick's mom, speaking with a good dose of Irish brogue inherited from her parents, taught her children to take life with a grain of salt, then "give 'em hell!"

I have an old newspaper clipping from the *Long Island Daily Press* dated February 10, 1957, announcing the death of Nicholas T. Nerich at the age of sixty-three from a stroke. It figures he'd die from *some* type of stroke. The director of the New York Athletics Club, Paul Pilgrim, is quoted saying, "Nerich was one of the great swimmers of his time." When he swam he took no prisoners, when he played piano the joy of life was expressed to its fullest, and in everyday life he was generous; that rare combination of athletic brawn and musical finesse was in the spirit of his American soul. To me, he's our family's all-American original. My grandmother expressed it best: "Nick was the *real deal!*" And she was no slouch in the water either. I have a first-place medal she won in 1913 for the 220-yard backstroke and another first-place medal for the 100-yard in 1914 when she competed in the National Women's Life Saving League. There was no tougher competition for women because the Olympics at that time were closed to them. If my grandmother and her brother were alive today they'd most likely be professional swimmers and/or musicians who'd swim and play for the same reason they did so long ago—because they loved it. That love for music, along with an inherited drive and talent for the water, passed through my mother to Dave, who got it in spades.

When we were in the water with our mom she always spent extra time with him. We all had our special thing with her and Dave's was swimming. She recognized his talent right away. We were on swim teams and our dad sometimes coached us. At first, I'd beat him because I was older and our mom would laugh and say, "Next year, you'll be in his wake." Swimmers like me fight with the water the way I do with just about everything in life. I couldn't keep my body from twisting but Dave could and he didn't fight the water but used it to grab, pull, push, and propel himself. After one race our mom said I did pretty good but had to work on my kick because, "you can't win for long with just your arms." But with Dave, the kick was already there.

One day she told him there was a movie she wanted him to see. It was the old 1932 version of *Tarzan* staring Olympic gold medal swimmer Johnny Weissmuller. Until Weissmuller came along nobody was able to touch Uncle Nick's friend The Duke's Olympic records, but Weissmuller broke them and, to boot, did the greatest Tarzan call of any Tarzan ever. We'd practice it up on the bank above the Saugus River, but no monkeys or elephants ever came, just a crap-load of mosquitoes. When the scene came on that our mom wanted Dave to see she sat on the edge of the couch, pulled him to her, and wrapped her arms around him as he became mesmerized with anticipation. She told me to keep quiet and this made me jealous. I'd make him pay later when she wasn't looking. When Tarzan dove in the water to rescue Jane from a tribe of cannibalistic aristocrats, the camera shot was a perfect view of Weissmuller from head to toe. He was a machine and you wanted to look at his upper body, but my mom pointed and said softly, "Look at his kick Dave, look at his kick." He understood exactly what she wanted him to understand.

The next day at the Lynn YMCA, where our mom was a lifeguard, she showed us a drill to make our kick stronger by holding a small surfboard out in front to go up and down the length of the pool by kick alone. I did it a few times and decided it was for the birds but Dave dug in and drove the thing with no mercy. He began doing this with the different kicks of the butterfly, breast, and backstroke, and there'd be a musical rhythm to the sound coming out of the water. He kept getting faster and stronger with the blood of our mother, Uncle Nick, and grandmother swimming through his veins.

"If you could be an animal, which would you be?" he asked me one night before we went to sleep.

"A bird, so I could fly," I said.

"I'd be a dolphin so I could fly through water," he replied. He was taking flight and metamorphosing into one right before our eyes. Our young and more important, our *aware* parents, gave us unremitting permission to explore and express our young passions from the earliest age as these years in Saugus next to a sad old river floated away.

When I was ten, Dave eight, and John five, our parents told us we were going to look at a house in the big city of Lynn next door. For years they wanted to find a place on Sluice Pond where my mom grew up, where our Uncle Nick would swim with his brothers and sisters when he came to visit and later our cousins too. Like most kids, I bitched and moaned about moving away from my friends, but every time Dave heard we might move to Sluice, a clean, spring-fed, deep body of water that was ideal for swimming—it had been our swimming hole our entire lives because our grandparents lived there—for him, it was a no-brainer. We'd already gone several times to look at houses but it seemed every one in a good location was too expensive and every affordable one was in a lousy location for swimming because it was too shallow or in a weedy cove. Well this time, the house was in one of the best locations on the pond. Unfortunately, it'd recently been in a fire so it didn't look so hot. We could sense our thirty-two and twenty-nine-year-old parents thinking, "Holy frickin' crap, if we can pull this off." They told the Realtor they could afford to pay such and such and he replied that because of the fire damage the owners, who'd already moved to Florida, might be willing to go a little lower but not that low. Our mom asked him to try anyway. He agreed and went into the house to call them or maybe eat a sandwich. As we waited outside, with the pond begging us "take me, take me," our mom said to our dad, "Oh Al, this would be perfect." She was never melodramatic or sentimental like that. Then she said, "Boys, if you ever wanted to ask God a favor this would be the time."

We'd never heard her say anything like that even though we were still practicing cafeteria Catholics. So when Dave and John closed their eyes and began to pray with all their might, I asked God if we could please get the house because it'd make our mom happy. It was an honest prayer. When the Realtor come out with a little mayonnaise in the corner of his mouth he said, "It wasn't easy but I talked them into it. The house is yours!" Dave, who until then had never said a swear word in his life, said, "Holy shit," and ran down the big cement steps and jumped in the pond with his clothes on. The Realtor started laughing and my mother kissed him, and then we all watched Dave flopping around in the cool early spring water like a dolphin on the old *Flipper* show that'd just found a willing female. Our dad said, "We'll never get him out now," and our mother, filled with emotion, said, "Thank God we won't have to." It was a day that changed our lives dramatically.

We drove back to Saugus with my wet brother in back wrapped in our mom's sweater and were informed we were going home to put on clean clothes and then out to eat. We'd never been to a restaurant before so this was courageous of our parents. We went to a fantastic seafood place two miles down the river from our house called Heck Allen's. We sat in a booth, John, our mom, and me on one side and Dave on the opposite with our dad so we wouldn't fight. We tried to kick each other under the table until our mom gave us *the look*. We could see in the kitchen where fish was being tossed into batter and fried and Dave asked our dad which one of the guys was "Heck." Our dad discreetly pointed out a cute, elfish little guy, you might like to pat on the head. "That's him!" he said. Heck looked like he spent a lot of time in The Crystal, the bar directly across the street, when he got off work. Our mom asked how the hell he knew that was Heck and he said, "Well, he looks like Heck." She laughed so hard it embarrassed her and told our dad to knock it off. We didn't get the joke but out of courtesy laughed too. We'd never heard our parents say anything derogatory or make fun of anyone ever and weren't sure if this was the case. But on the way home our mom started giggling and said, "You know, hon, I have to admit, the guy did look a bit like a haddock."

"Yeah, especially from the side," our dad replied.

They knew we could hear but talked in quiet voices which meant we weren't supposed to listen. This became one of those goofy recurring stories our family shared through the years. Later, after Judi died, I'd have a heartstring pulled when I'd hear it because it dawned on me that while I was safe and sound in Heck's with my parents there may've been a cute little blond girl with green eyes alone in a car waiting for her dad to come out of The Crystal. Even now I can't bear the thought and can't help having it.

We lived in Saugus a couple more weeks, but immediately began cleaning up our new home so we could move in and repair the fire damage. Our parents couldn't afford to have someone do it. Once we began, our dad discovered the damage was more cosmetic than structural so the repairs went smoother than anticipated. Luck and God or maybe a little of both had shined on us. The remaining weeks in Saugus allowed me to say good-bye to my old haunts, like The Iron Works and the marshes. In the marshes, among the bulrushes—basically acres of cattails—we made paths with secret passages along the river. We constructed forts with these bulrushes, and in secret rooms used them as spears and clubs to kill bad guys. We really lived a rural, barefoot sort of way that we'd never totally leave behind.

The last day there I went down to the river to say good-bye to the tree branch that reached out to and saved Dave four years earlier. For the last couple of years it'd grown strong enough to climb to the tip to fish for minnows, which appeared by the millions every spring. When the chemical company was dumping it killed tens of thousands but when they weren't putting too much crap in the water for a day or two you could catch a bucketful with a string, safety needle, and bread balls. Then you could take them to the local bait shop where they'd buy them for a quarter. Then you'd take the quarter to a little variety store where it only cost a dime for a package of Hostess Cupcakes and another for a package of Twinkies and with your remaining nickel climax this joyful load of delectable all-American junk food with a bag of Boyd's Potato Chips, which were made in Lynn. Of course you'd make sure to have an extra half bucket to buy a twelve-cent bottle of Fanta orange soda or Squirt to wash it all down for the best stomachache minnows could buy.

So I climbed out on the branch for the last time in the spring of 1961 to say good-bye to one of my sacred thinking places. I had many of my best Civil War fantasies when I was perched on it, looking over the river. I'd pretend to be an older boy of sixteen living in the Deep South on a tributary of the mighty Mississippi River just before the outbreak of war. I wouldn't be catching minnows for cupcakes and chips but "catchin' a batch of catfish to bring home to maw, paw, and my brothers 'n' sisters so we could eat somethin' good 'cause it was my turn to fish while they worked the corn, bean, and squash fields. Hell, we didn't have no slaves and if'n we did we'da let em go if'n they wanted to go and if'n they didn't, maw and paw woulda treated 'em kind like they do every livin' creature on the farm so it woulda been all right all round. And when the war came, I know'd it's all the damn Yankees fault cause they want to take away our blessid way of life that God and George Washington gave us. The Yanks said we cain't take our way next door to the territories cause it ain't no good to take anywhere no more no how, and that got us so mad 'cause who's they to say that about us? And now, just cause old Jeff Davis is saying 'We're outta here' and 'All we want is to be left alone' 'cause we ain't hurtin' no one, Mr. Lincurn's sayin' we'd end up hurtin' the whole world if we split, but how can that be by just askin' to be left alone? Mr. Lincurn ain't thinkin' right and all I care about is I ain't lettin' no stinkin' Yankee steal my family's fishin' hole."

Then off I'd go to war to fight alongside Jeb Stuart, Lee, Longstreet, Johnny Yuma, Little Joe Cartwright (even though he wasn't in the war, it didn't matter), and all the other cavalier, chivalrous Southern buckaroos to fight against those no-good, two-timing Yankees who wanted to take away "everything that made life worth living," which was the actual way Lee stated the case and that included my fishin' hole. And if that wasn't bad enough, those damn Yankees insulted our sacred Southern Honor and no one could get away with that. I knew what Southern Honor was because it was explained to me one Saturday morning when I was eight while my brothers and I ate Rice Krispies and watched a Looney Tunes cartoon. In this episode, the ever bombastic, Southern blowhard rooster, Foghorn Leghorn, was a Confederate general in command of a prisoner-of-war camp. One of his Yankee captives was his nemesis, little Henry Hawk, a young chicken hawk who doggedly looked for a chicken to eat but didn't know what a chicken looked like and so relentlessly pestered Leghorn to point one out to him. Leghorn, irritated as all hell, shooed him away saying, "I say, I say, I say, boy, go away, you bother me!"

Every time General Leghorn made the rounds little Henry would say, "Good morning General," and the general would slap him with his gloves and say, "Boy, I say boy, I say, I say, boy, you've just insulted my Southern Honor." This went on for quite a while until one day the little Yankee prisoner asked, "General, what is Southern Honor?" And General Leghorn replied, "Why boy, my Southern Honor, why it's, why it's . . ." and then, thinking to himself, "Hmmmm, what . . . is . . . my . . . Southern Honor?" He then proceeded to pace back and forth in deep contemplation of the question, then stopped to look straight out our old black-and-white TV set in Saugus, Massachusetts, to see three little shit-heads eating Rice Krispies. Then he shrugged his shoulders, went back to pacing, while scratching his chin and muttering to himself, until a light bulb went off. Finally, all cocksure of himself, he strutted back to Henry, slapped him several times and said, "Why boy, I say, I say, boy, my Southern Honor, why my Southern Honor is the thing you've insulted." Slap, slap, slap.

And as he walked away, he turned to those kids eating cereal, shrugged his shoulders, and walked off the scene. And maybe this is why Lincoln so often used yarns and humor to make a point that couldn't be made better any other way.

Somehow I'd be one of the lucky ones to miraculously survive the worst fighting of the war, with only a half dozen scars and a slight limp due to Yankee shrapnel still in my leg. And at the age of twenty-one, I'd make my way home accompanied by a beautiful Yankee wife I met behind enemy lines when I was on a scouting mission. She hid me in her root cellar from some bad old Yankees that stole her livestock. We fell madly in love in about three minutes and I told her I'd come back for her after the war and she said she'd be waiting. It didn't hurt none that she looked like Donna Reed or Gary Cooper's wife in *Friendly Persuasion,* although someone like Jane from *F Troop* or Julie from *Lost In Space* or Ellie May Clampett or Maryanne or Morticia Adams would've been cool too, but my wife was more like Reed than anyone. Within a few short years, I'd once again be coming home from the fishing hole with a stack of catfish on a stick and there'd be smoke coming out our Thomas Kincaid(ish) cabin's chimney and the cutest little girl, who'd have Donna's hair, would be waiting at the door with her two older brothers, ages under eight, playing checkers on a Confederate flag rug by the fire. Above the mantel were portraits of Generals Lee, Jackson, Stuart, and Leghorn, along with Jeff Davis, George Washington, and Jesus.

After supper, with stomachs full because no Yankees were ravishing the countryside, the kids would ask me to tell stories of my hair-raising adventures with old Stonewall, Lee, and the rest. As it got close to bedtime they'd plead, "One more, Paw," and I'd look over to Donna, only her name was something like Kate, and she'd be rocking by the fire knitting a pair of tiny socks as a way of telling me something. When I noticed them I'd give her a Rebel wink and say to the kids, "You young'uns need your sleep now in order to grow big and strong in case we have to fight the Yankees again." Then as I looked at Donna, I mean Kate, I'd say to the kids, "Someday soon we'll have a whole

Rebel Company made of brothers right from this cabin, now hit the hay." After they scampered to bed the missus and I would sit by the fire with sassafras tea and her head on my shoulder and she'd say in her Yankee accent, "Oh darling, the war was such a terrible hardship but it caused one good thing to happen, it brought you into my life." And I'd say, "Yup, I reckon it did. It somehow made all the hard fighting worthwhile." And as I turned to plant a big wet one on her parted lips a minnow would tug my line.

My precious truth was, due to my mother's wisdom, compassion, and honesty there *never* was any controversy in my little-kid mind out on the branch about why the war was fought. I was already on a journey of preparation that would serve me well in adulthood, when I'd meet a strong yet overly vocal minority of "misguided brethren" unwilling to teach their children that, just as pollution in an old river might not be readily apparent until they fell in and swallowed it, there was a deadly pollution in the psyche of too many Americans, in the North and South, that caused the bloody mess, which people like Lincoln had warned about time and again. For every minnow tossed in the bucket, I assumed the entire United States viewed the war the way I did. I never considered there were radically different views of what caused it, but my mom taught me that history *did already* have it right but again, not everyone was ready or willing to listen. I couldn't know then, and still don't now, why that was so. But these were my innocent years before learning firsthand the true horrors of slavery by watching Dave and Judi become slaves, and experiencing the implications of people not being honest about it. Naively, on that glorious lifesaving branch, I thought everyone knew slavery caused the war and accepted it because opposing leaders Abraham Lincoln and Jefferson Davis repeatedly said it did, and that was good enough for me and still is! Sure, not everyone in the North was fighting to get rid of it but the South, beyond a doubt, fought to protect and spread it and said so many, many times. *The South was honest and I believed them!*

I fully accepted the Gray guys fought the Blue guys because they were ticked off the Blue guys wouldn't let them bring slavery into the territories. For decades the Gray guys had been saying "we're outta here" if a president came along who wouldn't allow slavery to spread. I knew, not only because of my mother, but also from what I learned from my incredible seventh grade history teacher, Sister Marietta, that this indeed was true! Historical facts became precious jewels to me, and the most precious was *knowing* the Gray guys tried to break away when a president they feared arrived by the ballot. The hypocritical irony, though, was that if the Gray guys' John C. Breckenridge got in, they would've stayed in the Union. They might've stayed, for a while anyway, if Douglas got in because he said slavery could spread to the territories if a *majority* of people settling there wanted it. But the sad truth was that Southern leaders said even that wasn't good enough. They wanted Breckenridge (an ex-vice president under Buchanan) because his presidential platform *guaranteed* slavery could spread even if only *a minority* wanted it to, and he wanted to amend the Constitution to make it so. But the new president said *no mas* to this insanity, and even a screwy little kid catching minnows could understand that.

But in some sense I knew the new president was talking about something far more sinister than my young mind could comprehend when he said slavery and cancer were the same thing. I didn't know what cancer was, but knew he'd been saying for years that slavery was the only thing that could destroy the U.S., so it had to be the worst thing on earth. Others had said it, too. It was an argument as old as the nation, and people had different ideas for how to deal with it, but this president was the first to not only say but *insist* that a good first step would be to stop encouraging the thing to spread, and that made sense to me. He said if there was an attempt to "rip out" the cancer all at once, the nation could bleed to death, and the war certainly proved he was right about that. But what I ignored out of youthful ignorance was my Gray guys saying that cancer/slavery was not a bad thing but a good thing, even sacred and holy. I ignored it because I didn't know what slavery was. It was "tucked away like a man hides a wen or cancer" to again phrase it like Lincoln did when speaking of it in the Constitution.

But my God, what I did have a grasp on was that, ever since the founding of our nation, my Gray guys cherished the ballot of democratic American elections. That is, until their guy lost, and this intrigued me to no end, that my beloved Gray guys were against American democracy. How could that be? Was it because, until then, it protected slavery and now that it was threatened they were splitting? The Blue guys said they wouldn't let the Gray guys split regardless of what anyone thought about slavery, because the new president won the election fair and square, so how could the Gray guys claim they were wronged by the legal American electoral process? Hadn't they honored elections since the time of Washington? Hadn't the Southern states carved on their representative stones in the Washington monument that "the Union" above all else was "most sacred?" So what the heck changed? When the Blue guys asked the Gray guys why they wouldn't abide by the 1860 election like they had all others, General Leghorn and his followers became insulted and tried to take their ball home, only it wasn't theirs to take. It belonged to all Americans and the Blue guys fought to keep it that way.

So holy cow, it truly was about "the divine rights of kings as opposed to the rights of common man" as the new president so eloquently said it was. And he made it perfectly clear that American elections meant something, that he ran on a pledge that the Gray guys wouldn't be allowed to spread their divine right one inch further—North, South, East, or West—than it already was. Yet even some of the staunchest haters of slavery said, "Let the South go." But the new president said, "We can't do that!" because we must prove once and for all that in the United States, the majority rules and that's what democracy is all about. Nobody quite understood that as much as the new president did. He hated slavery and was not about to let what he called "the monstrous injustice of it" destroy democracy. Nobody thought he had the gonads to stick to that principle but *he did* and then some. This was how a young minnow catcher understood beyond measure there was a difference of opinion between *his* Blue and Gray guys and about how the new president said American democracy was the fairest way to address that difference. He called slavery evil! My Gray guys called it sacred and for them the ballot, that was no longer adequate, became the bullet of cancer/slavery and it saddened me.

After 10,000 nightmarish battles on land and sea, during which the Blue and Gray tried to annihilate each other, the Blue guys prevailed and a kid on a branch over a polluted river thought the side that won might have had God on its side because their side made it better for both sides. And though they were wrong, I somehow knew God loved my Gray guys because he knew they were crazy, so I loved them too. Phrasing it this way was decades away from my young psyche but even then I sensed *what we say and think about the American Civil War tells us very little about the war but tells us everything about ourselves.* I was lucky by birth to know this war is one thing no American should be wrong about. Because if we are wrong about it; we can be wrong about everything!

Lincoln said, many times in many ways about facing the truth of the war and slavery, that "The way is plain . . . if we do this . . . we cannot lose . . . and the world over shall call us blessed . . ." It's what justice is; the light of truth shining on the eternal Civil War within us so we can find our way. To be a slave to anything can be deadly. To spread it, *always* is!

The Best Swimmer
I Ever Saw

Moving to the big city brought all the stereotypical implications one would think of to kids used to running barefoot in the summer. Our parents, who had taught us to be honest and that it was okay to be wrong because everyone makes mistakes, instilled a realistic, rustic fortitude I was only partially aware we had. My brothers knew it better so they were more comfortable with the move. I came carrying the burden of caring too much what people thought. It's good to a certain degree, but not to the extreme I did and in many ways still do. But the option to remain passive was there, so I took it. I had a hard time adjusting but my brothers slid right in. Little John made friends instantly. Later, in high school, he'd be elected "class gentleman" because of his courteous manners and the pleasant atmosphere that has always surrounded him. The fact that in his yearbook he had hair as long and golden as Duane Allman and Robert Plant showed he was one cool, hip dude and that hasn't changed, although his hair is shorter now. Dave never cared what people thought or got hung up on things he perceived as phony, selfish, or goofy, and he easily made friends too. My brothers took things as they were but I didn't know what I didn't know and was too shy to ask pesky questions I thought would expose how screwy I was. Dave and John didn't carry that nonsense with them.

Because of our twenty-one-month age difference, Dave and I traveled in different circles in our early years in Lynn until music glued us like epoxy. We shared the same upstairs bedroom till he moved to the basement to get closer to the record player. We were on the same swim team and all three of us attended St. Michael's Catholic Grammar School, so we had some things in common. I couldn't swim like Dave (nobody could), but I could run fast and throw a baseball pretty hard and catch and hit a little better than average, which is not to say I was a great baseball player but I did okay. Dave and I were on the same Little League team and our dad was the assistant coach. This was how we first came in contact with tough, swearing, cigarette smoking city kids. From them, we learned how babies were made, how to buy "butts" even if we were twelve and ten, which girls that hung out at the park kissed with their mouths open, and all sorts of information you couldn't get anywhere else in 1961 and 1962. When the coaches weren't around we'd hear the seven swear words George Carlin said you couldn't say on TV.

One episode typifying my adjustment to the city was when, after practice, I was excited about sun turtles hatching on Sluice Pond. I asked our dad if I could ask the team over to catch some. He said it probably wasn't a good idea because "city kids might not be into that sort of thing." But I persisted until he reneged, and when I asked the guys the most prominent member of the team asked me, "What are you, some kind of fuckin' faggot or something?"

No coaches were around but all the kids were and I asked, "What's a faggot?"

"Are you stupid? It's a guy who jerks off another guy!" he replied.

I said, "Nooo sa!"

Then he challenged me to fight because, by doubting him, I somehow insulted his honor. He must've had a little General Leghorn in him. He got in my face and pushed me to the ground and before I could get up Dave was in his.

"If you do that again I'll kick your fuckin' shitty underwear ass all over the field, now screw!" said Dave.

Our teammates started laughing, which made the embarrassed bully sulk away. Later I thanked Dave and told him he didn't have to do that, although I was glad he did because the kid was much bigger than me, and therefore much bigger than Dave.

"No sweat, the guy sucks and I kinda wanted to kick his ass anyway," Dave said.

"How long have you been swearing like that?"

"Since today!"

The shitty underwear kid, a decent ball player, never bothered me again but he kept kissing up to the manager's son in an odd, phony way and none of us knew why. Ours was the worst team in the league so it was no major accomplishment to end up leading the team in batting average, home runs, and stolen bases, but somehow I did because I'd finally gotten a little comfortable in my new surroundings in the second half of the season. In the end, each team picked two players to represent it on the all-star team and I thought I'd make it because of my stats. But our manager picked his kid and shitty underwear boy. Now I knew why Shitty chummed with the manager's kid. To be fair, Shitty's stats were good, just not as good as mine. At the team gathering where it was announced who made the all-stars, Shitty gave me a "screw you" look when his name was called. It didn't bother me as much as surprised me. My dad, who seemed a little perturbed about it, said, "It's politics!" I didn't know what that meant, but it felt like the right answer.

Soon, a lot of kids started coming to our house for a variety of reasons. Some even asked about the turtles. Our forever young renaissance parents were another reason. It felt funny at first but I grew to love kids calling our mother "Ma Foster." Later, when she became a history teacher, hundreds of kids called her that. Dave had the stereo in the basement, and we always had the hippest music blasting on the old turntable, so kids came to listen and they'd bring their records too. This, along with having a beautiful pond in our backyard to swim in during the summer, meant kids were always at our home. We taught those who didn't know how to swim, and we taught quite a few. Our dad hooked up a spotlight on a tree hanging over the pond, so in winter, when the pond froze, we'd play night hockey and that brought more kids to the ranch.

A lot of us ended up going to high school together, along with Shitty who spread a rumor about a nice, shy, awkward, gangly classmate getting kicked out of McDonald's for masturbating in the men's room. The rumor spread like wildfire to the point where no one would sit near the kid. Even the nuns heard about it, so he was miserable. All through school he was taunted, and the upper-classmen were merciless. On graduation day, I was saying good-bye to everyone and he came up to me and thanked me for never making fun of him. I said it was too bad he got caught in the men's room, and I'll never forget his expression of sadness when he said, "I wouldn't mind if it was true, but it's not! (Shitty) made it up because I wouldn't give him answers to a test in the ninth grade." He said I was the only kid he could tell because he somehow knew I'd believe him. The irony was he didn't know of my Little League experience with Shitty. This tortured kid died a few years ago and Shitty's probably still tormenting some-body somewhere. So my dad was right, "it's politics," and Shitty's an aristocrat!

All through our mid-teens, Dave swam harder than ever. When he wasn't in the Olympic-sized fifty-meter pool at the Y he'd be home training in Sluice Pond, in a makeshift lane my dad built by inserting two thick slabs of plywood into the water twenty-five meters apart. This meant Dave had to do two extra flip turns every hundred meters, which made his turns a powerful weapon in his arsenal. The underwater thump of him driving off the wood felt like Ringo's and Charlie Watts' bass (kick) drums, and you could tell the stroke and type of training—speed or distance—from the intensity and frequency. Sometimes our mom, who'd be watching from the yard, would yell down something like, "Keep your head down near your finish, a hundredth of a second can beat you the same as a minute."

When I graduated from St. Mary's High, our parents took Dave out of it and John out of St. Michaels and enrolled them both in the Lynn public schools. Dave entered the eleventh grade and became the captain of the Lynn English High School swim team. This hooked him up with Pete Sawin, a local swimming coach legend and a friend of my mother. Today there's the Pete Sawin Trophy, awarded to swimmers who go beyond expectations. Just recently an entire swimming complex was named after him, the Peter A. Sawin Natatorium. He came to our home to talk about Dave and our mom got a big kick out of him because he could play the piano and banjo. He knew my mom was an incredible piano player because she was a history and social studies teacher by now, and she'd often play for her students, and Pete, also a social studies teacher, would hear her. He coached thousands of kids, and many went on to have brilliant college careers. When he became Dave's coach, Dave began tearing up the eastern Massachusetts high school competition and was often in the sports section of newspapers. Pete said to our mom that Dave was "the best swimmer I ever saw" adding, "his determination and 'coachability' are unique."

Our mom replied, "He'll need that in college!"

Dave got a swimming scholarship to the University of Connecticut and chose to go there because of its great program. The coach, who was a friend of Pete's, liked what he saw of my brother on film so much he invited Dave to train with the team in the early spring before his freshman year.

After one of his first trips down, he came home with a slight limp. He said he'd been experiencing a little pain in his hip that seemed to go away with his morning swim. He was also popping Tylenol, which was unusual. Nobody was too concerned, but to be on the safe side our mom took him to our doctor. X-rays revealed cysts in his hip and he was prescribed medication that was supposed to make them go away. It was probably some sort of steroid. It worked, but shortly after going back to college, the medicine, or whatever it was, lost its effectiveness. The school's athletic doctor didn't like this and recommended my parents take him to a specialist for a biopsy, whatever the hell that was. To our utter shock and horror, he was diagnosed with an aggressive form of bone cancer, which sounded bad on its own but, because I'd never known anyone who'd had cancer except someone old when I was little, I didn't know the implications. I knew modern medicine cured many things, but the look on my parents' faces was something else altogether, and I heard them groan. My best friend's (the one I'd been with in the car accident) girlfriend was a nursing student, and when I told her Dave had bone cancer, she asked if they could operate. I told her they couldn't and she burst into tears. I didn't expect that. Her honest reaction indicated Dave might be in deep water trouble. Somewhere dark, in a place I didn't know I had, a sickening, warm, heavy, twisting feeling told me this could be the end of my dolphin brother. But on the surface I wasn't ready to think that, because those kinds of things didn't happen in real life.

As soon as I was alone with Dave I asked him if he was okay.

He said, "Yeah, but Ma and Dad are shitting bricks, and I hate that!"

"The doctors will fix you, so don't worry too much," I said, not totally believing what I was saying.

He said, "I'm not worried about me, I just hope I'm okay for their sake."

You mean for all our sakes, I thought but said, "You will be!"

"I hope so. I don't want to miss my first swim meet because of this crap. At practice the juniors and seniors are strong and fast as hell, but I keep up with them easier than I thought I would, and I haven't even opened it up yet." He had several gears! "To tell you the truth, I don't think anyone on the team can beat me, and I'm anxious to see how I do against 'the monsters' around the country. It'll tell me where I am and where I need to go," he said.

"Well, I'll talk to you tomorrow, I've got a gig tonight at U-Mass with that Top 40 band. Their bass player is still sick, and I agreed to fill in one more time," I said.

"I know, Ma told me. Me and Jimmy"—his best friend—"are going. It's cool seeing you play that music, even though a lot of it's goofy," he said.

We both laughed and I said, "Yeah, but Steve's an excellent drummer, and we mix it up enough so we don't fall asleep and that's fun. And besides, it keeps my chops up and that's all I care about. But don't you think you should stay home and take it easy?" I asked.

He replied, "Take it easy for what?" It wasn't a question.

The next day in the early afternoon I went to the Lynn Y to practice for a swimming test I had to take in order to get my lifeguard license. I'd already squeaked by the written test but for the in-water part of the exam I needed work on the stroke a lifeguard uses to bring a victim to safety. When I pulled into the parking lot I saw Dave's ugly, glorious, 1960 Chevy, the "Blue Bomb." It was where it usually was when the water in Sluice was too cold. He'd gotten the car for a couple hundred dollars. The previous owner had painted it a hideous color of nonshiny, dull sky blue with a broad brush and what looked like latex paint. It was so disgusting it was cool, unless you lived next door, then it was just disgusting. When he brought it home we all laughed and asked what he was going to do about the paint job, and he said, "First, I'll let it dry, and second, nothing." He put in a great radio with FM stations (relatively new things) and an 8-track tape player (another new thing), and said that's all that mattered. How he kept it going and passing inspection no one knew.

His cool girlfriend (the first and only one he ever had) had a deep love for music and always came to wherever I was playing. Sheryl became a good friend of Judi's and mine and the four of us went to dozens of concerts and did a lot of hiking, camping, and mountain climbing together. She lived in the beautiful upper-scale town of Marblehead next to the upper to mid-scale town of Swampscott, which was directly next to our beloved hard-scrabble working-class city of Lynn. Her parents would've preferred she had come home with a nice Jewish boy, but Dave's lethal smile changed that and they welcomed him. He liked her parents and told me, "They're cool, like Ma and Dad. They're not hung up on prehistoric religious and racial crap." He got the biggest kick driving his shitbox eyesore, the Blue Bomb—I had to say the Blue Bomb one more time because I loved him so very much—to pick up Sheryl, when he'd either get dirty looks from what our half-Irish grandmother (Nick's sister) called the "hoity toity," or when someone would laugh or just shake their head. Judi and I were with him many times when he'd notice someone repulsed by the Bomb and he'd say, "Some people just don't know class when they see it." When he saw people laughing, he'd laugh. You had to admire him, a nineteen-year-old college kid with little money but a car that went.

Somehow the Blue Bomb was able to make it to and from the University of Connecticut, so there had to be something in the tank, but I never suspected that after this visit home, he'd never go back. His limp was getting worse, and our parents scheduled appointments with specialists to determine a course of action to deal with his "cysts." I avoided calling them tumors because of the way Lincoln referred to slavery as a cancerous tumor that could destroy the nation. To me, my brother was indestructible, and some annoying little cysts weren't going to destroy this force of nature. If I'd known he'd never return to school, I don't know how I would've reacted when I pulled into the parking lot next to the Blue Bomb. As it was, I didn't react too bravely when I saw him in the water doing what he did as naturally as a dolphin does what a dolphin does.

The Y was always a busy place, but Dave was a water rat and I a gym rat, so we knew when to go when it wasn't too crowded. When I entered the pool area, there weren't many people, but one powerful dolphin was *flying* through the water as if it were effortless. Of course it wasn't effortless when you knew the tremendous amount of work he put into it. He was at a unique point that few athletes get to, where swimming was his art and water his canvas. The average person can't realize the amount of time, sacrifice, and effort an athlete, musician, historian, writer, or anyone seeking physical, artistic, or academic fulfillment must endeavor to get to the level Dave had reached with swimming. But with him, there was no sacrifice because it was what he was supposed to do and he knew it. His only investment was *time,* which he gave freely. To see him

146

swim was witnessing one who uses the gift God, the universe, family genes, or luck (it doesn't matter which) had given him in a way that says "Thank you" to God, a gratitude that exudes love. Seeing him *experience* his art was seeing the fullest expression of the eternal!

As I walked the hall from the locker room to the pool I heard the muffled sounds of his *swish* through the water. Normally I'd have pushed the door open as if I owned the place, but the emotional reaction of my best friend's girlfriend to his diagnosis was haunting me. The more it sank in, the more frightened I became, so when I got to the door I stopped to gather my witless wits while I wiped fog off the little window to peer in to see my brother doing fifty meters of the back, then butterfly, then breast, and then his specialty (just like his Uncle Nick), the freestyle stroke. He was magnificent in all. When a person learns the butterfly stroke it's like battling the water to get out of the way. With the backstroke it's telling the water, "Okay, I'm in your hands now and I'm trusting you so please let me through." With the breaststroke it's, "I trust you but just in case, I'm keeping a close eye on you and I'll caress you, embrace you, and apologize for sweeping you aside, and if I have to I'll plead a little but that's it, so let me through." And last, with the crawl, you're on all fours and, depending on what kind of person you are, as stable as you could be on dry land. The water's slippery, lubricated, unpredictable yet controllable, and lets you slide through its fingers. That's how some first experience those strokes. And for most, like me, it's never totally one way or the other, which is okay if you love the water as much as your capacity to love allows. Then, water becomes magic!

But every once in a while a dolphin is born in human form, and those descriptions are inapplicable because a dolphin never informs the water he's coming through. The water has already invited him. He never tells the water he trusts it because there's already trust that need not be spoken. He never pleads or sweeps aside and has no need to caress and embrace because that's permanently and automatically taking place anyway, and it's not the water that's slippery or unstable but those on dry land who can't tango or waltz without caring who leads. They're fluidity, and they birth each other. That's what I saw through the window that faced the pool, and I began to cry.

He was in the water holding the diving board with his left hand while he counted his neck pulse with his right hand fingers as he looked up to the time clock above the pool. He did this for thirty seconds and then was off for another two-hundred-meter medley to end up hanging for another thirty; not even breathing hard but idling like a racing car pulled into the pit for a quick engine check. He was speed training and breathtaking. The more I watched, the more I became engulfed in the unexpected, uncontrollable sadness inside me, and the more I cried. I couldn't stop and thought, *Shit, this is not good!* Because when I cry my eyes become red and I couldn't let him see me with red eyes now, though he'd seen me with them plenty of times before in those days of flowers and war, but for different reasons. I couldn't let him see that *cancer* was making me weep.

I began to scheme like I do in times like these. Thank God I feel guilty afterward, so maybe I'm not as big of a cowardly, hypocritical psychopath as I'd be without guilt. I decided as soon as he started another two hundred meters I'd slip in the pool and either have my swimming goggles on to hide my eyes, or could blame the chlorine in the water if the subject came up. By the time he was half a length down the pool I was in at eye level with the water. He was even more impressive from this vantage point. It's one thing seeing a football game or concert from the stands, but it's quite another to see them from the field or stage level where you can smell the passion that make these people do what they do. He was amazing and I was in the corner with bloodshot eyes, my secret kept. Once again he held the diving board, looking up at the clock, and I called over, "Looking good brother!"

Still looking at the clock, he said, "Yeah, but I *need* to look better. The college teams are not like high school teams."

"Well don't let me interrupt you," I said.

"I won't!" he said. Then he looked over and asked if I was there to swim laps for exercise and I told him I was going to use the floatation dummies to practice for my lifeguard test. Like our mom had been, he was already a life-guard so when he heard why I was there he let go of the board, swam toward me, and said, "Frig the dummies, I'll help you!"

"No, that's okay, I don't want to take time away from your speed training."

"Don't worry. I've got all the time in the world!"

There are no words to describe the impact of that moment. He said it while looking directly into my bloodshot eyes with his so-beautiful-it-was-scary Dave smile. My brother John is the only person who knows the look the way I do. Dave was so intense but even here he kept the atmosphere light. He did and thought things most people are afraid to discuss, including me, but I tagged along because when you were with him you felt alive, safe, and nervous. He inspired! To put it bluntly, there was no bullshit with him and he was careful not to frighten with his intensity. He knew the fringes of thought he found interesting were too much for most, and that a large part of the human race lived their entire lives in a world of make-believe, superstition, and silliness. But, when the chips were down and the situation, no matter how dire, required "cold, calculating reasoning," there was no one better. His Lincoln-esque qual-ities allowed him to see the world as it presented itself; a world not set up to have rational discussions because of all the nonsense people believed. He lived a way that revealed that if those rational discussions ever took place, unnecessary human-created suffering would vanish. The intimate discussions he had with himself, he had with me.

It was fitting that he'd written "Know Thyself" above his bed; he knew who he was like no one I'd ever know. It was as if, in his short existence thus far, he understood the universe at nineteen far better than most at ninety. He embraced the contradiction of it all and made it rational, so when he said he had "all the time in the world," I had the distinct feeling he wanted me to know he was aware of his situation. It broke my heart and took all my strength to hide it as I accepted his offer. He understood his situation far better than I did and perhaps better than our parents, because knowing him, when he had the doctors alone he told them to tell him what they thought and conveyed that he'd know if they were jerking him around. He was incapable of operating on any other field of battle where facts, as they were known, weren't faced. Swimming hard helped him gather his thoughts to think clearly, to stay in shape for the struggle he saw coming. But it was also who he was and that trumped all. Now, helping me, trumped even that.

A lifeguard only enters the water as a last resort if he can't reach a victim by extending a pole or throwing a lifebuoy. Entering creates the potential for two people to drown. He told me to go to the deep end and thrash around like I was in a panic. As I did I stole glimpses of him swimming straight at me, head held up, strong and steady with intense brown eyes never losing sight of me. In an incredibly quick, smooth, safety-conscious move, he had me on my back with his right arm around me and my chin cupped in his hand and my head tilted in the exact angle that would allow me to breathe and prevent additional swallowing of water on our way to "shore." I felt like I was being pulled by a small motorboat as he explained the hold, side stroke, and scissor kick techniques he used. In the shallow end he went into detail and we did this exercise several times until he was satisfied I understood. Then he told me to go back to the deep end but this time to not only thrash around but grab him anywhere I could—bathing suit, hair, goggles, flesh—and not to be gentle about it, to use my strength.

My first thought was, no way was I going to do that, because not only did I not want to hurt him but I was very strong at the time; usually when he was in the pool, I was down the hall in the weight room. Just over a year prior I'd come in second place in the Mr. Massachusetts bodybuilding contest. I never set out to be in a physique contest, it just evolved. I was one of the scrawniest kids on the high school football team; among the weakest of the weak. Our coach put us on a weightlifting program and said I needed it more than anyone because he didn't want me to get killed. I wasn't as brave as he thought I was but I ran hard because my grandfather taught me the harder you ran, the less you got hurt. The coach thought I might make a good running back if I beefed up. I liked receiving punts and kick-offs and one time ran ninety yards for a touchdown, but they spelled my name wrong in the paper, which was okay because I really wasn't that good anyway, and also our team lost way more than it won. The truth was, I wasn't that into it, but played because my buddies did. The coaches tried to convince us football would give us the best memories of our lives and maybe that's true, but if I had to do it again, I'd probably pass. But for some unbeknownst reason, the first time I lifted weights I had an instinctive knack for understanding far more than the coaches or anyone on the team how each exercise and angle affected the various muscle groups. I told the coach I thought I'd do better on my own at the Y than I would with the team at the school gym and he said okay.

By sheer coincidence, the Lynn Y happened to have some of the top body-builders in the country working out there, so when I went into the weight room I was a boy looking at men. I never would've dreamed they'd become my friends. There were two Mr. Massachusetts, Johnny R. and Jerry C.; two Mr. New Englands, Joe S. and John Mc.; and a host of others. Members of the Boston Patriots football team (now the New England Patriots), including lineman Ed Toner, back Pete (Pistol Pete) Pedro, quarterback Mike T., and others trained there. The weight room was open to all, but kids were not encouraged because it was small and could be dangerous if you dillydallied or got in the way. It wasn't a place to screw around. It was all business; it's why they call them workouts. I was and still am clumsy in social settings but for some reason I knew how to negotiate and stay out of the way of these great weightlifters and athletes. There was never a lift I didn't understand the purpose of and slowly, when these guys saw how polite I was (because of my parents) and how hard I was willing to work, they took me under their wings. So in 1967, at the age of sixteen, I had professional football players and Mr. New Englands asking me, "Hey, kid, can you give me a spot?" and then asking, "Hey kid, do you need one?"

Somehow I was accepted into this fraternity of giants who did what they did because it helped in their profession but also for the way it made them feel.

Later in life I'd learn this lesson from people who had the same passion for music and history, and to this day I know where to go when I need a physical, musical, or historical "spot." Here, I began to figure out that I'm most comfortable surrounded by people of passion, intensity, and curiosity. It's why I loved my brother so much—no one epitomized that like him.

I became the boy prodigy of the gym, falling in love with the way exercise made me feel, and not just weights but cardio too, and that love is as strong now as it was then. To this day exercise strengthens my temple and clears my head while meditation frees my spirit. Eventually, after three years of methodical work, someone suggested I represent the Y in the Mr. Boston contest. I thought this was silly but managed to come in sixth place and couldn't believe it. Six months later, after doing double sessions six days a week, I came in second in the Mr. Massachusetts contest without the aid of supplements or steroid-like drugs. I was "totally clean"; only my mother's good cooking fueled me. Steroids were on the scene back then and were suspected of killing bodybuilders with liver and other organ cancers. I knew of two. A few times I saw the aggressive, irrational, destructive behavior and emotional havoc steroids can cause. But ours was considered a "clean gym," and I'll always be proud that I never, ever tried "roids." Somehow history had taught me that Hitler gave steroids to his Nazi storm troopers and the allies reported them as wild out-of-control monsters, and that's all I needed to know. I also felt that taking "roids" would be cheating.

I was absolutely mortified getting all greased up to do muscle poses during competition in front of crowds under hot stage lights at the Huntington Y in Boston, but there was no way around it. I was too embarrassed to invite my parents, who might've thought it a bit over the top, but the guys from the Y were there to cheer me on and my biggest fan, who was *always* there, was my brother. So, in the pool when he said to grab his arms, legs, hair, or whatever, he knew it wasn't going to be a weak person grabbing. I gently asked, "Are you sure?" He got stern and said, "This is your life and you can't screw around with it!" It hit me hard, like always, that he was worried about me, not himself! In the deep end I thrashed harder than ever because I needed to thrash something and every time I grabbed his bathing suit or anatomy he'd combat it with a swift technique using my strength and momentum against me. No matter what I did, before you could say *Flipper* I'd be on my back in the arms of my brother, on my way to safety.

In the shallow end he emphasized how important staying calm was because calm muscles floated and tense ones sank. Kind of like too tense Civil War kids, loading and clogging their rifles because they forgot to shoot the previous round and so sank dead. There *are* times you have to stay calm when your heart's pounding and adrenaline's flowing but still there's no guarantee, just a better chance. He emphasized that a lifeguard has to control the situation but, even then, is never out of danger. Everything he said overpowered me with emotion. He asked if I understood and was okay, and I said I was, and he said we should review by doing one last thing. He told me to go to the deep end and relax by doing the dead man's float. This gruesome-sounding way of floating reminded me of a pirate, but really it's simply floating facedown with arms and legs extended in a natural position. Most of the time the floater is dead and has resurfaced but sometimes they're alive, so you must get to them quickly, turn them over, give them the breath of life, and get them to shore in order to get the water out of their lungs.

I could always hold my breath for a long time, so I took a deep one and floated facedown. Everything was peaceful and silent as I let my body go limp. But the way Dave had said "dead" when referring to the dead man's float made me realize that, if his disease was as bad as it might be, he'd be dead before me. It overwhelmed me with a sadness I never knew. I began begging God to let me trade places with Dave and if that wasn't possible to give me cancer too so he wouldn't have to have it alone. I thought of all the times he stuck up for me, taking on the largest, meanest neighborhood bullies who snuck up on me, like when I was on crutches after falling out of the tree when I made my mother groan like she had at Robert E. Lee. A bully saw me helpless in our yard and ran to pummel me because he'd been trying to catch me for years. Dave happened to be on the porch and saw the whole thing. In a split-second he was on the bully's back like a swarm of bees and our mom, hearing the commotion, had to come out to rescue the bully. Later I heard her tell our dad how strange it was that Dave and I fought so violently, but as soon as someone threatened me, he defended me like no other. She laughed a little and said Dave looked like King Kong on the back of the Tyrannosaurus that was after Fay Wray in the 1933 movie classic. Now, a little more than a decade after defending me like Kong, he was on his way to rescuing me again, only this time something was in his body that could pummel him to death, and I wanted to fight it with my life.

For the first time I had reckless courage combined with the new experience of irrational, visceral hatred to fight, but there was no one to fight. Facedown, I started to cry in the least conducive place for crying, and I began to choke, but before I could lift my head I was on my back in the arms of a brother I loved beyond words. He asked if I was okay and I lied, saying I just swallowed water. As he brought me to safety, he explained everything we'd done and I heard every word, but noticed tiny drops of condensation hanging from pipes parallel to the pool ceiling, as if trying to make up their minds if they needed to fall. There are times when things that were never apparent before become profound because a situation brings an understanding that love is all that matters, is all that's worth fighting for, where droplets are miracles. And, in the nick of time, a young kid in Gray finds truth lying facedown on Malvern Hill, paralyzed from the neck down from a Yankee bullet that severed his spinal cord. His eyes, in a head turned to the side, see a blade of grass as stunning in majesty as any mountain or ocean and he thinks, *Why haven't I noticed this before? It's so beautiful, I want to share it!* and exhales his last. He's found *what love is.* But I was alive in the arms of my brother, with water atoms making drops that fill pools, ponds, and oceans that allowed him to express himself in what love is. The day was a gift to me, so I could love him with all my might while droplets and dead men kept my secret that my innocence was drowning.

When we got to the shallow end, he asked if I wanted to do everything in reverse, this time with me rescuing him, but I said I felt secure enough to pass the test. The truth was I had to leave because I was getting too emotional and didn't want him to know. When he asked, "How much water did you swallow?" I knew it was time to go. But I would've found strength to stay had I known this would be the last time I'd ever see him swim. Leaving, I turned to see a dolphin doing the butterfly and the floodgates of emotion opened and I couldn't close them. He was swimming the way a professional fisherman fishes on vacation, as a historian goes to his history club on his day off, as a musician plays when no one's listening, as a writer reads after putting down his pen, like a guru meditates long after nirvana; swimming for love as I stood under the shower to wash off chlorine and I cried like never before. But I had to get a grip. He'd soon be done and I wanted to be gone before he was.

As I dried off, one of the thousands of odd little lonely guys who live in Ys around the country came into the locker room. In his sixties, Charlie had a sad story but no one to tell, though eventually he'd tell me because even then I was a person people liked to tell things to, and I don't know why. I'm trustworthy and excellent at keeping secrets because I don't like them, maybe that's why. He said hello in his friendly way as I gruffly blew by and sensed it upset him, so I went back to say, "It's not you Charl, I just can't talk right now." He was always kind and liked hearing of my youthful adventures that made him laugh. If I could go back in time I'd tell him, "I'm sorry Charl, my brother has cancer and I don't know what it means, and not knowing things makes me crazy."

From the Y I went directly to the Lynn Public Library, a beautiful, peaceful place. There was no Internet in those days so the librarian helped me find books, magazines, and medical journals on bone cancer. We looked for "how to cure" articles but couldn't find any. I wanted to learn about the different types of tumors because of the way Lincoln used the words "cancer" and "tumor" to describe slavery. Somehow I knew this was the key to understanding the bloody war in the way he did. The more I read, the more terror and despair I felt. True, new therapies and treatments had merit and were being discovered all the time, which gave me hope, but the key was, you had to stop it from spreading or it was curtains. *Cancer truly was slavery,* but I found a little false comfort in that I did not know exactly what kind of cancer Dave actually had, although I knew the word "aggressive" was in the diagnosis. "Malignant" was a word I read a lot so I looked in the library's dictionary to learn that it meant "likely to cause death," "having an evil influence," and was "harmful to the whole." It hammered home how right Lincoln had been in describing slavery that way, because he always said it could cause the death of our nation, but my mind was far more on Dave than Lincoln. The definition of "malignant" registered deep, though. The list of "omas"—carcinomas, blastomas, gliomas—went on and on. So many tumors ended with "oma" that I decided if I ever had to drive from Chicago to Texas I'd drive around Oklahoma to avoid its "oma," even though it's a beautiful state. I left the library numb, dejected, and overwhelmed.

I went home to a cute little apartment Judi and I had on South Street. It was a stone's throw from the South St. Baptist Church where the family of the great black abolitionist, Frederick Douglass, attended services when they had a home in Lynn a little more than a hundred twenty years prior. Another stone's throw from the church stands the Frederick Douglass Bandstand where he gave gut-wrenching antislavery speeches on Lynn Common. A beautiful plaque commemorates it. A victim and escapee of slavery, Douglass went on to educate the nation, including his friend Lincoln, on how truly insidious the thing was. As a free man, he was subjected to physical danger and verbal abuse from Americans who believed slavery was not a bad thing but a good thing and, though I found this hard to believe as a kid, it was sadly true. Now I was in the beginning process of finding out the hard way that anyone who believed slavery/cancer was a good thing hadn't *experienced* it or had anyone they loved suffer from it. But Douglass and the heroics of my tired old city that gave his family refuge were the last things on my mind as I walked in the door.

What a sight Judi was for a weary traveler. She hugged me and said I looked like I'd seen a ghost. "Maybe I have!" I said, then briefly explained what I'd learned at the library. She became very sad, but had a great pasta supper with her homemade sauce all ready. We had each other so the sharp edge of my despair was dulled a little, though the hilt was buried to my soul. She was deeply affected because Dave was her brother, too. But I was home, which was wherever she was, where I could rationally process information, although that's debatable. She provided sanctuary that made it possible. One of the greatest gifts I constantly received from her was the feeling of safety, besides having *my trusted someone* to share my joy and sorrow. We carried burdens together, and they were almost always mine because I was the selfish one. To this day, she knew more than anyone, even my parents, brothers, and daughter, that I was not the happy-go-lucky person people thought I was; that I agonized and worried over big issues but also over stupid, mundane things that caused my stomach to turn and my head ache; that I was an expert at making mountains of molehills, and assigned too much anxiety to future events (still do) that later turned out to be a total waste of energy because nothing was as bad as I could anticipate, except slavery, which would be beyond anticipating. If the song "Tears of a Clown" is applicable to anyone it could be to me, but because of her comfort and understanding, Dave's inspiration, meditation, the exhilaration of exercise, music, and history, I at least had some tools to deal with my emotional paranoia and gloom.

Thankfully, history had taught me that Lincoln was also a tormented man in his early twenties. He had concluded that he had to acknowledge his torment or die. He said to his closest friend, Joshua, who shared a similar torment, that acknowledging their nervous dispositions for the realities they were might be a way to live with them, because there was no escaping them. I believed then and do now that it's why his favorite poem was "Mortality" by William Know, because it asks the question in the first line and again in the last: "Oh! Why should the spirit of mortal be proud?" Every line in between tells the truth that there is nothing new under the sun; that all thoughts and emotions we think are new have been before. So this means that pride keeps us from asking for help, because we think our generation's version of joy and horror and whatever else existence conjures, good or evil, is somehow different than it was before. But it isn't, and that's "the rub"— Lincoln's term for the truth of a situation.

The eternal can only be entered by understanding the present, and the present can only be understood by knowing the past. The key can be a poem or it could be a Dave or Judi. Either way, my saving grace was recognizing early on that *there's nothing healthier than an open mind.* But I was weak (still am), yet somehow Judi kept my mind open so I had a prayer.

London Calling
Uncle Joe's Left Foot

After supper I got the mail. Two letters from dear friends in England had arrived. Word from the other side of the world always made Judi happy, so I handed them to her. My having no inclination to be happy made her realize how much trouble I thought Dave might be in. Knowing less about cancer than I did, which was next to nothing, she was shaken by my apathy. She hugged me and said, "Don't be afraid!" But I felt worry in her embrace as she put the letters on the kitchen table and said, "We'll open them in the morning with tea."

With our first cups, I opened one and she, the other. Colin wrote, "Hello, mate" but I heard "'ello, mate." He told me of a great job opportunity for the right person in my chosen profession—one I loved beyond *all* activities. The other letter-writer, Stephen, like Colin, was in the profession too and his letter asked Judi when we were coming back to England. He asked, "Coming home?" We weren't supposed to stay away as long as we had. Judi made her little motherly giggling sound she always made with Stephen when we were "out and about" in London, or having tea at his mum's, or rolling around the Oxford countryside. I'd lived there for a year and Judi for half a year when she came to visit and I wouldn't let her leave. This all occurred because of what I am, a musician. If I've ever been anything besides human it would be a musician. I've been intimately involved with music since my parents brought me home from the hospital. Their passion for classical music exposed me to the truest language of God from day one, and maybe before that if one can hear from the womb.

My earliest recollection is lying in a child's carrying chair underneath the keyboard of an upright piano and next to sustain and mute pedals in my grandmother's living room in the early 1950s. The whole Nerich clan was gathered as Uncle Joe, Nick's younger brother, led the way on piano. His siblings and in-laws played guitars, ukuleles, and fiddles, and sang, danced, or some combination thereof. My mother put me there because there was no place else to put me. I remember the laughing, singing, and my mother's deep red lipstick emphasizing a smile that told how much she loved being with her aunts, uncles, cousins, musical mentors, and Olympian swimming heroes. They passed songs around like families pass stuffing on Thanksgiving. Every few minutes my mother's beautiful face checked on me; it's how I remember the lipstick. But what I remember more was the small, shiny-shoed left foot of her mother's brother, Uncle Joe, tapping a rhythm that controlled what went on in the room and for all I knew, the entire world. I somehow sensed it was the heartbeat of *everything*.

It conducted the sound coming out of the wood above and below me. When I wasn't looking at the foot I saw cuff links (strange things) on Joe's shirt sleeves where white skin led to hands to fingers to things making music. When he picked up a cigarette to hold by his right knee, smoke rose and I felt my individuality, that *this being alive stuff is pretty cool.* This stopped the splashes (chords) and quick, staccato bursts sounding like voices, but his left hand kept vibrating the mantra. Walking, bluesy, boogie-woogie bass lines woke me from when before an impulse of God set off the big bang. They connected me to murmuring voices of tribes gathered around fire since the beginning of time. I'd already been exposed to the classical melodies of *Carmen, Clair de Lune,*

Bolero, and hundreds of others the world can't spin without; but Uncle Joe's foot tapping seductively subtle and not so subtle, silky, slinking rhythms unleashed my *peculiar* nature that would give me gumption to sit next to Beethoven— not to tell him to roll over because who can do that, but to inform him in no uncertain terms there's room for two at the piano, so slide over. Joe's right hand connected me to God, but his left, which gives music legitimacy and authority, connected me to life.

In the spring of 58, at age seven and already long bonded with Uncle Joe's left foot I was next door, up the old road along the river, when my friend plugged in a portable record player he had received for Christmas. Songs came out of the speaker that stunned, excited, seduced, and transported me to a different dimension. They were Elvis's "Jailhouse Rock" and "Hound Dog." I asked him to play them again and again and after a half dozen times asked, "How long have you had these?"

He said, "Since Christmas."

"Why didn't you show me then?" Aggressive questions from a non-aggressive, tentative little kid. The yin and yang feeling I had while asking was foreign yet familiar.

"What's the big deal? They're just songs about jail and a dog." he asked.

I couldn't understand his response because I hadn't heard a single lyric so I asked him to play them again and he was right, notes had words *attached* to them and two were "jail" and "dog." Being a child of Uncle Joe's left foot meant I was inherently different because words in songs were the last thing I heard. After the two snare hits in "Jailhouse," it was all she wrote when the bass line came in.

Lyrics were an afterthought because the interaction of the bass, drums, piano, guitar, and melody made me want to climb a tree, run, punch, hug, destroy, create, love, and fly through the air. Without knowing it, I listened to music from the inside out, the opposite of most people. I could listen my friend's way, from the outside in, which gave me *some* juice, but I liked my way better because I got the whole fruit. If seeds, stems, bruises, and skin came with it, so be it; it rocked! Spirit, passion, and desire came from imperfection and I felt it. One day I'd live with and love people who felt music like that, and later those who felt history, warts and all, from the inside out. I'd come to learn there was no difference between them. My mother was both and I now knew what it was like to drink a tall cup of coffee or snit something stupid with a straw up my nose. I couldn't sleep that night and was wired all the next day in school. I couldn't wait for the bell to go home so I could feel the thump of the jail and the dog, but my friend was at his piano lesson so I had to wait. I felt desperate, lonely, and impatient; feelings I didn't understand because I had no clue I experienced music differently. The physical, organic, explosive rush was hard to get used to; like riding a rocket to destinations unknown yet somehow familiar. When my friend finally got home to inject the needle into the groove, I was the vinyl and the groove my vein; it was "aaahhh" for a new junkie having his first taste of the day.

Now I needed a supplier and my paternal grandparents helped me find one that summer. We'd sit on their back porch in Saugus and listen to the Boston Red Sox on a little single-speaker 6 transistor GE radio you could hold in your hand or shirt pocket. I was fascinated by it and noticed that by turning a dial, my grandmother could change it to a station with music when the game was over. I asked to try it, and when I stumbled on Chuck Berry's "Johnny B. Goode" I discovered the way to Shangri-la. I asked for a radio like that for my birthday, and when I turned eight they got me one. Now I had my own window to the world of modern pop music. It had a one-ear extension so I could listen without anyone hearing and, because music wasn't in stereo back then, one ear at a time was okay. No one except my grandmother, who always kept my secrets, and Dave knew I snuck my radio into bed with me every night from 1959 to 1962. It's probably the only secret I was able to keep from my mother. I was extremely careful and sneaky about it. I didn't want to lose my guilty pleasure for a moment. And as long as I let Dave listen to a song or two, he wouldn't rat me out. He liked the music I liked, but somehow was able to fall asleep whereas it took me a while to calm down after I turned the music off, which I never did till a goofy song, like one about itsy-bitsy bikinis, came on. I had a system!

I became saturated in and infatuated by "Johnny B. Goode," "Whole Lot of Shakin' Going on," "Great Balls Of Fire," "Lucille," "Summertime Blues," "Rock and Roll Music," "Money" (that drove me wild with its power), "Good Golly Miss Molly," "Sweet Little Sixteen," "What I'd Say," "Love Potion No. 9," "Shakin' All Over" (that song put me over the edge and made my lower lip do a tough guy look), "Stay," "Stand By Me," "The Wanderer," "Green Onions," and too many others to mention. My neighbor told me there were tons of Elvis songs we could hear at the movie theater so I persuaded him to persuade his mother to persuade mine to allow us to go to the old Warner Theater in the big city of Lynn. My mother agreed and said she'd take us and pick us up, but told me I'd be disappointed by the music. It was the first time I ever thought she could be wrong about something, but that wouldn't happen till The Beatles came on the scene.

When I and three of my eight-year-old Confederates packed into our 54 Plymouth and were dropped off, it was my first movie theater experience. The anticipation was unbearable. After previews of Vincent Price horror movies, Elvis came on in a goofy beach movie. It was thrilling seeing bikini girls, though I felt mortified thinking my mother might find out, but how could she? Elvis was cool and confident and his voice was so smooth, but my mom was right, the songs, rhythms, and instruments felt so ridiculous I couldn't stand it. There was plenty of fabricated, manufactured energy but no *natural, honest* oomph or prisoner-take-all punch to inspire doing something courageous. If it hadn't been for the bikinis, nothing besides the salt and butter on the popcorn would've appealed to me. When my mom picked us up the guys were already making plans for the next week's Elvis movie but I kept quiet. She knew what my silence meant. When we got home she laughed and said, "I told you, you wouldn't like the music but at least you got to see some girls in bikinis" which made it more horrible than it already was.

She said Elvis was tremendously talented and she liked his early hits "Jailhouse Rock" and "Hound Dog," which made me feel a little better. Then she said a scoundrel (my term, not hers) named Colonel Parker got hold of Elvis when Elvis was too young to know better and "The Colonel" controlled what songs and movies Elvis did. I felt a *nah . . . this ain't right* feeling about the notion that you could lose your freedom by signing something called a contract. She said I shouldn't feel too bad though, because at least Elvis had a choice because he wasn't a *slave* (that word again). A decade later when The Beatles met Elvis, Lennon asked him why he made those silly movies. I never found out Elvis's reply but the question was a good one. But it was the music, not him, I was interested in. The more I learned, the more I realized how much great music he never recorded because a contract said he had to dance with bikini girls, so maybe in a mild way he was a slave but who can say? Though, considering the tragic way he died, maybe it wasn't so mild. Elvis belonged to the previous generation more than to mine but "Jailhouse," my first love, got and still gets me going!

In 1960, at age nine, when I was just getting comfortable with my classical piano lessons, I asked my mother if I could learn to play the music Uncle Joe played because it was so similar to the rock piano I heard on the radio. I got a little nervous because she looked shocked yet pleased and asked, "You remember that? You were only a baby when you heard Joe play." I wasn't that young I thought, so when I said I remembered she sat down at the piano and said, "You mean like this?" Her left hand played the most wicked bass line I'd ever heard. It made the hair on my arms and legs stand up. Then her right hand sounded like a buzzing bee. I was blown away because all I'd ever heard her play was Beethoven, Mozart, Brahms, Liszt, Strauss, and stuff like that. When she was done I told her it sounded like a bee and she said, "That's why it's called 'The Flight of the Bumblebee.' Do you want to hear another?" Then she played a bluesy up tempo three-chord progression, the kind guys like Jerry Lee Lewis and Chuck Berry's piano player Johnnie Johnson played (so Chuck could have hits).

I wasn't going to be sleeping that night and said, "Yeah Ma, like that!"

Then she said something as important as anything she ever said to me. "You can play whatever music brings you the most joy. It'll tell you *what* you are. I just hope you won't forget classical music."

"I won't, Ma." It was a promise easy to keep.

She talked to my piano teacher and when Mrs. McLaughlin, a lady in her seventies, agreed, I was on my way. Mrs. M. said it surprised her that I wanted to play the "peppy stuff" because I was such a "shy little thing," but she added that when she was young she liked the "snappy beat" too. Her terms for *my music* embarrassed me for some reason but she was an excellent teacher. She didn't attack notes the way my mother and Uncle Joe, who owned and possessed them and weren't afraid to pick 'em up, twist 'em, to *respectfully* put 'em back where they belonged, did. Mrs. M. gently borrowed notes with every intention of not disturbing, which was okay because she taught me songs, scales, time signatures, and what notes were what. But I somehow knew that when I'd play the "peppy stuff" I'd own notes like my ancestors because they were begging to be had, like the girls in Elvis movies pleading with glances that said "take me, take me now." I was discovering what I was and my teachers were notes, wanting to be ravished and loved. But my coming of age took a long, terrible, dark and unfortunate detour when I was ten and in the fifth grade at St. Michael's.

I was always one of the youngest kids in class and I struggled to keep up. Many times I wasn't able to, but I never got in trouble because I was too scared to. The nuns in their seventies and eighties probably should've been retired. Some were kind, others not. One day in music class the school secretary came in to tell our wonderful, young music teacher, the only lay, or non-nun, teacher in the school that she had a phone call. She knew Mrs. M., who must've told her I was a pretty good piano player because she said I could play for the kids while she answered the phone. My classmates egged me to play so I started with a Jerry Lee Lewis bass line, then went off as best I knew how, left foot tapping and all. Kids ran to the sides of the piano, smiling and dancing and it made me so happy. For the first time *ever* I felt like I belonged and was contributing something good to the world. Then, without warning, I experienced the worst pain since falling out of the tree of Robert E. Lee. From behind, I was picked up so hard by my ear that I felt and heard cartilage ripping. It was absolutely excruciating! The kids ran to their seats as our innocent teacher returned in time to hear Sister Superior, the principal, yelling at me. "Who gave you permission to play Satan's music?"

Before I could say "nobody" our teacher said, "I did!" but Superior turned back to me and said, "We do not play evil music in this school! Do you hear me? DO YOU HEAR ME?"

I said, "Yes, Sister, I hear you, I'm sorry!" while my ear was on fire.

She told me to stop crying and I partly succeeded but the pain was awful. Her words ripped my self-esteem to shreds. I'd never made anyone so mad before or since. Then she grabbed the hair on the back of my head, pulled it back so my face looked up to the crucifix with Jesus nailed to it, hanging on the wall above the piano, and said, "Apologize to God for your betrayal!"

The "ancient dogma" of the word "betrayal" in the Catholic psyche is too powerful to describe because of its inherent implication to Judas. If it's possible to crush the spirit of a kid *forever* with a word, that's the one. Until then I believed the "snappy beat" honored God. How could I have been so wrong? All this time I'd been a Judas and didn't know it. Then she turned me to face the class to apologize for playing "evil music" and made me promise to never, ever play it again. Our teacher was in anguish and I did as I was told. Then Superior stormed out and we sat in awkward silence for the rest of the class. Afterward, our teacher told me how sorry she was and I told her it wasn't her fault and not to let this get back to Mrs. M. because then it'd get back to my mother and I didn't want to disappoint her. My shame, self-loathing, and, worst of all, confusion were beyond words! At home I told my mom I wasn't taking piano lessons anymore. She didn't believe me and tried to get me to tell her what was wrong. I lied and said that I *never* liked them and was done.

"I thought you loved it," she said.

"I hate it!" I said and went to my room.

Having been taught that nuns were literally the brides of Christ (making Jesus a Mormon?), I had committed the worst sin by loving "Satan's music." I offended Jesus so much that one of his wives almost ripped my ear off. The thought of it terrified me and I was too frightened to tell the person I trusted most, my mother. I wouldn't touch the piano again for four years and my relationship with it would *never* be the same!

In the sixth and seventh grades in 1962 and 1963 I kept a low profile; horrified around Sister Superior. I noticed other students and teachers were afraid of her too but maybe it was "just my imagination, running away with me." It seemed every kid who had something that made them happy annoyed her. Meanwhile, I added to my guilt by continuing my secret life with my 6 transistor radio. I stopped playing evil music, but couldn't stop *listening* to it. I wasn't sure if I was a slave to it or not, but I knew I was sinning. Religion was teaching us that purgatory was a place we'd go to suffer when we weren't quite bad enough for hell so maybe I could squeak in there to pay for my sin and still have a chance for heaven. But then God *had to* be convinced my repentance was sincere and how could I do that? So I was screwed!

Years later when I told these things to Judi she became agitated, I can't say mad because I never saw her mad, which sounds ridiculous but is true. She said, "If you didn't play evil music, we wouldn't have met." Ironically, she said this as we were on a beach under the stars after I'd spent the night playing Satan's music and getting paid for it, which made it extra sinful. After I told her of my ear-ripping adventure I told her of all my fears and silly dreams along with my every disgusting, guilty, perverted, selfish, egotistical thought and she relieved me of the burden by not running away and by saying, "Hon, everyone's screwed up and people who deny it usually have the most trouble.

You're okay and I wish you knew it like I do." At the time I was reading a lot of Mark Twain and found further relief that he *wanted* to go to hell because most of the people he found interesting were there or heading there. But as a kid I didn't have Judi or Twain and I felt terrified, isolated, and helpless.

Things got a lot better in the seventh grade. My teacher was the sweetest, kindest nun in God's creation. When Sister Marietta started off the year by asking if we'd heard about an exciting new band called The Beatles that *she loved,* I almost hit the floor. From day one I hung on her every word. She was the first person to suggest I had a knack for history and should speak up in class. She told me my mother was the "coolest"—she used that word—mother she'd met on parent's day. I trusted her, but was still too traumatized to heed her advice about speaking up. Sister Superior would be my eighth grade teacher and that pending cloud hung over me.

On November 22, 1963, the school secretary came in and whispered something to Sister M. that made her reach into her robe for a large white handkerchief to bury her face in and weep. We all ran to her and I was the last but plowed my way through to get into the lap of my dear friend only to feel tears on my neck and hear her cry, "Oh, God, please, not this, please not this!" She'd always hugged kids who performed an act of kindness or if they were scared or sad and, when she did, you felt you were in the safest place in the world. On this day she held me as her body convulsed with grief and I felt there was a woman underneath the head-to-toe attire worn by nuns of her order. I'd never thought of a nun that way and knowing her feminine humanness, my admiration and affection only grew. Eventually she composed herself and told us to go back to our seats. She stood before us in a long silence searching for words for kids she called "my precious babies." Everyone was crying except me. Finally, as if it was her fault, she said, "Oh children, I'm so sorry this has happened to you. President Kennedy has been killed." Our age of innocence was over and nothing would ever be the same. When our mom picked me and my brothers up she had a handkerchief too and that's when I cried.

The next day Sister Superior said over the intercom, "Everything happens for a reason and is part of God's divine plan. The mysteries of faith *can never* be understood, but if we put our faith in Jesus everything will be all right." This somehow made me feel sorry for her because history was teaching me that things didn't happen for mystical, unexplainable reasons, that there were very specific, solid, understandable reasons why things are the way they are, and if we worked hard, we could know them to make rational choices to contribute solutions. It's how Abraham Lincoln looked at things and, even though I didn't fully know that like I one day would, I could sense it because my mom and Sister M. felt that way too.

A few days later I asked Sister M. if she was still sad.

She said, "I'll always be sad about hate in this world."

When I said, "I don't believe what happened was part of God's divine plan."

She said, "Neither do I!" giving me a taste of freedom that only love can give.

When we studied the Civil War, she was so cool. She allowed a strange, eccentric kid, Irving L., who was into Gothic decades before anyone, to keep a small Confederate flag in his inkwell. If Eddie Munster and Pugsly Adams had a brother, Irving would've been him. Years later he'd drive around the city in a hearse he bought from a funeral home. As far as I knew all he had in back were musical instruments. In seventh grade he'd ask me about notes and what instruments made what sounds and I always shared what I knew. Sister M. let him keep his flag there as long as he understood what it stood for. She wanted us to know that above all things, the war was caused by the dispute of whether or not the *sin*—her word—of slavery should be allowed into the territories, and that the North said "no" and the South said "yes." Irving, sounding like the quintessential '60s TV beatnik Maynard G. Krebs, said, "It's a deal, Sis!" She was the only nun who'd let him get away with a comment like that. She said, "If I was your sister, you'd be in big trouble!" and this made us all laugh. With her, learning, especially history, was pure joy!

Before we got out for the summer I asked Irving why he flew the Reb flag.

"Because I think they look so much cooler than the Yanks," he replied.

"I do too. I wish we learned more about them than we did."

"I can help!" he said.

The next day he gave me a grocery bag full of magazines, precursors to today's *North & South, Civil War Times, The Monitor,* etc., that history professors, students, and the curious subscribe to if they're interested in that period of U.S. history. He said I could keep them over the summer, so the four books I was supposed to read never got read. I learned so much about who was who in the Reb Army and government. And that, yes, many of them looked swashbuckling, cool, sexy, and forbidden. No kidding, some even had feather plumes in their hats as they led a charge. It was a good summer for a kid with history and music becoming intricately, permanently entwined in his spirit no matter who or what religious dogma was scaring the hell out of him.

In 1963 and 1964, "She Loves You," "I Want To Hold Your Hand," "I Saw Her Standing There," "Please, Please Me" (all by The Beatles), "Louie, Louie," "Surfin' USA," "Blowing In The Wind" (a profound and beautiful song even to a kid), "You Really Got A Hold On Me" (the melody felt like a beautiful waterfall,) and grooves like that of "Dancing In The Streets," "Heat Wave," "Nowhere To Run," "Going To A Go-Go," "Shotgun," and "Mustang Sally" were physical and spiritual experiences that temporally overpowered my trepidation of Sister Superior. Great songs kept coming and I lost so much sleep. My studies, never good to begin with, went down the tubes and I decided, like Civil War Naval Admiral David Farragut when he entered the deadly waters of Mobile Bay, "Damn the torpedoes, full speed ahead!" And I didn't have to sneak under my covers to get my fix because music was exploding; in cars, friend's houses, on TV, everywhere, all while Vietnam was sucking us in, so war was wafting through the air too.

My brothers and I were now "jin-you-ieenne" big city citizens and our parents bought a new stereo for their classical music that my brothers hijacked

for ours. And we found an infinite reservoir of the *forbidden* in the new phenomenon: FM radio. These stations were dedicated to what we were into and
my brothers felt no shame playing them louder than our parents preferred,
because they didn't suffer the demons I did. They were sane and didn't give a
damn if music was evil or not. Our dad tolerated it, which meant everything
as our forever-curious mom grudgingly yet respectfully became enthralled
because, despite the fact that most of the musicians couldn't read and weren't
classically trained, though some were, there was no denying the incredible
melodies and sometimes brilliant lyrics she heard.

When The Beatles came out she said, "Now they're very good," but predicted they'd be a "flash in the pan."

I said, "No Ma, they're just getting started, you'll see."

"Okay, we'll see."

I knew I was right because I'd seen Lennon's foot tapping like Uncle Joe's
on *The Ed Sullivan Show,* and you don't get to tap like that unless something
permanent is in your blood. The sound Lennon and his three Confederates
made, made the world feel like a better place than Sister Superior wanted us
to believe it was. They were the "real deal," and somehow we belonged to the
music and it to us. With The Beatles, there was no doubt and not even my mom
could convince me otherwise, which was an earth-shattering contemplation!
But she never tried; she was a student of history, and as hip as they come. In
the music was my solace; too powerful for all the Sister Superiors in the world
to disturb. I felt happy again and entertained the idea that when I went back to
school Sister Superior would like me and that her feelings had all been a mistake
because nuns weren't supposed to hold grudges toward anyone. I decided I'd
be extra good my last year at St. Michael's and on the first day I'd say, "Good
morning, Sister Superior" in my friendliest way and everything would be all
right. But it was a pipe dream of youth. In September she was as dour as ever.
When I said my good morning as planned her silence shouted repugnance,
making me miserable from day one, with guilt impossible to describe.

In a split second I was back to my usual state, an absolute mess, and my parents kept asking what was wrong, but I said nothing. The entire year was torture, and my dad was very disappointed in my grades, only he didn't know I was too. I couldn't climb out of my fear until a new kind of savior came to my rescue that somehow captured my fear and turned it into a shield to help me withstand Superior's gaze of dislike. "All Day and All of the Night" by The Kinks was a different kind of animal. The opening riff—power chords—was uncontrollable, long imprisoned, released rage that made me sit up and take notice. The aggressive, hacksaw, mechanical sound, grabbed and root-canalled my fear. The drum part before the guitar solo gave me supreme confidence (still does), to tell my parents the truth of my troubles with Sister Superior, but in the mad rush to get to school on time it faded, so I never got the chance. The Beatles' "A Hard Day's Night," The Animals' "House of the Rising Sun" and "We Gotta Get Out of This Place" (my theme song for St. Michaels) all combined with The Kinks to make a Confederacy of sound that helped me make it to the end of the year. When Eric Burton sang, "I'm just a soul whose intentions are good, oh Lord, please don't let me be misunderstood," it was my prayer to God to protect me from the wrath of Sister Superior. Those words like no others until Lennon's "Help," taught me it was okay to throw myself on the mercy of the court, exposing heart and soul. And dear God, I missed my piano but stayed away because there was no way to play it and not love it.

Somehow I made it to the end of the year unscathed, but on the last day before graduation Sister Superior gave me a going away present. All year she had me sit in the last row in the corner so she wouldn't have to look at me. She had each kid stand, one at a time, and told them what she envisioned they'd be when they grew up. Many were to be doctors, lawyers, firemen, policemen, and a surprising number priests and nuns. When she got to me she told me to stand without saying my name. I looked at the old wooden floor and wished I was a bug so I could crawl into a crack. She said, "I don't have any idea you'll amount to anything, but I'll pray your parents' sacrifice to send you here wasn't a waste of money. Sit down!" She crushed me! I wanted to tell her I hadn't touched the piano in three years so there was no need to hate me but I started crying and couldn't help it. Maybe by being a bride of Christ, she knew I hadn't stopped listening to evil music like I was supposed to and my demeanor told her I was still sinning.

I sat down in a heap of misery and just before she dismissed us for the last time a classmate, Joanne D., who'd stood next to the ear-ripping piano, got up and said, "Sister what you said to Robert is mean and not what God expects of you. The only reason he played the piano for us was because we asked him to! You shouldn't hate him for that."

I couldn't believe she said that or had the courage to or that the incident was still on anyone's mind. Then her friend Jeannie W. stood up and squeaked in, "We liked his music!" and quickly sat down. They were two of the future nuns Superior had predicted. But I only wanted forgiveness because I thought that's what Christianity was all about.

It proved too much for Frankie M. sitting next to me. He'd gone through more abuse than I had because his sin was having a wicked sense of humor. He found irony in everything. It'd been a joy seeing him make Sister Marietta laugh till she had tears in her eyes. The year before, during history class, she'd said, "You know children, Abraham Lincoln felt that laughter is the best medicine!" There's more truth to that than anything else history can teach! But in the eighth grade laughter and irony weren't allowed. Frankie now got red and started shaking and said to himself, "I hate her guts." He then exploded at Superior, "I'm not going to be no stupid fireman no matter what you say! You don't know us and you act like you were the one hanging from the cross! You don't know anything about it. Why don't you go up and hang from it to see what it's like being frightened to death, then tell us how to think."

It was an awful, pathetic scene but Superior was unfazed and simply dismissed us. She'd done the best she could to save our souls and in a war with Satan, *you can't win 'em all*. The difference between Sisters Marietta and Superior was like love versus the "honor" of old General Foghorn Leghorn.

Kids in Catholic schools today aren't treated like we were because some of the sins of the church have been exposed. We were in the last desperate gasp of the dark age of secrets where fear wasn't only the norm but the rule, where Popes were infallible, incapable of error in deciding church doctrine and what the faithful had to believe in order to find salvation. His decisions were perfect and final, yet we were taught there was only one perfect person ever born and he died for us, so how could the Pope also be perfect? There was no answer except to not ask the question. It was like our nation during the Civil War, when the Confederate government, schools, and churches taught children their society was the most perfect, infallible one ever evolved by mankind, while Abraham Lincoln said nobody's society was perfect. The standard of perfection that Sister Superior preached was unattainable and some, like Frankie and I, cracked.

In old photos of those years I see some confused, frightened little kids and one who looks like he lost his piano forever. He was really a good kid who wasn't allowed to know he was. He never did a mean thing to anyone unless they were his brothers. He'd grow up to be one of those strange people who's never had an enemy and wouldn't think of Sister Superior as one. There must've been something that made her so angry. Maybe it was what Lincoln called "ancient dogmas" that went against all estimates of rationality and common sense, that would push anyone over the edge had they had to give up the joys and pleasures of the "snappy beat" of life, only to find out too late it was the worst mistake of their life because innocent children everywhere revealed God wants everyone, especially nuns, to have a good time meditating the wonder of it all by loving everyone. Did Uncle Joe's left foot make her feel she wanted to be free, but slavery to dogma make her interpret that craving as an evil to be avoided at all costs instead of a gift to liberate the spirit? Was it infallible church doctrine that, to this day, had the beloved last pope, John Paul, saying even Bob Dylan's music was evil? In '65 "Like A Rolling Stone" brought me closer to God but

Sister Superior wanted us to believe it was actually a step away. Thankfully, the song is a sacred sacrament to me now that I love with all my heart!

Today my old church is making John Paul a saint as it continues to pay lip service to one of the worst cover-ups in criminal behavior, perpetrated on "the least of my brethren," while it rewards the Cardinal who hid the molestation of four of my little league friends in Saugus. God help me, I don't get it and, having known a real saint, never will.

In the end, like the old Confederacy died an empty shell of its self-perceived perfect self, St. Michael's is a long abandoned building. If a crumbling, cobwebbed, upright, out of tune piano is deep in its bowels with ghosts playing it, that's good because the 11th Commandment that Moses accidentally left on Mt. Sinai states that *it's a sin to waste a good piano!* And if it's only home to a mouse, there's use in that too. Some classmates, old and gray now, are convinced that that time long ago is the basis for their neuroses and addictions. Gratefully, I'm not one. Yet, when a dear friend who liked the way a kid tickled the ivories in her fifth grade class says, "Thank God our children and grandchildren don't have to go through what we did!" all I can say is "Amen to that!"

FREEDOM TASTES
OF REALITY

To be free, to be born again, to get a second chance on the most sacred day of the American calendar, April 9, the day Robert E. Lee surrendered and signed a paper in 1865 that will always be the true signing of the Declaration of Independence because it declared what being human would forever mean in the United States. Then one hundred years later to the day, to have The Beatles release "Ticket to Ride" declaring what kind of human I was, was the core of my rebirth. Riding the opening notes, I entered a new galaxy of hope, leaving my old confusing world behind. Lyrics about a girl *"going away"* were unimportant to a kid who listened to music from the inside out. But if they had to be about someone they could be about Sister Superior leaving me, even though it was the other way around. The feel and majesty of the perfect song illustrating a sum of sound that far surpassed the sum of what each instrument played when added together was how I discovered what magic is. No one had to explain it to me, and thank God I didn't have to *take it on faith*.

Ticket was lightning in a bottle that couldn't be stopped from getting out no matter how hard the lid was tightened. It lifted me and made me whole, wanting to rip my clothes off and run to the ocean on a sunny day to dive in and thank God I was alive. Sister Superior be damned? No, no way, that's not what I wanted; it was about forgiving, saying, "Take my hand Sister, be my friend, my guiding light, and swim with me, thanking God that when we thank him separately it doesn't come close to the sum of our thanks when given together." This holy song was the sound of that summer and although other summers would have theirs, this was the first love I'd marry. Unlike the "Jailhouses" and "Hound Dogs" that were more than puppy love for sure, *Ticket* was true, mature love that would get me to St. Mary's High, where a magnificent church organ waited. Where the air was fresh and I'd somehow fit in with kids as equally brainwashed as I, with pimples oozing through peach fuzz, beards, and cracking voices; with unexpected, unwanted, hard-to-hide spontaneous erections, with girls with pimples and peach fuzz too. Some girls looked like women and some looked like girls. All glorious chaos in September of '65, with a song as cool as any breeze, "The Sound of Silence" by Simon and Garfunkel, allowing it to make sense in a way lyric and word alone never can.

The song recorded or mixed with reverb (echo), told us we were in a wide universe of possibility, that if we stuck together, we'd be all right in a world getting sucked into Vietnam and deception. *Silence* was a meditation of the times, but just to make sure we didn't get too hippie-dippie-ish about it, an abrupt sliding bass line came in like sharp reality, reminding us not to get too comfortable no matter how much goodwill there was in smiling "upon your brother." It trumpeted alert; to be on the lookout, and those who heard it like I did became my fellow Confederates. Some hung out before school, during lunch, and after school behind dumpsters smoking pot, butts, exchanging pills and cough syrup, while others played on athletic teams or had noses in books or were on debating teams or were experts in science labs or some combination thereof. The music connected us like "Sentimental Journey" connected our World War II–era parents. All was now and immediate as we banded together and marched to distant shores, intent on discovering what we were while keeping step to the beat. Somehow (maybe thanks to Uncle Joe) I could bridge the gap between musicians, historians, philosophers, scientists, politicians, charlatans, gurus, aristocrats, drunks, and junkies, for I had a mother who found commonality in all, who'd teach in her history class that everyone deserved to be heard because *all* had a song!

But before we could get too intimate with each other, a song came out in November that smashed everything. It didn't slip out of the bottle like *Ticket,* but blew it up into tiny shards too small to bruise and impossible to dig out of embedded skin. Like the marriage of hot and cold, heaven and hell, love and hate, and good and evil it didn't entice, soothe or invite; it disrupted and assaulted with the violence of war, with power too intense for the tiny ball of matter to contain that exploded into the universe we know, love, and fear. Pete Townshend wrote it, Roger Daltrey sang it, and Keith Moon and John Entwistle delivered it. "My Generation" *was* our generation, written by a kid not much older than us. He'd felt the after-rumble of Nazi bombs on his island nation when he was an infant, and was old enough to see the rubble of war that somehow inspired or tortured him into leaving rubble on stages. When asked for an explanation for the song, he wrote another, "I Can't Explain," to spare timid inquisitors the truth, that *slavery* is the cause of war! And if that's not what was on his mind, it was on mine because I somehow knew it'd been on Lincoln's.

Now, The Beatles, The Stones, The Kinks, The Who, Led Zeppelin, Hendrix, Dylan, and the rest spared no one, for even they couldn't stop the music the universe was writing. "Hope I die before I get old" meant I hope I die before I become a slave to bigotry and ancient dogma by ending up an aristocrat. Music was exorcising my spirit of superstition but I needed a foundation of compassion, otherwise it'd be too dangerous to me and those I loved. I was given the most sacred one in December on my fourteenth birthday. John Lennon's "In My Life" was the most beautiful thing I'd ever heard from "my generation." Dear Lord, how could anything so beautiful be evil? *Knowing* it couldn't be, freed me to start my Civil War battle through fear back to the piano and maybe to what reality really was while proms, winter frolics, spring socials, and summer dances sponsored by schools around the city greased the skids with music provided by my fellow Confederates, some sitting next to me in school.

One of the most popular bands (by far) was the youngest, a quartet made up of three guys from my class and one older guy (eighteen) who'd dropped out of public school. Wherever they played I went. There were two dozen or so other bands from the city also good enough to play dances, and new ones were popping up all the time. Surrounding towns like Swampscott, Saugus, Peabody, Salem, Revere, and Beverly had bands too, and I checked out every one as soon as I heard "the buzz." All were made up of guitars, bass, and drums but none could touch the young quartet. A few had organs so they could play The Animals' and The Doors' songs or "Time Is On My Side" by The Stones and even silly things like "96 Tears" and "Woolly Bully."

Unbeknownst to me, the young quartet decided to add an organ and asked Frankie M., my old St. Mike's classmate who was now at St. Mary's, to join them after they heard him play piano at a school function. I never found out why, but he declined and suggested they ask me. So, out of the blue, the leader of the band, of whom I happened to be in awe, asked me and I was flabbergasted considering I hadn't touched the keys in four years. The Catholic guilt of playing the piano (or organ) was something I couldn't shake. To make matters worse, all the parts I would've played would've been easy because rock is more *feel* than anything. Technically, it's simple addition and subtraction, with the occasional fraction and decimal point added for "coloring." The truth is, rock, country, and the blues aren't nuclear science, physics, or brain surgery like (some) classical and intricate jazz can be. *It just has to be catchy!* I could've handled the gig, and it made me miserable. I was too screwed up to say yes so I avoided the guy who'd one day become my best friend.

Eventually he cornered me and I lied, "I don't think I could handle the parts."

"Well, you could learn them," he said.

He had me there, but I somehow squirmed away and hated myself for it. How could I tell him that what an old nun had said and done years ago had made me afraid to play the keyboards? In an irony of ironies, within a couple of years a similar thing would happen to him when a warped form of Christianity enslaved him, making him afraid to play some of the greatest songs of all time.

Soon after, another Confederate invited me to a party where he and his older brother were providing some of the music on electric guitars. I was so used to seeing school bands and The Beatles and The Stones with three guitars—a lead, rhythm, and bass—that it seemed strange these guys only had two. Without a bass they sounded empty. When records were played I managed to have the first slow dances of my life to "make-out songs" like "Don't Let The Sun Catch You Crying" and "You've Lost That Lovin' Feelin'," but without the fringe benefits other Confederates were getting in dark corners, having their hands pushed away or guided to special places.

I had something far more important than my first taste of sex on my mind, and I worked up the courage to ask the brothers, "How come you guys don't have a bass player?"

The older brother said, "We're looking for one. Do you know any?"

Out of my timid mouth I heard someone say, like a goofy cliché, "Yeah, and you're looking at him!"

The fact that I didn't have a bass or know the first thing about the beast was immaterial. I was "in the band," which is the greatest feeling you can imagine. In the early, innocent stages of one's musical life, auditions aren't necessary. It's simply an agreement and if it works out, great. If these guys needed a lead or rhythm guitarist, I would've been that but they needed Uncle Joe's left hand, which was like asking a dolphin who'd never been allowed to swim, if he'd like to take a dip. Possessed, I dove in and immediately began doing extra chores at home and at both sets of grandparents' houses to make money to get a bass and amp. In six weeks I had them, after scoping out every music shop in town to find a bass that not only sounded good but felt comfortable in my hands, like a baseball bat or hockey stick that was the right fit for my body type. Somehow, instinctively, I knew this. Learning to play was hard because I was asking my fingers to do strange things, but the guys were patient and showed me what they knew, which was quite a lot. The few piano lessons I'd taken years before taught me the bass functioned pretty much like the left hand of a piano and the lead and rhythm guitars like the right. Uncle Joe's foot taught me when they pull together they make music instead of noise. Like me, my band-mates were from a musical family which gave us a huge advantage because we understood music was a language. We went at it and they were never satisfied till it felt right, and then, it usually sounded right and vice versa. We listened and dissected music for hours, but playing was how we communicated. When they heard what I was trying to do they asked how I knew what I knew and I said, "I used to be a piano player." When they asked if I still played it I firmly said *"No!"*

One day I came home from "rehearsing" and my mom handed me a new acoustic guitar. For months she had me saving green stamps, which substituted for money in stores that honored them back then. She didn't tell me why until she gave me the guitar she'd purchased with them. She said the last four strings on an acoustic were the same as the four on a bass, only in a higher octave, which I knew, and it'd be easier on my fingers to practice my runs on an acoustic. It made my learning go much quicker while it introduced me to the acoustic, which I instantly fell in love with. To this day it's the instrument I'm most comfortable with. Years later she said the other reason she got it was because the constant rumble of my bass was getting on my father's nerves, though he never said anything. Also, the loud vibration was knocking things over and she didn't want her antique vases over the fireplace destroyed. We laughed and I said it would've irritated me too. I went at it with a vengeance and loved it! The acoustic let me work out bass parts at all hours without bothering anyone, while Dave, even at night, was under the spotlight in Sluice Pond or at the Y pool. If I wasn't practicing I'd be at the Y working out with weights, and that's when our paths crossed. He would poke his head into the weight room, or I'd poke mine in the pool to say "hi" while our mom nurtured her fanatical sons.

It's not cool to say but I got pretty good, pretty fast. In several "battles of the bands" I participated in during high school I always came in at the top. For one at the old Jewish Community Center auditorium on Market Street, my dad let me get out of bed with walking pneumonia when the doctor said I was past the stage I could give it to anyone. The day before I had a fever of 103° (sounds like that old Foreigner song) and was weak and delirious, but I insisted on playing. The pull of music was too strong and I had to ride the wave. I studied and emulated the greats, like Paul McCartney, Jack Bruce, John Paul Jones, John Entwistle, Stanley Clarke (a monster if there ever was one), Jack Casady, and many others. Eventually I developed my own style by discovering that the bass, first and foremost, is as critical to the rhythm section as drums, but it also plays notes so it can play a song (a melody) within a song if done in such a way that it doesn't go overboard and detract from the whole. McCartney in "Something In The Way She Moves" and "Come Together" are cool examples. Guys like Bruce and Entwistle sometimes went over the edge in concert with Cream and The Who, and I loved it because they did so in a musical way; defining and exploring the boundaries of an instrument only a couple decades old, which in many ways was replacing the upright bass that'd been around since the Garden of Eden. Some historians speculate that it was the upright that got Eve all worked up, not the apple.

To me, no one combined those ancient boundaries with the new like John Paul Jones. He never wasted a note or threw one in that wasn't needed. Zeppelin's highly sexed "The Lemon Song" from their second album in 1969, which should never be listened to with parents or children, is an excellent example. But all were great teachers because they loved their instrument with a passion you could hear. So different from say Bill Wyman of The Stones, who sometimes sounded as if he were tagging along, trying to figure out the song. But that was okay too, and part of their "mystique." To be fair, when

Bill knew the song, he was just right. What I discovered later about the guys I loved, like McCartney, Bruce, Entwistle, and Jones, was that they played piano when they were kids. It's how they understood the bass in context of the song because the piano truly is the gateway to understanding *all* instruments. Above all, they *always* sounded like they were having fun.

In January of '67 a miracle happened by way of a Stones song that brought me back to the piano. In the tenth grade, when I heard "Let's Spend The Night Together" for the first time, with Keith on bass for this one, I just about lost my mind from its infectious, driving, longing desperation. It still affects me that way when I'm driving down the highway and it comes on like a gift from the gods. Our class had several excellent piano players far better than I ever was, but none quite had the left hand of Uncle Joe. At lunch, I was walking by the music hall and heard a classmate, Richard, playing. He and Sister Timothy (some nuns take names of male saints) were the Glee Club piano players. She played the classics and he took over for the modern. He was a kind, sweet, geeky kid with a high IQ and covered with pimples (I was covered too but without the IQ). He wore thick coke-bottle glasses and embodied enough awkwardness for the entire class, with a high-pitched, irritating, nasally voice because he suffered terribly from asthma. When he sneezed you ran for cover so a mollusk wouldn't end up on your lapel, but if you talked to him you fell in love with him. Creepy upperclassmen made cruel fun of him but he never squealed. He was like the elephant man; underneath, cool as hell, and he was trying to figure out the new Stones song. He was very good, technical and precise but wasn't playing with the passion it needed. If any song needs passion with lesser amounts of precision, "Let's Spend The Night Together" is one. If it doesn't rock, precision doesn't mean much. It has to be played in the primal way it was written. I went in and instinctively reached over his shoulder to tell him to play the right hand while I played the lower octave Ds with my left!

From the first instant I felt his body tense with excitement, like he was driving a sports car with no speed limits; he controlled the stick and I the clutch. Our tandem was loosely perfect. Kids (but no Sister Superior) came in to surround the piano and he couldn't stop giggling and sniffling. "This is very cool, Robert, thank you so much!" He was in his glory because girls were there and he was kicking butt. The music announced, "There's a man behind these telescopes on my eyes!"

It made me so happy seeing him accepted. Kids said, "Go Richie, go!" I could hear his nose whistling and maybe it was wishful thinking but his runny honker sounded a little like the organ Brian Jones actually played on the song.

He could blow me away on the piano but when the bell rang he asked, "How do you know how to play like that?"

"Make believe you're riding a ferocious bull and *never let go* of the rhythm no matter what."

He said, "I love that!" as if I'd said something profound, but I hadn't.

Back in class I realized I had touched a piano and no lightning bolt had struck me down, and nobody picked me up by the ear to make me apologize to Jesus for doing it. I cried and somehow felt God saying "Well done!" And I realized that Pete Townshend was right, "freedom tastes of reality."

Later at home I sat at the piano to figure out the right hand so I could play it myself. My mother heard me, came in, and said, "Try it like this." She made corrections and before she turned back to the kitchen she kissed me.

"How do you know that song?" I asked her.

"I've heard it several times coming up from Dave's room. How does it feel sitting at the piano?"

"Great!"

No more was said. The next day I played it for Rich and he said it sounded just like the record. I told him my mom helped me figure it out. Years later, in a beautiful coincidence, Rich became a history teacher in the same school as my mom and he told her this story. When tragically he died several years ago my mom reminded me of it and it made me smile to remember two pimply kids rocking the house at the old St. Mary's High music hall. What my mom didn't know was that when I was showing him the song, our very nice, six foot four—Lincoln's height—open-minded music teacher Sister Timothy came in and asked what we were playing and before Rich could say anything I lied and said it was "Let's Spend 'Some Time' Together." I didn't want her to get mad at the words "the night." My mom laughed and said "smart move."

The week before, Ed Sullivan hadn't let The Stones sing the real words on his TV show because they were too provocative and that's how I got the idea. Ironically, a few days later Sister Timothy asked me to play "that new song 'Let's Spend 'Some Time' Together'" for the class so I did and it became a running joke. I never got in trouble for it because nobody ratted me out, not even the "Holy Rollers" in the glee club. I believe my band-mate Richie had something to do with protecting me. I remember Sister Timothy's head bopping to the rhythm like it was yesterday. My demons, for now, were caged! And because the musicians in school now knew I could play the piano, I somehow started to believe it too. But by this time I was so into the bass and acoustic guitar that they were now my primary instruments. But I'll love the piano for the rest of my days because, in essence, it taught me everything and not just about music.

I still didn't realize that the way music affected me was unique and strangely intense. But I was beginning to suspect something was up because I'd listen to "Foxy Lady" by Jimi and "Jumping Jack Flash" by The Stones and "I Can See For Miles" and "Magic Bus" by The Who and other violent songs before a football game because I needed something to get me fired up to give me courage for when I received kick offs and punts. I'd time it so just before I left my house on game day I'd still have enough fire in me at game time to run with reckless abandon, propelled by the music in my head. But, by the time the second half came, my musical high had subsided and I'd run like a wimp. My coach correctly called me a first-half player and I had no argument. I was beginning to think I was a little weirder than I thought or maybe blessed, cursed, or lucky.

At the end of tenth grade the two brothers and I teamed up with a drummer who couldn't keep proper time but had a great Gretsch drum kit. He was a classmate of mine and the younger brother, and he knew an excellent singer from another school who joined us. The older brother who played lead guitar was uncomfortable with his limitations but we somehow got hired to play dances in Lynn, Saugus, Revere, Salem, Beverly, and several in East Boston. The drummer's father managed us and got the gigs so we were stuck with a timekeeper who couldn't keep proper time—not that mine was perfect. I found out the hard way that a bad drummer is a bass player's worst nightmare. All night I'd stand in front of him with my back to the dance floor to guide him the best I could. The band thought this was hilarious. Sometimes music just isn't "in the genes" and it's no one's fault, but our drummer thought he was the second coming of Buddy Rich and his father did too. Being in a band can be the coolest thing but, because it almost always involves other humans, it can turn into a soap opera.

At one gig the truly great band leader, who had asked me to play organ two years earlier, came to see us. He was now without a band because, among other things, his drummer, who was older, got drafted to fight in Vietnam. He said he'd gladly play with us if we wanted. The older brother thought this was a terrific idea because he could then switch to organ and we'd have one of the best lead guitarists in the city added to our band. Suddenly I found myself in a band with a musical hero and I couldn't believe it. I was so proud to be associated with him and, to boot, the older brother began playing a pretty decent organ. Everyone's skills were improving except our drummer's. As we got into our senior year, turning eighteen and finally old enough to play in clubs that served alcohol, our drummer began getting paranoid because people, i.e. club owners, were questioning his playing. To add fuel to the fire, his father still had us wearing goofy pirate-like outfits of off-white corduroy pants held up by belts with huge gold buckles that scraped the backs of our guitars. We also wore Beatle-type boots and long, black, ruffle-sleeved shirts with white vertical stripes and collars. The problem was that the world of music was changing rapidly and we wanted to change with it, except we were under strict orders not to grow our hair or "play any of that new psychedelic crap." When everyone else in town was playing Cream's "Sunshine Of Your Love" we were stuck in the dark ages playing "Midnight Hour"—a good song for sure—in pirate suits with me, the rhythm and lead guitarist now, lined up behind the singer and the four of us doing synced dance steps that didn't help me in trying to keep our drummer in time.

After a gig in East Boston our lead guitarist told me he was thinking of forming a band with three instruments, like Cream, Hendrix, Led Zeppelin and The Who. We'd grown very close and he was teaching me so much. At our next gig in Lynn, he, the younger brother, and I decided not to wear our outfits or do the goofy dance steps and to extend the guitar solos whenever we were in a good groove. Well, our manager went ape-shit over our "hippie" attire and was disgusted by our improvisations. He went absolutely ballistic at the end of the night when, on our last song, "I'm A Man" by The Yardbirds, our guitarist took off on a three-minute solo I wish we had gotten on tape. There was a cool descending bass line off a high note I loved doing as he came out of his solo but this time he looked at me and yelled, "Okay Beau"—my new nickname—"now it's your turn!"

By sheer instinct, because I didn't have time to think (always a good thing), I didn't come down off the high note but stayed on it like a mantra and stepped forward as far as my cord would allow. And because we were on a basketball court with no stage, the kids on the dance floor circled me while I launched into a bass solo for several minutes. It must've been okay because our drummer (almost) kept time as the other instruments dropped out.

I'd been playing around with it for months but never expected to play it live. I never thought I'd have the opportunity. The kids around me went nuts and at the end I went back to the high note to do the slide to end the song as usual. We couldn't have planned it better. Kids started yelling for an encore and it felt like a "jin-you-iieenne" concert instead of a CYO (Catholic Youth Organization) dance. I couldn't help it, I tore into "Sunshine Of Your Love" and our guitarists jumped in on the second bar. Our organist yelled at our dumbstruck drummer, "Play the fuckin' thing!" so he half-assedly joined in and off we went. From behind someone put a fedora hat on my head and a lit cigarette (I didn't smoke) in my mouth that I tucked under a machine head, or tuner, of my bass. I saw Uncle Joe's smoke coolly rising with my spirit and felt a freedom I couldn't comprehend. For the past year our guitarist had been encouraging me to play what I felt and now that I had our manager docked three of us half our pay because only his son, our singer, and the organist had worn their outfits. Not to mention the solos, fedora, and cigarette would forever give us a bad name, according to him. If it happened again, our manager assured us, while looking at me, "You'll be out!"

Our guitarist said, "If he's out, I'm out! And if what we did was so wrong, why did we get our first encore?"

Our manager said we'd discuss it the next day. That night our guitarist and I wrote a song list in case we ever formed that power trio. We came up with over eighty no-brainers without even trying.

The next day we went to the meeting to hear what our manager had to say, but we had every intention of telling him we were through. He made it easy by saying all was forgiven; that he realized this "new psychedelic crap" was a passing fad we'd grow out of, and though it "disgusted" him, he'd tolerate it for a while. Then he said something as pathetic as it was ridiculous that gets funnier as the years roll by. He unveiled a chart revealing a new pay scale for the band based on what each guy did on stage. The singer sang so he did one thing, the two guitarists, the organist, and I each used two hands and sang backup so that counted as three, but his nitwit son (I say that because he went along with it) drummed in crappy time with two hands, two feet, plus sang flat backup and that counted as five. That meant our drummer would be getting more pay than the rest of us from now on. Dear Lord, how priceless some memories are!

Before anyone could respond, our guitarist shot up, walked over, put his finger in our drummer's chest, and said, "I *know* this was your cockamamie idea." He then turned to our manager and said, "And you, you're a fucking idiot. I quit." This was the first time in my life, besides Frankie M. and Sister Superior that I'd ever heard a kid my age stand up and talk to an adult like that. I thought, *Holy crap, this is frickin' great!*

As he started to walk out our manager jumped up and said, "Wait, we can negotiate."

Our guitarist replied, "Negotiate with yourself, I never played for money and never will!"

Then we all, minus a drummer who did five things, walked out. None of us were mad and we started laughing as soon as we were outside. We got some beer and went someplace to compare notes about how our manager had been bad mouthing each of us in order to divide and conquer, only to end up conquering himself.

I now knew that if I was ever to be in a band, it could only be with people who *knew* music was sacred. This was my first lesson that the business side of it, perhaps as in all things, could be cutthroat, even in small-time versions. But, like in every vocation that's worthwhile, I'd learn there were far more wonderful and interesting characters than I could ever imagine. Having a true-blue love for what I did, if it made people happy or somehow lifted their burdens, even if only by making them dance or simply listen to something that helped them escape their sorrows for a moment, it was very important in a world getting nastier because of Vietnam, bigotry, and racism. I now knew I could only get involved in an *artistic* venture with those whose love was true.

THE BIG, SAD FIZZLE

The guitarist and I left our pirate buckles behind and formed a new band with one rule: no rules! If somehow we made a single penny playing music we loved we'd split it three ways, but we would've played for free. The economy was healthier back then so, after graduating high school, our dads, who were both in management at GE, got us jobs where we made enough money to purchase huge, powerful equipment no other bands on the North Shore of Massachusetts had unless they were a touring band from a major record label. We were over the top and felt good about it. I had a 500-watt stack with eight 15-inch speakers and our guitarist had matching power with twelve 10-inch speakers on the other side of the stage. We went through several drummers until the guitarist's former drummer came home from Vietnam, and then we had our guy. He was a man of twenty-two years and we were eighteen and we got along great.

Almost immediately I witnessed our full-blooded Native American drummer face racism and learned that he had experienced it in the Army in Nam too. I couldn't fathom anyone getting drafted to fight for *his* country to come home to face racism. I thought a thousand times, *What the hell is wrong with white people?* even though I knew color had nothing to do with it and ignorance, everything. I saw it with club owners who thought it was funny calling him Geronimo, Crazy Horse, and Tonto. Once we were just about to play to a packed house and the club owner was so obnoxious with Indian jokes I was about to tell him to take the damn gig and do a Johnny Paycheck—he did that song "Take This Job And Shove It"—but our drummer grabbed me and told me to let it "roll off my back" or else we'd never play anywhere.

As a result of a lifetime of this crap, he had a hard edge about him and came home from Nam even harder with demons, but I never knew a vet who hadn't. To us, though, he was soft-spoken and gentle as a lamb with a unique, cool look on and off stage. He wore bandanas, some with peace signs, that held his jet-black, beautiful, all-the-way-down-his-back hair, and there was a constant aroma of marijuana and Marlboro cigarettes about him. He was rock 'n' roll thin and we used to kid him that we never saw him eat. He had a cool ashtray setup next to his drum kit hi-hat so everywhere we played he had the comforts of home. He always seemed in control yet cautious, but when he played he let go of the caution. He was also an excellent piano and guitar player and had a terrific voice. By now our guitarist and I had shoulder-length red and blond hair, and if someone wanted to paint a Norman Rockwell–type picture of two late '60s or early '70s white rockers and their Native American drummer, we would've been perfect.

We quickly became popular and had bookings just about every Friday and Saturday night at high schools, colleges, and clubs around Boston. We were very loud, aggressive, and sweaty, yet somehow likeable. People said we were fun to watch, too. We weren't in any way a Top 40 band but managed to get gigs by playing power versions of things like "Day Tripper" by The Beatles, "Jack Flash" by The Stones, a Who(ish) version of "Summer Time Blues," but also ballads like The Beatles' "Something In The Way She Moves" and The Stones' "Love In Vain." We never approached shows as mere gigs, but always thought of them as concerts whether they were or not. When we got encores we either did a mean version of "Sympathy For The Devil" or something like "Little School Girl" by Ten Years After. From our inception we introduced original material we'd written, and somehow this brought more people our way who made requests for it. Some brought little recording systems and asked permission to record us so they could listen to the songs later and we'd say, "Go for it!" We were too immature to worry about copyrights and figured that if someone stole a song, we had plenty more and could simply write a new batch. It was so cool getting invited to parties after gigs to hear the host playing our music that he'd recorded that very night. It's how we met a great friend, Ken P., who became our manager. He got us a ton of work and even let me drive his dark green Corvette on occasion.

My brother and his friend Jimmy, nicknamed "The Jimbo Fling" because he could fling any size speaker cabinet onto a truck with grace to spare, were with us from the very beginning. They took me in the Blue Bomb to one of our first rehearsals, and kept smiling the whole time.

On the way home they informed me, "We're your new road crew!"

And I just said, "Okay"

Music was always responsible for making me and Dave spend time together because we listened to it in the cellar, but away from home we'd only run into each other occasionally. Now we were inseparable! He and The Fling were at every practice and gig and were incredible at moving and setting up the equipment. They'd somehow been doing roadie work for the great band Mountain when they toured New England, so as young as they were, they weren't rookies. My brother became my constant companion and biggest supporter. When I asked why he worked so hard he said, "Your songs are as catchy as anyone's and I want to help get them out there."

Our mom hadn't seen this band, so when we were booked for the Summer Outdoor Concert Series on the Lynn Commons I told her she should go. I overheard Dave telling her, "Ma, you should go see Bob play. He really gets the crowd going and the songs are catchy as hell."

On the day of the concert we were backstage watching people arrive and Dave said, "Hey, Ma's here," so I had him bring her backstage. Someone was smoking pot nearby and I said, "Sorry, Ma" and she made me laugh saying, "No problem, I smell it on some of my students and I've smelled worse things." I told her if she saw the show from behind the stage she wouldn't get her eardrums blown out and she pulled out a pair of earplugs and said, "Don't worry, I came prepared." Then she told me not to say anything about her from the stage because many of the kids in the audience were her students. She didn't want me to embarrass her and it didn't bother me a bit because I knew this loud, bombastic kind of rock was so different from what she'd grown up listening to. We had mountains of classical, boogie-woogie, rhythm and blues, and Uncle Joe music in common, but I tried to imagine what it had been like growing up in the time of Benny Goodman to now see The Who on TV smashing up equipment after playing "My Generation." The contrast was too stark to comprehend.

Somehow the show went off without a hitch and we got two encores. Afterward, our mom introduced me and Dave to her students. "These are my sons," she said. It was a magical day for us.

Later I asked her what she thought of the show and she said, "It was too damn loud even with earplugs, but you and the drummer had a nice groove going that made it work. You know some of those bass lines you were playing aren't new . . ."

And I stopped her and said, "I know what you're going to say, Ma; Uncle Joe, right?"

She laughed and said, "Right!" Then she said, "It just proves you *can* pay attention when you want to."

"It's a good thing I'm not one of your students, right, Ma?"

She smiled. "But you are!" Then she gave me an American jewel: "I was very proud seeing the Frederick Douglass bandstand plaque above you and your drummer." She was right; I *was* her student and thank God, always had been.

From then on she became even more curious about the music coming up from Dave's room. A week after the concert I looked up the stairs when we were blasting "Sympathy For The Devil." The door was cracked and I saw her head bopping, listening intently.

Later she asked, "Isn't that song about the Devil one you played last week?"

"Yes. It's by The Rolling Stones."

"They sound like hillbillies, but are very entertaining."

"Exactly!"

"The lyrics are historically poignant. The line about the Kennedy assassinations is emotionally moving."

I told her to listen to all rock bands like they were *mostly* self-taught musicians who had talent, something to say, and the courage to say it.

And she said, "And not only that, that's how the Devil would sound introducing himself. Whoever wrote those lyrics is very clever. They reference the inhumanity of Russian Czarist history and British Colonialism." It made me laugh because my historian mother understood more than I did, but then again, she always had. She became fascinated with The Who's *Tommy* and even more so by The Kinks' epic *Arthur* opera about the rise and fall of the British Empire and England's place in the post–World War II world. She fell in love with the folk, jazz, and blues sounds of Traffic and the jazz, rock, and traditional English folk sound of Jethro Tull, with their mischievous, medieval, whimsical presentations, and too many other bands to mention that combined a wide variety of musical elements.

When she heard the opening piano notes of Joe Cocker's version of "Feelin' Alright" she came down the stairs and said, "Now that's very good, for a minute I thought Uncle Joe was here."

"He is, Ma!" I said.

As our band continued to grow in popularity, we got more and more requests to play original material. We decided to go into a real studio to record a dozen songs despite not knowing the first thing about recording. We wanted to see how we sounded on professional equipment. Our first of many mistakes was booking a studio too small for our massive equipment. Our second was insisting we needed all of it to record. I sang the songs I mostly wrote and the guitarist did the same. The first thing that jumped out at me on play back was how much I disliked my voice. It sounded very different than I thought it did on stage or on live recordings, but the guys said that's the way I sounded. I asked Dave and The Fling why no one had told me before and they said, "Well, it's not that bad." But to me it was an embarrassment. The engineer said he'd recorded worse voices. "We can 'fix it in the mix,' with reverbs and delays," he said. From that day on I'd wince at the phrase "fix it in the mix," because when you sound good without tricks, there's nothing to fix and tricks can only enhance. I was fussy about the music, too, and could hear tuning and timing slipping. We all could, and it would've been a problem if we hadn't. But my singing bothered me the most. I was reaching for notes I had no business reaching for and my overall God-given tone didn't appeal to me at all. However, the songs sounded pretty damn cool when things were clicking, almost pro and tape never lies (in theory anyway). But we concurred we had to sound pro all the time if we ever wanted to get a recording contract. This experience taught us, especially me, that you can't hide behind volume and bombast like on stage; that passion only goes so far.

We pre-paid for a few hundred cassette copies and passed them out at gigs and to friends, though I would've preferred scrapping them. I knew if we were back in the studio we could've done so much better. But still, people played them at after-gig mind-altering parties, and I'd cringe every time I heard my whiney, nasally, sour voice but nobody seemed to mind, so maybe there's truth to the old adage, "the more they drink the better we sound." But as it was, with Dave and The Fling being roadies for Mountain, they gave some cassettes of the flawed songs to their roadies and one somehow got to Mountain's manager at Windfall Records in New York. A few weeks later, out of the blue, we got an invite "to meet for an hour if interested in receiving constructive criticism of your music."

We never expected this but our guitarist—by now my best friend & partner in crime—and I flew to New York in a DC-10 propeller plane and had the honor of meeting Mountain's manager. His skyscraper office was covered with gold records and pictures of him with musical icons we worshipped. A few were of him with Santana because he managed them at one point, I'm pretty sure. But the thing I remember most was him laughing when we walked in. "Jesus Christ, you're only babies!" he said, reminding me of Sister Marietta calling me and my classmates "her precious babies." True, we were young Confederates, both in the second half of our eighteenth years, so maybe we looked like babies but damn, babies our age were getting killed in Vietnam.

We ended up staying almost three hours. He put our music on so we could go over it together. Right away I wanted to take it off because I could hear the flaws more than ever and his sound system was ridiculous. He said it sounded like it was probably our first time in a studio and suggested better mic placement for the drums and going directly into the board with the bass and other technical things. He said my voice was not a lead singer's voice but was good enough for backup vocals and that our guitarist sang well but getting a great lead singer would be even better. He suggested we add keyboards for coloring like Mountain had, and that appealed to us. He noticed the same time lag and tuning issues I had, but surprisingly didn't mention too many other criticisms, which made me think I might know how to listen to music even though I didn't know how to record it. Everything he said made sense and he seemed to care. He said he'd invited us because he thought the writing had "great potential" and some of it was genuinely "catchy as hell" (Dave's term, and I couldn't wait to tell him). The last thing he said was that we were a little self-indulgent with six- and seven-minute-long songs that could be shortened to four and five. He chalked it up to our youthful hormones. Then he asked if we agreed with "anything" he had said. I replied with a strong "Everything!" and he said, "Good," and that we could bring music to him anytime, his door would always be open. We said we would and he said, "Make sure you do!"

He then asked if we had any questions. I had one: "What about our playing?" He said that was the least of our worries because we sounded like naturals, and to just be careful about timing and tuning. Then he added that he could tell from my playing that my interests were far and wide, and that he suspected I had some classical piano training. I told him, "A little." Then he blew me away by saying he wouldn't be surprised if our guitarist had played a wind instrument before he took up the guitar, and my friend said, "I started out on saxophone." Something I never knew. This guy was the real deal.

On the flight home I told my friend music was something I wanted to do for my life's work, and he said the same. We felt empowered by our visit to NYC, but also knew we had a long way to go and couldn't wait to get started. The band had its first and last meeting (when things are good, meetings aren't necessary) to discuss things, and I asked if we could start practicing four or five nights a week as opposed to the two or three we did on weeks when we weren't gigging. All of us thought it was a good idea, but I felt a slight tug of resistance from our drummer. Dave said, "Let's go for it!" At our next rehearsal he showed up with a little two-track recorder and laboriously recorded a full rehearsal each week so we could hear our progress, or lack thereof. I also got a metronome that we played to on acoustics, with our drummer on bongos and this made our timing issues go away. We noticed the hormone issue too, because the metronome revealed that we would speed up when approaching an exciting part. Someone joked it was "premature anticipation." Now we gently slid into things.

However, not all was wine and roses in this time of flower power. A few months into this hectic schedule we found out that the reason our drummer never ate was because he'd come home from Nam with a life-sucking monkey on his back. He was a *slave* to speed (meth). He snorted it in the morning to get going and supplemented it with pot and butts to stay calm throughout the day, and then took barbiturates at night so he could sleep. We found out about this vicious cycle by accident when he showed up extremely agitated, out of character, and couldn't rehearse because he was out of his supply. He confessed all, saying he hated to sleep because nightmares came and that before Nam he never did hard drugs; "only a little weed but it was so messed up over there" that he got "into the heavy shit." Now, because of our schedule, he was unable to make his usual connection so we canceled rehearsal. We didn't know what the hell to do but the cat was out of the bag. Truth revealed is better than truth hidden, but it got worse. He got fired for shooting up at work from a well-paying day job he'd had since coming home from the war.

It was so sad because he'd lived on his own since he was young, and there was no family we knew of that could help him. We looked up to and admired him, not just because he had his own place where we could crash, bring girls, smoke stuff, and listen to music but because he truly was a good older guy who knew the ways of the world. And very selfishly, I was afraid of losing a great drummer, which any young bass player learning his trade needs to play with or he ain't going nowhere. He was my friend and rhythm partner, and it made me miserable. I could always make him laugh so hard he'd get embarrassed, and our guitarist was ten times funnier than me so they really got along. But when he lost his job, he went downhill quickly. He began showing up late for rehearsals, and at times, between songs, we thought he'd keel over. The band was the only legitimate thing he had going, so when we finally decided he had to clean up or leave, it was horrible to contemplate. We told our manager not to book any more gigs, but that we would try to finish the ones we had. I hoped he'd put the junk down before it got to kicking him out. I didn't realize how much slavery truly was the disease Lincoln said it was!

After making the agonizing decision not to book more gigs without telling him, we still had a busy summer and were somehow able to get through unscathed. Some shows, I thought, were quite remarkable. Because of our situation we only halfheartedly looked for a lead singer and keyboard player. The uneasy, sad, lurking atmosphere of playing with and loving someone who was enslaved hindered our confidence in that pursuit. We didn't know what to do and it drove me crazy. To add to my confusion and overwhelming surprise, at the beginning of the summer our guitarist fell in love with a strict, self proclaimed, born-again Christian, who unbeknownst to me, was critical of cover tunes and several original songs we played because "they offended Jesus." I never learned how she knew that, and it put tremendous pressure on my best friend— pressure *we* didn't need! She was remarkably consistent, being equally critical of my songs as well as her boyfriend's. Songs we wrote together, Jesus downright hated.

Almost always, I decided and the guys approved the song list for each show. In an irony of ironies, it was this same list that irritated Jesus that attracted Judi a month before we officially met. In this swill of blind faith, in my opinion anyway, mixed with turmoil and the anguish of slavery, religion, and Nam, we were booked to play the first of our last half dozen gigs at the end of the summer of '71 at the Outdoor Summer Concert Series in Cambridge, Massachusetts. It was a gig with tons of exposure, and I fantasized that if we pulled it off, maybe it would somehow fix things and inspire our drummer to kick his demons. And maybe, too, our guitarist's girlfriend would be persuaded that our music wasn't so "evil" by seeing a large crowd of happy people enjoying it.

Because of local sound ordinances, we couldn't do a soundcheck so all we had to do was show up a little before showtime, plug in, and let it rip because Dave and The Fling would have the stage all wired, duct taped down, and ready to roll. The three of us (band members) traveled to the gig in the same van and I felt really good, like before a sporting event I was prepared for. I did push ups, sit ups, and chin ups in the van to calm my nerves, and our guitarist tuned up his guitars while doing his usual incredibly funny impersonations of Lyndon Johnson, Richard Nixon, and Jimmy Stewart. Even our drummer was in a good mood. He was sitting on a crate with his drumsticks tapping the sides of his bony legs, which was a good sign. He must've hooked up with his dealer. Plus, because he was no longer concealing his demons, he was hanging out with us a little more. I suggested that, if we got an encore, we'd do our power version of "Sympathy For The Devil."

Well, I wouldn't have believed it possible but our guitarist said, "I can't play that anymore, it's sinful."

Our drummer laughed and said, "Yeah, right."

"No, I'm serious I *can't,* it honors Satan," said our guitarist.

"When the fuck were you going to tell us?" our drummer asked.

"Right now, I'm seeing the light" was the reply.

I looked up, but the truck light was broken. Our drummer loved playing the song because he started it with an infectious African/Celtic/Indian tribal-type beat that hypnotized every crowd, that for him was the high point (not that he needed another) of our gigs.

"Is that the crap you're learning from your girlfriend?" he asked.

"It's not crap!" our guitarist replied.

After several seconds our drummer said to himself—but we all heard it, including our manager driving—"If she was my girlfriend I'd kick the crazy cunt to the fucking curb. She's the kind of brainwashed bitch that'll ruin your fucking life with her *deadly* superstitions. *I've seen it happen!*"

Despite him already doing a good job of ruining his own life without anyone's help, this was the first time he ever referred to his past, so it carried enormous weight and in some sick, perverse way I was glad he said what he said, just not with the words he used. I thought our guitarist was going to pick him up and break him in two, but he showed remarkable restraint. Maybe it was the light he was seeing, or that he knew part of his friend's brain was enslaved by drugs. I now knew there was no redemption for our drummer or any of us even if he cleaned up. This was not a good way to approach an important gig, and I felt a heat wave rush come over me that I only get when I learn someone I love has a deadly disease.

I knew our guitarist had been attending mysterious bible meetings with his girlfriend, but I never asked about it. It was none of my business anyway, and I thought it was his way of getting on her good side but this new, frightening attitude floored me because he was my musical mentor, hero, and safety net. He then told us (but really just me) that after the show he'd give us a list of songs he'd no longer play because he was "going back to the Lord." As I was trying to digest everything, we were announced to a great crowd on a beautiful late summer's day. A Cambridge newspaper took a picture of us going onstage and I looked stunned, perplexed, and sad. It felt excruciatingly uncomfortable. Somehow though, we loosened up because music, volume, sweat, power, movement, work, and audiences have a way of soothing and inspiring. We began to play well and by the end managed to get an encore we probably didn't deserve. It could've been people just wanting to dance a little more.

Backstage I said, "Let's do 'Little School Girl,'" by Ten Years After. Our guitarist, who sang it, said he couldn't play that either because it had "too many un-Christian sexual references."

Now I piped in because I was pumped from the crowd. "You've got to be shitting me!" These were the first harsh words I'd ever spoken to the best male friend I ever had next to my brother, but he didn't take offense. Then our drummer threw down his cigarette and said to him, "Fuck that no-good bitch and the shit she's brainwashing you with, I'm fucking playing 'Sympathy'!" He walked out to the front of the stage pounding his heavy sticks (clubs, we called em) over his head to set the tempo and the crowd got into the groove right away and began clapping to the beat. *It's a sacred trust* when an audience follows you.

He always sounded great on the song, but this time something was different. He ripped off his bandana and his peace sign fell to the floor. His hair fell over his face and bare shoulders when he put his head down to pound himself into his drums. Dear God he was beautiful, majestic, and terrifying. My "real deal" American friend made woodchips and sawdust fly off his sticks while ferociously beating drums of war against a dogma that killed thousands of his ancestors. Few musicians have the privilege to play with a drummer like that; there are no words to describe it. He was a Reb the Yanks called "a demon possessed," charging cannons, yelping the Rebel Yell that was a cross between an Irish/Scottish banshee and the yip yip of a *true* American taking scalps off soldiers that rode with that brave, idiotic ex-Civil War general

Armstrong Custer, who had ordered his soldiers to kill innocent, defenseless woman and children.

The sound was more sensual than the greatest sex, more holy than the holiest place, more ominous than any storm. The crowd began a desperate weave dance to the intoxicating rhythm of evolution all the while having no clue what song was coming. Our guitarist said, "I told *him*"—He didn't say "you guys," which told me he wasn't completely lost to me—"I'm not playing that fucking song!" He started to storm off but I grabbed him while making a circling motion to our drummer to keep playing but he wasn't looking and wasn't going to stop till the earth ceased spinning. I looked into my friend's eyes and asked, "Are you listening to that?" It made him sad as it would anyone caught between *knowing* and *believing*. I pleaded, "Play it for me this one last time and I'll never ask you again." With our pupils locked, he pondered what could've been a mathematical equation and said "Fucking God, forgive me!" and I followed him onto the stage.

With his back to the crowd he yelled at our drummer, "You suck!" but our drummer only heard the spirit of the eagle as our guitarist strapped on his guitar to play the opening chords of an ode to the Devil. The bass was the last to come in so I strapped it on and kissed our drummer on the top of his head because when a drummer plays like that I have to kiss someone. He gave me a sad smile like he knew he wouldn't come out of this alive. My band-mates loved each other but one was going North, the other South. I did a descending bass run, like a missile from Nam hitting the open "E" and the stage from a five-foot leap off the drum platform, and the bass and drums became one. Dave, oblivious to the backstage bullshit, jumped in the air like I had just scored the winning touchdown in the Super Bowl. Behind him the guitarist's girlfriend burst into tears as if she'd lost her mother in a train wreck. We were in *The Twilight Zone,* but I didn't care. This was what I lived for! Maybe it was the sense this might be our last hurrah, Pickett's Charge, our high water mark—whatever it was, we tore it up. If this was to be our last time playing it, our guitarist let it rip and the rhythm section blistered till smoke signals rose. The crowd went crazy and called for more but I shook Dave, "No!" and he and The Fling immediately began tearing things down.

Our guitarist ran backstage to his girl who was crying hysterically, "You promised me and Jesus you wouldn't play that song." He kept saying, "I know, I know, I'm sorry." I told her it was my fault, not his. I thought he'd tell her she was overreacting, but he just said he'd meet her back in Lynn. As the band got in the van I was about to tell him I wasn't sure she was right for him, but before I could he said he was marrying her and asked me to be his best man. Stunned, I said I'd be honored. On the way home no one said a thing. Our drummer looked like he was going to keel over, and I sympathized with him because his ancestors had been obliterated by Christian missionaries thinking, "You're going to accept Christ if we have to kill you to make you do it!" It was my young, naïve way of trying to figure things out. Or maybe it was a simple matter of slavery to drugs and/or slavery to a misunderstanding with Jesus. Either way, the band was headed to oblivion.

In a quick, thirty-second, phony-baloney meeting with our manager the next day, we agreed to finish the few gigs we had left then break for a few weeks and meet later to see if continuing on was feasible. Thank God we did those last shows, because at one of them I'd say hello to Judi for the first time. But inside we "all knew" (what Lincoln said in his second inaugural about slavery being the cause of the war) this meeting would never take place. We kicked the can for sure, but because we truly loved each other the last gigs were better than expected. We didn't play certain songs but we didn't offend Jesus either. Still we did "Day Tripper" and "Jack Flash" so we were able to do *some* damage. We were determined to go down in an atmosphere of camaraderie, good fellowship, and gallows humor.

Our last show was at Catholic Merrimack College and it was a blast. We got invited to a party afterward at a mansion deep in the woods of North Andover. Here were smart, hip, upper-crust kids and some had been following us for the last year. There was drinking, smoking, people having sex in closets, and trays of food that were surprisingly ignored by everyone except me, Dave, and the Fling. Someone was passing out hallucinogenic mushrooms like candy and people, ourselves included, took them. When it seemed like everyone was peaking—*Fleetoscrammin'* as Dave would say—our guitarist, whose girlfriend wasn't there so he was letting loose big time, began doing his Jimmy Stewart, James Cagney, Jack Benny, Stan Laurel, Cassius Clay, Lyndon Johnson, Richard Nixon, and Ed Sullivan imitations. I was always involved as the straight man interviewing this cast of characters. People heard the laughter and came into the large central room where Jack Benny and Cassius Clay were arguing about Nixon while Stan Laurel looked on. It was so damn funny people were rolling on the floor laughing and saying, "I can't take this." He had a way of contorting his face to make his ears look bigger than they were and you'd swear you had Lyndon Johnson in front of you. I don't think I ever laughed so hard.

Eventually he had to stop because everyone's face was hurting. Kids lit joints and someone put on The Beatles *White Album* and cranked it. The last song on one side was Lennon's "Happiness Is A Warm Gun," with the lyrics, "Mother Superior jumped the gun." When it ended I said to Dave, "That always reminds me of Sister Superior." Someone heard me and said, "So you had a Superior too, we all frickin' did!" These were Catholic kids like us. Then, in the strangest way, everyone got reflective and quiet and for some reason I told them of my ear ripping incident with my Superior and others told similar stories. At the end it became weirdly silent and intensely unbearable because we, being Catholics, felt guilty talking about our "Superiors." Also, the mushrooms (peyote) magnified that guilt many times over.

You could've heard a pin drop when Dave asked, "Hey, what the fuck kind of name is Sister Superior anyway?" Someone who didn't want to laugh did one of those "irrepressible" nose-snorting laughs that led to a long crescendo of laughter from the souls of forty kids. When it became calm again Dave asked in his nonchalant way, "I mean, why aren't there any Sister 'Inferiors' and Father 'Mediocres' around?" This led to another explosion. Those who hadn't passed out after that ended up talking till dawn about everything our generation talked about; from Vietnam and The Beatles to race riots and religion. When the sun rose someone showed up with a bucket of coffee, and we came safely down with sore faces. It was my last psychedelic waltz that somehow always seemed to revolve around our band.

In time our guitarist and his wife had several beautiful children but ended up divorcing, and that made me so sad. He was someone who liked to have a good time and make people happy, and maybe he couldn't do that anymore. Either way, because I'll always love, honor, and respect him, I haven't used the band's name. But in our city, and in places north of Boston, for a brief moment, we ruled the power rock scene with a guitarist loved by everyone, especially me. These decades later when I'm on my road bike, walking the beach, running, or mountain biking in the woods, and a stranger or old friend calls out the name of the band and mentions an original song, and says, "Man, I thought you guys were heading places!" it moves my heart, and I ache bittersweet for what might've been and sometimes say, "Me too!" A few years ago at his dad's funeral, our guitarist embraced me and wouldn't let go, and I didn't want him to! And sadly, our much loved drummer recently died. This American soldier lived the last years of his life on the streets, homeless. Sometimes, I thought I'd seen him in the shadows and it killed me. There was a service at the Vietnam section of the Pine Grove Cemetery in Lynn that I couldn't go to, but I went to his grave the next day and we jammed in the pouring rain!

After word of our band's "big, sad fizzle" got out, I got calls from several Top 40 bands to join or at least fill in. I had to play much quieter and some of the songs were goofy schlock like "Crimson and Clover," but I also played with great Berklee College of Music musicians too, doing everything from show tunes to Blood, Sweat & Tears-type things. It wasn't my cup of tea, but I learned a lot and loved the obscurity of hiding in back, melted into the scenery behind sunglasses. But I missed playing original songs and was discovering that my favorite thing was not playing music, but writing it.

The Berklee guys would ask me how I came up with riffs and grooves and I'd always tell them, "I don't know! Sometimes I just hear something or stumble on it by mistake on the piano or acoustic but once I feel the tug, I'm somehow able to reel it in." I also had to feel an emotion like love, fear, lust, anger, and joy, and that maybe made up for the lack of an education like the Berklee guys had. I needed to be motivated and, with my love for history, it was impossible not to be by the never-ending ugliness and beauty of everything there is and ever was. Without planning it, I began writing on the acoustic in Dave's room and at Judi's house. When I wrote on the piano at home my mother would come in and say, "Jeez, that's melodic, what is it?" And I'd say, "Something I made up." At first she'd say a surprised and maybe proud, "Really?" But that soon changed to, "You're over writing that," "That's pretty but you should simplify it," "Don't get too fancy," or "You have two or three songs in that one idea."

Somehow I began playing coffee houses in Boston, Salem, Marblehead, and Beverly and it was so easy because all I needed was my acoustic and Judi. If a place had a piano, all the better. There was no drama of slavery to drugs or agreements with Jesus. I could go on stage and be a fool all by myself while Judi, Dave, and my mother were convincing me I might want to try doing something more with my songs. I was about to investigate the Cambridge scene because people said it was conducive to what I was doing but somehow I decided to try London. I'd read there were hundreds of above and below ground coffee/tea houses and pubs where acoustic acts could play original music, so I went on a rampage to write four sets with twelve songs in each. I already had three with tons of ideas on tape so the goal was achievable. And by singing against an acoustic and piano I was able to learn my voice a little better. I'd never be a great singer, but if I stayed within my range maybe I'd be good enough to display my writing abilities.

Dave and Judi were the only ones who knew of my plans. They were my fellow Confederates all the way. When I had my sets down, I told my parents I was going to England to see if I could somehow be a part of the acoustic scene.

They didn't believe me because I'd never been away from my mother's home cooking, and I wasn't sure I believed me either. It was one of those things that once you say it, it carries you along whether you change your mind or not. Every time I thought of chickening out I'd think of a classmate in Nam whose birthday didn't pull the right draft number like mine had. Bob Dylan was right: It was a "simple twist of fate," but man, what a twist!

LOSING MY RELIGION

In the spring of 72, at the age of twenty, I flew over the Atlantic to God knows where. I had a few casual clothes I thought would look good on stage, my new Martin D-35 acoustic, a thousand dollars converted to English pounds, and a return ticket I could use within a year. I planned on staying a month or two. Dave and Judi had brought me to the airport and as the plane pulled away I wanted them with me more than I can say, but I was "in the army now." Somehow, as soon I landed in England to begin an adventure that would change my life for better and worse, I received a good omen from the gods.

At customs I was guided to a table to sign a form stating my intentions for coming. I'd been advised by college students back home to say I was a tourist and would be staying at a youth hostel in London. As I wrote, a large, bony, long fingered, black hand appeared on the other side of the table to fill out the same form. A voice belonging to the hand said, "Nice guitar!" after having recognized the D-35 guitar case glued to me. I looked up to say thanks, peered into the eyes of Chuck Berry and brilliantly, said, "Are you Chuck Berry?" Reminding me of a Lincoln phrase, he said, "The beast himself," and then, "See ya 'round, kid" and was off. *You've got to be kidding me. How cool was that? Wait till Dave and Judi hear this,* I thought to myself. I thought I'd see some famous musicians because this was London, but this was too much. That Berry was an American didn't matter. He seemed friendly despite his reputation. I found out later he was touring England and never brought a band because he used local musicians from wherever he was playing. The all-American, three-chord blues progression of his music made that possible, because once you knew the key, it was off to the races.

I took a bus from Heathrow Airport to an agency in London that helped students find places to lay their heads. I was disappointed to learn I came at the busiest time of year. The agent, a friendly girl in her twenties, spoke with an English accent (surprise, surprise) that was so cool I didn't hear what she was saying until I snapped out of it to hear all the hostels were full. She saw my chagrin and said that, if she hadn't offered the floor of her flat to several students already, she would've offered a spot to me. I asked what my alternatives were and she said sometimes students took temporary rooms at places like the Stockwell YMCA in southwest London. She gave me her card and said she'd probably have a place for me in a day or two.

When I got off the tube at Stockwell Station it seemed like a great idea because a YMCA was something I was familiar with. Maybe I could even work out with weights a little, so this would be perfect! When I inquired about a room I was told there were plenty so I got a tiny one on the top floor. When I put my things on the bed and looked out the window I thought, *Wow, I can't believe I made it to England!* There was an alarm clock radio on the nightstand so I flicked it on and Mick was singing, "What a drag it is getting old." "Mother's Little Helper" wasn't a song I was crazy about but The Stones sounding the same in London as they did in Lynn 4,000 miles away brought me comfort. Then I locked my room and went down to find out where I could send a cable to let Judi know I was safe and living at the Y. Strangely, it felt like I'd been there for several days already.

On the way back, I ate fish and chips out of a paper wrapper and it was fantastic. I also learned that for 25p (about 70 American cents), I could get supper at the Y cafeteria from 5 to 7 o'clock. What luck! There also was a weight room with basic equipment and, lo and behold, a music room with an upright piano. It was extremely out of tune, with broken notes but it was a piano. I discovered it by hearing someone playing it and following the sound like a rat follows a piper. When I pushed the door open I met my first English friend, Nigel, a boy my age and quite a good piano player. He was disheveled with greasy, wild hair, very white pasty skin, like it hadn't seen the sun for months, with red blotches covering his face, neck, and hands. I startled him and had a feeling that not too many people went in when he was playing. I got the impression many things startled him. He had a paranoid, frightened look so I said, "Sounds great!"—the two greatest words to settle a musician's nerves wherever in the world it is!

"I sound better on me mum's piano," he said.

"Where's that?" I asked, causing him to look dejected.

"In Sussex."

"Can I sit?" I asked.

In a very English way he said, "Suit yourself mate."

I introduced myself by my nickname for the first time. Usually I use "Bob" or "Robert" but people had been calling me "Bo" after Bo Diddley because a high school classmate (today one of Lynn's best high school basketball coaches and good guys) started calling me that. I told him Diddley wasn't a bass player but he said it didn't matter, so everyone started calling me Bo. I thought it would go away if I didn't object, but it didn't. I was introduced to Judi as Bo and it stuck with her too. When she heard my family calling me Bob she said, "You don't seem like a Bob to me." She made me promise I'd introduce myself as Bo in England so I did to Nigel, though I felt goofy about it. To add confusion, Judi spelled it B-e-a-u, saying it meant "beautiful" in French, proving even she could be wrong sometimes!

For painful reasons I surmised, Nigel had lived at the Y for years. When I told him why I was in England he told me to get a *Melody Maker* newspaper because it had the "goings about" of London's music scene. He seemed to enjoy our conversation and was far more intelligent than his eccentricity displayed. I felt he was very lonely and just needed someone to talk to, but I wanted to get back to my room to write to Judi. When I said, "I'll see you at supper!" he brightened and replied, "Okay, mate!" Later, when he walked into the cafeteria he looked straight at me but sat off by himself, so I went to him and this made him happy. After our meal, which was similar to American pot roast (the potatoes and carrots tasted extra good), I went back to my room to get my acoustic because Nigel asked to hear some songs. Everything looked safe and sound so I took my guitar to the music room where he was playing a bluesy thing on the piano. I tried to play along but the piano was so out of tune it sounded awful, and he said, "It's good no one can hear us, Beau." That's when I knew he was a musician. I played a dozen or so songs because he kept asking for another, which was good because it gave me a chance to play, helping the little dexterity I had to stay sharp.

When it got late I was feeling the day and Nigel said, "You should have no trouble getting a gig, mate." This made me so happy. I went back to my room around 11 p.m. and everything was peaceful. I felt content and confident, like I could live there my entire stay in England, no matter how long it might be.

Around 3:30 a.m. I woke to a nightmare, wet and itchy. I got up and turned on the light to discover I was covered in blood and my bed was swarming with what I'd later learn were vampires, otherwise known as bedbugs. They were in my hair, armpits, up my ass, everywhere! It was an absolute horror show. I didn't know what to do except pick them off. I was a young Confederate on the Peninsula in 1862, attacked by "jiggers," and disgusted to the point of nausea. My American anger kicked in and, even though people don't think of me as a person with a temper, on rare occasions when it blows, it blows. I violently shook out and reluctantly put on my clothes and went down to the front desk where an elfish old guy was dozing. I pounded the desk. "Wake the hell up!"

I didn't mean to scare the crap out of him with my loud, angry accent, but he shot up. "What is it, sir?"

I said, "I've been attacked by thousands of bugs that came out of my mattress. I want my deposit back and plastic bags to separate my clothes. After I shower I'm outta here." He wasn't surprised and said he'd accommodate everything except giving me my money back. Maybe I shouldn't have, but I informed him if he didn't give it to me that very second I'd hop over the counter and take it. He said he could be "sacked" for doing so, but gave it to me.

I went back to my room and picked off hundreds of little bastards from things I had out and then took the plastic bags, suitcase, guitar, and myself to the showers. When I turned on the water I found out the hard way they only ran hot water certain hours of the day and I almost cried. I had no choice; I took a brutally cold shower, which was the last thing in the world I was in the mood for. By the time I left around 6 a.m. I'd gotten the blood off but noticed blotches like the ones I saw on Nigel. It hit me hard! He knew what he was sleeping with and I wanted to rescue him and tell him to come with me, but where? In a foreign land, "You can't always get what you want." I found a Laundromat that hadn't opened so I went to a little park down the street and fell asleep. When I woke the Laundromat was open and I washed everything; even the clothes I had on; changing and hiding in back. As the last of my things dried I got a *Melody Maker* (MM) at a newsstand. With that and a chocolate bar I went back to the park to look for places to play, not places to sleep. My priorities were intact!

Fortunately, it was a sunny day so before I went anywhere, I spread my clothes on a bench to look for vampires in the sunlight and didn't find any live ones. A Bobby (policeman) approached and before he could ask I said, "I got attacked by frickin' bed bugs last night and I'm checking to see if I got rid of them."

He said, "Sorry Yank, they're a bloody public nuisance."

"Officer, where's the good music clubs for acoustic acts?"

He laughed and said, "Well, if I were a foreigner trying to make a name for me-self, I'd head to Fulham, Hampstead, or Kensington."

"Much obliged," I said and then thought how strange it was that I'd used that expression, because I'd never said it before. I got off the tube in Kensington near one of the more prominent acoustic clubs in London. I wanted to try a smaller venue first, but I didn't have the luxury of time to be selective. Musicians saw my Martin and told me, their fellow Confederate, that if I wanted to sign up for an open mic spot I'd better do it now because there was only one left. On the sign-up sheet, under "where from," I wrote America and spelled my name the way Judi wanted me to.

Most of these clubs had similar setups. You'd play for fifteen minutes and if the audience and club owner liked you, you'd get invited back the following week to play an entire night or to share it with one or two other acts. There'd be a "pot of gold" or something like that, where patrons would hopefully throw pence in and maybe the occasional quid—slang for a pound, like buck is to a dollar—then you and whoever you shared the night with would split it. The only way I could stay in England longer than the money I brought from home allowed would be to generate cash. Being a Rebel *with* a cause, I'd only need a little. By the luck of the draw I got the eighth spot, with the executions beginning at 8 p.m. I didn't know that much of London shuts down at 11 p.m. An hour before showtime I washed my hands in the men's room because nothing dulls guitar strings faster than grimy fingers, and the mirror told me why people were backing away from me. My vampire bites were oozing blood and gunk, trying to scab. I cleaned them the best I could and went outside to find a sidewalk to tune and loosen up. Musicians stopped to listen or maybe check out my Martin, but none got too close.

Pulling the eighth spot would give me a chance to size up the competition and also get a feel for what tempo songs worked best, but my spirit took a tumble with the opening act. He was a local guy who had stopped to listen to me warm up outside. He was so damn good his musicianship intimidated me. I thought, *I can't go on after this.* His original songs were excellent but they didn't intimidate me. It was his musicianship and singing that blew me away. After the second act I felt better. She was a French girl trying too much to sound like Joni Mitchell. Her guitar was way out of tune and she didn't seem to know or care. Then a German guy played Southern American blues. He was cool but I decided German wasn't the best language for the blues. Finally I heard, "Now, from the States"—I never thought of my country by that name but liked the sound of it—"Beau Foster."

Hearing that goofy cowboy name made me feel embarrassed and home-sick, but I went up. When the stagehand adjusted the guitar and vocal mics I felt surprisingly comfortable. Normally I would've been a nervous wreck, but maybe because of exhaustion, desperation, and anger at vampires I played with the confidence of a dying man with nothing to lose. I opened with an uptempo Jethro Tull-ish type song called "Death Of A Knight" about a knight in the days of old who dies rescuing a damsel. I thought it might be cool playing it in England and got more applause than I thought I would. Then I dedicated a ballad called "Who's Coming Round?" to my girlfriend back in the States. My mother had told me, "Make sure you play that in England."

Before the last song I said, "I'm glad it's dark in here because if you saw my skin you'd see I was attacked by a thousand bloodsucking demons at the Stockwell YMCA last night."

"It's not that dark, mate, you look like you've got the bloody plague," someone yelled from the audience.

I said, "I feel like I do!"

Someone else said, "Stockwell's notorious for that!"

"Well I found out the hard way and now I have no place to stay. If someone could let me sleep on their floor for a few quid I'd be forever grateful. I've showered and have been to the Laundromat to wash everything and found no bugs after laying everything on a park bench under the watchful eye of a policeman." This made people laugh and a musician who was part of an Australian duo going on after me said, "You can come home with us, mate."

I said, "Thank you so much, I will." Then I played my last song, an upbeat, friendly, folkish protest song about Vietnam (if there is such a thing) called "I Love America Even If America Don't Like Me" which was also the words of the chorus. Halfway through people began singing the chorus. Something I didn't know about these clubs was that patrons loved to sing along. Somehow it turned out to be a magical night, and quite unexpectedly the club owner informed me that, if I was "still in country" the following week, I could share a night with the opening act and the Australian duo that followed me. I was so happy.

I stayed with the Australians (kind and awesomely funny guys) for a week and their girlfriends fed me, which was an extra bonus. At night we went to clubs for open mics and were able to get gigs like the one we got that first night. So despite a bloody start things were going better than I could've hoped, but I wanted my own place. I called the girl at the placement agency every day to see if she'd found one. She mentioned a flat available for six months because the tenant was going on sabbatical, but it was twice as much as I told her I could afford so she had been reluctant to mention it. I took it sight unseen. I thought if I played five to seven nights a week I could just about swing it. The landlady, Mrs. Briggs, had to meet me first and I liked her immediately. She was a retired teacher in her eighties and proudly British with a portrait of the "Queen Mum" in her living room. Over tea I learned her husband was long dead and their only child, a son, had been "killed by Hitler." She had wisdom and experience in her eyes, with the saving grace of Abraham Lincoln because, like him, she never forgot how to laugh.

My new home was a tiny, third-(top) floor flat on a side street off busy Russell Square. It had a bed, sink, hot plate, and radio, but no television. The bathroom and tub on the second floor were shared by me and Mrs. Briggs, but not at the same time. The word "spartan" was invented for a place like this. It had the cutest little enclave outside the window were I could strum my guitar on a rooftop Mary Poppins may've landed on after passing Peter Pan in his search for his shadow. Here, I was inspired by the same London moon that's caused so many to morph into werewolves. Just around the corner was a small jewel of a park known only to the neighborhood. Directly below our flats at street level was a popular pub with liquor stores on either side. If you wanted to develop a drinking problem this might've been the perfect place, but it was peaceful. The pub served good food and when I could afford it I ate there. But mostly I learned to make more things on my hot plate than you could imagine. Every penny from gigs went to rent and food so I didn't tap much into the money I brought from "the States."

Something that alone would've made my trip to England worthwhile was that my new home had a bookcase with rows of "For Women Only" romance novels from the 1880s and 1890s. Sexually, they sizzled as much as anything today and were mesmerizing page-turners. I learned from Mrs. Briggs that the woman whose flat I was living in was an English professor and the books were hers. I asked Mrs. B if she thought the professor would mind if I took a peek at them and she said, "I think she'd be pleased to have a male read them because she's always lending them to her girls." So I read them all; some before gigs and some after. It hit hard how universal the ideas of love, loss, betrayal, and redemption have always been. The themes had surprisingly modern feminist slants in hilarious, irreverent, racy humor which described men as "God's worst invention." But until "she" came up with something better, they were still "God's greatest gift to women."

One afternoon Mrs. B said, "You must've been reading those books last night." I asked how she knew and she said she heard me laughing at 2 a.m. The books felt like long lost relatives and brought me so much joy along with insight into human nature at a time when I was becoming more aware that no matter what was happening, this time of being on my own was revealing what Judi wanted me to know: that I had a good soul because I was treated more than fairly by everyone I met. The only thing missing was her. In a way, this time alone showed me how much I loved her. Her selfless, encouraging letters gave me consolation and I found solace in knowing I'd never let myself be without her for any length of time ever again!

When I finished the romance novels I discovered I was now an official member of a lucky club addicted to reading. I'd entered a society Abraham Lincoln belonged to, and I felt honored. My dad had given me two books by Alan Watts and two by Krishnamurti, aka Murti, his favorite Eastern philosophers. He said, "If you ever feel lonely in the crowd over there, these might help." I was reluctant to open them, thinking they might be beyond my comprehension, but late one night after a smoky gig, I opened Alan Watts and fell so much in love I devoured them in a week. Watts and more so, Murti were the most liberating, brutally honest books I'd ever read. They introduced me to the idea that we're *not* born sinners at all but are an integral part of, not separate from, what God is. That being taught we're born as sinners separates us from God, and it's the root cause of the Civil War within us. That God is found in relationships with everyone and everything and turmoil (war) in the world stems from corrupted thought passed down from generation to generation from time immemorial. Even now, their liberating message makes me think of what John Lennon said days before he was murdered, that the world we see is an illusion *but* it's an agreed upon illusion that we can agree to change for the better. The first step that *should be* the easiest is acknowledging it's possible to *give peace a chance* if we consider for a moment there's *"No hell below us . . . above us only sky,"* and no boogeyman under the bed unless we put him there and that maybe Christ was right, *the kingdom of heaven is within all of us.*

In my tiny London sanctuary Watts and Murti were teaching me I was not my thoughts! That thought is never new but *always* old, because thought is the shadow of memory and memory the shadow of experience, so thought is a shadow of a shadow whereas *experience* is now. But thought fearful of being overruled by experience creates a desire for a past sunset in order to *compare* it to the one now, allowing the beauty of now to slip out the window. *Now* (being present) is what meditation is, *if* it's anything. Meditation is not comparison! Comparison creates conflict.

This didn't mean thinking was bad, because without it we wouldn't remember our way home or Aunt Mamie's recipe for soda bread or who won the '51 pennant. But it meant one has a personal responsibility to know what thoughts were unhealthy to one's life; for instance, in my case, that being a Catholic made me different from a Jew, Muslim, Hindu, or Buddhist. Every label and belief put upon me by my parents, my country, my world, my teachers, and myself that I believed made me who I was, separated me from God. Ego tells us to believe we're our name, nationality, sex, religion, social order, democrat, republican, liberal, conservative, Yankee, Rebel, Beatle, Stone, believer, nonbeliever and not simply a child of the light; part of "The All" contained within God's love. Thought or, as Abraham Lincoln put it, "ancient dogmas," tell us we must adhere to certain beliefs or we'll never find fulfillment or get into heaven. This Confederacy of thought becomes more selfish as it's brought into the light by love, which exposes it for what it is: slavery of the spirit. So the ultimate question is: If love is not the answer, what is?

Ancient dogmas were barnacles on my spirit that I had to scrape off. I'd always used my ex- Reb friend Mark Twain's phrase to understand the Confederacy: "Loyalty to petrified opinions never freed a human soul and never will!" Now I applied it to everything because petrifying something meant converting a living, breathing, organic substance, be it plant, animal, or human, into stone, making it lifeless, stupefied, paralyzed, or at best confounded with fear. Maybe that's what had been happening to me since birth. I wanted to be done being petrified without my knowledge and consent! I wanted to "think anew and act anew," as Lincoln said America must in order to "disenthrall" itself from slavery and the notion that the Declaration of Independence didn't apply to all. For the first time, I wasn't too petrified to ask what the bloody hell Paul had been thinking in First Corinthians when he wrote, "If Christ has not been raised then empty is our preaching; empty, too, your faith." Was he saying the message of love, the Golden Rule and doing "for the least of my brethren," wasn't enough? That we also needed supernatural zombie hoopla to seal the deal when my heroes and now my heart were singing, *"All you need is love?"* Wasn't the laying down of one's life supernatural enough?

Could believing Judi was too good to be true be a thought of my paranoid, pessimistic nature? So screw it, just love her, be with her, accept her, and be done with it. But *that* attitude was an unhealthy thought too, so I let it go and into the vacuum came the seeds of peace. She had taught me that "when things are right, you can feel them," so I decided I'd send for her to float across the ocean because I now knew I could be good for her. It would take awhile for her to arrive and I could continue to question in a new gentle way everything I'd been taught to believe. This new "pesky" questioning somehow brought me a lightness of being, not like being "born again" *into* faith, but *out* of it, into the light of rationality, reason, and love and, thank God, with a sense of humor. All of it happening in a foreign land where my love for America had a new addition; that there were indeed other places in the world in which I could feel free to evolve. Then something good happened, as if on cue, just as Alan Watts said in one of his books, "When a student is ready, a teacher appears."

On my way to a gig my eye caught a tiny posting on a message board through the window of a fish and chips shop. It had the word "meditation" on it. I went in and saw that the posting advertised free lessons to anyone who wanted to learn how to meditate. I don't know why; maybe because George Harrison spoke of it so fondly, or maybe the word meditation had such an honest, organic draw to me, but I copied the number down, put it in my pocket, and forgot about it till the next day when I pulled the paper out while making morning tea. Mrs. B let me use her phone and I called the number. Someone sounding like an American male answered. He said I could come that evening if I wanted to learn how to meditate. The address was in a rough section of Soho but I had no qualms when I rang the bell for the top floor. The same American voice that answered the phone asked over the intercom, "Is that you, Robert?" It was the first time in months I'd used my label "Robert" instead of Beau. It felt good and right, just as Judi and England calling me Beau now felt good and right. When I said, "Yes," he said, "Welcome."

I was let into a flat by a short Indian girl who looked sixteen but could've been thirty. She wore a purple robe and sandals and had a red dot above and between her eyes that I believed signified Hinduism. Above all she had a beautiful, peaceful smile. The place was stereotypical of the late '60s, early '70s hippie mindset, complete with beads between the doorways. Incense burned and quiet sitar music played in the background. I don't know why, but I've always loved the comfort of that setting. She led me through the beads to a small parlor where she told me to sit and relax while she brought tea. I could hear the chaotic, hectic London traffic and nightlife four stories down but felt it couldn't disturb a thing where I was. When the beads parted I turned to see a young white guy wearing a turban, Indian robe, shawl, and sandals.

He sat down next to me. "Why do you think you want to learn meditation?" he asked.

"It's simply because, as I understand it, it might help me live a more honest and genuine life," I replied.

"Are you not living one already?"

"*I don't know,* maybe sometimes. But if there's a way to find out, I'd like to *experience* it."

He laughed. "Experiencing *it* is what it's all about."

"If I'm not mistaken, your accent is of someone from Wisconsin." He sounded like a Green Bay Packer fan.

He laughed and said, "You're right, and when I go home to visit, I put on my *cheese head.*" We both laughed hard and I immediately liked him. I said I was an insanely curious person and he said that was a good thing and answered my questions that he just happened, by chance, to attend a lecture on meditation at his high school by a swami and/or guru from India who was touring "the States." The guru offered to teach meditation to anyone who wanted to learn and from that day on he'd been in love with the practice, peace, tranquility, and order it brought into his life. After a couple years of practicing at home he was so in love with it he decided to go to India to study under his teacher to become a guru himself.

I said, "That blows my mind!"

He laughed. "It blows mine too!"

He was only in London a few days, then off to Amsterdam, Paris, Madrid, and Lisbon, then home to the Green Bay area of the United States. The loving way he said, "The United States" gave me a powerful pang of homesickness.

"How many people are taking you up on your offer to learn?" I asked.

"Not enough!" He explained that people thought meditation was a mysterious hocus-pocus thing that would lead them away from their beliefs and religion.

I said, "I'd think the opposite is true if their beliefs and religion are based on love."

"That's because your curiosity has made you smart!"

"I'm not smart; I've just been reading a lot." He burst into laughter. Meditation was about to teach me the universe has no greater purpose than to *experience* love and laughter.

My new friend taught me my first form of meditation. I've since learned others I like better, but this brought me deep peace. He guided me through a series of steps focusing on different parts of my body to gradually bring it all together to a point between my eyes like the spot on the forehead of the girl who had let me in the door. As I focused on that spot, I'd inhale and think, "I am" and exhale, "that infinity." When thoughts arose, as they do, I wouldn't fight them, I'd just gently return to my breathing. I went with it and found an incredible essence of wellbeing; like coming home to a place beyond my mother and father; one we all come from. The experience was profound because I was ready and in good hands with my teacher. My only desire was to have none, to be nonjudgmental and genuine. Maybe I'd learned meditation but no one can truly say, and that's the beauty of it. I had my first experience of loving *not knowing* and, for someone who wants to know everything; this would turn out to be a lifesaver. After sitting with my breath for thirty minutes of the sixty I was there, I asked how much I owed and he said there was no charge, "just spread the word." I asked if I could donate and he said it wasn't necessary but I left a few quid anyway. I felt this would open me to things that were priceless. He walked me to the door and told me to call or come back if I had any questions.

"Even though I'm a Boston Patriots football fan?"(They became the New England Patriots in '71.)

He laughed. "There's some things meditation can't help!"

Over time I'd keep the "I am" when I inhaled but "that infinity" evolved to "this" when I exhaled. It felt a little less dogmatic. Back on the street everything appeared different, more alive. People whizzed by to nowhere or somewhere and I began thinking that by and large most people created their misery and their happiness, and I was good at misery because I thought too much. I laughed, thinking of Lincoln saying, "People are about as happy as they make up their minds to be," while compassion told him it wasn't that simple for people with intellects enslaved by the disease of slavery; calling those who thought slavery was a "sacred blessing from God," "our wayward brethren." But for me, tormented by ego, grandiosity, ignorance, and ambition, his saying was a great place to start because it suggested if certain thoughts caused damage to my peace of mind, maybe those thoughts weren't good for me. I suddenly realized to my great and everlasting relief that I most likely never had an original thought in my entire life and probably never would. That my thoughts were acquired things passed along by a world that couldn't help but acquire them. So maybe it was enough for my wellbeing just to be grateful for the way I observed the world because, certainly, no one had my eyes, and through that observation I might find a way to help "spread the word."

On my way home under the streets of London I had an epiphany. I thought of Christ going off to the desert to meditate for forty days before going on his mission, and how very sad it was that meditation wasn't emphasized in my religious education with the same vigor prayer was. I felt giddy irony that this simple practice of following my breath might ease the anguish my ancient faith caused me, but *for the first time* that feeling wasn't accompanied with guilt, fear, or betrayal but joyful gratitude instead. I felt unexpectedly calm, awake, and excited within that irony in the gentlest loving way; like I'd dodged a bullet—my faith. When I went to bed, absent was any desire to ask God for anything. All I wanted was to say, "Thank you, thank you, thank you." Prayer had always been a chore because I'd been taught God already knew my every wish, so why, I wondered, should I ask for something he already knew I wanted. I'd always felt guilty bugging anyone, let alone God, for anything. Now I felt that, by being warm in the winter, well fed, with good health and family, I already had everything anyone could want and here, in a foreign land, home resided in my heart.

I never made a conscious decision to stop praying, it just evolved as I practiced meditation. I was aware that Christ said every honest prayer was answered and found humorous joy that maybe that's why a lot of my prayers hadn't been answered, but maybe they had been. Prayer now felt like knocking on the door of a room where God *might* be waiting and hoping I'd get invited in. But meditation was *knowing* the right door was wide open and always had been, and knocking wasn't necessary because God had already invited me to come sit and have a cup of tea. Meditation was the walking in and when I sat, God didn't want to be worshipped, only loved because the stronger and wiser never require the lesser to worship them, for what kind of friendship would that be? So thank God, hallelujah; God was not an aristocrat! And if the teachings of my ancient faith said believing that was my ticket to hell, then sign me up!

The lock on the door that always felt shut was the fear my religion put into my heart, so I began to let it go because part of meditation is letting go of fear. I was in no way, shape, or form thinking my ancient faith was bad for everyone. I was simply realizing that, just because others felt it essential to their wellbeing, it might not be essential to mine. That maybe mine was a happier soul without faith because, as far as my salvation was concerned, I couldn't think of a single thing I wanted to be saved from and if I did, *it was just a thought!* My God, I thought, here I was living in London making just enough pence for food, my own flat, and dare I dream it, all from music I'd written. I felt grateful beyond words and when I felt scared I didn't have to believe or wish upon a star, I could sit, breathe, and have a cup of tea with God.

The only beef I had with my old faith, with "beef" being too strong a word, was that you couldn't get out of the club without acquiring a nasty reputation. It'd always been tricky, but somewhat permissible, to think others *could* get into heaven by means other than Catholicism but the deal was, for those of us born into it that had the privilege of "the truth," to then walk away was a betrayal of the highest magnitude that could mean the loss of one's eternal soul. My ancient faith appeared to be an extremely sore loser even when the game was played fairly. Actually, especially then! I began to see the absurdity of the guilt and if that absurdity came from my doubts, fine, because along with it came a feeling of wonder and an irreverent, glorious freedom that made me happy just to think it was possible to live free from the guilt created from absurdity, and to do so without the confederacy of aristocratic thought that feeds it.

I felt sadness for a wonderful, kind nun in my old science class who loved science for all the right reasons, who taught us Einstein believed in God but wasn't allowed to teach us that to him, it all depended on one's definition of God. From another book on the shelves of my sanctuary above Russell Square, I'd found a quote by Einstein saying he believed in "a God who reveals himself in the lawful harmony of all that exists *but not* in a God who concerns himself with the fate and doings of mankind." Einstein distanced himself from the idea of a Christian-styled God because he wanted to preserve his own freedom "to wonder at and respond to the universe in a full-bodied way." He said that religions professing a meddling, controlling God did so by making "childish analogies." To me, this somehow meant Einstein didn't want to be a slave to concepts that couldn't be proved or disproved but wanted to marvel, investigate, and learn from the structure of things to find God in relationship to everything. It felt almost cruel the nuns didn't teach us Einstein's personal perception of God instead of towing the party line of "ancient dogma" that might not be "adequate" for world peace in the long run, or my salvation, which was fast losing its appeal to me.

I was realizing the image I'd had of myself was way off-kilter, and if everyone had a false image of themselves it was compounded further by having a false image of others, which meant we looked at one another through four false images. Dear Lord, I wanted to share all this with Judi. Almost every time I meditated there it was, peace, sometimes in a big way and sometimes just a speck. I was riding without training wheels (my teacher) and that's the way I liked it. To think, this beautiful gift had been given free by a *cheese head* dressed as a *guru* with both *images* being false because the true image was one of a compassionate human being with a great sense of humor, helping a curious one find peace and doing so out of love.

Now I had a sense of it, that not having to know, understand, believe, or possess, that that insight, once attained, could never be taken or given away—misplaced, maybe, but never lost. Meditation was allowing me to trust that Judi was right to love me because she knew I was not what I thought I was. She trusted me; so here for the first time, I'd try to trust me too.

KARMA'S PROUD WANKERS

Every morning now began on a high note of tea and meditation followed by three hours of playing and writing music, but I needed exercise. I'd known for years it was not only healthy for my body but acted as an antidepressant for my mind, so I went to a sporting goods store and bought a pair of running shoes. Soon I was venturing five miles a day in all directions in a city that was home. My lifelong love affair with running had begun. I'd start in the little park near my flat by stretching, doing push-ups, sit-ups, squats, and chin-ups from a tree. Pigeons and regulars watched at first but soon I'd hear, "Where off to today, governor?" and I'd say, "I'll find out when I get there."

I don't have the skeletal structure for distance running but my heart, lungs, and brain didn't care; they kept whispering that "thank you, thank you, thank you" I now whispered to God, the universe, or whatever to describe the indescribable. I saw so many sights and sounds I could fill an encyclopedia. On one run in the Earl's Court section of town I heard the rumble of a bass guitar and kick drum from a large indoor sporting arena and thought; *damn, those guys are doing the best imitation of Led Zeppelin I've ever heard!* I ran down the alley between large lorries to hear better and, it *was* Zeppelin doing a soundcheck for a concert that night.

My gigs were now comfortable routines where club owners greeted me with, "Hey Beau," and locals requested their favorite songs. I was meeting great musicians and songwriters and one in particular, Stephen Clarke, became very dear to me. I shared a bill with him one night and he was terrific. He was a folkie through and through and liked guys like Pete Seeger, early Dylan, and Tom Paxton. He wrote a lot of sing-a-longs full of sarcastic but never nasty jabs at British politics and society that made people laugh and jump right in. I don't know why he was attracted to me because I'm not a folkie but a rocker to the core with a mix of classical, pop, and blues influencing everything, but he bought me a pint after the show and we hit it off. I invited him back to my flat where we stayed up all night critiquing each other's songs and ideas. I always sneak a peak at people's feet to see if they're into it, and he was tapping away like a madman. He turned me on to many more places to play.

Early one Sunday he called and told me to meet him that night at historic St. Martin's Church in London's Trafalgar Square and to bring my guitar. I thought there might be a small underground pub (and there was), but he led me into the church.

I asked, "What's this?"

He laughed and said, "Don't worry, Beau, we're going to the crypt underneath, not to mass." We proceeded to descend ancient rock stairs to a large hall where there must've been a couple hundred people sitting in folding chairs and a stage with microphones set up for acoustic music.

Everyone seemed to know him and he said, "Beau, I got a forty-minute spot for you. These people will love you!"

"Stephen, I'm not prepared to play tonight and I don't know if my brand of music will go over here."

"Don't be silly, mate, *I know*. Just do what you do!"

The first two acts showed it clearly was a folk crowd that liked sing-alongs. Each taught the audience the chorus, which was the sing-along part, before they started the song. Stephen had prearranged to introduce me, so when it was my turn he said, "This is my good mate Beau Foster from America." I got a big hand and decided to play songs I thought had a folkish flavor with major chords and maybe a minor here and there, but no 7ths, 9ths, or diminished-type things. I couldn't believe how well I was received. My "I Love America" went over really well, even though I forgot to teach the audience the chorus but they caught on right away. Stephen was offstage giving me the thumbs-up and when I didn't know what to play for my last song he whispered, "Beau, play that rain thing." So I threw caution to the wind and played a sing-along idea I'd been kicking around called "Before It Blows Away."

The verses sang of people complaining of summer heat and winter cold (metaphors for everything) and every once in awhile, as the bridge suggested, we should go outside to *"dance in the rain."* Rain was familiar to everyone in England so the chorus went, *"Everybody's got to go outside, to see the rain before it blows away."* This time I taught the audience the chorus and to hear it come back at me in that underground crypt, echoing off ancient rock walls and ceilings magnifying every peep—it was amazing. The verses weren't completed so I literally finished writing it as I sang it, which was a reckless gamble you might pull off once in a lifetime. The crowd really liked it and I was asked to come back for the following week and ended up doing an eight-week stretch. I wanted to keep this gig going so Judi could see it. Stephen was the final act and the crowd loved him. They knew the words to every song. Afterward, he said, "I know you're a rocker, Beau, and this isn't your particular cup of tea but I wanted you to know you could do it." What kind of friend was this? It astonished me that in almost every place I played after that I'd get requests for "the rain song."

A few weeks before Judi arrived something happened that would affect her, me, and Dave for the rest of our lives. I got invited to an all-night jam in southwest London by a couple I'd met where I was playing. We got off the Fulham Broadway tube station to enter an ordinary house in a row of like houses, connected together for space and heating purposes as per custom in British cities, on Hartismere Road. Here I was engulfed by American music played by some of the most incredible musicians I'd ever meet. The crammed room had mattresses and all manner of muffling paraphernalia up against the walls to "kill" the sound. They did a double take at my Martin but didn't stop playing, so I found a spot in the corner. These guys were the real deal, as comfortable with their instruments as a master plumber with his tools.

When they stopped playing they put on a record of America's Steely Dan, who were huge in England, and collectively decided, "Okay let's do this with it here and this with it there." Then they'd play the song for half an hour or so, incorporating their own syncopations and chord changes as they went. They were pros! I was next to the records they chose from and saw Blood, Sweat & Tears, Chic Corea, Taj Mahal, Crosby, Stills, Nash & Young, The Allman Brothers, Tower Of Power, Elvin Bishop, Al Cooper, Ry Cooder, Mike Bloomfield, Frank Zappa, Chuck Berry, Johnnie Johnson, Wilson Pickett, Willie Dixon, Otis Redding, Al Green, Smokey Robinson, Robert Johnson, Koko Taylor, Muddy Waters, Albert King, Bo Diddley, and a host of others, but no British musicians. The way they made the songs their own blew me away. When they played something they didn't like they'd laugh and say, "Sounds too bloody British!" I found it so ironic that I, an American, was there because I loved British bands and here they were emulating American bands; a case of the grass being greener if there ever was.

As I listened I thought of God and thought, *Thank you so much for letting me live this life* on an island peopled by musicians and artists somehow infused in the city of thinkers, writers, and seekers such as Chaucer, Shakespeare, Samuel Johnson, and Dickens; a city with the tenacity of a Victoria and bulldog grip of a Churchill; the last bastion of freedom in Europe against the insanity of the biggest aristocratic believers of slavery imaginable: the Nazis. And I, born free in the land of Lincoln who, when asked to describe his religion, said, "When I do good I feel good, when I do bad I feel bad; that's my religion." So, *if* I had to have a religion let it be Lincoln's, for what blew me away more than anything was that the kinder I was to my fellow human beings, the deeper, more peaceful, and loving were my meditations. This was a system too good to be true. My body and mind were in a union of shared life that couldn't secede from each other and the best way to enjoy it was with loving intent.

I observed these four incredible musicians, the same age as me, playing with no fear of hitting a wrong note, even if some were sour, because they knew there was no such thing when played with hope, passion, and above all, a sense of humor. They knew a sour note could teach more than a good one. I thought, Wow, *they're so comfortable in their skin, and maybe I'm becoming comfortable in mine.* And as flaky as it sounds, I was thinking that possibly there was such a thing as karma because the only thing they didn't have was a bass player. The keyboard player, Julian Colbeck, was playing bass lines on a Fender Rhodes electric piano, which is a great instrument, but in no way was it adequate in providing the oomph of a real bass, which they needed. I assumed their bass player was on his way because there was a bass on a stand plugged into an amp just begging to be played. When they finished another jam the drummer, Jimmy Matthews, said, "I hate playing without me bleeding arse covered. Where is the fucking wanker anyway?" Andy Winfield, one of the two brilliant guitarists and an incredible singer as well, said, "He's probably banging his bird." And Jimmy said, "Or he's home wanking himself, the bleeding wanker," making everybody laugh.

Having been in England for six months, I recognized by their dialects that one came from upper-crust society and three from working class. All were likeable (actually lovable), and wickedly funny in an irreverent British way. Nothing was too sacred to abuse and they abused themselves more than anything, making me smile inside and out. I kept thinking of Judi saying that "when things are right, you can feel it." I understood the music they were playing as well as they did because I had American red, white, black, and blue blood running through my veins. They were far better disciplined musicians than I was, who could not only rock but, I thought, would have no trouble sitting in with *The Johnny Carson Tonight Show* band. It seemed that along with everything else, they had strong jazz backgrounds in their quivers, something I'd never had. But I had Uncle Joe's left foot, a better (homegrown) feel for the American way they wanted to sound; an arrogant thought no doubt, but without malice. So when another break in the music came I somehow blurted out, "Hey guys, I can fill in till the wanker shows."

My nasally American accent brought silence. They looked at me in a hilarious, curious way. Colin Fletcher, the other guitarist and perhaps most talented of the bunch said, "Oooorrhh bloody 'ell, mates. We go' a Yank 'ere who wants to fill in for the wanker, should we le' 'im?" parodying a cockney accent they all did when they wanted to be silly. I didn't know that, which was good because I might've otherwise thought they were making fun of "me" accent. That would happen soon enough, without mercy. They said, "Come on up, mate," so I got up and strapped on a Rickenbacker, which was a larger bass than I'd ever played but, like with a baseball bat that's too big, I choked up.

I said, "I've never played one of these before. I prefer a Fender or Gibson."

Jimmy laughed and said, "We do too, mate!"

As I figured out the volume and pickup knobs I heard them giggling, imitating my accent. Then I said, "I've only been playing an acoustic and piano the last six months so this feels like a beast; can I warm up a bit?"

"Go ahead, mate. We're here till dawn." As I was learning the fret spacing I said under my breath and meant for no one, "Thank God I'm a wanker." This brought a huge laugh.

Jimmy said, "That's the bleeding trouble with our bass player. We're proud wankers and he's not. I mean if you can't enjoy a good bleeding wank in life, who's gonna do it for ya, mate?"

I laughed so hard I choked and said, "We have them in America too and they usually end up playing elevator music at weddings and bar mitzvahs." I regretted saying that immediately because it was snide and cruel. Then again, seeing musicians who think they're God's gift to wine, women, and song can be extremely embarrassing. These guys weren't remotely like that and Jimmy, saving me from my faux pas, said, "Yeah, or end up playing at me Auntie's bleeding Sheep, Turnip, and Brussels Sprout Convention; the bleeding fucking wankers."

Musicians can tell right away if someone can play by the way they warm up or even tune up. With my back to them I did a few sustained and staccato walking bass lines up and down the neck and slapped an occasional string. I could hear the tribe murmur in the universal way musicians murmur—it sounds like a cross between great sex and eating a dripping Mississippi sandwich with all the fixins. It says, "Oh oh, we're in deep trouble, thank God hallelujah." I knew what I was doing, not for the sake of trying to impress, but for the quickest way to say, "Thanks guys, you don't have to worry." As I got used to the bass, Jimmy said, "Bloody hell I need a smoke." When I turned I thought he was rolling a joint but it was tobacco because a lot of people in England rolled their own. I was relieved because pot could turn me into a nervous wreck and make me play in a wimpy manner, especially if I didn't know the material, so this wasn't the time. From my experience, musicians who thought they *needed* pot to play well usually didn't. Clearly, there are greats who partake, but they also play well when they don't.

Colin suggested an up-tempo 4/4 blues jam and asked what key I liked. I said, "I like 'em all but how 'bout 'E'"—it would let me utilize the lowest note open E string. Then I asked Julian, "As long as it's all right with you?"

He laughed and said, "That's the first time anyone's been concerned about my bloody feelings around here." Then Jimmy started a cool funky beat and no one came in so I did a trick I sometimes did in my old power trio back in the States by playing two chugga-lugging steam locomotive bars on the open E, then tuning it down to do an open D for two, then back to an E to begin an Uncle Joe line on the one beat of the fifth bar. When I did this, the whole bleeding Confederate Army attacked on the seventh. It was magical. Jimmy looked so damn funny with his ugly little cigarette dangling from his lips. His squinty eyes gave me the look that June Cleaver gave Ward when Wally and the Beave were out causing trouble with Lumpy, Gilbert, Whitey, and Eddie. He made a smooching pucker at me as if to say, "Let's go upstairs while we have the time, I love you; where've you been all my life?" I made one right back and their girlfriends got up and started dancing.

The jam was not a courtship but a spiritual, hormone-driven honeymoon that went on for forty minutes through a myriad of twists and turns, showing how each reacted to the slightest musical innuendo or undisguised blatant playing of the other. When it ended I heard comments of "bloody hell," "I've got to change me bleeding underwear," "holy Christ," "blimey," "good God, mate!" and that sort of thing. My American feel oiled and loosened them up for sure, but I'd shown them all I could. Every jam after I was the one learning. We played a variety of tempos and flavors until the sun came up. Julian or Colin would shout a chord as we went and Jimmy and I would sense when to do a syncopated off-beat passage and we'd laugh like little kids when we nailed it. Their girlfriends supplied constant pots of steaming tea. My lifelong love affair with *real* tea had begun. To this day I only buy loose tea, no bags for this bloke! Finally, when we sensed shadows on London streets we retired to the kitchen, which was good because blisters from plucking were painful and my left hand was numb; good war wounds. I didn't know how I'd play my gig later that night but I didn't care.

Andy asked where I lived and I told them of my flat near Russell Square, which I was losing in two weeks. Mrs. Briggs's tenant was coming back. Colin said, "Why don't you live here, mate? There's a room upstairs another bass player is moving out of. I'll talk to our landlord and you could move in today."

I asked what the rent was and it was less than half what I was paying for my flat so I said, "I hope it's not your bass player who's moving out. I wouldn't want to cause any trouble."

Jimmy said, "No, it's not the bleeding wanker."

Colin said, "Don't worry mate, the bloke is the bass player for Uriah Heep. They're going on a world tour." I'd heard of Uriah Heep but didn't know their songs. I knew they hadn't found much success in America but were huge sensations in Scandinavia, Germany, Russia, and Japan. Then I said, "The other thing is my girlfriend is coming from the States in three weeks and she has to live with me."

Colin replied, "Of course she does, so that settles it. I'll tell John, (the landlord), you're moving in in two weeks and your lady will be joining in three." Colin calling Judi a "lady" and not a bird might've meant the way I talked about her showed I was deeply in love, but it was more likely because he was one of the kindest and classiest of gentlemen Judi and I would ever know. He also happened to be one great, smoking guitarist.

One of the girlfriends handed me a cup of tea and asked, "What's your lady's name?" When I told her she replied in a very civilized English manner, "Oh, how delightful, we girls will show Miss Judi the sights of London and a good dose of the countryside while you and the boys play. I hope that's not too presumptuous of me?"

"Oh no," I said. "She'll love it. She's more of a social butterfly than the stick in the mud I am. But how do you know 'the boys' want me to play with them again?"

She laughed. "Well, look at them, haven't they just swallowed the canary?"

And Colin said, "That was the best jam we've had yet, mate. Didn't it *feel* right to you?"

That settled it, I'd move in in two weeks and the love of my life would be there in three. The timing was perfect. I hadn't had a place for Judi and I to live and now I did.

Then Jimmy asked, "Beau, my man, what the bleeding hell is a 'stick in the mud'?"

I said, "I'll tell you if you tell me what a 'wanker' is."

"You're joking me, mate. It's a bleeding fucking wanker, that's all it is!"

I laughed till I cried and said, "That's what I bloody well thought!"

Then Jimmy said, "Colin forgot to tell you about Jonathan. Your room is next to his. He's one of the most brilliant classical and theater pianists in England. He travels abroad quite a bit and is often gone for weeks." Now everyone began shuffling and snickering because Jimmy was tiptoeing in a manner he wasn't used to, because when a drummer finds a bass player that understands him, it's sacred and he didn't want to scare me away by anything he said. "Well, he's raaather flamboyant for conservative palates, and someone with a closed mind might find him a bit disturbing but we love him."

"Then I'll love him too! I don't care a flying fig if he's gay." I said.

The only issue I've ever had with homosexuality is the cruelty of those who say being gay is not as natural as being straight is for straight people and then proceed to use that wrong-headed fact to deny equal rights. Before I was out the door I heard them laughing, trying to say "flying fig" with an American accent. On my way home I couldn't stop smiling, knowing they'd keep trying till they got it right! By their loving Jonathan, I'd met Confederates who rebelled against hate and ignorance; unlike my innocent, beloved, American Rebs who were brainwashed to protect it during the American Civil War.

The next night I shared a bill with Stephen at the club where I had played my second night in England. This time I wasn't covered with vampire bites. The last set was mine because we were flipping coins to see who got it. He always wanted me to have it so I said I'd flip for it because without him guiding me through the London pub scene I might've vanished with a wish. To my surprise, Colin and Jimmy walked into the smoke-filled room for the last set and I waved to them from the stage. The blisters from the night before made me drop my guitar pick a few times and when I played a few songs on the old upright piano they had it felt like playing with tiny balloons on the tips of three right-hand fingers but I survived. Afterward I introduced Stephen to Colin and Jimmy and felt like a "jin-you-iieenne" English subject introducing his fellow citizens.

Colin invited Stephen and me back to Hartismere and I almost said no because of my blisters, but we went anyway. On the way Colin asked if I'd written the songs he heard and when I said yes he said, "I love them."

Stephen said, "See, Beau!"

Jimmy of course was more interested in my bass playing as every good drummer should be, and when he said something about it Stephen said, "I didn't know you played bass, Beau." In my heart I was dying to jam but playing bass is an athletic event and I needed time to heal, so when we got there it was a blessing to hear the rumble of a bass from inside the house.

Jimmy said, "Bloody hell, the wanker's here."

Colin said, "Bollocks" with disappointment not anger, which I believed might've been an English swear word. When we got inside I introduced Stephen to everyone I knew and took him to my usual spot in the corner. They played a lot of things we had the night before, and Stephen leaned over and said, "Christ Beau, they're fantastic." I nodded yes but thought, *if you think this is good, you should've heard us last night!*

The wanker seemed like a good guy and technically there was nothing wrong with his playing except there wasn't much bounce, swagger, humor, or "damn the torpedoes" sense of adventure to it. He provided an adequate bottom, but seemed irritated playing a sour note instead of laughing it off like the other guys did. This was a jam, not a bleeding recording session so I kept thinking, *Loosen up buddy, have some fun. That's how you learn.* But all of them, including the wanker, weren't amateurs. They played for different bands that hired them and also played on television commercials; it's how they met our landlord, a BBC cameraman. These jams were what they wanted to play on their time, not the clock's. It was peculiar no one mentioned our jam of the night before but when the wanker went to the men's room Jimmy told me he might get sensitive if they did. Plus, I thought, I used his gear without permission and he might get upset and I wouldn't blame him! I sensed they weren't having as much fun as we had twenty-four hours prior, and they knocked off early.

Over tea in the kitchen, Colin whispered, "Beau, come tomorrow night; the wanker doesn't know we're getting together and we'll play all night!"

When Stephen and I left he said, "I don't think they know how good they are, and if they did it wouldn't affect them." The next day good karma continued, because I found a cheap, banged up, bloodied, little second- or third-hand (I like 'em like that sometimes) Fender P Bass that turned out to be so much fun to play. It was all I could afford, and after I put new strings on it sounded great. Still, I had to sneak using the wanker's amp.

And so it went; we had our secret jams while the universe under my feet was about to shift. Judi was coming to England. I was dying to feel her in my arms in the worst way, and talking to her would mean even more than that. My last two weeks at Mrs. Briggs's were bittersweet because we'd grown close. Of the 180 days I lived above her we must've had 178 cups of tea together while we talked about everything. I've always loved talking to older women who are smart and forever young because I had two grandmothers like that. She was sad to see me leave and made me promise I'd bring Judi by for "a cup." She wanted to meet the girl I described as "very unusual, inspiring, and the most natural person I ever knew." It was a promise I kept.

Because I was a gypsy, the move from my flat only involved a guitar and a suitcase. Every morning I'd have a cup of tea and great conversation with a guy who lived there named John Taylor. He was deeply into the music scene. His girlfriend, Susan, was a schoolteacher and told me that a few years before she'd taught at the same school where John Lennon's son Julian had gone. I don't remember if he was her student or if it was in Liverpool or London, but what was interesting was that she said she'd held the picture Julian had drawn of a girl and titled "Lucy in the Sky with Diamonds," that supposedly inspired his father to write the song. I thought that was so cool. One morning I asked John if he liked living at Hartismere and he said, "Oh yeah, it's why I bought the place." That's how after a week I learned he was the landlord.

At night if I didn't have a gig I'd write songs or jam with "the boys." During the day it was quiet so I meditated, wrote songs and letters, and read. I found great places to go for my morning runs, and even a little gym where I lifted light weights, doing high reps to keep toned. I loved an open-air food market just down the street on Fulham Road where farmers and fishermen brought fresh meat, fish, and produce, so I ate very well. I was a typical spoiled rotten American because I always bought plucked chickens even though I could've saved a few pence plucking them myself. I loved puttering in the kitchen and when I cooked it brought people to the table, so I always had company. My housemates would often ask if it was an American holiday because of the lavish meals I made—which I thought were average everyday suppers—and it hit me like a ton of bricks that Americans probably ate too much. But I made healthy food and shared it with everyone.

When none of us were gigging and we couldn't all get together to jam, the guys would bring me to rock clubs where I felt even more at home than I did in the acoustic clubs. In my mind, the original songs I played in pubs were meant to be played by a band. I just played them the way I'd show a song to a band. I've always loved the power, vibration, and bombast of loud amplified music but I knew for many of my favorite writers, like John Lennon, Pete Townshend, Jimmy Page, Steve Winwood, Keith Richards, and Ian Anderson to name a tiny few, that some of their hardest rocking music originated quietly in their laps on an acoustic or at a piano because their bands were in their heads and they could hear it all. Being introduced to the London rock scene by guys that knew it like the back of their hands was beyond description. They took me to the best clubs and I got backstage at all of them and met musicians they knew because, like being in the Confederate Army, it seemed that everyone knew each other in a clannish family way that was so very cool.

The club that really blew me away was perhaps the greatest rock club on the planet where everyone from The Stones, The Who, and The Kinks to Hendrix and Bowie had played; London's famous Marquee Club. I couldn't believe how small it was and estimated it could only hold several hundred people if you packed them in like sardines, and they did. The stage was tiny but the sound system could rip you to shreds. There was a cool little lighting booth in back, above a bar tended by people with blue, red, green, orange, and purple hair, male and female and some where it was hard to tell the difference; a disgusting men's room and a no-frills dressing room for bands not much bigger than the men's room that was just as disgusting. In every way, it was the stereotypical *perfect* rock club of the late '60s and early '70s both in theory and practice. Bands on the way up to fame and fortune and those on the way down played there. Bands at the pinnacle of success tried out new material there too. I met members of Small Faces, though not Rod Stewart, and Ten Years After. I told the latter's drummer, Rick Lee, about Dave and I seeing them at The Boston Tea Party. He said he loved playing Boston and, "I still can't believe Fleetwood Mac opened for us on that tour. What an honor!" I saw Jethro Tull guys but not Ian, and some Black Sabbath guys but not Ozzie. I met Yes's keyboard player, Rick Wakeman, a few times. He was tall, loud, and could down pints in a swallow. When he talked you wished you had an umbrella because of the spray, but most famous musicians were smaller than I expected.

One night I somehow had a conversation with a cool little guy named Archie who talked like a pirate if Popeye was a pirate. He worked the lighting at The Marquee when he wasn't on the road with Black Sabbath as a roadie and light guy. He came to one of my gigs and told me that any time I wanted to get in The Marquee for free to knock on the back door and ask for him. A couple nights later I did, and he brought me up to the booth and I helped him do lights for a band whose name I can't remember. He worked the main spotlight and had me put the smaller one on anything interesting, with the stipulation that when the guitarist soloed we should both be on him.

During one solo he yelled, "Beau, why are you on the bass player's right hand so much?"

I yelled, "I'm trying to see his technique!"

He yelled, "Why didn't you say so!" and put the main light on the guy's hand till I said okay. He was not only funny but so very kind. It was the coolest thing to be sitting in the booth with him. When Judi came we tucked her between us.

I adjusted to life at Hartismere quickly even though I didn't know everyone who lived there. It seemed peculiar when I'd hear a key turning in the front door, someone coming in, saying hello, and then I'd never see them again. But then a momentous, positive force of nature turned the key late one morning as I came out of the bathroom after taking a bath in the deep, old-fashioned, glorious tub on the first floor. Because everyone did, including some of the girls, I came out with only a towel wrapped around my waist. As I walked down the hall to go up to my room I heard the front door lock turning. It was very sunny out so when the door opened all I saw was the silhouette of a six-foot-four man with travel bags over each shoulder. We just stared at each other. I was not built like I had been eight months before when I was first runner-up for Mr. Massachusetts because you have to work out twelve times a week to be in that kind of shape, but still, as arrogant as it sounds; I had the six-pack abs, chest, and shoulders of a muscular professional athlete.

When the staring contest with the tall mysterious pillar of salt became monotonous I stepped forward and put my hand out to introduce myself to a prematurely graying man in his mid to late thirties looking at me with a goggle-eyed Barney Fife-ish expression. His mouth and eyes were wide open and I said in my American accent, "Hey man, I'm Beau." Suddenly, he dropped his bags and screamed like a squeaky six-year-old girl, with arms flapping at his elbows and feet dancing like a four-year-old boy trying not to wet his pants. "Oh my God, Jesus, Mary, and Joseph, I can't do this, I can't do this, oh my God, oh my God." He ran to the kitchen pushing open the swinging door, came out still flapping, ran halfway up the stairs, then back down, approached me and said, "Oh my God, I can't do this." He then ran up the stairs to slam the door shut to the room next to mine. It was the funniest damn thing I ever saw. I'd officially met Jonathan. He left his bags by the door, and after Andy and

Julian arrived hours later we heard his door crack and to no one in particular he yelled down, "Could some precious darling pleeeease bring my bags up? And for heaven's sake tell that American boy to keep his shirt on or I'll never be able to come out." We laughed hysterically and the fact that he could hear us told my instincts I'd met a dear friend.

The next morning I was alone having tea in the kitchen when Jonathan walked in disheveled from sleep. Like a cat meowing he said, "Ooohhh Beeaaaauuu darling, John told me about you when you and the boys were playing last night. I'm so sorry I reacted the way I did when I saw you but it was immensely cruel no one gave me fair warning, but how could they I suppose? No one knew I'd be arriving from Heathrow at that supreme moment so please forgive. The vision will keep me warm at night, until I have the real thing, that is. Now, am I to understand you have a lady friend coming from America that you haven't seen in six months, and you expect me to sleep in the room next to you as you no doubt perform Herculean acts upon her innocent body? Well, I won't have it, mind you, and if I can't win you over for myself before she arrives, I'll stay with a friend until you children get everything out of your ravenous systems. I'm taking a pot of tea to the bath and you're welcome to join me, but I have rehearsal so it may not be wise, but you'll be joining me soon, won't you?" Now it was my turn to stare Barney Fife-ishly. I hadn't said a word and I couldn't drink my tea because I couldn't stop giggling. Here was someone formidable who I would grow to love very, very much.

The day before Judi arrived I couldn't contain my excitement. I was working on ideas with a classical flavor on the upright piano in the music room. The melodies weren't something I'd play in clubs, but I wanted to tape them on my cassette recorder so I could listen to them. I like privacy so I can sound ridiculous when working on new ideas and I thought the house was empty when the door slowly opened and Jonathan poked his head in. Like a Cheshire cat imitating Peter Ustinov after getting his paw caught in a cookie jar he asked, "Ooohhh Beaaaauu, what've you been playing?" I was so embarrassed, and it was good I hadn't heard him play because I wouldn't have had the courage to do so in front of him if I had.

I said, "They're just ideas."

"I was afraid of that!" he said.

"How much have you heard?"

"Everything darling, my room is above this one."

He asked, "May I?" and before I could reply sat next to me and played note for note the first idea I'd played an hour before, and then abridged versions of the others. Then he said, "And I particularly like this one."

"You mean you like my ideas?" I asked.

"Oh yes, darling!"

"Then why'd you say you were 'afraid of that'?" I asked.

"Because now we're obligated to do something with them, which means I must behave myself around you and that's the last thing I want to do!"

"You don't have to behave around me, but what the hell are you talking about?" I asked.

He looked skyward and sighed. "My goodness, why do they only make them like this in America? Well, first, darling, we'll go to my friend's studio sometime in the next few weeks and we'll get these ideas of yours on proper tape." Then he asked, "Can I show you how I'd fill them out if you let me play piano?"

"Of course," I said. A minute before he played my ideas exactly the way I had, in my—compared to him—chopstick fashion, but now he played them like a concert pianist would a nursery rhyme. I was so blown away I couldn't speak. His large powerful hands were up and down the keyboard in panoramic crescendos and arpeggios, but first and foremost my melodies and rhythms weren't lost but enhanced in the safe hands of a master. He garnished with light, color, and wonder and I was stunned. Stunned, too, that he remembered every idea.

Then he said something only Dave and Judi knew; that he guessed my favorite thing was not playing or performing music but writing it. I said, "You're right, Jonathan, if I could stay home and sit at a piano or with an acoustic guitar in my lap, with a cup of tea, writing songs in my pajamas all day, I'd be the happiest man alive! I don't care about performing. I get bored with it quickly, but I wanted to come to England to see if strangers would like my songs. So I have to perform so they can hear them. Sometimes there's so much music bursting inside me that performing gets in the way, because I have to play a song that's already written instead of writing one that isn't, and there's not enough time in the day for both and I feel all balled up. It's one big pain in the ass!"

"Oooohhhhhh darling, I wouldn't phrase it that way but you mustn't worry; write when you can and understand that not everyone can write music others want to play, but you can! Your ideas aren't an attempt to write something real, they're real! What I'm hearing can't be taught, and people like me are always looking to play melodies that haven't been played before. Beau darling, I can't come close to composing what you can."

"That's ridiculous!" I said.

"No, it's true, that's why I want to go into the studio with you, because I want to show these ideas to a producer friend of mine." Then he got up to leave and added, "The thought of you in pajamas makes me weak! Can we do the session in pajamas?"

"Of course," I said.

The next morning, after a great pub gig with Stephen and an even better all-night jam with my fellow Confederates, we were having tea and I told them of my Jonathan experience. They said, above all, Jonathan was honest as the day is long, and wouldn't have offered if he didn't like my songs. When Colin said he'd go into the studio too, everyone volunteered. I never asked or expected this. They told me Jonathan was a child prodigy and considered a musical genius who had perfect pitch and could play a song after hearing it once days or weeks before. Sometimes, they said, on his way out he'd poke his head in the music room to say, "Colin, your B string is slightly flat and your A's a bit sharp and Andy your G is too tight as usual and Julian your F sharp

2 octaves down is dour." Then he'd be gone in a flash. When they checked he was *never* wrong.

Somehow I was living in a world where every conversation was about music. I was in heaven. Even an opened or closed hi hat technique on the radio was discussed. Now, the guys began coming up with ideas for songs, because they'd been inspired to try at a party a year or so before after having heard a demo that became a hit in America. The writer's name was Reginald. They asked if I knew the song. I said yes, it was "Your Song" by Elton John, but added that I didn't know his name used to be Reginald. Hearing stories like that combined with all the musicians I was brushing up against, I'd think, *I can't frickin' believe this. I wish Dave was coming with Judi!* The truth was, things were utterly fantastic for a greener than green kid from Lynn, Massachusetts, who came to England with only his Uncle Joe's left foot and a few tunes in his pocket.

HOLY CRAP, I'M MARRIED

I'd wanted so desperately to share my adventures with her, and finally I was heading to the airport to pick her up. Stephen's little car only had room for four so he, Colin, and I went. I sat in back with my heart pounding like Charlie Watts's kick drum. I wasn't so much nervous as alive and I was nervous as hell! The guys talked, but I didn't hear a word. We arrived to see her flight float to earth. When she exited the plane Stephen said, "Blimey Beau, she looks like your sister!"

"That's what everyone says," I said.

Colin asked, "Are you sure she's not?"

She was the most beautiful sight I'd ever seen. With her were My Family, the American Flag, Apple Pie, the Boston Red Sox, Patriots, Celtics, Bruins, New England Seafood, Sluice Pond, Lynn Woods, White Mountains, the Ocean, Fourth of July, Nicky's Pizza, *The Boston Globe* and *Lynn Item,* and everything else I loved about home. We threw our arms around each other and it felt like we floated off the ground. We hugged and kissed until she said, "Honey, there's two guys staring at us and it looks like they're crying." I waved them over and she handed them tissues. There are no words to say how happy I was. I said it felt like a lifetime since we'd held each other. She smiled and said, "Sweetheart, it's been six months!"

On the way to Hartismere I peppered her with questions about home, using too much American slang for the guys to understand. They got the biggest kick out of us. "Blimey bleeding hell, now we've got two of 'em. Pretty soon we'll all be talking like cowboys. Are you using a foreign language, Beau?" they asked. Judi talked to them like she did everyone; like they'd been her lifelong friends, casting a spell, as she would on everyone in England. When Colin asked about her flight he turned to look at her and she put her hand on his arm as she answered and he smiled the biggest smile I ever saw him smile. My mates were falling in love.

It was an early Saturday afternoon so when we got home the guys and girls were waiting and they swarmed her. Tea and pastries were set up in the kitchen and we all crammed in. Judi sat and asked, "Where's Jonathan?" and out of a corner came a sheepish, "I'm here!" She got up and gave him a big hug and said, "I've been looking forward to meeting you very much!" His towering figure melted over her five-foot-five frame. He said, "Oh God, I'm such a flaming fool." And Jimmy said, "You're a flamer all right!" and the kitchen exploded.

I can't, so I won't try to describe the feeling of home she brought to the place. I now felt a sense of security and legitimacy I didn't know I was missing. Eventually we went to our room, which became our private universe for the next half of a year, and among other things, we slept till the early evening. The guys had gigs and I intentionally had nothing scheduled for the next few days. I just wanted to be with her. Around 8 p.m., on his way out, Jonathan knocked on our door and Judi opened it. He said, "Beau has probably told you I can be foolish."

"No, he hasn't, but if he did that would make two of us." She kissed him on the cheek and he said, "Goodnight, my darling" and left. They'd become the best of friends. That first night was not all passion and roses, though. She got very upset seeing a hundred little scars on my skin from all the English women I'd slept with, assuming half those bed bugs that attacked me six months earlier had been female.

The next morning we walked for hours around southwest London and stumbled on a beautiful little park where we sat and watched the world go by. "This reminds me of Cambridge," she said. I thought so too. She said I looked thin and healthy and everybody back home was thinking of me. She'd seen my parents and brothers every day and said Dave was missing me very much and swimming like a dolphin possessed. He told her he played the tape of my old power trio before he trained because it made him swim harder. When she said that, I felt a strong pang of missing him and wondered out loud if my Uncle Joe's left foot made *his* brother, Uncle Nick, swim harder? She said, "I bet it did!" There was so much to tell her, but first and foremost was about meditation because I wanted her to experience it. She said Chuck, a very good friend of ours who did some roadie work for my band back home, had become a transcendental meditation teacher and he told her to tell me it was right up my alley; a coincidence from across the ocean and a sign of the times, too. I explained how meditating allowed me to not wrestle within myself so much and she said, "That's good, but you shouldn't anyway!" I asked if we could learn Chuck's technique when we returned to the States and she said she'd like that very much. Then I told her of my musical adventures and what Jonathan had said about my writing ability and about going in the studio, and the guys volunteering too and she said, "It doesn't surprise me. Just wait till they hear your new music!"

"What new music?" I asked.

She said, "The music you haven't written yet!"

I shared my insecurities with her too, those that have plagued me my whole life, that she was familiar with more than anyone. I said the past six months had felt real, yet somewhere deep inside I felt like an imposter. She said it was just my pessimistic, paranoid nature rearing its ugly head. Then she asked, "Do you feel that way now or when you write music, study history, meditate, or work out?" I said no and she said, "Well that goes to show that if you do what your heart tells you, you'll be all right. You're the type of person who should listen to his heart more than his head. I learned that about you when I started following your band. I wasn't interested in you, you know. I liked your music but thought you were stuck up because you never said anything to anyone during your breaks. You always snuck off to some corner or the equipment truck to read a newspaper, magazine, or history book. It was cute at first, but it got weird because you did it all the time. I couldn't figure it out because you looked so confident, sociable, and aggressive on stage. But when we met, you were a shy little kid bursting with ideas and a strange cloud of guilt hovering over you that I wanted to tell you was nonsense, but I didn't know you well enough. But now I do! Somehow you were slogging through, and I began to see that learning things was how you coped with your demons. Knowledge excited you and you'd say something funny like, 'Ahhh, so that's *how* everything got so messed up!' You didn't care a flying fig *why* the world was so mean to itself because that muddied the water. You said everyone had a different opinion about *why* and was entitled to them. And, if their *whys* lead to war, that meant they were based on lies."

"You said history teaches *how* the world got so screwy and that opens a window to know how to fix it. It's how you were able to leave your pessimism outside when you came to my home. Mine was a world you never knew existed, but your curiosity brought some peace to the chaos. You made my mother, sister, brother, and even my father laugh in the last days of his life, and you did it for me. I knew what was going on inside you the first time you came, but you didn't run away like most everybody did. You became *the truth of all things* to me and that truth is in your music and in the way you treat people and how they treat you. You were so happy when you discovered Abraham Lincoln was plagued by self-doubt, 'nervousness,' and paranoia and how reading, humor, and action helped him deal with it and made him want to contribute something good to the world. Hon, that's what you need to do, and music is your way to do it. But no matter, you need to know I love you and that you're okay and when you're not, *I'll always be there!*"

It was the first and last lecture, scolding, or whatever she ever gave me. It was the first time I realized how lucky I was to share Lincoln's sentiment that everything of value in the world he had learned from a woman. It made me cry.

The weeks rolled into months and one by one the guys, including Stephen, took us to their homes to meet their families and everyone fell in love with Judi. They were from the Abingdon area outside Oxford, so we were treated to ancient, picturesque countryside scenes that have made writers and artists reach for pen and paper. A thousand times Judi said, "I love this place!" In London she'd go out with the girls while we jammed and sometimes I'd hear, "I've never had so much fun, if you go back to America, Judi, please take me with you!" On nights I gigged she came or showed up later with one or two of the girls. Club owners loved her and one rang a bell above the bar announcing, "Princess is here!" when she arrived.

My fellow Confederates continued working hard on songwriting and the better they got the more they seemed frustrated with the wanker. I thought if I hadn't told them I'd be returning to the States they might've given him the boot. And man oh man, every time I threw a riff at them during a jam they'd jump on it. I told them they could have them. When I heard them using one with the wanker it didn't have the Uncle Joe drive, but I was honored.

About four months after Judi arrived I'd almost forgotten about Jonathan taking me into a studio. He was so busy in the orchestra pits of the theater district, as well as doing session work. Also, he was serenading children a few days a week on a British television show similar to *Sesame Street,* which Judi and I got the biggest kick out of watching. One time we didn't know Jimmy was going to be on it, but there he was playing drums with little kids dancing around his kit. It's what music's all about. But late one night Jonathan knocked on our door and said he finally had a free night to go in the studio. He hummed four of the melodies I showed him and told me they'd be enough to show his producer friend. I asked when we should rehearse and he said not to worry, that we'd go over things in the studio, so I said okay. Saying he remembered melodies four months later sounds preposterous, but the guys said he was a genius and they were right. I've never known anyone with that kind of musical memory.

He gave me an address and told me to meet him there the next night at midnight. After my pub gig I found him waiting outside. He'd just finished work and was dressed in the elegant clothes of someone who worked in an orchestra pit, complete with polished black shoes and white scarf. I had on dungarees and a flannel shirt people thought was part of my American shtick, but they were the only clothes I had, so we were quite a contrast. We entered an incredible studio with the largest mixing board I'd ever seen. There was a grand piano for him and a stool for me with mics for my acoustic and vocals. He had me play the songs as he took notes and then said, "Okay, let's play them together with acoustic guitar." I had told him I'd written accompanying parts, to which he said, "Oh fabulous darling, simply fabulous!"

We ran through one and it sounded so cool in the headphones. Then he said, "All right, Beau, let's play all four straight through." So we did. I thought the engineer behind the glass was still getting levels when he gave Jonathan a thumbs-up and Jonathan said, "That's it darling, good job."

Incredulous, I asked "We're done? I haven't changed into my pajamas yet."

In the mixing room Jonathan was all business, and I could tell he and the engineer were good friends. We listened back and I couldn't believe how well things blended with just the right amount of reverb. The engineer suggested I play the guitar part again on a fifth, unplanned song that on a whim I'd asked to record. He wanted to double track it so he could pan it in stereo. I'd never double tracked before, but was back on my stool and thinking to myself said, "I don't know if I have the ability to play with myself," meaning guitar on guitar. When I said it I saw Jonathan and the engineer explode in laughter but I couldn't hear them. I felt like an idiot and was so embarrassed. I said to myself, "you frickin' nitwit," and they kept laughing. Jonathan pushed the button, "Remember darling, these mics can hear your heartbeat, so we hear everything you're saying."

"Oh?" I said.

The engineer told me to relax and just play along, that it'd be easier than I thought and he was right. Once you get a *usable* track down the rest is usually cake, although very hard work sometimes. When it was over I asked the engineer how much I owed him and he said, "Nothing!"

Jonathan said, "Beau darling, this was my idea."

We did the session in three hours and left with a reel-to-reel and several cassettes. On the way home he talked about Judi the whole time, saying, "Pleeeeease don't bring her back to America, Beau."

"Well, I can't leave her here."

"Why not?" he asked sternly.

The next afternoon at tea he played the session for the house and everyone seemed impressed. The guys insisted, "We're playing on the next session!" I was so happy. Judi later asked why, on the fifth song, I changed the lyrics of "Who's Coming Round" where I usually sang *"She'd never cry"* to a whispering, *"She'd never die, if she left me!"* at the end. I told her I never sang it like that before; it just came out without me knowing it.

She said, "Well, it's one of your better songs, but I'm not dying and I'm never leaving you!"

"I know, hon, I don't know where it came from."

A few days later Jonathan took me to a building that looked like it'd once been used for industrial purposes. We were buzzed in after he said into the intercom, "It's me Mark. I'm here with the American lad." As we entered, a huge painting of an angelic man with wings confronted us. It looked like the logo of Led Zeppelin's new Swan Song Record Label that'd soon be the label for Bad Company and was currently the one for Maggie Bell. Bad Company would become a world renowned super group while Maggie was already popular in England. To her dismay, she was often introduced in concert as England's answer to Janis Joplin. She's the powerful, smoking, sultry voice you can hear singing, *"Every picture tells a story don't it?"* with Rod Stewart, long before he got goofy. It was rumored, too, she was the inspiration for his song "Maggie May."

As we headed to the elevator I said the logo reminded me of Zeppelin's and Jonathan said, "Oh, it is theirs darling! They're a crash, boom, bang outfit that fancy themselves after American blues artists. They're popular in Britain and shamefully their first album sold more than The Beatles' first, but I can't tell you a single song. I don't suppose you're familiar with them. My friend produces records for their label because we all have to make a living somehow. He's currently working with Maggie something or other but he's better known for the song Lulu sang in Sidney Poitier's movie *To Sir With Love,* because he wrote it. He's been listening to your songs and wants to meet you!" *Holy blankety blanken crap Batman,* I thought as we stepped off the elevator. Zeppelin might've been a "crash, boom, bang outfit" to Jonathan but to me, like The Beatles, The Stones, Jimi, Cream, The Who, Kinks, Tull, and Traffic, they were the epitome of what rock was meant to be. Just as I wondered, *How in the hell did I get here,* I thought of my mother who loved and admired Sidney Poitier and suddenly I was shaking the hand of Mark London who had written *To Sir With Love,* a number one smash hit in 1967.

He saw I was blown away by all this and quickly put me at ease. When Jonathan went to the men's room I told him I was a huge Zeppelin fan and he laughed and said, "Don't say that around Jonathan." So right off we were Confederates. He said he was excited to be working at Swan Song because it was a new label that had some clout behind it and he wanted it to succeed. He said he'd listened to my songs "a good half dozen times" and thought I had the makings for a songwriting career. He told me good songwriting "can be groomed, but not taught."

"So I'm told," I said. I told him I'd rather write music than play it, but if I didn't play it no one would hear it.

He laughed. "I know just what you mean!" He asked why we recorded the five songs we did and I said they were just ideas Jonathan happened to hear when I didn't know he was listening. I said I didn't think they were my best ideas but were just what I had in my head at the time.

He asked, "How many songs have you written?"

"About one hundred fifty so far."

"Well, 'Who's Coming Round' is very beautiful."

"It's about a beautiful person."

Then he said, "The others have good seeds for songs, and the only criticism I have is overwriting because you have two or three songs in every one, but that's a good problem. I'd like to listen to any ideas you have. My door will always be open so, please come back." I said I'd love to and thanked him very much. Before we left I asked if any Zeppelin guys were around because if I met one I could tell Dave. He said, "Jim and Robert are here a lot because their manager Peter Grant's office is down the hall, but they're on tour at the moment!"

The elevator down was like descending from a cloud. I asked Jonathan, "Why the hell didn't you tell me we'd be going to Led Zeppelin's record company?"

"Ohhh Beau darling, I knew that wouldn't impress you but Mark would. I mean, at least he's legit." This made me laugh so hard I cried. He knew one side of me but not that I loved the riffs of Zeppelin almost as much as Beethoven's. My musical/historical comfort zone has always had Mozart and Robert Johnson as its east and west and Yanks and Rebs as its north and south—all within reach.

Five months had flown by since Judi arrived and I was very homesick. I'd come to England with a half-baked idea of playing things by ear and not only hadn't gotten thrown out of the country for being a crook because it was illegal to make money from gigs (as little as it was) without a work permit, but I'd found a home away from home. I had a lot to digest and our visas to stay were coming to an end. I missed America and especially Massachusetts so much it hurt. It surprised me, though, how little enthusiasm Judi had for going home. She was more in love with England than I was, and I loved it very much. Knowing we'd be coming back made leaving bearable. I concluded that in some weird, wonderful way London was the best place for me to chase my dreams.

A few weeks before leaving I did the smartest thing I've *ever* done: I asked Judi to marry me. I had decided to do this long before she came to England and thought that because her mom couldn't afford to help us pay for a wedding it would be easier all around if we got married before we went home. That is, if she'd have me. I didn't propose but more or less ran the idea by her.

She asked, "Are you kidding? Why do you want to do that?"

"Because I want to be with you forever!"

"Yeah, well, what does getting married have to do with it?" she asked.

"Well, nothing, but at least we'd be able to legally take care of each other if something happened," I said.

"Well, that makes sense, but it wouldn't change anything."

"I know," I said.

She thought about it for too many uncomfortable seconds and asked, "When *do you* plan to do it?"

"Before we go home. Wouldn't it be cool getting married in England?"

She liked *that* idea and said, "It *will* be cool but remember it won't change anything!"

"That's why I want to do it."

If her attitude toward marriage seemed cavalier and careless, it wasn't! This was the early '70s when the hangover of the senseless killings of the Kennedys, King, and Malcolm X still hung in the air. Race riots in the land of the free were broadcast around the world while the spirit of the '60s was being squashed by the sight of kids coming home from Nam in body bags; some were our friends and loved ones. Those of us who thought we had some historical sense were rebelling against a society we loved, because it was so misguided in a confederacy of ignorance and fear that it dropped napalm on villagers in grass huts in a witch hunt for something that didn't exist. Senator Joe McCarthy's "fire-eating" insanity against communism was alive and well twenty years after he'd spewed it, just like John C. Calhoun's had been a century before. This was the world of our Vietnam generation, in which every institution considered sacred by "The Establishment" carried embers of mistrust whereas Judi could only incarnate trust.

She believed in love, decency, and fairness and represented the best of it. She *was* a true-blue American flower child who didn't have the naïveté of those who thought they were because they liked the novelty of it. She was the real deal, a natural! She was not against marriage or any institution per se, but saw the hypocrisy of a society that thought their brand of living was perfect and everybody else's wasn't. She loved America with all her heart, but loved the world even more. She *felt* what Lincoln meant when he warned Americans that when they thought they were perfect, they were doomed. She epitomized his sentiment that Americans should always ask, "How can we do better?" She knew it instinctively and I knew it historically, and somehow we knew we were right for each other. She could've gone to San Francisco with flowers in her hair and been everything good about the spirit of the age. Instead she floated east because her future husband was there and she believed in him. Sometimes being a Confederate in rebellion *is* a sacred thing, for there was no Civil War within her spirit about anything. She was "the cause" and my inspiration. Plus, I loved her so very much!

It may be strange for a couple so young to want to get married, but I was as sure about us as I was about the sun rising. I'd experienced being without her for six months and knew what that was like. And aside from love, we simply enjoyed each other's company. As unrealistic as it sounds, and I *know* it does, we never fought about anything. The more I thought about getting married, the more I found relief in joining a club of people that no longer had to be concerned about things so many are concerned about, like finding the perfect political, intellectual, spiritual, and sexual partner. I'd been around just enough to know those were worthy goals, but knew that so many search their whole lives for what they perceive as perfection and suddenly find themselves old, gray, and alone. In their search for a shadow that didn't exist, they missed out on so much joy they could've had in abundance, with or without someone. But for me—I don't want to say this because it destroys any shred of credibility I might have, but I *have to* because of the truth of it—I found perfection in *not seeking it*. It's hard to explain, but there was never a feeling of uncomfortable desperation, jealousy, envy, or any of that nonsense in our relationship. Still, because of my ever-annoying, curious mind, whenever I asked her why she was so good to me, she'd say I deserved it and to this day, I've never been able to accept it.

Somewhere deep remained that old lingering feeling that our relationship was too good to be true. I tried my best to ignore it and sometimes was successful. Everywhere we went people told us they'd never known a couple better made for each other, who got along so well. I *know* it sounds like the syrupy recollections of a sentimental old fool, but there's people today in England who can vouch for this and friends and relatives here at home who remind me of it whenever Judi's name comes up. The thought of marrying her somehow made that "wayward brethren," misguided, paranoid whisper in my soul go away. And because only an insane person believes he can see the future, and her acceptance of me meant I was not insane, it made that feeling go as far away as it had ever gone before, at least for awhile. So I made arrangements that, in 1973, on November 9, my paternal grandfather Abe's birthday, we'd get married in the Court House of London's borough of Camden.

We decided not to tell anyone except Colin and Stephen because we needed two witnesses. A few days before the event I asked Colin to be mine, and Judi asked Stephen to be hers. It didn't matter whose was whose, we just wanted them there. We explicitly told them not to tell anyone because we didn't want anyone to fuss. But on the day, we woke at 9 a.m. like any other day and at 9:30 there was a knock on our door. When we said, "Come in," the girls marched in with a tray of tea, toast, oranges, and a rose. Then Valerie, Julian's girlfriend, came in with the coolest dark navy blue dress embroidered with bouquets of red roses. When she hung it on the clothes rack that served as our closet she also put down a classy pair of smart, friendly, sophisticated, and sexy women's shoes that went with it. Then she left only to return with a man's gray suit, white shirt, and tie with similar roses along with a pair of shiny, new men's black shoes.

I asked, "What's this?"

Susan said the clothes were our wedding gift. "Today you'll look like a British couple fit for a royal wedding."

We were moved beyond description!

Valerie said, "I'm almost positive everything will fit." And it did.

We had to be at the courthouse by 1:45 for our 2 o'clock ceremony. Stephen said he'd take us but a taxi showed up at 1:15. Little did we know that, when I mentioned to our landlord John that someday I'd like to ride in a British taxi because they looked so cool in those goofy Beatle movies, he decided that part of his wedding gift would be to have us picked up by one and the other part would be that when we got to Camden he'd be there to take pictures, having prearranged with the driver to open the door as we exited. And, because John was a BBC cameraman he took the most incredible pictures of us doing just that. I looked like an English Mod or dandy who'd make Roger Daltrey proud and Judi looked like an elegant Jean Harlow, the great Hollywood star of the 1930s, only prettier, in a dress that fit like a glove and showed off her shapely, athletic figure. Thank God I have pictures of this cherished day. Some are on the wall of my home beside pictures of my Hartismere Confederates and Abraham Lincoln.

The taxi waited outside while the Deputy Registrar, who was the Justice, preformed the ceremony. She said we were the happiest couple she'd seen all week and Colin laughed. "They're always like this!" John got a picture of us smiling within seconds of our "I do's" and we're radiating. When it was over he took pictures of us outside and then had the driver take a few of the five of us. Then he said, "We'll see you back at the house." When we got back in the taxi the driver turned and told us the third part of John's gift was to take us for a historic ride through London before returning home. This was so wonderfully surreal because not only was the driver funny, but his historical knowledge of the sights and sounds was far more than what you'd think was typical. I asked him about it and he said, "Well, I'm supposed to know a good bit for the tourists but the truth is I've been a history junkie all me life. If I give too much detail tell me!" Judi then said a magical thing, "There's no such thing as too much historical information *for my husband!*" The word "husband" made me think, *Holy crap! I'm a married man in a London cab who just married the greatest, most adventurous traveling partner in the world.* I asked her how she felt and as usual her thoughts were of others. She said, "I can't believe they did this for us."

We got home around 5 p.m. and thought we'd have some peace and quiet, assuming everyone had gigs that night. But when the driver opened the taxi door we heard the opening notes of "Exile On Main Street," the latest Rolling Stones record blasting from inside the house, which was very unusual.

I said, "What the?" and Judi said, "They're playing that for you Beau!"

When we opened the door the house exploded with congrats and Jimmy said if I didn't carry Judi over the threshold, he would. A pint of bitter (beer) for me and champagne for Judi were put into our hands before we said hello. Jonathan, his engineer friend from the pajama(less) session, and the guys and girlfriends were there with food and drink set up in the kitchen. When we cut a marvelous cake Stephen's mother had made, Colin toasted, "To Beau and Judi, two people made for each other if there ever was. They've brought a taste of America to us and now we want to go there. With much regret they're going home, and a piece of us is going with them. If we're lucky, they'll be returning soon." To which everyone held up a glass and said, "Here, here!"

I asked, "What's this, the bleeding parliament?" This brought a howl and The Stones back on.

They'd been partying since before we got there and it was the first time I'd ever seen any of them buzzed. I don't know how to say it any other way except that they were so cute, silly, genteel, and civilized all at the same time. Jonathan was carrying a glass and bottle of champagne and kept congratulating us with tears, smiles, and slobber. When "Tumbling Dice," the fifth song on side one, came on I got up to play air guitar and dance. Jonathan said, "Beeaauu darling, the boys are trying to convince me you like this music and it makes me want you all the more. But their instruments aren't properly tuned so I have to drink bubbly to tolerate them." This made me laugh so hard I almost fell down.

I said, "Jonathan, think of them as a bunch of off-key whiny tomcats crying on your back fence. If you can do that, then see how great the songs are, despite the way they sound and see how it makes you feel." This seemed to turn a light bulb on because he began dancing, but most likely it was the champagne. We partied till the wee hours and when Judi and I were finally alone she said, "That was the best wedding party I've ever been to."

"Me too," I said.

Then she asked, "Do you feel any different?"

"No, do you?"

"No, and let's keep it that way!"

"Definitely," I said.

TIME WAITS
FOR NO ONE

In the weeks before returning to The States we finished my gigs and said good-bye to club owners, goers, Mrs. Briggs, and our good friend Archie at The Marquee. Then we took time for ourselves with a two-day train sightseeing tour through the most beautiful vistas one could imagine. When we waved good-bye to Colin and Stephen at Heathrow Judi said, "Look, they're crying like the first time I saw them!" I was missing my fellow Confederates already but couldn't wait to see my family and, most of all, Dave.

I assumed he'd be picking us up at the airport, but we saw my parents on that cold New England mid-December afternoon. Judi said, "They're here because we got married." We'd just about forgotten about that but had written home with the news and this was the first time I felt a pang of guilt for not getting married among family. It dawned on me that it must be a big deal for parents when their firstborn comes home with a bride. I thought that somehow, someday, in some way I'd make it up to them and Judi's mom. When they greeted us though, I couldn't recall ever seeing them so happy, so maybe I hadn't disappointed them too much. As we walked to the car I thought of the time a year before when I asked my mom what I should get Judi for her birthday. She'd held up her engagement ring and said, "If you don't get her one of these someday you're a knucklehead!"

Now I teased her, "Hey, Ma, maybe I'm not such a knucklehead?"

She laughed. "Not at the moment!" I missed talking with my history teacher, musician mother very much.

We prearranged to stay with Judi's mom until we found a place of our own. On the way there I couldn't believe how big everything was; from the width of roads to the size of buildings, houses, people and cars. America is one huge place. Anyone who's lived in Europe knows what I mean. When we got to Saugus we stopped at Heck Allen's, still the greatest seafood restaurant on the planet. My parents treated us to gargantuan proportions of food. My mom said we looked skinny but healthy, but I couldn't remember ever once going to bed hungry in England. They beamed at us the whole time, looking at Judi, maybe trying to imagine what their grandchildren would look like. As we sat with gorgeous mounds of seafood in front of us I took in the sights and sounds of this busy all-American restaurant. For the first time I heard with some objectivity that nasally, glorious, New England accent in a way I'd never heard it before. It'd only taken me a few days to get used to British accents so I knew I'd only have an hour or so to enjoy this perspective of my birth dialect, and I soaked it in.

I began having an epiphany of what nationalism truly is when I had my first taste of Heinz Ketchup after a year without. In England I panicked when I learned they didn't have Heinz or Hunt's because I couldn't see how I could survive without them. Now I was home loving my Heinz, but wishing I had a bottle of British ketchup too, as well as the amazing malt vinegar I doused on my fish and chips. It hit me hard that if you had a comfortable life, no matter where in the world, and you were taught there's no place like it on earth—which is okay until the words "better than" or "the greatest" are used in a way that makes you look down on other nations—that that's where half the turmoil in the world comes from. If my family had been English, we most likely would've had lives as equally rewarding, and our love for our country would've been as strong as our love for America was. Then I went a step further, because I can't help myself, that this would've applied had I been born *white* in the American North or South during the 1830s or 1840s, and I would've fought for the side where I was born in the Civil War. So, Lincoln was right, it *was* parochial! I now understood with certainty that traveling the world was the greatest education because it allows one to walk in another's shoes. But damn, nobody, nowhere had seafood like this.

This epiphany of nationalism made my musical mind think of John Lennon's "Imagine," which was becoming a meditation for me in much the way the Our Father prayer was. "Imagine" suggested breaking down barriers of nationalism between nations and the Our Father suggested breaking barriers between heaven and earth and above all, that it's possible! I was beginning to grasp that Christ was absolutely right when he said the kingdom of heaven resides in every heart and the Buddha was right that meditation was the best way to find out if it's true. "Imagine" was only two years old at the time, and not the accepted world-wide anthem it is today. It was controversial and many U.S. Bible belt stations refused to play it because religious people thought it sacrilegious while secular people thought it holy. But I loved two nations now and would love them all, if democratic, so I saw neither view of "Imagine" as helpful because John wrote it to ask both sides to simply *"give peace a chance."* Days before he was murdered he asked an interviewer, "Can you imagine a world without countries and religions?" His wife would later explain he was trying to move the world toward the idea of "one country, one world, one people" so there'd be no more wars.

As hippie-ish as that might sound, it's essentially the message of Buddha, Christ, and all the sages who've *known* what love is, that God must truly be *peace, love, and harmony.* Lincoln said the American Civil War illustrated better than any war what happens when that message is ignored. And history teaches the seeds of that war were racism and bigotry, while Webster's dictionary explains that *"racism* is prejudice expressing either favorable or unfavorable bias and/

or race hatred; a doctrine or program of racial domination and discrimination based on the assumption of racial superiority of one over the inferiority of the other." And that a *bigot* "is a hypocrite, one obstinately or intolerantly devoted to his own church, party, belief, or opinion." Lennon just rolled the ball a little further by suggesting that nationalism in the extreme can be a perpetuating, *enslaving* disease. Then my dad asked what my plans were and I mistakenly put an onion ring in my mouth. I've never been a big fan of them, but at least it had Heinz on it.

When we got to Judi's mom's house it was late and we were pleasantly surprised that her brother, sister, and a very dear friend of Judi's parents from down the street, who had lost his wife the year before, had done a lot of work on the old cross in Cliftondale. The house looked terrific. Within a year Judi's mom would marry this wonderful man and he'd become a good friend of mine, despite being a New York Yankees fan. Judi's mom beamed at us like my parents did; maybe trying to imagine what her grandchildren would look like. When we opened the shades the next morning I told Judi how good the place looked and she said, "That's because you've brought life to it." But I couldn't see how I had anything to do with it. Later that morning we climbed the old hill nearby and tried to assess the past year as we breathed in American air flowing in west from the Atlantic. In the afternoon her sister and brother came by. They were my family now and I felt so comfortable with them, as I always did!

Within a day I called our friend Chuck, the transcendental meditation teacher and told him I'd learned a meditation technique in England and wanted to know if he could teach me, Judi, Dave, and his girlfriend transcendental meditation. I told him I felt that if everyone meditated there'd be no wars. He laughed. "There wouldn't! Come Saturday." His compassion and empathy had inspired him to become a great special-ed teacher in the Saugus school system, and his lightness of being made the course so much fun for us. I loved this form of meditation because the simplicity of experiencing a mantra was a relief for someone like me, who concentrates too much as it is, usually on nonsense.

Without question, learning meditation was the best thing that happened to me in England before Judi arrived. I wanted the people I loved to experience the peace and relief it brought me. And also that it didn't solve everything, which is part of the beauty of it.

We had a wonderful holiday season getting together with Dave and his girlfriend just about every night. By late January we found the cozy little place on South Street in Lynn, a few hundred yards from the Frederick Douglass bandstand on Lynn Common, which again, honored the great abolitionist, ex-slave, and friend of Lincoln's. Douglass lived and gave speeches in our town in the 1840s, feeling *somewhat* safe here. Judi then got a job as an assistant for a dentist she caught using laughing gas on himself, and I got a job at a local hospital delivering food to patients, so I put on a few pounds. I quickly got gigs doing fill-in work on bass with bands in the area. My Hartismere Confederates helped me develop chops to go along with my harder rock ones so I felt I could handle just about anything. And I began writing songs with a vengeance. We lived very comfortably but simultaneously got homesick for England and started planning to go back as quickly as possible. Seeing that everyone in America was safe and sound made our desire to return powerful and Judi's desire was stronger than mine.

As I wrote I put every lyric in a notebook and filled dozens of cassette tapes with drafts and riffs for songs. My portfolio of ideas was growing exponentially and I finally figured out how to calm down a little, to not overwrite so much. Verse, verse, bridge, chorus, middle, bridge, chorus extended and out with only minor fluctuations, like an intro or verse after the middle, depending on what the song asked me to do. This was rock, not classical or intricate jazz so it didn't have to be complicated, just catchy. Judi liked everything so she was not the best one to critique my work, but Dave told me what got him fired up and what didn't. He didn't spare any feelings I might have. I mentioned to him how much I disliked my hospital day job and this was when he told me that if I got my lifeguard license he could get me a job for the summer. He'd been a lifeguard the last two years and was friendly with the guy who did the hiring. Having the greatest swimmer in the city for a brother had advantages. This was also when he was driving the Blue Bomb down to UConn to train with the team because he'd be swimming for them in September as a freshman. At least, that was the plan.

It was in this late spring that he began walking with a limp that would lead his body to wage a Civil War on itself. It's what cancer does. But before the implications were known he'd help me in the pool so I could get my lifeguard license and make enough cash to return to England. It was part of our childhood dream. He'd told me long ago in no uncertain terms, "If you make it in music, no matter what I'm doing, I'm going with you to watch your back." Music and blood bound us, and I was trying to figure out how to make it happen when the letter from Colin arrived. He wrote that session work with Charisma Records might be available if I passed an audition. I had just come home from reading about bone cancer at the library. A few weeks later another letter arrived urging me to come. I received it shortly after coming home from the library again where I was learning about chemotherapy. As I read his latest letter I began to intentionally and/or unintentionally lie to myself and my God in order to make the greediest and worst mistake of my life.

Colin didn't go into detail. If he said something was good for me, it was all I needed to know. Playing for Charisma would be momentous and might be part of the catalyst to make that dream my brother and I had come true. Words about cancer and chemo at the library were more powerful than words in letters from England, but they *wouldn't be* if I ignored them. It was true, I didn't know how bad Dave's disease really was, but part of me had a sense of it. Judi had taught me to feel when things were wrong, so the only way around it was not to pay attention to my feelings but to rationalize my way to justify going back to England. I began to think that, even if Dave's disease was as bad as it could be, coming back and forth would be no more complicated than a long bus ride, assuming I got the gig and made the cash to do it. If I didn't pass the audition it'd all be moot and I'd just come home, so case solved. And chemo would most likely cure him (a lie I told myself), so taking off might just be okay. Also, I rationalized, because Dave knew I had plans to return to England before he got sick and knew about the letters from Colin, I figured if I didn't go he'd assume I thought he wasn't going to get better. And if I did go, he'd assume I thought the opposite. Then I created more torture thinking: If I got the gig I could send him pictures, letters, and tapes of the music I was playing and that'd be a big pick-me-up if he needed it. Via self-deceit and selfish rationalizations I had it all covered, but words can't describe how confused I was. The excuse that I didn't know then what I know now about cancer is one thing, but ignorance aside, if I had known, I would've had a whole different life than the one I do now. This life suffers indescribable remorse and shame to this very day.

In late September, just before his twenty-first birthday on the 28th, Dave had been on chemo but the effects hadn't gotten to him like they soon would. He and I, the Fling, and a few other guys were out on the tip of a jetty that juts into the Atlantic at Preston Beach in Marblehead. It was 2:30 a.m. and I had just finished gigging in Boston. We sometimes did this after a day at the office. It was weirdly warm for that time of year, and the moon was full. Dave was lotus sitting; meditating like a Buddha at the very tip, silhouetted by the moon and waves. I couldn't stop looking at him, thinking there was no way I could leave him.

As I thought this our friend came up to me and said, "Hey Beau, Dave's tripping!"

"What? That can't be true, we stopped doing that Timothy Leary shit years ago." And he said, "No, it's true!"

The thought unhinged me in every way one can be unhinged. What kind of lunatic does a thing like that knowing he has a deadly disease running through his veins? As crazy as it was, I thought, *who the fuck has the gonads to do that when they're in that condition? It's inviting a bad trip!*

It frightened, twisted, and destroyed any gyroscope or kilter I might've had. I didn't want it to be true because it didn't make sense so I sat, held my stomach, and stared at him. Finally I couldn't take it. I got up, went to him, and asked, "Are you tripping?"

He turned, smiled calmly, and said, "Yeah, but don't worry, I'll never do it again. Besides, there's worse shit flowing through my body, affecting me a lot more than tripping."

"Then why the hell are you at a time like this?" I asked.

Then the bastard did his Dave thing that only a crazy person, angel, mystic, soldier before battle, or brother can do; he asked, "What do you mean by 'a time like this'?"

When I began to melt so I could slither into the ocean like the coward I truly am, he laughed his wicked, beautiful laugh with his dilated brown eyes searing through me and said, "I'm sorry, I'm just screwing with you, I'm okay, really, don't worry. I wanted to *visit* this one last time *to check something out* and decided I'd better do it now *just in case.*"

You crazy son of a bitch, I thought. Not because he was, but who the hell has the balls "to check something out" and do it now "just in case." What the hell did that mean?

My God, I couldn't take it so I sat and 'mantra'd', my made-up word, and breathed in and out with the waves and tried to calm the hell down when finally a tiny piece of the peace of God entered me, or maybe it was my idiotic imagination. It somehow allowed me to smile a little and look at my crazy-ass brother and know there's no greater love than the one a brother has for another when they're like this before battle, with me, just behind, held in reserve. He was an American soldier at Malvern Hill, Gettysburg, and Cold Harbor just before Bob Lee and Sam Grant ordered those insane charges that achieved nothing except an enormous waste of life. A thousand historians today, with a hundred I know personally, will tell you there were rational reasons, in that most irrational of times, for those charges, and I know those reasons as well as they do. But damn, not many of those sacred truth tellers and dear friends knew their brothers' bodies were about to be torn to bits so not only did I know it, I felt it. But Dave was not only an American soldier Blue and Gray; he was an American Indian with his war paint and peyote, participating in a ritual as old as the world, preparing for death and I had no right to criticize because "the great spirit" was with him if she was ever with anyone. He wasn't the coward I am so he wouldn't run because he didn't know how. If he did, it would've bored him to death. Then it hit me, "just in case" meant he knew he could very well be in the process of dying and he didn't want to miss any of it. God help me, I couldn't stand it.

We sat in silence like a couple of frickin' Buddhas or numbskulls until he said, "Hey, maybe I was once a kamikaze. That must've been a trip and a half!"

Now I was ready to kill him. I said, "Shut the fuck up!"

He said, "No, really, if I knew *it was it* I would've dove right for where the fuel or ammo was located so I'd make the biggest bang."

"Yeah and I would've dove and chickened out at the last second to fly away in shame with a pair of Admiral Nimitz's underwear hanging from my wheels."

He laughed. "Maybe so, but think how inspirational that would've been for the Japanese Fleet to have those goddamn underwear flapping on a flagship flagpole next to the rising sun. You might've changed the course of history and written a song about flying underwear that little Japanese kids still sing today."

"That's true. I hadn't thought of that!" And I hadn't. Then I got up and went for a walk and learned for a fact that Pete Townshend was right, *"A beach is a place where a man can feel he's the only soul in the world that's real."* There was no way I was going back to England while my kamikaze brother was preparing to dive.

When I headed back to the jetty it was 4 a.m., the time Civil War generals on both sides liked to begin battles if they could. Dave watched as I approached. Before I could say a word he asked, "So, when you going back to England?"

The bastard, I thought, and then said, "Oh, I don't know, maybe not for a while or at all. I've been meeting incredible musicians here at home"—which was true—"who have the same ideas as us, so maybe I don't have to go anywhere!"

"Yeah, but nobody here is offering you session work with a major record label that might help get your songs out. You can stay here and hope you find opportunities breathing the same air as J. fucking Geils or go where you've already been invited and breathe the air of the frickin' Beatles and Stones, for Christ's sake."

I couldn't say anything for awhile. But then I said, "They're always looking for guys over there; it's no big deal!"

For three seconds he gave me his wild, incredulous, Dave look, then gently but firmly grabbed my arm and said, "If you don't go and get that session work I'll haunt you for the rest of your life!"

"I'd want you to haunt me forever!"

"Yeah but I'll be a real pain in the ass and I'll dive so hard there won't be any fucking underwear to be found!" he said.

"You suck!" I said.

"Big time!" he said.

Like someone from the famous Breckenridge and Crittenden families of Kentucky before the Civil War, we were brothers about to join opposite sides of a war within a family. For all my torment of bluff and greed, if I was sick and Dave the banjo player there'd be no way he'd leave me. It was the truest truth of all! I was joining the Rebs despite having been to the library to better understand the issues and consequences of cancer. I was abandoning what I knew to be true, that *there's nothing more important than family*. The rationalizations of a fool with the courage of a coward were my weapons when a final letter from Colin said, "You'd better come *now*, if interested." I got plane tickets for Judi and myself that very day. I'd enlisted in the Confederate Army and there was no turning back. I went for glory instead of integrity and would attain neither.

The late October day before our flight was cold, damp, and miserable when Judi and I went to say good-bye to my family. Dave and his girlfriend were in the music room in the cellar. He looked skinny, tired, and anxious but said, "Check this out, it kicks butt!" He put on the new Stones record and the first song, "If You Can't Rock Me," kicked so hard it made me want to put my fist through the wall. Dave gave a fist pump, feeling it too. It was the last ass kicker we'd ever hear together. After the song I lifted the needle, something I'd never done before with a new piece of music. I had to say good-bye now because, like Judas betraying, I had to do it quickly or I wouldn't have been able to do it at all.

"Nice hair," I said. It just slipped out and I couldn't put it back.

His girlfriend said, "See, Dave, I told you, you look okay." He had a wig on because the chemo had made his hair fall out.

He said, "I don't give a sweet shit how I look. Ma got the wig so people wouldn't freak!"

Judi said, "It really looks okay, Dave."

He said, "You Jude, I can believe. Are you guys all set?"

"Yes," she said.

"Who's got the tickets?" he asked.

She said, "I do."

"Good. Don't let your husband touch them, he might lose them," he said.

"I won't!" she said.

I asked if he wanted to go for a drive and a bite to eat but neither appealed to him. "Maybe we'll hit the road then," I said.

He asked, "Can you stay for one more song?"

"Of course!" I said.

"I've only listened to the album once but there's a song that makes me think of you," he said. So I sat on the couch and looked at the mantel piece with our weightlifting and swimming trophies, Civil War soldiers, and knickknacks that only had significance for us, and he put on something so, so very beautiful, "Time Waits For No One." It was the last song we'd ever hear together. When Mick sang, *Time waits for no one and it won't wait for me!* it was Dave singing to me. Some songs are time machines, some miracles, and some both. When I hugged him good-bye he said, "Don't forget what I told you at the beach."

THE WORST MISTAKE
OF MY LIFE

As soon as our jet lifted off American soil I knew it was a mistake. I don't remember a thing about the flight except holding Judi's hand. When we got to Heathrow Colin and Jimmy were waiting on a day as dismal as our last day in America. It must've floated over. Seeing their sweet welcoming faces made me smile. They asked if we were queasy from a turbulent flight and that told us how we looked. We went straight to Hartismere and everyone, including Jonathan, was there. They swarmed Judi with hugs and kisses and after awhile noticed I was there too.

One of the girls said, "This time we're not letting you leave."

Judi replied, "I hope not!"

Susan asked if I was okay and I said I was just a little tired. She said, "Well, I've got just the thing for a cold, rainy day!" She told us to bring our things up to our old room and, after we got settled, to come back to the kitchen.

When we came down, everyone was mulling around the old row house and she put two large bowls in front of us that were filled with steamed cauliflower, brussels sprouts, and carrots, all from her mum's garden; so sweet and delicious,

271

smothered in velvety cheese sauce with a tray of toast for sopping and a large pot of hot as hell English tea. This somehow cheered me up a bit and I leaned over to Judi and said, "It seems like we're back in old England."

She said, "It *feels* like we're home!"

After a few bites of heavenly food and our first cups of decent tea in many months, Colin said, "I'm glad you brought your own basses Beau. How's your chops?"

"Better than last year's. I've been playing a lot in the States."

"That's good mate. The audition's tomorrow afternoon."

The next morning at tea Colin had one of London's main radio stations playing quietly in the kitchen. A lot had happened since we were last together and he wanted to tell us about it. He said a month or so after Judi and I left, a singer I vaguely remembered as "Pre" (short for prima donna because that's what the guys called him after he would leave our jams) started coming all the time.

I said, "That's the guy who wore scarves, makeup, and platform shoes," which was all perfectly okay except this guy got out of bed looking that way. Well, as the guys started putting together original songs, Pre insisted on writing lyrics for one Julian and Andy had written and were planning to record as a demo. He asked/informed them he was going to sing it and that's how he invited himself to join their band. He was a good enough singer all right, but Andy was tremendous. But Andy wasn't the pushy type.

Eventually they recorded a half dozen songs with this guy singing, and when his bass player friend from Uriah Heep came back from touring he thought the songs were good enough to take to his A & R friend at Charisma Records. The record company liked the songs enough to sign the guys to do two singles and an album. As Colin was telling us this, he got up and turned up the radio because a song came on that sounded familiar. The drummer was doing things Jimmy liked to do, and when the guitar solo came on there was no mistaking it was Colin. It was their first single, a song called "Gemini." When they were signed they didn't have a band name so someone picked Greep because apparently Richard Nixon said it by mistake instead of the word "group" when he was telling yet another lie. It was reported in the British press on the day they needed to pick a name. This was all in the middle of the Watergate mess.

Colin said that even before the song was released the band began experiencing dissension—"a load of bloody rubbish" was Jimmy's description—with the overbearing singer. Somehow the wanker sided with the singer and when it got too much, the band decided to either break up and start from scratch or throw the singer and wanker out. They chose the latter just as the song got airplay. It must've been brutally painful for them because none of them liked turmoil. They just wanted to play music while Pre and the wanker were more interested in being rock stars. I neither knew nor wanted to know the sordid details but I trusted everything Colin said to be true and found out later, it was. For these humble guys, having a record contract was not all it was cracked up to be. Judi and I had arrived just as their single began getting substantial airplay, which would've been a dream come true for anyone, but instead was a "load of bloody rubbish."

The record company was ready to shoot them because of all the money they'd invested. But they agreed to give them another chance by supporting the band in a British tour that'd already been announced to start in March, though only after the guys' manager, Dafford, convinced Charisma to let the guys try to find a new bass player and let Andy sing lead. The reason the tour was so far away was because the band was supposed to already be on tour in Holland, Germany, France, Italy, and Australia, to come home hot as hell to tour on home turf. The "rubbish"—no one says that word better than an Englishman—canceled all that. I felt so bad for the guys because only Julian had been out of the country and I knew they would've loved to have seen more of the world.

After hearing this sad story, Judi and I returned to our room to digest it. I said I wasn't sure I should go through with the audition because if I got the gig it'd be more than session work for Charisma, it'd be a commitment to my

Hartismere Confederates and touring would make it difficult to go back and forth to the States to see Dave.

She saw my confusion and in her motherly way said, "Why don't *we* take it one step at a time and do the audition anyway, because you might not get the gig. As Colin said, none of the guys will be involved in the decision; it will be up to the record company. If you don't get it, we'll just go home. But if you do, things could turn out differently than you think and they might have a solution for us to see Dave."

"I don't think that would be the case, Jude, but either way, I don't want them to know about Dave. They have enough, 'crap'"—no one says that word better than an American—"on their plates. But you're right, we came a long way so I'll do the audition and we'll see what happens."

That afternoon Judi went out with the girls and I found myself in a studio with the guys, another bass player who'd already auditioned but was asked back for a second look, Dafford, whom I hadn't met, and the producer from Charisma who'd produced their single. The other bass player was the nicest guy. He said it was down to me and him and at least he could say he beat out sixteen other bass players that'd already auditioned. The process was simple. We'd go in one at time and listen to a recorded song, then play it with the band. Supposedly it'd be a song we'd never heard. He went in first and Steely Dan's "My Old School" came on. It didn't seem like he was familiar with it but he picked it up extremely well. Then the band played one of their songs and he played along. I could hear the rumble and thought he'd be a great fit for the guys. After thirty minutes he came out, wished me luck and said, "They're great blokes!"

"I know!" I said.

As soon as I went in the same Steely Dan song started blasting, which didn't seem fair because I jammed it with the guys the year before. When it was over I tried to tell the producer to play another song so the competition would be fair but before I could get a word out Jimmy yelled, "Beau!" When I turned around he started the count and we were off and running, playing "My

Old School." Jimmy and I did a funky little triplet at the perfect time during the staccato part and it made us laugh like we'd just played it the day before. When the song got to the end we didn't stop but morphed into a jam, and I saw Dafford and the producer laughing like coaches in a dugout when someone drives in a run in the 9th. Dafford came out, shook my hand, and said, "The gig's yours, Cowboy, if you want it. *What say you?*"

In my euphoria I was lost to the reality of this world, as I am when I play music, and I said, "I'll take it!" The guys hugged and congratulated me but I could see the other bass player packing to leave. He was deeply disappointed but so very gracious with a handshake. Seeing his expression made me sad even though I knew this was the nature of things.

It's hard to describe the sound of any band but in my opinion we were a bit like a cross between Steely Dan and The Average White Band (without brass), but with a heavier sound from my harder rock influence. Somehow it worked. Nothing was contrived and when we played we were happy. I thought their song "Gemini" was very catchy, though a little tame, and attributed that to Pre and the wanker. Still, it was pro and to have it played on London radio during the day impressed the hell out of me. With me joining and the other two gone, the sound changed threefold in a natural, unforced way. Maybe it's why, when the producer came out holding a tape of the audition, he shook my hand and said, "This is special!" He was going to play it for the president of Charisma that evening and then get back to Dafford. But, as far as he was concerned, I was "their guy." On the way home I asked Colin and Jimmy whose idea it was to play the Steely Dan tune and they giggled in cockney, "'aven't a clue, mate." All along the fix had been in and even though they were devious about it, it made me happy to know they really wanted me. Being in a band can be a soap opera full of jealousy and pretension or be a beautiful band of Rebels where all is for one and one is for all. We were the latter and I loved them dearly.

That night, Dafford came to the house after meeting with the record company and explained that on the producer's recommendation they'd finance the British tour with me playing the role of a hired gun bass player. And if I agreed to a temporary contract where I'd be considered a session player, at the end of the tour, if all went well, I'd be offered another contract to officially join the band. He said he had to know right away and then went downstairs to have a cup of tea so I could decide. Judi said the scenario might be perfect because at the end of the tour we could go home to see Dave. Then she brought Colin to our room and I asked him what he thought and he said, "That's how I thought it would go, Beau. We're all happy about it. We've been through the mill and haven't been able to enjoy a bloody thing. Charisma wanted to dump us and who could blame them? They've invested thousands of pounds in us but 'Gemini' going over so well makes them reluctant to let us go. The tour will pay back some of the money. Then we'll make another record with you and nothing will stop us!"

So that was it. Judi asked Dafford to come back to our room and I signed the contract. He said this would make it easy to get a work visa so I'd be legit in every way. Then he hugged and thanked me and out of the blue handed me 60 pounds in cash, about $150 at the time, and said every week I'd get a stipend from the record company for that amount. This floored us. It may not sound like a lot, but back then, combined with the spartan way we lived, we suddenly felt rich. Later we found out this was precisely what the band got and they insisted I get the same. I told Dafford I felt like I was getting paid to be alive and I'll never forget what he said. "You are!" Immediately we wrote home with the news.

This opened up a whole new world for us and we had a weekend of celebration. Julian was from a wealthy family that owned an estate outside Oxford, and he invited us to an extraordinary dinner in our honor. Their large, luxurious, seventeenth-century thatched roof home was situated on a hill with a perfectly groomed lawn and English garden. The only thing missing was a moat. At dinner Judi and I thought we were in a movie because they had a maid and a butler, and some of his parents' elderly relatives and friends dined with us. It was quite a contrast from the year before when the other guys had brought us home. Some of the houses in their neighborhoods still had outhouses in the backyards. I was uncomfortable at the table because I didn't know which fork to use, but somehow Judi did so I followed her lead. An elderly couple sat across from us and the lady looked like Margaret Thatcher, only older. You could tell she was born with the silver spoon and wanted to talk American politics after having several tall glasses of wine, saying how "appalling and shameful" it was that the American press, "a horde of hooligans," were going after "poor Mr. Nixon." Judi gave me a gentle kick under the table which meant "Keep quiet, I'll handle this," and then proceeded to charm the crap out of the misinformed aristocrat. "Oh you're such a charming young woman *for an American,*" the windy one said. And I got another kick.

We started with pheasant soup and when I took a courtesy sip I couldn't believe how good it was. I haven't had it since but would in a second. Then "Margaret" went on a spiel about how upset she was that "youthful homosexuals" had stolen one of her favorite words, "gay," as if it belonged to her personally, and how she wanted to "take it back." Judi, not missing a beat, said, "Maybe we'll just have to steal one of their favorite words and we can negotiate."

"Oh marvelous, my dear. Would you be our negotiator?"

Judi said, "But of course, I'd consider it an honor!" and I couldn't help but smile.

After dinner Julian and I went outside and he said, "Sorry about my aunt, Beau." We laughed like blokes in a band. Then he took me to his family's musical library, which matched the one my family had in Dave's room. Where our parents contributed classical albums, Julian's contributed American and European jazz and show tunes. He then handed me a book with a man at a piano on the cover. The man looked familiar. He identified him as "our Jimmy's father." Jim's dad had been a jazz pianist in the 1930s and 1940s and he died from wounds, a gift from Hitler that eventually caught up to him just before his son was born in the early 1950s. Julian said Jim's dad was a famous musician in England and the book was written by someone who thought he shouldn't be forgotten. It affected me deeply because I couldn't imagine growing up without a mother or father. It brought home how close the war really was to my sweet English brethren; mentally and physically, and how the cause of all the suffering came from across a small channel of water my ancestors and brother could swim. The war was initiated by a madman; the biggest proponent of slavery in our parents' and grandparents' generation. Its sad aftermath was all around me and it made my love for Jimmy and hate for slavery all the more real.

That night Judi and I slept in a luxurious room at the estate. The next day the band arrived with a photographer from the record company. We went to the countryside for publicity photos but ended up using one taken in an alley behind the guest house. Two days later we were in the London music papers with a caption indicating that Greep was continuing with Andy Winfield taking over lead vocals and a new American bass player, Bea*n* Foster. It was a typo that Judi thought was so funny. She called me her "Little Bean" for a few days. I said it was her fault, because spelling my name Bea*u* instead of Bo was her idea and this made her laugh all the more. It was spelled correctly in the accompanying article and, thankfully, "Bean" never caught on. I sent a copy of the band picture to Dave. Today, it hangs next to a wedding picture taken just after Judi and I cut the cake. It's right above a picture of Abraham Lincoln.

For the next few days things were quiet. Dafford had to find new rehearsal space because Hartismere was too small for the equipment the record company bought for the band and the studio where the audition had been held had already been booked. Space in London was not always easy to find, even for a successful band. In the meantime, I met "Whittle and Steve," the roadies who set up the equipment, kept the truck running, and did too many indispensable things to mention. It was so cool that they'd also worked for Traffic on occasion. I asked if they'd been at the Tea Party when Traffic played Boston, and they remembered that "a baseball team" (the Red Sox) were playing across the street. The fact that they were there when Dave and I were made the world feel smaller. Now they were on Charisma's payroll doing what Dave and the Fling did for bands back home. And like all great roadies, they could fix just about anything with duct tape.

A week later we received letters from home telling us how proud everyone was, but one letter to Judi from Dave's girlfriend said Dave was rapidly losing weight and feeling like crap. It put a corkscrew chill down my spine, but I persuaded myself that as soon as the chemo treatments were over his hair and appetite would return. I was lying to myself and somewhere deep down, I *chose* to believe what I couldn't escape in my sleep.

When Dafford found rehearsal space we finally had a chance to play. For two solid days they showed me songs they'd written with Pre. I'm a slow learner anyway, so trying to absorb twenty songs made my head spin, but things were gelling. Late on the second day, Andy, the most soft-spoken, asked, "Why are we trying so bloody hard to sound like Pre and the wanker are still with us? We sound so much better now and these songs have their smell all over them. We can do better and should be true to ourselves." I wholeheartedly agreed but said nothing.

Jimmy said, "Let's go eat some grease and figure things out over a gallon of tea." I said I'd go for a walk so they could talk things over, but Andy said, "No, Beau, we need your opinion!"

I said, "I'm not in the band and you guys know what you're talking about more than I do!"

Jimmy said, "Beau you're in the bleeding band no matter what a piece of paper says."

We went to one of those glorious little shops that smell of bangers (sausages), bacon, fried potatoes, and onions and had a meeting "over a gallon of tea." Boldly, they decided that, because the tour wasn't starting until March, if they started at that moment, it being November, that by breaking their "bloody arses," they might just have time to write a new batch of songs by January. I was stunned. Their "audacity" had an absolutely Robert E. Lee feel to it. It was a huge gamble that took tremendous courage. They'd risk all to sink or swim on their terms, and my admiration for my fellow Confederates went through the roof. We had another day of rehearsal space so we decided to have fun and let it rip. This set the tone for them to start their quest for the summit of songwriting Everest. When we played "Gemini," the only song we had to keep, or so we thought, we rocked it like it'd never been rocked. Later that day the producer from Charisma came by to listen and was all smiles. Julian told him this would be our last rehearsal for a month because he and Andy were "going into the bunker" and wouldn't come out till they had twenty new songs. He couldn't believe it, but said that when we played to our full potential we smoked, so we had his blessing. He was supposed to report everything to the record company but I got the feeling he'd keep as much as he could close to his vest.

This aggressive plan of attack gave me time to write letters and do a dozen or so gigs at my old haunts with Stephen Clarke. A few people recognized me from the papers and some remembered me from the year before. I heard the old refrain, "Hey, Beau, I didn't know you played bass." Stephen said I didn't realize how big a splash "Gemini" had made in England. I reminded him I was no part of it. "But you are now, mate!" he said, and it started to sink in a little. By the third week of December the guys had about sixteen songs, and Colin wrote a couple, too. When he took me and Judi home to have Christmas with his mum and little brother, he played me his songs. They were excellent. He asked if I'd been writing and I said, "I'm always writing!" So he asked me to play something. He hadn't heard me since the session with Jonathan and the time he saw me at a pub gig the year before. I sat at his mother's short octave spinet piano and played a half dozen songs straight through. His mum came in from the kitchen to listen, reminding me of mine doing the same. I ended with a song I'd written that week at Hartismere, and it made Colin's mother emotional. "My Way Home" was about Dave.

The letter from Dave's girlfriend was breaking me to bits. The first verses sang, *"I wish that I could find my way back home. And if I get there will the people I see, see me? Or will they see the broken man inside of me?"* Colin said, "Christ Beau, that's beautiful. Can we show the band?" and I said, "Sure." After a wonderful Christmas dinner, plum pudding and all, Colin and I went to his room where I played more songs on an acoustic. He said, "Beau, I love your bass playing but your writing is from another planet. Can we let the guys hear these too?"

The next day, Andy and Julian played us the new material and it was spectacular. I couldn't believe the feat they'd pulled off. They were exhausted but exhilarated Rebels. The music had elements of their old stuff with none of the weaknesses. It was catchier and beefier and I loved it. We began rehearsing immediately. By December 28 things started to cook. On the 29th we went into the coolest little four-track studio to make a live recording so we'd each have a cassette to listen to so we could pick the songs apart. Not much picking was necessary, but the tapes showed where we were and helped us become more intimate with the material. I'd gotten one song mixed up with another a couple of times, but "the feel" was awesome. The tapes were for no one's ears, but I sent a copy to Dave so he could hear what his big brother was up to. Years later, I learned he was so proud that he played it for everyone, while explaining, "Mind you, this is only a rehearsal!" The thought gives me a lump in my throat!

On December 30, Jimmy and Colin casually mentioned that we had a gig the next night. I asked where and Jimmy said, "Not far down the road. It's a New Year's Eve charity event. It'll be a blast." I thought they were kidding, but Jimmy said they'd played it the previous year and a lot of musicians were there.

"Like who?" I asked.

He said people like the guys from The Faces (Rod Stewart's band).

I said, "I'll be a nervous wreck; I don't feel ready to play in front of people like that yet."

Jimmy laughed. "If bloody Rod Stewart shows up there's no need to worry, mate. It's just a party; no one important will be there. We'll just jam so people can dance. There's a band going on before us and by the time we go on everyone will be half pissed. Think of it as our first stage rehearsal."

I thought, *No one important will be there; who's he kidding?* To me, if Rod Stewart showed that'd be important! So I asked, "Well what if Steely Dan, Tower Of Power, The Doobie Brothers, or any American band you admire showed up, wouldn't you be nervous?"

He said, "Of course! I'd probably shit me-self!" and this made me laugh.

The next night Judi, the guys, the girls, and I arrived at a huge dance hall where people had on wild costumes with the occasional female breast popping out to say hello, which only surprised me and Judi a little. We were getting used to it because this was Europe where bare breasts were even on daytime soap operas and nobody seemed to care. "They're only boobs, mate." And what a contrast we were walking in. Without realizing it, I was a bad influence on the guys. They thought I looked cool in my American jeans and casual shirts and were starting to dress like me. It's so ironic, because to this day everyone who knows me knows I don't have a clue how to dress for anything. And this was when The Stones were wearing globs of makeup and sparkle and David Bowie looked like an androgynous alien from outer space while we looked like a Seattle grunge band from twenty-five years in the future because that's all I had for clothes. To top it off, our record company tolerated the way we looked so by accident, we adopted it.

There was a smoking blues band already playing, and our gear was set up behind them looking so cool. I've always loved looking at gear before a show. Andy could tell I was nervous and said, "As far as I know, no one from our record company will be here, Beau. Dafford asked us to do the gig because we did it last year and they wanted us back, so we'll just have some fun." This somehow took my worries away, and listening to the other band got my competitive juices flowing. I said to Judi, "I think I'm gonna kick some butt!"

Backstage I asked Colin if he thought Rod Stewart would show.

He said, "I don't know, he might've last year, I can't remember."

Then I looked through the curtains and thought I saw Ronnie Lane (bass) and Ian McLagan (piano) of The Faces and maybe Cozy Powell, the great drummer who played with Stewart in The Jeff Beck Group. Next thing I knew, we were being announced to a great ovation. Halfway through the first song I had an epiphany: *Just do what you always do no matter where it is, because that's what the guys are doing.* I loosened up and saw Judi give me the 1-4-3, "I love you!" sign.

And not to brag, but she was the coolest dancer on the floor. Every guy and several girls wanted to dance with her. She had such cool grace with absolutely no goofy movements; more classy than sexy, but very sexy too. We played till the wee hours, extending songs into jams so people could dance. Between songs someone yelled, "You groove like an American band!" It was a great night and broke a lot of ice for me despite Rod Stewart not showing. Having Judi with me, though, was the best part of the evening, and after the show we walked home in the cool night air. We weren't far from home and felt safe. People weren't in love with guns like some in the States. Police didn't even carry them, and we never got used to that. London wasn't crime-free of course, we just felt safe as I brought home the prettiest girl at the dance.

A couple of days later we took our morning walk to the open market food stands down by Fulham Road. On our way back we passed a cute little knick-knack shop we must've passed a hundred times and Judi wanted to go in. It was the coziest place with all kinds of arts and crafts. A little old lady said, "I made most of it myself!" and Judi said, "I love this place!" The lady said she'd been there for many years but was "closing shop" because she was getting too old and couldn't find anyone to run it. Judi blurted out, "I can run it!" The lady immediately trusted her and within ten minutes the deal was sealed. Judi would run the place from 9 to 5 Wednesday through Sunday but could close up whenever she wanted because the lady lived upstairs and could take over. I know how improbable this sounds, but that's how Judi affected people. You had to see it to believe it, and I saw it all the time.

On the way home I asked why she wanted to do that and she said, "Well, I have to do something while you're in Devon in a couple of weeks for two weeks of rehearsals."

I asked, "Who told you that?"

She laughed. "Dafford! He tells us girls everything. We know more about what's going on than you guys do. He's booked a place far from everything where you can concentrate on the music. It's on a farm that Yes, Ten Years After, Jeff Beck, and other bands use when they want to get away from it all. The record company's paying for everything, even a cook."

It made sense and would give us time to work out the little kinks some of the songs might have. The thought of being on an isolated farm far from everything sounded great, but I hated the thought of going without Judi, and told her so.

She said, "Me too, but now we'll both be busy!"

"I could ask Dafford if you could come with us."

"He already said I could, but I'm staying in London because I have a job now and can't quit before I start. Plus, I have plans with the girls, so don't worry about me!" There was no doubt she wanted to go but she also wanted me to concentrate on my job because it was that job that had brought us into each other's lives in the first place.

We had no surprise gigs for the next two weeks so we unplugged and rehearsed at Hartismere with acoustics, Julian's soft Fender Rhodes piano, and Jimmy, the little beatnik, on bongos. Like natives around a campfire it helped tighten up some loose ends and we knew playing amplified in Devon would be the icing on the cake. When we broke for lunch, I'd walk down to see Judi at *her* shop. During one break the guys wanted to see her so we walked together. I felt a little like a rock star or rather someone walking with some (silly, I know), because a few cars beeped and waved but Jimmy said they were just flipping us the bird. At the shop the guys bought scarves and things they later hung from microphones and amps wherever we played. It was so cool! Judi had the place buzzing. We watched her make a sale, saying to a customer, "I can let it go for a little less if you get this to go with it!" I smiled and thought, *Not only is my wife the coolest person in the world but she can be one hell of a goofball too!*

It was about a two-hour drive to Devon and on a whim I asked Whittle and Steve if I could drive with them in the equipment truck. I wanted to hear rock 'n' roll stories. They said, "You can always go with us, mate!" So Dafford and the guys went in the van and I went with two of the funniest roadies on the planet. From the get-go they had me almost peeing in my pants with stories and so many horrible sheep jokes, none of which I can repeat. Going through that part of wool country we saw thousands and each flock brought a new herd of jokes. The landscape was breathtaking. Devon is part of the peninsula at the bottom southwestern corner of the old isle that juts westward into the Atlantic as if reaching for America or, at other times in British history, to poke it away.

When we pulled into the courtyard of Langley Farm I thought I'd died and gone to heaven. It was a working farm with a rehearsal room attached to the main house. Each had a thatched roof, as did the barn and another small house across a cobble-stoned courtyard, where the farmer and his wife stayed when bands were there. The band Ace—they did that song "How Long Has This Been Going On?"—left that morning, and now it was our turn. The place was built with stone in the seventeenth-century. Inside, the walls and low ceilings were whitewashed plaster with wooden beams. The farmer told us to watch our heads on one particular beam because Rick Wakeman, Yes's keyboard player, bumped his head on it, but none of us were that tall. The rehearsal room was just big enough for us to stretch but no more. The farm's remoteness, in a valley that absorbed sound, meant we could make as much noise as we wanted 24/7 and there'd be no one to disturb except a cow poking her head in the window to moo a critique, "Hey, you guys can play the middle section better than that!" This was a place I needed Judi to see.

Toward the end of the first week of incredible rehearsals Dafford came back and I asked if it would be okay to invite Judi down for the weekend. He said, "Of course, Beau, and you'll have the place to yourselves. Jimmy and Colin have a wedding to attend and Andy and Julian would just as soon go home. We'll be back Monday." I didn't know this and thought, *Holy South Devon cow, Batman.*

If Judi came, we'd have this fairytale place to ourselves, except for the farmer and his wife who we'd hardly see. I called the shop and when Judi asked the owner if she could go I heard, "You'd better go lass, my husband and I honeymooned in Devon. There's no place like it!" So on Friday afternoon, after a great morning rehearsal, Judi got off the train where I was waiting. We took a taxi through rambling hills and fields between high and low hedgerows, passing a road sign identifying it as Black Dog which was the title of a Led Zeppelin song. It made me wonder. When we pulled into the courtyard and got out she spun around, "Oh my God, sweetheart, thank you for bringing me here!"

"Thank you for coming!"

She threw her arms around me, told me she loved me, and asked where the guys were.

I said, "We're it!" Somehow Dafford and I kept it a secret. We then entered through the centuries-old threshold to our new home. I had peat that the farmer had supplied from a bog down the road burning in the fireplace, and a kettle of tea ready to heat with fresh cream courtesy of my new musical cow critic friend. The place seemed to absorb Judi, and she it. She was more at home than I was and I was never so at home in my life. After tea I showed her around as if I owned the place, introducing her to all my new animal friends. Then we had a light supper of scrambled eggs and toast. After, we took hot baths, and then sat by the fire with wine and the flame making shadows on the walls, half expecting Snow White and the Seven Dwarfs to come trouncing in.

I told her how well rehearsals were going and how amazing I found it being so far from home, taking a bath in a tub famous musicians like Jeff Beck had taken one in.

She said, "That's why I let you take the first one!" which made us laugh. I'm so goofy like that. To this day I get a thrill looking at things like the boots Joshua Chamberlain wore at Gettysburg when I see them at Bowdoin College in Maine. Or Lincoln's pocket knife in the Lincoln museum in Fort Wayne, Indiana, or his boots and long coat from the night a lunatic shot him, in the neat little museum under Ford's Theater in Washington, or Stonewall Jackson's stuffed horse, Little Sorrel, next to the black rubber Yankee coat he (not Sorrel) was wearing when he got shot.

When it got late there was still light outside from the latitude of earth we were on. Ocean currents from the south that keep England and Ireland milder than New England, even though they're farther north, were more tepid than usual this winter so we never saw snow. I took Judi to the window next to the fireplace and held her from behind to point out a small mountain, large hill, rim of the valley, or whatever it was, that'd beckoned me to climb it since I first saw it. I asked, "Isn't it beautiful?"

She read my mind and said, "We should climb it in the morning!" We loved climbing the White Mountains of New Hampshire with Dave and his girlfriend, so this appealed to us very much.

It's probably silly qualifying things this way, but if I had to pick the best day of my life, to that point anyway, we woke on it the next morning. The weather was dreary but, like in Ireland, it can change in an instant, so after a breakfast of tea, toast, and oranges we embarked on an ancient path with short slate walls on either side, made just for us, meandering back and forth up the valley wall. As the sky cleared the view got more spectacular with each elevation. When we reached the top we discovered the path continued on a plateau till it dropped out of sight. We were encased in blue so brilliant I understood why John Lennon sang of watching "The English Sky." From the shade of color reflecting over it, we could tell what direction the ocean was in. Silently, in awe of the beauty, I pointed west. "Dave is that way!"

Before she could reply a voice from behind us said, "Beautiful day to be alive!" We turned to see an elderly, leathery, little man in homespun woolen clothes and cap, who looked like he'd sprung from the soil. "Yes it is!" I said and was about to apologize for possibly trespassing on his land when he looked at Judi and smiled an ancient smile. "She's too pretty to have you for a husband or boyfriend, maybe your sister or cousin then?"

"Everyone says that!" I said.

"Don't flatter yourself, me boy" he scolded, followed by, "So what is it then?"

I said, "She's my wife!"

Then he got face-scrunchingly serious. "I don't believe you; she could do *soooo* much better!"

Judi laughed. "Unfortunately, my husband believes that too!"

This made him laugh so already they were in cahoots. "So we're a couple of Yanks up from Langley, musicians I suppose?"

Judi said, "He's the musician, I'm a fan."

"So he has one then? Well at least she's pretty. Does he play songs you like?" he asked.

Judi laughed. "He does, and takes requests too."

"I see, so you have him trained, that's good, very good! Keep it that way and things will be all right!"

We introduced ourselves, saying we were from Lynn, Massachusetts.

He said, "My name is Liam but you can call me Liam. Isn't Massachusetts the only state in *your union* that didn't vote for that *royal pillar of honesty* Richard Nixon?" He then laughed like the leprechaun he might've been. Now I was in cahoots and willingly under his spell. I laughed and said, "That's right! And a lot of states regret their decision. Massachusetts doesn't always vote for a winner but when they do they almost always turn out to be a decent president!"

"Ahhh so we're a bit of a historian, are we? It fascinates me, in general terms, that more musicians, historians, philosophers, scientists, and writers lean liberal than not. I sometimes wonder if that's because of their creativity, curiosity, or both. I me-self prefer a liberal bowl of pudding to a conservative one," he said and laughed.

Then I might've given him more of a reply than he wanted, but his theory excited me. "Well, I hope that's why! The more I learn the more I lean liberal and probably too much for my own good. But every time I try seeing things from a conservative bowl I'm disappointed and hungry because conservative presidents like Pierce, Buchanan, Harding, Hoover, and as you say, Nixon, to name a few, seemed to care more about the rich who don't need help. Somehow I want to participate when I think of liberal ones like Franklin Roosevelt, Truman, and Kennedy because they tried to help the downtrodden. My favorite president, Lincoln, called this difference, 'the divine rights of kings as opposed to those of common man.' And, like Roosevelt and Truman, he knew how to fight and win a war."

Liam laughed hard. "Speaking of, we appreciated your help in the last one! You mentioned presidents I don't know but my Jane would've. She taught history and would've enjoyed talking to you." Then he blew me away. "As for helping the 'downtrodden,' I wouldn't mind having a cup of tea with Lincoln. I'm almost old enough to have. My Jane had her students read *Uncle Tom's Cabin* so I did too and was deeply moved, as was Lincoln. And if I understand correctly, he never left *his* country but reading helped him know universal truths of compassion."

I said, "That's right! Sadly he was talking about visiting foreign lands just days before a man opposed to those truths killed him."

"What a shame!" Liam said.

I then asked if he'd ever been to America. He said, "Never thought of it. They say it's a great place."

"The greatest!" I said.

He said, "I feel that about this country!"

"And you're right too!" We learned his farm of many generations was just over the ridge and he took this walk every day, and as far as he was concerned, "There's no prettier place in the world."

Judi said, "There isn't!"

Then he said, "Hang on to her, she's your better half!"

"You mean ninety percent," I said.

He laughed. "I was attempting to be kind."

He then pointed to a spot on the edge of the ridge. "If you sit real close, there's a pocket with room for two. When the wind shifts you can smell the Atlantic.

My Jane and I sat there." Then, as quickly as he appeared, he turned for home. "Goodbye, Liam." His weathered hand rose and the earth gently swallowed him like *"castles made of sand, melt into the sea, eventually"* that Jimi Hendrix sang of.

It was so beautiful above the valley of fields and farms separated by ancient rock walls. Each patchwork a different shade of the richest green as far as the eye could see to the unseen ocean. I'd never been to a more beautiful place unless it was in the fall of New England's woods. We were in awe and talked about how lucky we were to be alive and luckier still to have found each other. I told her that when I was little my mom said I'd meet a little blond girl someday and live happily ever after because I was her little blond boy and mothers knew of such things. And that we'd have little blond children.

She said, "Yeah, I know!"

I asked, "How'd you know that?"

"Your mother told me!" she said.

"When did she tell you?"

"Oh, not long after we started dating," she said.

Incredulous, I asked, "Oooohhh yeah, how long?"

She said, "Oh, I don't know, maybe after the first date." Then she threw herself back on the blanket of grass in Liam and his Lady Jane's pocket of the world and laughed like a little girl. "You were putty in our hands, so easily led, and your mother said your father was the same way. You didn't have a prayer in the world." We laughed till our faces hurt.

I'd never been so happy. We talked about what we'd name our children and the kind of parents we'd be. We promised each other we'd raise our children to be citizens of the world and teach them that even though America truly is "The Last Best Hope Of Earth," it's not the only place with goodwill and a generous spirit; that, no matter what a person's skin color, religion, nationality, or social status, *all* have equal value as a human being. Then I said, "Jude, let's vow our children will see a view like this, even if something should happen to one of us."

She said, "Absolutely, but don't be so morbid. I'll never let anything happen to you and nothing's going to happen to me!"

"Is that a promise?" I asked.

"It is!" she said. (To that vow; when our daughter graduated from college in 1997 she and I rented a car for eleven days and drove where the wind took us up and down the west coast of Ireland to see scenes like the one her mother and I saw from Liam and Jane's pocket above the valley.) Then we sat in the most beautiful silence there is, that's found between the notes of music you can only *feel* when you're with someone you love.

The next day we got up early and walked to a little village and had a joyous time. When we got home it was time to call a taxi to take her to the train station. Before she left she said, "I hope you don't mind honey, this came in the mail right before I left London. It's from Dave. This place made me forget to give it to you when I got here. I hope that's okay?"

I said, "It's actually a good thing. Writing back will give me something to do tonight. This place won't be the same without you, but we'll be busy getting ready for some gigs in London that Dafford set up before the tour starts."

She said, "Yes, sweetheart, I know."

I said, "Oh yeah, of course you do."

When she disappeared into the landscape I went in, made a cup of tea, sat by the fire, and opened Dave's letter. The writing was a little shaky. He wrote, "I wish I could swim over to see you. I could use a good long one but this cancer crap has me tied up. I keep playing your rehearsal tape, it's awesome! I can't imagine how great the album will be. Now I won't have to haunt you (ha, ha). Everyone is doing the same as when you left except I won't be swimming for UConn this year because some shit spread to my lungs so I get winded easily. Other than that, everything's fine. Say hi to Jude and tell her I'm okay. Keep up the good work! Dave."

Did he really write "other than that?" Did he have to use the word "spread" in the same way Lincoln did when he said cancer and slavery were the same thing, and the only way it could kill the nation would be to allow it to "spread." Did he have to use it like that? Of course he did, otherwise he wouldn't have been Dave. I wanted so, so, so desperately to feel him physically like I felt him when I was in his arms in the pool, when he said, "This is your life and you can't screw around with it!" If Judi had known what was in the letter she wouldn't have left me. I needed her, someone, something, or some God to hold onto because I was as isolated as if I were on *the dark side of the moon.*

I must've sat for a long time. It was light out when she left, now it was dark and my tea was cold. I got up and staggered outside to hear an owl. "Whoooo are you to abandon your brother to chase silly dreams?" Before I knew, I was kneeling on the barn floor next to my musical cow friend as she chewed a piece of straw. I needed my hand on someone with life in their veins. It didn't matter if they were human. Her warm blood somehow reconnected me to myself but only partially; some connections were severed forever. I wept uncontrollably while my friend kept on chewing.

A World
Where God Cries

Before the sun woke the valley, I went back to the house. The guys would soon be arriving, all full of piss and vinegar, and rightly so. They knew if they didn't screw up they were on the precipice of rewarding careers and exciting lives. I tried to sleep but could only think of what I'd learned about cancer at the library back home. I asked myself over and over what kind of person gathers the best information available and then ignores it if it interferes with his ambitious narcissist agenda. The answers were a coward, fool, or worse, an aristocrat! I was blessed to have a history teacher for a mother so there wasn't much chance of me becoming an aristocrat, but no mother can prevent her son from becoming a fool when ambition blinds him. Guilt began tearing me to bits. I felt like a driver in a hit-and-run death and the weight was suffocating me. I wanted to turn myself in, but to whom? I'd ignored the facts of the slavery of cancer just like Confederate slave-owners did and I was so ashamed, and still am.

All of these thoughts were going through my head as Jimmy walked in. "What happened to you, mate? You look like you slept in the barn."

293

Soon we were rehearsing and the music made me feel better. During a song I thought, *Hey, maybe the cancer was already in Dave's lungs and the X-rays missed it and the chemo will make it go away.* I was aware my pessimistic nature had always made me worry needlessly but at *Langley* I was really lying to myself about *the true nature of things.* I was a mess, yet, by midweek, the band felt ready to hit the road. Julian and Andy arranged the songs in a very cool concert set list, and we ran through it several times each morning and jammed in the afternoon. As beyond distracted as I was, I thought we sounded hot as hell. The guys kept asking if I was all right and I lied and said "yes." After supper we relaxed and watched *Monty Python* and other ridiculously wonderful, silly and funny shows. When news from America came on, it somehow made me feel close to Dave. The guys got a big kick out of my intense interest in the Watergate fiasco, which was big news there too. "Americans know Nixon's lying, right Beau?"

On our last night there I was extra quiet, sitting by the fire in a ball of self-loathing knots for abandoning my brother when Colin asked, "Beau, can you play us the songs you played at my mum's on Christmas?" I didn't feel like it but Andy said, "Yeah Beau, Colin said you have some great songs. Don't feel like you're imposing, we're asking. The more material we have the better. Julian and I 'shot our wad' for awhile writing the album, and we'll need more for the second." This made me laugh a little so I got my acoustic and serenaded my sweet, generous Confederates for half an hour. Halfway through Julian asked, "Beau, why are you playing bass instead of just writing?"

I said, "I love playing bass and you guys needed a bass player when the wanker didn't show so I jumped in!" and they laughed. Then I played "Blue Is Just A Word," a song I wrote in Saugus a week after my new bride and I got home from England the year before. As always my acoustic was next to our bed and when I woke with *the feeling* I asked Judi to push "record" on the cassette player. "I think something good might come out." I thought, *Thank God the tape's rolling!* Some songs arrive with great effort, but every now and then one slips out and you wonder, *Where the hell did that come from?* Andy said, "Bloody hell, that's got to go on the first album." Then Colin asked me to play some piano songs so we marched to the rehearsal room. When I played "My Way Home," Julian said, "That's got to go on the album too!"

In bed that night I thought, *Wait till Dave hears about this!* but my annoying mind that always analyzes things to death kept wondering why, if Dave didn't want me to worry, did he tell me what he did in his letter? Then it hit me. *I* was the only one he could talk to the way he *needed* and felt free to because everyone else got the crap scared out of them by his intense honesty. He never lied to himself like people with their heads in the sand or up their "bloody arses" or wherever they put their minds to protect self-serving superstitions. If you gave him a chance, and took a genuine leap of faith to see how he came to what he came to, it was the most liberating experience and sacred privilege. And I was the luckiest of all to be trusted in the way only a brother can be trusted. He wrote what he did because there was no one else he could say those things to and I wanted to go home to him so bad it hurt!

Returning to London and Judi brought some comfort, but the guys kept asking if I was okay. I said I was just a little homesick. They said after the tour I should go home for a week and that cheered me up a bit. I let Judi read Dave's letter and, though she still didn't know much about cancer, sadness grew on her face and she said the worst possible thing: "This doesn't *feel* good!" It was a knife to my heart! But in my lying mind, I kept hoping a letter would arrive saying, "Good news, the chemo's finally kicked in. I'm feeling better and went for a swim today." But that letter never came! The music kept me moving though, which was Satchel Paige's sage advice "when something is gaining on you!"

The most important gig before the tour started was the first one in London because the president of Charisma Records would be there. He'd never seen the new lineup because everything was done through Dafford and the producer of "Gemini." I spotted him from backstage and thought he looked like what a powerful music mogul should look like. He was a big, heavyset man with jet-black hair, probably in his late forties. He wore the coolest, tannish, three-piece suit and he oozed confidence. To top it off he actually smoked a big fat cigar like the band Boston would later sing about. Either he'd come from an important meeting or was impeccably dressed because seeing us was a big deal. I heard people calling him "Stratt," which was a nickname for Tony Stratton, if I recall correctly. As I looked at him Jimmy said, "That's the big guy. I've never spoken to him because Dafford handles the rubbish." That somehow put me at ease for a second.

But this wasn't any old gig. It was a real concert in a jam-packed, smoky London club. The guys were anxious but I, a kid from Lynn, Massachusetts, was nervous as hell. Every gig I ever did, even if it was playing air guitar in front of my steamy bathroom mirror when I was ten was a prelude to this. But the guys were pros, and London being their home turf made their ridiculous, casual, outrageous humor calm me a little. Just before we went on I said, "I'd feel better if a frickin' Langley cow mooed her head in the window," and they started mooing as we were announced. When we walked on stage they were still mooing and people in the front rows started laughing and mooing too. Someone added sheep noises, maybe Whittle and Steve, and I couldn't help but laugh. Then Andy turned to Jim and said in that funny, exaggerated, cockney accent I first heard at Hartismere, "Awwll right luv, let's get it up!" Jim set the tempo with his sticks and off to the races we went. I could see the girls off to the side jumping like fleas on a Confederate hot plate. As soon as the vibration from my bass hit my brain through the wooden stage, Uncle Joe arrived on the scene and I hung on!

Everything was going smoothly when halfway through the show I got the surprise of my life. Andy announced, "Our American bass player, Beau Foster, is going to serenade you with a song he wrote. He played it for us one night around a fire in Devon and we thought you should hear it. It's called 'Blue Is Just A Word'." As he said this the band walked off the stage while Whittle and Steve set up microphones within half a minute. I had no clue this was going to happen and thank God I hadn't. When Steve finished adjusting the mics—acoustics were played over mics in those days because decent pickups for them hadn't been invented—Whittle handed me my guitar and I mouthed to the guys off stage, "You suck!" They just laughed and mooed.

I said, "Well, here's the song." Everything got quiet because it starts with gentle finger picking. As I played I began to feel like I was in some sort of meditative cocoon; safe, warm, distant and protected from myself like I was back in bed with Judi in Saugus where I wrote it. When the song picked up to the big bang strumming part conclusion I felt like I was with my old power trio back in Cambridge, Massachusetts, combined with being with Stephen in The Crypt underneath St. Martin's Church. When I finished there was a moment of silence before the applause almost knocked me over. Andy hugged me from behind and said, "Christ, Beau that was better than in Devon," and then to the crowd, "That's our cowboy!" I looked for Judi and she was crying proudly with the girls hugging her. We gave each other the thumbs-up. As soon as all the moo cows were back on stage, Jimmy goosed my butt with a drumstick and clicked the tempo for the rest of the show. We finished with "Gemini" as the encore. Somehow I'd made it through a real rock 'n' roll concert and I couldn't wait to do it again.

The girls came backstage and Julian asked Valerie, "How did Stratt seem?"

She said he had a smile from ear to ear and had been tapping his hand on his table.

Julian asked, "You're kidding, right?"

"No!" she said.

Then Dafford appeared and said, "Beau, Stratt wants you to have a pint with him!" I asked the guys if I should and Jimmy said, "Go for it mate! He can afford to buy you a pint. Look at the bloody three-hundred-quid suit he's wearing!" Everyone laughed and I went out to shake a huge hand with huge rings on huge fingers.

"So you're the hired gun bass player we have on payroll. Nobody told me you could write!"

I said, "No one told me either. I'm still trying to find out if I can."

"The song you played indicates you can. Did you write it yourself? How many have you written? How often do you write?" he asked.

"Well, that one popped out on its own without my involvement. I just got out of its way. My wife captured it on tape before it could escape. I've written a couple hundred so far by either hearing things or stumbling on them," I said.

He laughed. "I hear that from writers all the time. Keep stumbling and come see me after the tour. Dafford will remind you." Then he added, "Everyone thinks writing a good song is easy, until they try it."

I laughed. "Well, I just try to uncover something that *feels* true. It can take ten months or ten minutes."

As we finished our pints he said the show was "a tremendous surprise" because when 'Pre' was in the band he was "the only showman of the bunch. Everyone else stood around, like mannequins on Oxford Street. Now everyone is moving and it's fun to watch. Dafford said the moving is your fault."

I said it was just how I kept time but, "I think the guys wanted to move anyway, they just needed a good groove." This made him laugh. Then he told me how impressed he was with Julian and Andy's writing abilities on the rehearsal demo from several weeks before and I said, "Me too!" He said having three or four writers in a band was very unusual and he was glad he hadn't dropped them from the label. "Well, 'cowboy,' you better get back to your mates. I'll be by in a minute to say good night to everyone and I'll see you after the tour if not sooner."

When I went back to the guys their curiosity could've killed a sabertooth. "What did he say, Beau, what did he say?"

I said, "Moooooo bloody moooooo!" Then conceded, "He said if I was smart, I'd leave you guys and start a band with Pre and the wanker," but I couldn't keep a straight face. "But I'm not smart. He said we were tremendous! He'll tell you himself before he leaves. Also, he asked me to see him when the tour is over!" This made everyone hoot and holler and we mooed all the way home. The next day our picture was in the newspaper with a caption, "Cowboy fits in!"

The next few gigs in and around London morphed right into the tour and it all seemed part of one, big, grand concert. I fell in love with the lifestyle. Depending on how far away the next show was, we'd travel either at night or first thing in the morning. I preferred night because I could sleep in and wake up to go to the local market before soundcheck to buy a piece of fruit and loaf of bread, and then check out the local museum or recommended historical site. Because music and history are first cousins to me, this became my favorite part of touring. It always surprised me when we traveled to the next city, town, or village, that when we came over a hill or ridge at 2, 3 or 4 in the morning, it'd be illuminated in energy-saving lights that produced an otherworldly color of dark yellow or light orange from the sulfur-based gas inside the bulbs. It reminded me England was in Europe and not the U.S.

I saw the Roman ruins, once baths, in Bath; the quaint streets and storybook architecture of Chester; the topography of Cardiff and Swansea; the valleys, coastline, and hills of Wales, with their canals and nature preserves; the industrial complexes of Manchester and Leeds; ancient chapels, so many castles they blurred into one and much more. The lifestyle made me feel sophisticated, which I'll never be. When the weather was bad I'd stay in my hotel room to read my Alan Watts and Krishnamurti books, or write music and letters. I kept busy.

Most of the shows were on the college circuit in athletic auditoriums that sat two thousand people or so, and sometimes we'd play a large music theater that might've held a little more. Quite often our day officially began at a local radio station and after the DJ played "Gemini" he'd interview the band with Andy and Julian doing the talking but almost always I'd be asked how I came to be in England. I think they wanted to hear my Boston accent. After several instances of not knowing what to say, except that I like British bands, I came up with my stock answer that I was "heading to France in a row boat and turned left by mistake." This sometimes brought a chuckle and stopped the questions but I always tried to find a way to convey how much I loved England.

We did an interview in Liverpool and everything made me think of The Beatles. I was beyond awed being there and as we entered the station I thought a guy across the street was about to commit suicide by jumping off a building. Jimmy said in his faked cockney accent, "'E ain't bloody jumping, Beau! 'E's a buildin' washer. Don't they 'ave them in the States?" Inside, the DJ asked me how it felt sitting in a chair John Lennon had once sat in, and I said, "Honored," only he didn't know how much. The only time I've felt equally honored was years later sitting in an Episcopalian church pew in Washington where Abraham Lincoln had once sat. My friend and I were walking by the church when we saw a custodian unlocking a door. Somehow I said something that made him invite us in. He treated us to a private tour and let me hold a rough draft (protected in plastic) in Lincoln's hand of the preliminary emancipation proclamation. He showed us things the general public is rarely privy to. One was a letter Mary Lincoln wrote a few days after her husband was murdered, offering food to a neighbor who'd fallen on hard times. It tugged at my heartstrings and made Mary forever feel like my neighbor.

The great thing about England being so small was that Judi and the girls were able to come to a lot of shows. It wasn't like touring America because England is about as long as California and I was told it was impossible to be much farther than sixty miles from the ocean, which puts things in perspective. Well into the tour we were playing near Oxford University, not far from the guys' hometowns of Abingdon and Wallingford, and the girls showed up. After the show we were invited to a party at a college dorm where Judi and I found out that in an adjacent dorm there was an international conglomerate of thirty or so philosophy and political science students who'd just been to our show. We slipped in back to hear kids from England, Ireland, Iceland, Germany, Africa, India, France, Scandinavia, the Middle East, and elsewhere having a late night roundtable discussion about Vietnam, the environment, capitalism, Watergate, and the general state of the world, with America being a catalyst for much of what was wrong with it. I strongly disagreed with a lot of things said, but not everything.

A cool kid from Germany named Hans was presiding over things and everyone seemed to respect him. He made sure everyone had a chance to make their point. Each criticism of America made me uncomfortable but also fascinated me. I knew what they meant by the arrogant attitude of the Nixon administration and "napalm bombs dropped on innocent civilians," but not everything wrong in the world was America's fault. Finally, after listening to both wisdom and nonsense (in my opinion anyway), with a good dose of the latter innocently induced by youth and maybe a little alcohol, even in this high-IQ crowd, I raised my hand and asked in a loud, frustrated voice, "Hans, I'm an American. Can I say something?" Judi and I were the only Americans there, unless a young William Jefferson Clinton was off somewhere not letting a mouthful of smoke slip past his uvula. My accent brought silence and Hans said, "Of course, you're one of the musicians we saw tonight who was introduced as an American cowboy when you played a solo song. Please speak."

"Thank you. There are a couple of lines in that song that go, *'Let's teach love to the world for what else is there to do when everyone's feeling blue. Blue is just a word that heaven's never heard, I'd like to make you happy, I'd like to make you happy.'* All I can tell you is when you, the most educated of our generation, criticize America for thinking it's perfect you are absolutely justified in doing so, but very few Americans our age think we're perfect! Our greatest president taught us that when Americans think of themselves as perfect the whole world suffers. We fought a war amongst ourselves between the antagonistic ideas of American perfection and imperfection, and the side that knew it wasn't perfect won. It's true, many of the criticisms here tonight are well-founded. Vietnam is a huge mistake! But more than any other nation, if it wasn't for the United States, warts and all, where would the world be? There's a good chance many of us wouldn't be here and no offense to you, Hans, or anyone else, but those of us who would be, might be speaking German. We're able to have these free and open conversations because no country on earth shed more blood on itself than the United States. We brought the ultimate expressions of freedom and suppression together in a war that almost killed us, so please try not to be too harsh about us till you've entertained an old American Indian proverb that teaches you can't understand another person until you've walked in their moccasins. We Americans are as guilty as anyone in that respect. But maybe the real problem, aside from this nation and that nation, is how we're all addicted to our nationalities, cultures, religions and Gods and never take a chance to learn how we're more similar than dissimilar. Maybe if we swapped shoes and beliefs every now and then we'd better understand each other. Or better still, if we meditated back to our innocence, before someone stamped us as Christians, Muslims, Jews, Hindus, Atheists, Americans, Europeans, or whatever label we think we are, we might find a moment to admit that none of us, or our opinions, or our nations, are perfect; that these manmade labels are the root of the problem and ignorance is the soil. It's not America, not Asia, not Europe, and not you and me that's the problem, it's all of us. After we tried to kill ourselves Abraham Lincoln said we were all guilty, and that *'reason with malice toward none'* was the solution."

Then I sat down and Hans said my proposal for surrendering those labels was not so easy because that's how the vast majority of the world knew itself. I replied, "Hans, the world doesn't know itself. It's why we fight wars over the same stupid things we've fought over for millennia, and our children deserve better. Shouldn't we at least look at our beliefs?"

Strong accents replied, "We should try!" and someone from behind patted my shoulder. The next night Hans and others came to our concert forty miles down the road. From the audience they waved me peace signs and I returned the sacred salute. When I played "Blue Is Just A Word" I dedicated it to "my United Nations friends from Oxford."

Judi stayed with me that night, too. Jimmy arranged for us to sleep at his friend Dan's flat in Abingdon because the guys would again be staying in their nearby homes. On the way there she held my arm extra tight and said she couldn't stop thinking about what I'd said to the students the night before. She said, "I want you to write down what you said so I can show it to our children someday." At Dan's she brought me a pen and paper. The next morning we walked along the River Thames and saw a beautiful deep green field with children playing soccer and she said, "I wish we could live here!"

When we got back to Dan's she told him how much she loved the town and he said, "You should rent the flat upstairs. It ain't fancy, but it's got heat."

She said, "Oh, I'd love to!" He handed her his address and phone number on a slip of paper and she held it like a precious jewel.

That afternoon our entourage arrived in the next town. We weren't too far from London so the girls planned to head back right after the concert. The venue was small and reminded me of my old St. Mary's high school auditorium. Judi said it reminded her of places she used to see me play before we met. As we were about to do a soundcheck to learn the acoustics of the place, I felt a powerful presence and turned to see a wild spirit woman looking like she'd stepped from the fields of a Jane Austen novel approaching the stage. She wore a long flowing dress, high-heeled brown leather boots that ancient Scottish warrior women might've worn had they worn heels, and a flowing shawl with a scarf on a head of untamed, primitive, reddish brown hair that flowed to her waist. She was followed by two man-boy protectors. When she got to the stage she called out in an accent so strong you thought she had golf balls in her mouth because every syllable came out round, "Where's the little baaarrstard, James Matthews?" Jimmy was backstage and came running out to literally jump off the stage into her arms crying, "Maggie!" Somehow he and Maggie Bell had been friends for years. With her new album just released on Swan Song Records, produced by my old friend Mark London, this was an event all around.

I instantly thought of the line in Rod Stewart's song "Maggie May," that again, was supposedly about her. *"You took me away from home just to save you from being alone."* I wondered how anyone like her could ever be lonely. She said she had a one-day break from her current British tour and was staying for our show that night. I was probably wrong but it seemed like most of the girls were a little intimidated by her strong personality. Judi wasn't, though. When Jimmy introduced us, Maggie and Judi (two spirit women if ever there were) hit it off immediately. When Jim said my name, Maggie said her producer had told her about me after learning from Jonathan that I was in Jim's band. Maggie said Mark told her I wrote cool songs, which made me feel like a big shot for half a second.

As we tuned up for soundcheck she and Judi sat together, laughing like school girls at God knows what. I got the feeling Maggie found relief in finding a friend she could be herself with. *Imagine,* I thought, *My wife goofing around with a British rock star. Who woulda thunk it?* But that's how Judi was, magic to everyone. When we began playing Maggie got up and started twirling in the aisle in a Stevie Nicks–type fashion, long before Nicks ever did and all I could think of was a Druid or Viking sorceress honoring ancestors around a fire centuries ago. She was the high priestess, strong, powerfully built, somewhere in her thirties, and not at all like the airbrushed version of her on her album cover. Here was the real deal, and she was absolutely beautiful!

After soundcheck, Judi, Jim, Maggie, and I went to a pub for lunch and Maggie asked if we'd play with her sometime because she thought we were a powerful rhythm section. She said we reminded her of the Muscle Shoals guys in Louisiana and I thought no way were we that good. Still, we had a groove that made you want to dance, without which, there is no dance. She also asked if we'd be playing any songs I wrote and I said, "We will!" When I did "Blue Is Just a Word" that night I prefaced it with, "This one's for Maggie," and I could hear her figuring out harmonies from the side of the stage where she and Judi were watching. After the show she hugged me and said in her heavy Scottish brogue, "Beau, your song and the tale it tells was fooorcking beautiful. I shed a wee tear."

Later Judi said, "Honey, Maggie thinks you're awesome." It made me feel wonderful. A couple of weeks later she came to another show that, coincidently, Judi was also at and they picked up right where they'd left off. I asked Judi why they got along so well and she said, "We have things in common!" I sensed

Judi might've meant they had similar childhoods, but I didn't ask. Maggie was a trusting, wide-open spirit that, like Judi, you could feel was genuine. After that show, Maggie reminded me and Jim about doing a session with her and we said we'd love to as soon as we came off the road. To me, that meant as soon as I got back from seeing Dave.

Dafford was constantly back and forth to London and always brought my mail. As the tour was winding down, letters from home frightened me, not for what they said but for what they didn't. All I read was, "Dave's hanging in there." I knew for an absolute fact he didn't want me to be distracted but I wanted details, so a few weeks before the tour ended I wrote by express mail to a trusted friend—the guy who told me Dave was tripping at the beach—asking what Dave was really like. A few days later, right before a big show, I read his reply. "Beau, please don't be mad. I can't go there anymore. I can't handle seeing him *go down* like this. I'm sorry. I feel like an asshole." "Go down"—did that mean what it sounded like? I started crying as the band was announced.

Playing in front of a large crowd was a day at the office by now. I understood how the 1927 Yankees felt, where nerves were not a factor but this was different! Usually I was all over the stage, mostly between Julian and Jim or doing a vocal harmony here and there with Andy on his mic, but this night I put on sunglasses and stood behind Jimmy like a "mannequin on Oxford Street," as Stratt would say. The guys liked me to announce a few songs because of my accent but when I was supposed to I shook my head no. At the end of one song I thought there was another verse and kept playing, and I got one song mixed up with another. Worse, my red, white, black, and blue American feel that propelled us to places beyond was lethargic at best. Uncle Joe had left the building. When Andy was about to announce "Blue Is Just A Word," I shook my head no again. Thank God the tour was ending. I was having a mental breakdown.

The guys weren't upset with me, which made it worse. They laughed it off, chalking it up to my not feeling well. I never told them otherwise. With only a few shows remaining in that late April and early May I couldn't stop obsessing about going home to Dave. I had no clue when I'd be able to return to my beloved Confederates so I made up a cock-and-bull story, asking Dafford for the phone number of the bass player I auditioned with and saying I wanted to ask him about "his brand of bass strings." When I called I told him there was a chance I might have to leave the band and that he should start coming to our shows so he'd be familiar with the songs. I desperately didn't want to leave the guys in the lurch. The next show the bass player came. He was sworn to secrecy and I hate secrets with a passion! As I remembered, he was a great, humble guy. And somehow, I started playing a little like my old self because I wanted him to know what the guys liked.

The first week of May 1975, shortly before the tour ended, Dafford surprised us by saying the record company booked a day of studio time to record the next single when we came to London. This was a monumental thing to me. We had a half dozen songs from over twenty road-tested ones we wanted to pick from, but the company wanted us to record one that the old lineup used to play called "Star." It was a great tune but because the guys had written so many songs we never got around to learning it. Dafford's assistant was supposed to have told us a week earlier to add it to the set list but he forgot. The guys thought we could pull it off and I did too, because we had two days of soundchecks to rehearse it. It had some tricky timing parts but I knew if I was in the studio next to Julian he could guide me with facial expressions and head tilts, and I could watch his hands. It's how I learned all the songs, so I wasn't too concerned.

The night before the session I decided to call Dave to tell him I was recording a single in London's famous Air Studios, where many of our heroes recorded, and that I'd be home to see him shortly after that. When our mother answered the phone her voice sounded like a Civil War mother's; ghostly, exhausted, defeated, beyond despair, and deathlike. She said, "Dave's sleeping and he's paralyzed and can't hold a phone. If you want to see him alive *you better come now!*"

I could only say, "Okay Ma!" and hung up. Judi saw my face and called to book a flight home. We'd do the single and remaining two shows and be with Dave in four days. Later in our room, I probably had a nervous breakdown. I couldn't sleep and shook all night like I was freezing while Judi held me.

The next morning, I found myself isolated in a recording booth in the most luxurious spaceship-like studio I could imagine. Instead of being ecstatic I was a wreck. The producer who'd seen me play many times asked if I was ill and I said no. We ran through the song a few times to get levels and he said it sounded okay. I was clearly not at my best but thought I could swing it as long as I recorded with everybody else. But this was 1975 in an ultramodern studio with a new 48-track board. Considering The Beatle's *Sgt. Pepper* and Jimi's *Axis* were recorded on 4-track boards (with some bouncing), it gives perspective. Like all the good ones, our producer wanted to record each instrument separately to avoid "bleed through" of one track to another. Nowadays a little bleeding is sometimes preferable because it sounds more natural, but back then producers were learning and experimenting with the new technology, which was okay as long as each guy knew the song inside and out. But one of us didn't!

Julian recorded his part first to a click track, or metronome, through his headphones. Then Jimmy recorded drums using the keyboard and click as references. They hated doing it that way and I found out why when I tried to record my track next. I felt lost without the vocals and guitars, which would've been fine had I known the song like I knew the others. I repeatedly made irritating timing mistakes, suffocating in a claustrophobic nightmare I couldn't wake from when this should've been a piece of cake. After several attempts, combined with self-loathing, no sleep or ability to concentrate, and guilt beyond description, I began to shake and sweat. I sat down to weep. "Guys, I can't do it!" Maybe I'm giving legitimate reasons or making phony face-saving excuses, but I hated myself for letting them down.

Nothing good came from the session except it was the last time in my life I'd ever, ever, ever allow myself to be unprepared, be it for a recording session, historical speech, or anything requiring me to be intimate with the subject matter. The producer was very kind. "Beau, don't be sad. Everyone has a bad day." But I was so messed up I asked Dafford to take me home. My playing had been as attractive as the *"toothless, bearded hag"* Mick sang about in "Jumpin' Jack Flash" and I needed to be with an angel. When she opened the door I said, "Honey, I blew it!" I went to our room, curled up in bed, and thought, *It serves me right for abandoning my family when they need me the most. What a worthless, selfish, person I am!* I was like a poor, slaveless Reb who learned too late that all the killing was for a lie. Yet he was able to desert and go home with some dignity because he now understood he'd been duped into fighting so one man could own another. But for me there'd be no dignity because I had duped myself!

An hour later Colin knocked on the door, came in, sat on the bed, and said, "Beau, Judi told us about your brother! Why didn't you tell us?" Andy, Julian, and Jimmy were in the doorway. Andy said, "We've known for months something was wrong because you never laugh like you did last year. Judi said you're going home in a few days and we don't want you to worry about your gig. It's safe with us till you come back. Take care of your family! It's more important than any of this music rubbish."

I said I was so sorry to disappoint them and Jimmy said, "Beau, the record company was going to dump us. You gave us a chance. We should've told them we needed a couple more days to get the song ready, it was cruel to throw it at you like that." "No it wasn't!" I said. I couldn't believe their generosity and understanding but that's how they were *all the time.* I told them I had invited the other bass player to our last few gigs and they laughed. Colin said, "We know, we saw him. He can fill in till you come back from the States."

Having everything out in the open somehow lifted a huge weight off me, but the overwhelming guilt of having abandoned Dave was beyond lifting. Now I could be openly sad with nothing to hide and I'd never believe in secrets again, unless they're unavoidable to help or protect someone. The truth for why things are the way they are is always preferable; it's what history is! The guys told Dafford about Dave and he came by to ask if I could still play the remaining two shows or if he should cancel.

"I'm surprised you want me to do them," I said.

He said, "For fuck's sake, Beau, we're better with you on a bad day than with the wanker on a good."

Hearing the word "wanker," which is truly a crude word, made me smile for the first time that day. I said, "Let's do the shows and blow some doors off." Silly bravado, absolutely, but I was going to play for Dave.

The next day we headed north with the girls to play in Leeds. It was the only show of the tour where we were the opening act. Headlining was Hammer, the band of one of England's most famous drummers, Cozy Powell. He played in The Jeff Beck Group with Rod Stewart and Ronnie Wood and he'd been in, or would be in, Rainbow, Black Sabbath, Emerson, Lake & Powell (when he replaced Palmer briefly), Thin Lizzy, and others. Because of him, some heavy hitters were backstage, the heaviest being Jeff Beck. We had a dressing room next to theirs and could hear them jamming on little amps when suddenly we heard a guitar solo Beck played on a recent Stevie Wonder album. It was Jeff all right, there's no mistaking his playing. He's the real deal, the crème de la crème; admired by rockers, classical and jazz musicians the world over.

I'd finally gotten some real sleep the night before and knowing I'd be with Dave in two days I almost felt good and was eager to play. At soundcheck, I requested we run through "Star" and by the third time I was nailing the parts I'd screwed up on in the studio. The band vibe felt particularly hot so I thought we might have a great night. From the opening notes of our first song Beck, Powell, Boz Burrel, the bass player from Bad Company, and others came out from their dressing room to see us and we were sizzling. When I did "Blue Is Just Word" you could hear a pin drop and when I finished the place exploded. I actually laughed and, as the guys came back on stage, I announced, "Here's a song we learned today. It's called 'Star'." Andy hugged me and said, "It's good to have our cowboy back." We played it flawlessly. Dafford and the producer were off stage, smiling and happy as hell. Ironically "Star" was the type of song with precisely the rough edge I loved to play. It was as if someone picked it to record to make me shine. It had a cool, nasty quality, like crossing a Steely Dan song with a song by The Stones. It got a great ovation and after a few more songs we got an encore. I was the last to leave the side of the stage because I talked to our producer for a minute. When I walked down the hall to our dressing room Jeff Beck was coming the other way. As we passed he smiled and said, "Excellent!" I'll never forget it! Judi said we never sounded so good.

Being the first act, we were able to head home earlier than usual, but not before hearing a few kick ass songs by Hammer. Steve and Whittle stayed behind with the equipment truck to head back to London in the afternoon the next day. For reasons of logistics we couldn't do a soundcheck for our final show, which was no big deal. We wanted to get home early because the next night was to be the culmination of what dreams are made of. We were to end our tour, in concert, at the world-famous Marquee Club where The Stones, The Kinks, The Who, Traffic, Jimi, Cream, and thousands of others had played. This would mean history to me and Dave. The stage had been enlarged for David Bowie, who had played there the night before, and Dafford said it would be left like that for us. I thought, *Good, I'll have room to move!*

At 7:30 the next evening Dafford picked the five of us up in the van, which was unusual. Normally it would've been Whittle, but we didn't think anything of it. The girls had left around 4:30 to take Judi out for supper and talk her out of returning to America. When we arrived at The Marquee it was thrilling to see Greep on the billboard that had so many great names on it over the years. We, David Bowie, and the opening act from the night before were on it. We went in the front door because this was a crowd of family and friends and were greeted with applause, yells, and some mooing. If the place could hold six hundred there must've been eight. It was so packed I couldn't see Judi but saw Jonathan there for his first time, near the door so he could escape. Mark London was with him, which was an enormous, wonderful surprise. Seeing Jonathan made me laugh and I teased him, "Hey luv, try not to touch anything and if you do wash it off right away."

"Oooohhhh Beau darling, you don't have to tell me twice." This made Mark and I laugh. Mark asked if I'd be playing "Blue Is Just A Word." I said yes and wondered how he knew about the song.

Squeezing through the crowd I spotted Judi at a table behind the last row of seats. She was with the girls and sitting on John Taylor's lap. When John saw me he winked and I snuck up from behind and said, "Who's trying to steal my Johnny boy?" Judi jumped up, threw her arms around me, and said, "Not me!" She, John, and the girls had a little buzz going because he'd been buying rounds for everyone. Judi was always extra cautious with alcohol because, in my opinion, it frightened her seeing what it had done to her dad. But she was sweetly adorable, trying to have a good time while, like me, she was full of mixed emotions. Stratt was at the next table with two "suits" from the record company. When he saw me he got up. "Good to see you cowboy!" I introduced him to Judi not only to be polite but because she always made me look good. Stratt said, "You look like brother and sister."

Judi said, "Everyone says that!"

He said to her, "I hear you're going home for a bit. Make sure your husband sees me as soon as you return."

"I will!" she said, while I thought, *Good. He doesn't seem too upset about me blowing the recording session.* Then he asked if I knew where our equipment, that he had bought for us, was. I looked at an empty stage and said, "I don't know!"

I then left Judi with John and the girls and went up to the lighting booth to see if my old friend Archie was doing the lights. He was and joked, "I plan on shining a lot of light on the bass player's hands, Beau, but I'm concerned there's no equipment on stage by now." It was fast approaching 9 o'clock and if we didn't go on by 9:30 there wouldn't be a show. Thanks to British law The Marquee, like other London clubs that served alcohol, shut down at 11. At 9:30 Dafford gathered us in the dressing room and informed us that Whittle and Steve were okay, but had been in a truck accident, and there was no way to get the equipment there on time so the show was canceled. The guys were devastated and groaned, reminding me of my mother's Robert E. Lee groan. Dafford said there was a possibility of us opening for Mott The Hoople or someone like that the following night (they did that song "All The Young Dudes") but the guys said, "Beau's going home in the morning!" Then Dafford groaned, "Oh, yeah."

Together, the band went on stage to announce the news and there was a universal groan mixed with compassion. Then people started applauding, which revealed how much these guys were loved. Stratt must've told Dafford who then called Andy to the side of the stage to tell the crowd there was an open bar courtesy of the band and that made some people happy, but I felt so bad for the guys. Not only was the record company there along with the press, but their families and friends were too. I didn't have anyone to worry about. I would've loved to say my bass blew the doors off the world-famous Marquee Club but it never happened. But the thought of seeing Dave in a few hours made me happy! For the first time in my life my priorities were straight.

I found Judi and said, "Let's get the hell out of here!" We snuck out like thieves in the night and I was starving. I always liked playing and writing hungry and perhaps the best thing about The Marquee besides the music was a great shish kebab place Archie turned me onto a few doors down. Judi got a small and I got a large. I inhaled it like Stonewall Jackson's famished men after capturing a train of Yankee "victuals." I said, "Jude, I was gonna play my butt off!" She said she could tell by the way I ate my sandwich, adding she hadn't seen me eat like that for the past eight months, which meant I was returning to earth. The truth was, by going home to Dave I was joining the Union Army, where I should've been since the beginning of his battle with cancer/slavery. But I was abandoning my beloved Confederates, who never abandoned me, who were impossible not to love once you marched and fought beside them.

At the airport Colin reminded me, "The new guy is only filling in, Beau!" An hour into the flight I opened a letter I received that morning from my dad. It said to be prepared for Dave's appearance and that, in his opinion, the reason Dave was still alive was because he wanted to see me "one more time." I handed the letter to Judi and it made her cry. We were about to learn in the most concrete way that Abraham Lincoln was absolutely right when he said slavery was cancer and cancer was slavery and right too that God cannot be for and against the same thing at the same time. Like Lincoln, we were to experience living in a world where God cries.

You're Going To
Have a Baby

Our flight landed late, but Judi's brother Norman was waiting. He brought us to my grandmother's on Sluice Pond where we had prearranged to stay. I called my parents to let them know we had arrived safely. My mom said ten the next morning would be a good time to see Dave because the visiting nurse would be done doing what she did.

I asked, "Okay Ma, but . . . how is he?"

"Not good!"

Her voice had the same dejected tone it had when I talked to her from England. I asked Judi if she wouldn't mind if I went to see Dave by myself and she said of course, that she'd go to her mom's. As I tried to sleep and failed, I thought of my youngest brother, John, and how hard it must've been for him to do his part, helping my parents care for Dave while I was gallivanting around the globe chasing nonsense. Guilt and indescribable anguish were closing in on me and this was nirvana compared to what I was about to experience.

The next morning Judi went to her mom's and I walked to my parents' on the other side of the pond. It was a beautiful, warm May day. When I walked into their driveway the kitchen window was open and for the first time ever I didn't hear classical music coming from one of my mom's favorite FM stations. It'd been eight months since I'd seen them and when I entered the kitchen all they could say was "hi." I'd seen them exhausted before but never defeated, and it killed me. In the dining room they had a hospital bed so they could better care for their boy. My mom spoke softly, "He's awake. He knew you were coming."

I then saw those beautiful, wild, brown, kamikaze, "Spanish Castle Magic" eyes that never looked away from anything and they were studying me. Words, music, and dreams can't describe it. If a sledgehammer hit me in the chest and head at the same time it would have been mild compared to this. I was transported to a dimension I've never really returned from. I entered a picture Abraham Lincoln carried in his pocket of a Union soldier liberated from Andersonville, who'd been reduced to an emaciated skeleton. The photo reminded him of the sacrifice his boys were making for the freedom of *"all men."* Rebs withered viciously in prison camps too! The suffering went both ways. Dave looked like the breathing bones of holocaust victims in WWII films of Auschwitz, who still had a remnant of life in them, only worse. He couldn't sit up or pull the blankets back. My sweet, loving, protecting brother was beyond liberating!

He was five-foot-ten and weighed 185 pounds when he was a dolphin the year before, swimming at speeds 99 percent of humans can only dream of reaching. Now caught in a nondiscriminating cancerous tuna net he weighed 80 pounds at best. He had a beard and looked like his head was shaved. The outline of his body looked like a sheet thrown over the frame of a fiber-less couch. I was horrified, and if we have a spirit, it was in shock. But those all-seeing David Joseph eyes followed me, and they were bigger than ever. Eyes are the only organ that never grow or shrink after we're born, even when our bodies are gnawed away by slavery.

Finally my lifeguard brother said, "Hi."

"Hi, good to see you," I replied.

315

"Good to see you too!" Then I sat and patted his hand.

"You can't touch me *anymore,* it hurts too much!"

It also hurt him to tell me that. The word "anymore" had finality like the word "dedicated" had when Lincoln used it among the most sacred words ever said when speaking of the dead on a blood-soaked field in Gettysburg. People don't realize that unless they understand that the most important history ever written is not in a book. It's in the heart! He asked me to close the door so we could be alone.

I said, "Ma won't like it."

He said, "I know, but I will!"

"Me too!"

He said, "I'm glad you're here! I can't say this to anyone. My whole body feels like someone is constantly pounding it with a baseball bat. The hardest thing is I can't scream because it would make Ma and Dad feel bad and *I can't do that!*"

Dear Lord God, my brother said "I can't do that!" He truly was a slave! But a slave can speak to himself so he continued, "I know this can't go on much longer and I'm ready to get the show on the road. Dying doesn't bother me; it's this ridiculous suffering that's the pits. It's not worth it. I'm a little curious if there's something after this shit but it really doesn't matter, know what I mean? Either way, ending this is a win/win and I'm ready! I have to sleep. Saying a frickin' sentence kicks the crap out of me and I haven't said this much in months."

"I'll see you later then," I said.

As he drifted into sleep he said, "Good!"

Before I left I memorized the sight of my brother and promised myself I'd never let it fade from my mind. Gone was a dolphin hanging onto a diving board looking up at a time clock while not even breathing hard, and here was a prisoner of slavery/cancer slowly suffocating, sharing his last breaths with the only person he could say certain things to. Yet if he were only a prisoner, it would've been an improvement because he'd serve his time and get out, but there was no way out, so truly, he was a slave and death was his only way to freedom, and he welcomed it.

Can it somehow be imagined that this welcoming of death was felt by millions in the not too distant past of our nation? Dear Lord, people should contemplate that so many held in bondage believed death was their only way to freedom. It's our best chance to better understand the absurdity of the racial ugliness still with us. But here, where time was suspended and the eternal revealed, I asked my parents how long the doctors said Dave had to live and my mom said, "Maybe a day or two, no more." Then I left because there was nothing I could do and I was too ashamed to ask if there was. As I walked to my grandmother's I realized that if Dave had died before I got home I'd never be able to live with myself, and he knew this. Living with myself wasn't going to be easy anyway, for I'd forever be a person who abandoned his family. The words of my dad's letter were true; Dave stayed alive so he could see me "one more time." Dear God, that meant he chose to live with this inhuman suffering in order to see me, and I was not worthy of that; never was, never would be!

In bed with Judi that night I tried to prepare her for what she'd see the next day. I said not even Christ on his cross suffered like Dave, because at least Christ could cry out, "Father, why have you forsaken me?" Dave had to remain quiet because he "couldn't do that" to his parents. And he never felt forgotten or asked, "Why me?" Christ's suffering was over in hours, but Dave's went from hours to days to weeks to months because Dave *was a slave,* whereas Christ was a servant. Yet their suffering shared something inexplicable in common. Dave had cancer of the body while Christ was trying to cure the cancer of the human spirit, which Lincoln said was caused by "the meanness within man's heart." Christ gave it his all and if his story is not the best example, whose is? For me, in the deepest region of my soul, if the story of Christ revealed true love, Dave revealed it too!

The next morning I called to ask when was the best time for Judi and I to see him. My mother said, "Soon, he's drifting in and out." Her voice was as sad as any Civil War mother's and what she said next is as clear now as it was then.

"Your brother was very disappointed in you yesterday!"

"Why, what did I do?" I asked.

"It's not what you did but what you didn't do."

"What was it, then?"

Like it happened a minute ago, I can still feel the tone of what she said of her long-suffering boy in his final hours.

"You didn't kiss him when you saw him!"

Oh my God, I'm so sorry, I didn't kiss him; how could I have been so stupid? I thought.

She said it in the gentlest way she could and I could tell by the way she was breathing that she didn't want to hurt her prodigal son, who frankly, deserved to be hurt. She said it without a drop of punishing insinuation but I could hear her justifiable, reluctant disappointment in me. To this day I never knew if Dave said anything to her about it because it doesn't sound like him, but does sound like our mother. She saw the shock on my face when I saw him and she didn't want it to make him feel bad. There are motherly instincts to protect that no man can fully understand, that I'd become privy to through no choice or heroics of my own. To say it one last time, Lincoln's sentiment that everything of value in this world he had learned from a woman is how I learned, in times like these, that the things we think are important, don't amount to much at all!

After I hung up I went down to the pond because I didn't want Judi and my grandmother to see me cry like I'd never cried before. It didn't matter if he wanted me to kiss him or not, it would be a kiss good-bye. But there was something my mom didn't know. Between brothers like us, it's never about things said or done but a connection that says, "I know you know and you know I know!" It's pure understanding, which is a love that lasts forever that's as powerful as any love there is.

When Judi and I walked into my parent's house she hugged them and went straight to Dave. He spoke first, "Hey Jude, I'm okay."

She asked, "Are you sure?"

"I'm sure!"

She said, "I believe you."

"Try to convince Bob. So Jude, tell me what it was like seeing him on stage in England in front of all those big shots."

She sat down while I went down to the pond to sit where a dolphin once flew. When I came back Judi was in the kitchen with my mom and Dave was sleeping. I went to him and closed the door. His breathing was more labored than the day before and when it stopped, I was surprised another breath came. The more I looked, the more beautiful he was. I somehow sensed this magnificent human who just so happened to be my brother would inspire me to work through my every fear. I wanted to thank him but didn't know how, so I went to the head of the bed and, though I wasn't supposed to, I gently caressed his face and bent to kiss his him good-bye. At that instant his eyes popped open like he'd been sleeping for centuries. He looked at me, smiled, and got in his last, glorious, dig of life.

"I was hoping it was the kiss of death, but it's only you."

I said, "I didn't kiss you yesterday because I didn't want to give you my cold."

He gave me a look like the look my father gave me after I told him some cockamamie lie about how I dented his car fender. It was crossed with the look my mother gave when I brought home my 108th piss-poor report card in a row that she wouldn't show my dad until after I went to bed. But it was the look of a brother too, so it had humor, compassion, and understanding, despite knowing how incredibly full of crap I was. There was no place to hide and he laughed his last laugh. "That's a good one." As he did he cringed because laughing reminded him that he couldn't laugh *anymore,* it hurt too much. Dear Lord, if Lincoln was right about anything, he was right that, "Laughter is the best medicine." If Dave couldn't laugh, it was time to go! Then he said his last words to me.

"I'm glad I can tell you this. Everyone knows I'm croaking, but no one wants to admit it *with me* except you. I know what people are whispering because I

319

can hear better than they think I can. I want everyone to know I'm okay with this, but I wish to hell someone would take a frickin' pillow and put it over my head to end this shit because I can't do it myself. Living like this is not worth it and hasn't been for a long, long time, know what I mean?"

I said, "I do!"

"I knew you would!" Saying this took Herculean effort. He added, "I need a nap."

"I'll see you soon."

He said, "I know!"

In a perfect world inspired by the love Jesus and Buddha taught, that can only work if it's based on Lincoln's philosophy of "cold unimpassioned reason," which is not cold at all but the warm light of common sense, I would've taken a pillow and ended my brother's bondage then and there. They weren't dishing out morphine drips like they do nowadays and if they had been, I would've put one in him myself. His last two words to me were two of the most sacred there are: *"I know!"*

The next morning when Judi, my grandmother, and I were having tea my parents walked in and my mom said, "He's gone!" As we cried I thought of Judi and I, and Lincoln saying the sentiment of death was different for the young than for the old because, *"In this sad world of ours, sorrow comes to all: And, to the young it comes with bitterest agony, because it takes them unawares. The older have learned to ever expect it."* But he also knew losing someone you love doesn't necessarily become easier with age. The deaths of his boys Eddie and Willy almost killed him. Here I learned my desire to protect came from my history teacher mother because she said, "We have to get a grip!" My parents had a burial to arrange.

Sitting with Judi at the funeral I didn't blame God one iota for Dave's suffering. And I didn't pity well-meaning, neurotic friends, neighbors, and relatives who'd given magic prayer documents, miraculous water from Lourdes, and even a tiny splinter of the supposed cross Christ died on, to my parents over the course of Dave's battle with slavery. All were gifts from loving, good-intentioned souls, trying to help in the only way they knew how. If some were too frightened to have ever asked a "pesky question," or embrace the miracle of life the way Dave did, or thought that if we all believed in Jesus a little more and prayed a little harder and did the hopscotch on our left foot and the hokey pokey with our thumbs stuck somewhere, if they thought those things would've cured Dave; how could I pity them for that? If I did, it would've meant I had contemptuous sorrow for all mankind. But it wasn't for any goodness within me but for the abundance of pity I had for myself; trumping everything. My shame was unfathomable!

There was no escaping. I'd abandoned my brother and was the most neurotic, hypocritical lunatic in the church. I didn't and still don't mind so much being a lunatic because I'm resigned to it. But to be a hypocrite brought such self-loathing, reminding me of how Lincoln used the word when he told Americans that slavery in our nation allowed the world to justifiably "taunt us as hypocrites." That not a single person treated me as the hypocrite I truly was, but instead loved, embraced, and welcomed me home made it worse. Yet, because miracles do happen, even to hypocrites, out of the darkness came the light of life.

Within a week of Dave's funeral I had a dream of him standing before me looking like he had in the cellar on the day before Judi and I went back to England. He had on the wig he disliked and Mick was singing, *"Time waits for no one and it won't wait for me,"* while Charlie expertly hit rim shots with the edge of his drumstick. I'm not a person who remembers dreams in detail, but I'll remember this one forever. We were looking at each other and it appeared he was getting better instead of the other way around when he smiled and said, "You're going to have a baby!" It was so real I jolted up in bed, but no one was there except Judi sleeping. "What the hell was that?" I kept it to myself but, like Charlie's superb timing, at breakfast Judi said, "I'm feeling queasy."

I said, "That's because you're pregnant!"

"I'm not pregnant, I can't be . . . we haven't even been . . . that much lately . . . and besides." (She had a medical problem that made getting pregnant difficult.) This made me laugh for the first time since Dave died.

I said, "Honey, I have it on good authority." Then I told her of my dream and she said, "Let's get a pregnancy test kit." It proved Dave was right! To say I don't believe in a thing I experienced is one of the great, beautiful paradoxes of my life.

Soon we found a wonderful husband-and-wife pediatrician team, the McDonalds. They verified everything except my dream. My grieving parents were deeply moved. The next week we found the cutest little apartment on the first floor of a triple-decker in a tough section of Lynn. Our landlord, his wife, and six children inhabited the second and third floors and they adopted us as soon as they spent five minutes with the expectant mother. To this day my daughter and I are family to them. We received condolences from England because I'd written of Dave's death. A few days later, letters from Colin and Stephen asked when they could expect us back but I was already thinking like a father. The thought of having a baby was the most exciting thing I'd ever experienced.

My instincts to protect were in overdrive, and even though we didn't have much money I made sure the little we had went to the healthiest food we could buy. I went to the library and the same librarian who helped me learn about Dave's cancer and chemo, helped me find articles about the best diet for an expectant mother and baby. Every Sunday night I'd plan out the week's menu and we'd stick to it like a religion. Judi got the biggest kick out of it because we'd always eaten healthy anyway. Meditation had allowed me to know that things we ingest affect everything. I was determined that our daughter would have the best chance, and I knew before anyone we were having a girl. I asked Judi if I could name her and she agreed if she could name a boy. She always wanted a little boy named Joshua but I said, "Hon, we're having a girl!"

I was selfish. I wasn't one of those expectant fathers that say they don't care if they have a boy or a girl as long as it's healthy. That's stating the obvious. I wanted a healthy girl, pure and simple and made no bones about it. I didn't have anything against boys per se, it was just that I was the oldest of three, and 99 percent of the musicians I played with were males so it was "enough already."

Men who had to have sons irritated me and more than once I saw it was their sons who paid the price for their father's foolish attitude.

My female cousins always made me wish I had a sister, so a daughter would be the pinnacle of joy in every respect. Another reason was, although I loved conversations with men who were smarter than me, which was most of the time, there was something sacred about my conversations with Judi, my mom, grandmothers, aunts, and cousins. I was blessed to be in a family of highly intelligent, self-possessed, socially aware women with great senses of humor and it doesn't get any better than that.

Judi's family was ecstatic about the news, but what surprised me was Judi saying, "I hope this doesn't mean we can't go back to England right away!" She was *always* the more practical one of us, but I felt going back while she was pregnant might not be the wisest thing. Also, it was still May, the month Dave died, and maybe because I didn't want to abandon my family again so soon, I said, "Hon, there may be legal and medical reasons it would be wiser to have the baby in the States with our families. Maybe we should have her here and get used to being parents, then go to England on surer footing!"

This somehow made sense to her so I wrote to Colin and Stephen and told them they were going to be uncles. Uncle Stephen wrote back right away with congrats and three weeks later we got a big card with congrats from all our beloved Confederate aunts and uncles. Colin said in a little attached note that the record company was bitterly disappointed with the band. He didn't give details and I couldn't handle finding out it was my fault. He said the fill-in bass player was "doing okay," but didn't elaborate. He knew my plate was full and I can't emphasize enough what a kind, first-class act he *always* was to me. I wrote back saying that as soon as the baby was old enough to travel we'd make plans to return. He replied that if he were in my shoes he'd do the same thing. So Judi and I immersed ourselves in our new American lives.

I got my old lifeguard position back, and also my hospital job where I was able to work enough hours to get the health insurance we'd need for momma and baby. At night I got quite a few fill-in gigs playing bass, so life was good. I was meeting incredible American musicians, too, who wanted to hear about my English adventures and this was the first time I heard that I should write about them, but I never did. Guilt for abandoning Dave had forever changed something. I had never mastered the art of accepting a compliment graciously but now I couldn't accept any. Somewhere deep I felt I needed to be punished and that feeling has never completely left. So keeping incredibly busy and over-joyed with the prospect of fatherhood was the best thing for me. But Dave was constantly on my mind because his spirit was and always will be *in* the music.

And wonder of wonders, nine months after her uncle told me in a dream that I was having a baby, Anna Gabrielle was born at 2:46 a.m. on February 1, 1976; a bicentennial baby weighing in at 8 pounds, 5 ounces. When her little face popped out there was no denying she was mine. I'd always hoped she'd have a toenail or something that looked like mine, but when I saw her face it was like looking in the mirror. I thought, *HOLY CRAP.* Thank God she was born with her mother's sweet disposition. Dr. Jackson and the attending nurses sang "Happy Birthday" and I was so crazy with joy I asked the doctor if he was related to Michael or Stonewall Jackson. He said, "Not that I know of. I wonder how those two would've gotten along."

After Momma and I held our baby for a few minutes a nurse put her in an incubator in the corner of the room. Judi was radiant but exhausted, so I went to look at my new little friend. She had a frown my paternal grandmother called "the Foster Frown" so I bent down, put my lips on the glass, and hummed Stevie Wonder's "Isn't She Lovely" and then the riff for The Stones's "Can't You Hear Me Knocking" and her little frown disappeared. Throughout her pregnancy, I'd held her momma around her waist to hum songs so she'd know her dad's goofy voice. I was pretty sure she knew it anyway from the yelling I did at the television a few months earlier as the Red Sox were losing yet another World Series, this time to the Cincinnati Reds who may've had a distant relative of mine playing left field. Judi said, "Beau, you just made the baby kick!"

The next morning I was supposed to observe my baby having a bath and thought the nurse was a little rough, though she probably wasn't in the least. Without hesitating I elbowed myself between them and said, "I'll take it from here!" As I bathed her the nurse laughed and said I was a natural. From that moment I was a hands-on dad. I gave her all her baths and fed her as soon as she was on solids. Diapers didn't bother me in the least. I always got her laughing or maybe it was the way I sang. In so many ways I was like a mother but, man, was Judi ever the real deal. If I was a natural she took it to another level. She breast-fed Anna for almost a year and her motherly instincts were superb. I have tapes of them conversing with each other and even though Anna couldn't say a word, they made more sense than some authors I've heard in recent years who say the Civil War was about economics. Nothing, absolutely nothing, could be further from the truth! And that's not to say there wasn't an economic element to the bloody mess but, as Lincoln said, that argument shuts eyes to reality. For how many ounces of gold is the life of a child and mother worth?

Having a baby changed the way I looked at the world in ways I never knew existed. It was similar to how meeting her mother had changed me five years earlier. It somehow completed me and, though I'd always be wrought with despair about Dave, with my girls I began to feel safe.

The power, responsibility, and magnitude of parenthood can only be understood by someone who is a parent. It made me wonder what it must've been like for mothers and fathers to send their babies off to war and, in particular our Civil War, to maybe kill a brother who happened to have joined the other side. It happened far more than a just God would wish. And then to have one of those babies come home in pieces, if pieces were all that was left, was too much to comprehend. But that's what happens when slavery of mind, body, and spirit rule the land wherever on earth it does. I now knew I couldn't handle caring for my precious little daughter to have, in an instant, the door slam open and a master walking in as he had every legal right to, to take her from my arms to never see again while the United States Supreme Court, sympathetic to slave-owners, ruled in 1857's dreaded Dred Scott Decision that *"blacks had no rights which a white man was bound to respect"* and never would. Dear Lord, how could any parent ever think the Southern Confederacy was right? And what does it do to their children who were taught it was? Never did I dream that one day I'd meet people who believed it.

I began to feel fatherhood suited me. I'd always loved kids and had an understanding that if God wants to send a message into the world, she sent it through children and maybe, on occasion, art. So I followed my instincts to never get hung up on whether I should be a parent first and friend second because why couldn't I be both or more of one when one was needed. The only rule I had was no matter what question came from my little friend, I'd give her an honest answer, with her knowing ahead of time it wasn't necessary for her to agree with me or know that I'm particularly right about a thing. That's never changed and it's meant I've learned far more from her than she me. We learned to laugh together and that means I must've done something right.

But before I give myself too many pats on the back I have to say Anna was born with so much of her mother's spirit, and so was easy to raise. I got way, way, way more credit for my parenting skills than I deserved. People would ask what I did to have such a good kid and I'd say she was born good and add, "I just try to stay out of her way!" Yet no one believed me. But my family and close friends knew it was so. Seeing her parents love each other was the key to her early years and I don't expect or even want to be believed, but that was something Judi and I never had to work at. We were an American family but more, we were citizens of the world just as we promised we would be high up on "Liam's Ridge" above the valley in Devon.

The days turned to weeks and in a blink nine months flew by while Judi was increasingly getting more homesick for England. I was still doing fill-in bass work several times a month and had also hooked up with an old friend, Dennis Tully, whom I'd met a few years earlier at GE when I heard him singing Who songs as he drove by on a fork truck. He thought I was kidding when I contacted him to form a duo. His vocal range was far superior to mine and we got a ton of work in Boston and on the North Shore that was so easy because all we needed was an acoustic, some mics, and small P.A. system. Plus, the money was terrific.

These gigs weren't as cool as my acoustic gigs in London where I only played original songs, but we'd slip one in here and there and soon got requests for them, which led to us meeting incredible local musicians. But Judi kept dropping subtle and not so subtle hints about going back to England because we were now hiking Lynn Woods with a little person in a pouch on my back, which meant we could go anywhere. What I never did a good job of explaining to her, because I wasn't fully aware of it, was I had a deep paranoia about going back to England because I thought something bad might happen, the way it did when I abandoned Dave.

"They've probably forgotten about me over there by now," I told her.

She was taken aback, "Are you serious?"

I was also finding cool musical opportunities here at home by discovering the best opportunities are the ones you make. But as karma would have it, if I was paranoid about returning to England, somehow England returned to us!

In the early summer of 77, in a decade with some very good but also very goofy music like "Y.M.C.A." and McCartney's *Silly Love Songs,* which revealed even a Beatle could write a clunker, we were having Sunday morning tea with the cutest little thing walking around the apartment when momma read in *The Boston Globe* that England's Swan Song recording artists Bad Company were playing the following week at the Music Hall and the opening act would be none other than her friend, "England's answer to Janis Joplin," Maggie Bell.

Judi said, "We should go!"

"I heard it's sold out and Den and I have a gig that night."

She said, "Well, you can find someone to fill in and we can call Maggie for tickets!"

I said, "Jude, what makes you think we'd be able to get in touch with her and that she'll get us tickets if she even remembers us?"

"Beau, I told you, she loves you and your music. Why do you think she kept asking you and Jimmy to go into the studio with her?"

"Yeah, well, you can call if you want but don't get your hopes up."

Then she said in her Judi way that always made me laugh, "I don't have to get my hopes up. I want to see Maggie and she'd love to see you!"

I said, "And you too!"

All that week Boston radio blasted Bad Company and played songs from Maggie's album too. One was a kick-ass cover of her singing an early Beatle song where she sang, *"I saw 'him' standing there."* On Friday, the day of the concert when Maggie was most likely to be doing a soundcheck, Judi said we should call the Music Hall and ask Maggie to leave tickets for Beau and Judi at the front desk. I wouldn't do it so she did. I shook my head when she left our phone number but lo and behold, an hour later the phone rang when I was changing either guitar strings or a diaper. Judi called to me, "Hon, how many tickets do we want?"

"Tickets for what?" I asked.

"The concert tonight."

I couldn't believe it. "Get three, we'll bring Den." Den had Maggie's album and was a big fan.

We got to the Music Hall right before showtime and it was a mob scene of scalpers, the smell of pot, tattoos, court jesters, and local Pirates of the Caribbean who liked their music erotic, catchy as hell, and loud enough to make ears bleed. This, thank God, was no phony-baloney 1970s disco crowd. Here were real deal Confederates and I felt right at home. I heard several "Hey Beaus" and "Hi Bobs." The crowd was as cool as any waiting in line at The Marquee. We had no trouble getting to the front of the ticket line because there was none, only a sign reading, "Sold Out!" Judi said to the person inside the booth, "We're the party of Beau and Judi."

"I've been on the lookout for you; here are your backstage passes. I'll escort you to your seats," he said.

We were led to the front of the stage where three empty seats in the middle of the first row awaited us. Judi said, "See hon, I told you Maggie would take care of us. She said she would, you know." We learned later that Maggie got us the seats by offering the people they belonged to backstage passes and they jumped on the chance. I was so glad Den was with us. He loved my English stories, and this one he was in. To this day he can tell it better than me but back then all he could say was, "I can't frickin' believe this!"

We sat down just in time to hear the announcer saying something goofy like, "You've heard her sing with Rod Stewart on 'Every Picture Tells A Story.' Now she's here to perform songs from her latest album *Suicide Sal*,"—I think it was her second solo album with some heavy hitters playing on it like Led Zeppelin's Jimmy Page, which was produced by Jonathan's friend, Mark London—"England's answer to Janis Joplin, Maggie Bell." When she walked out among 5,000 screaming banshees, she waved to us and grabbed her mic like a mongoose grabs a cobra before it can strike, and in her beautiful round Scottish brogue said, "I'm nobody's bloody answer to anyone." Then looking at me said, "Beau, this is for you!" She turned to her band and stomped, "1, 2, 3, 4," launching into "I Saw 'Him' Standing There" and rocked it like an ancient sorceress riding an untamed dragon. Judi yelled, "I told you, sweetheart, I told you!" while Den's jaw dropped to the floor. The show was fantastic and she got an encore which wasn't easy for an opening act in the States. As she left the stage she nodded for us to come backstage.

When we entered her dressing room she was with her band. She hugged us and asked, "Beau, didja catch the tune I played for yer? It's from the album with Mark. You dedicated one to me last year, d'yer remember? It was your 'Bluuue' song." It was so bloody good to see her. She introduced us to her band and gave us invitation-only passes to an after-concert party at the Neponset Drive-In Theater in Dorchester (it was still in use and Swan Song had rented it). Then she and Judi took up gabbing right where they'd left off, so Den and I went to the side of the stage to watch Bad Company tear it up. Later in Neponset,

Den's jaw was still hanging because too many to mention local DJs and music celebrities were mingling, or rather stumbling around, but in my eyes they didn't come close to Maggie and Bad Company, who made my jaw hang too. It was a beautiful night. Maggie told me Judi promised to bring me back to England right away and that people who cared about me and wanted to help thought I'd "vanished from the earth." I asked about Jimmy and she didn't have details, but heard the band either broke up or got dumped by the record company. This made me sad and guilty, but being among so many English accents, and one Scottish, felt like home. It made me miss my Hartismere Confederates more than ever. As we left Judi said to Maggie, "We'll see you soon!"

The next night Den and I played a little club up on Route One in Saugus that hired acoustic acts to play for the late-dinner crowd as a bridge into the drinking crowd. It was the type of gig I promised myself I'd never do, but it paid well and I had my girls to support. I was always glad when no one from the old days saw me play these gigs. I know that's arrogant but I never enjoyed playing goofy songs I didn't write for people eating baked stuffed shrimp. Judi disliked these gigs more than I did, but came to this one because our upstairs neighbor was able to baby-sit. She arrived just in time to see a drunk heckling us to play the song "Amy." I figured the damn thing out during the break and this is arrogant too, I'm just not an "Amy" type of guy. Well, just as we started playing a half-assed version of it the heckler went to the men's room and missed it. When he came out he staggered to the stage and asked, "When the fuck are you playing 'Amy'?"

I said softly, "We just played it when you were taking a leak."

He said, "What are you, an asshole?" and took a swing at me, missed, and fell over. Before he knew it, he was bounced from the place. I looked at Judi and she was very upset so I gave her the "I'm okay" sign. Later at home she was quiet and I thought the incident had been forgotten.

The next day was a beautiful Sunday and she was still quiet on a hike in Lynn Woods with a little person on my back. She said, "Honey, I've been thinking. One night we're with Bad Company and Maggie Bell and the next you're playing silly songs to people taking swings at you. It's moving your career backward, not forward. You always said you didn't want to get old and find out too late you didn't contribute something useful to the world and that music was your way to do it. I know you feel guilty about Dave and want to punish yourself. And I know I can't talk you out of feeling the way you do, but you have to realize you did what he wanted you to do. He wouldn't like seeing you play in places like last night anymore than I do." (Den and I *did* play in some very cool places though, but she was right!) "I'm writing to Jimmy's friend Dan to see if we can still get an apartment in his building in Abingdon."

I said, "Okay, Jude."

Ten days later we heard from Dan that there was as a flat next to his on the first floor but even if it got taken we could stay with him till we found a place so "come no matter what." We didn't bug the Hartismere guys about staying with them because that was like a college dorm and we needed a home for our daughter. By hook or by crook, we were going back to England.

Deep in my soul I was excited yet leery, but chalked it up to my pessimistic nature. A humongous thing though, had me so fired up over the prospect. I never stopped writing! I had a whole new batch of songs to show the guys, the girls, Stephen, Jonathan, Mark London, Maggie, Dafford, Liam, Stratt, Archie, Nigel, Mrs. Briggs, The Crypt, a crapload of pubs, a cow in Devon, a million sheep, pigeons with British accents, and anyone who'd listen.

I went on a mission to work extra hours at my hospital day job and took as many gigs as I could handle. There was no way I'd take my girls to England without a big stash of cash in case things didn't pan out. I was no longer a vagabond, I was a father and that trumped everything, except being a husband. With Judi in my corner, things always worked out.

I don't know why, but midway through that summer, out of the blue, I began paying extra attention to her in ways I never had before. I observed more closely her interactions with our daughter and noticed more and more how utterly graceful and natural she truly was with everyone and everything. It was weird and backward of me, but I'm weird and backward anyway. I began to marvel at her and she'd ask, "What are you smiling at now?" and I'd say, "You!" I was falling in love with her in a new romantic way and my feelings toward her were stronger than ever. All along our love had been based on trust, passion, and camaraderie but now I began seeing stars and hearing music like in an old Grace Kelly movie. I tried telling her about it and she'd laugh and I'd say, "Don't laugh, I'm serious!" She'd smile in her motherly way and say, "Well, I think it's great because it makes you happy." Then it dawned on me, I could kill two birds with one stone (a horrible term if there ever was) by asking her a question.

I'd always felt bad about her mom and my parents not being with us when we got married, so I thought if I could marry her again in a church in front of our immediate families it would be a great thing to do before we went back to England. It just felt right and she couldn't argue with that. So I asked her and she said, "Okay, but this is the last time!" She thought I was silly but I went to St. Mary's Church where I met Father Tom for the first time. He said he could marry us in a month if it was to be as small a wedding as I described. And that's what we did with my parents, my brother, her mother, her new stepfather, her sister, her brother, and our landlord's daughter who always watched our little one. I was feeling like my old self for the first time since Dave died and I wanted to rock!

In the fall we received letters from England saying they couldn't wait to see us. I remember well, because a Moody Blues song always makes me think of it. It was on a Tuesday afternoon that I got a call at my day job from Judi, which was *very unusual.* We weren't an obnoxious couple that called each other every hour to discuss if the side dish for supper should be rice or mashed potatoes or that something taken out of the kitty litter box looked like J. Edgar Hoover if you looked at it from a certain angle. All she said was, "Honey, come home!" and I didn't ask any questions, I just said, "I'll be right there!" When I walked into our apartment she was sitting on the floor next to our hand-me-down couch.

The little one was beside her playing with toys. "What's wrong?" I asked. She said she was arranging the curtains and suddenly got dizzy and fell. She wasn't hurt but something was wrong with her balance. She'd been having headaches and one was so bad the week before that I took her to the emergency room. The doctor said she had an inner ear infection and prescribed medicine that she was just now finishing. I thought she might be pregnant. I stayed home the rest of the day and she felt a little better as it went.

The next day, Wednesday, was my day off. I loved it because I got up early with the little one so momma could sleep. As I was feeding her oatmeal Judi called, "Hon, please come here!"

When I did she was sitting in bed and said her head was killing her. A "drop of blood" had trickled out of her left ear so I wiped it off with a tissue and, God help me, she said, "That's good, I don't want to scare the baby," and then added, "It's weird. I couldn't feel you doing it; I think the left side of my face is numb."

I said, "We're not screwing around with this. As soon as you're up we're going to Mass General." (Mass General was perhaps the best hospital in the world.)

Her response frightened me to the depths of my being because there was no resistance, she said, "That sounds like a good idea!"

Within an hour we were on our way. We decided to take the little one, which doesn't sound like a good idea but turned out to be one of the luckiest things I ever did. We also didn't want to alarm anyone till we knew what the hell was going on.

Her balance was way off when we walked into the emergency room so I carried the little one with my left arm while momma held onto my right. Before we could say a thing to anyone a nurse came with a wheelchair and told Judi to sit down while she smiled at Anna.

"What seems to be the problem?" she asked us.

I said, "My wife's been having terrible headaches. We've been to the doctor but yesterday she fell down. This morning there was blood coming out her ear and the left side of her face is numb. The doctor said it's a bad inner ear infection but I thought it best to bring her here."

She knelt, looked into Judi eyes, and asked a few questions. Then she got up and looked directly into mine and said, "It's not an inner ear infection and you were right to bring her here."

I asked, "What is it then?"

She said, "I don't know but we'll find out. I'm taking your wife to an examination room and you and the baby can join her after you check in at the desk."

Check in? I thought.

She looked at Anna and said to me, "She looks like you but you and your wife look like brother and sister."

Judi said, "Everyone says that!"

"Thankfully she takes after her mother," I said.

The nurse gave Anna a sympathetic look that puzzled me, then she whisked momma away. We never saw this nurse again but if I learned that her name was Dorothy Dix, the great Civil War nurse, it wouldn't have surprised me.

After the secretary took our insurance information we went to Judi. A nurse was rolling a cookie-cutter device up and down the left side of momma's face while her eyes were closed.

"Can you feel it now?" she asked her.

"No!"

"How about now?"

"No!"

When it got to the top of her head she could feel it. Then the nurse said she could open her eyes and when Judi saw me and Anna she said, "Hi, sweet pea. Momma's okay."

"Okay Momma," Anna said.

We sat and watched Momma follow a pencil while holding her head still. When it got too far in any direction her eyes shook in a frightening, erratic manner. Judi whispered to the nurse so Anna wouldn't hear, "I have to stop! It hurts and I don't want to get sick in front of the baby."

The nurse said, "That's enough for now anyway, we'll know more in a day or two." Then she looked at Anna and gave her the same sympathetic look the first nurse gave and said to momma, "You can see she's daddy's girl."

"From day one!" Judi said.

The nurse said someone would be along to take Judi to her room. Momma wanted to hold Anna so I put her in her lap and followed the nurse out of the room. "You mean she has to be admitted? What's wrong with her?"

She gently but firmly said, "This is the best place for her and it's good you brought her when you did. The best thing you can do is go home and take care of your daughter. We'll call you tonight with a game plan."

"A game plan for what?" I asked.

She said, "It all depends. First, we have to rule out a brain tumor!"

Dear God, a flush of hot, twisted, unwanted electrical heat (the only way I can think to describe it) flashed through me, almost picking me up. For a second I thought I heard "brain tumor" but that couldn't be.

To make the understatement of all understatements; this was beyond surreal and happening too quickly to fathom. But then, those powerful instincts to protect my girls kicked in and took over. I went back into the room and Judi handed me the little one and told me not to worry, which was my first glimpse of what it truly means to be a saint because the last person a saint thinks of is herself. I took this as a good omen because no way in hell would a just God ruling any universe allow something so sinister as a brain tumor to happen to someone like this. And, I was positive God knew there was no way a cowardly fool like me could handle it.

Instinctively, Judi and I acted as normally as we could for our little one. But the words "we have to rule out" had me in their sights. I was too petrified to move, encased in a chaotic, confusing nightmare where nothing made sense. The kind guys like Freud and Jung convinced science was the mind's attempt to resolve some deep-seated issue, but somehow never does. The kind that when you wake you thank God it's only a dream, but as the fog clears it's not! It's real and there's no God to thank. The seed of torture was planted in my soul because who was I to be concerned with my thoughts and feelings, for *what was momma feeling?* Hadn't Lincoln taught me, the voice of a slave is *the only voice that matters?*

Momma's concern for us was a rock-solid guarantee that if Billy Joel's song has a shred of truth that *"only the good die young,"* then I was scheduled to live a long life in the emotions of shadows that would announce darkness inside me for the rest of my days.

Before an orderly took her away I kissed her. When Anna kissed her, Momma said, "Kiss the other cheek darling." She wanted to *feel* her daughter's kiss.

Good Doctors

Stunned and stung outside the beehive entrance of Mass General with our little one's head on my shoulder, my feet couldn't move. Humanity whizzed by in its haste to nowhere and I wanted to scream for it to stop. Didn't anyone realize it's not every day a saint came here. After reflecting, they could go right back to the world of racing rats. But no one slowed or even gave a crap. I was lost in the melee of battle smoke until a little voice said, "Daddy, I'm hungry," and the kind of autopilot only a parent can know kicked in. We walked to a Burger King.

I watched her pick up French fries with her palms more than her fingers as little kids do. "Can I have one?"

"Uh-ha," she said and she pushed one towards me.

I wanted to yell, swear, smash, and break out of this nightmare. To say I couldn't believe what was happening doesn't cut it but the thought I had from the very moment of meeting Judi, that she was too good to be true, entered my mind and I would've lost it then and there if it wasn't for my little savior eating greasy processed potatoes. Oblivious to my panic, she trusted she was safe, and how could I tell her otherwise?

"Is it okay, if we have a few days to ourselves sweetheart, just you and me?"

"It's okay daddy."

Maybe I should've gone back into the hospital to tell them we'd do this some other time, say in twenty-five to thirty years, after I walked my little friend down the aisle, but I didn't have the foresight.

Later at home the hospital called when Anna and I were having supper and told me to come in the next day at 10 a.m. to meet the doctor who'd be handling "your wife's case." After I put the little one to bed I called Judi, and it was so good to hear her voice. Her first question was, "What did you guys have for supper?"

"Green beans, squash, and chicken breast," I said.

"That's good. I was hoping you wouldn't sneak off to a Burger King." She said the doctor wanted to do a test and needed to discuss it with us.

"Have you met him?" I asked

"Yes, he's very cool and you'll like him a lot. His name is Dr. Richard Young and he is very young."

"How are you Jude?" I asked.

She said they had her hooked up to a steroid drip that already made her headaches feel better. I didn't like that because I knew how dangerous 'roids could be from my old bodybuilding days. Then she said, "I'd be doing better if you were here."

"Me too! I'll see you in the morning and stay all day."

"Who will watch Anna?" she asked.

"I don't know but don't worry." We decided not to tell our families anything until we had definitive information.

The next morning I left Anna with our landlord's family upstairs and had to tell them Judi was in the hospital. Their eleven-year-old daughter Maureen embraced her. When I got to Judi's room she wasn't there because she was taking a coordination test. A nurse told me Dr. Young wanted to see me as soon as I arrived. I liked him immediately. He looked directly into my eyes and not only did I see sympathy, but also compassion and understanding. He had a curious nature and this battlefield was the canvas on which he pursued his art for those who needed help. I felt like Stephen Douglas when he first met Abraham Lincoln. Douglas said he knew he'd met a man he could trust and even come to love. But where they'd come to disagree on the nature of slavery/cancer, I knew there'd be no friction whatsoever between me and Dr. Young. "I want you to be straight with me. I can handle it."—My first and only lie to him—"It appears you think my wife may be in big trouble, is that right?" I asked.

He said, "Yes. Let's go someplace quiet to talk."

On the way to a private lounge he told me he used to live in the Hampstead section of London so I knew he'd been talking to Judi. Then he said in a questioning way, "I've only spent a half hour with your wife this morning so that I may explain what I'm going to explain to you, and I have to say she's quite remarkable. In medical school we're taught to keep our professional distance but with her you can't. *She's very unusual.*"

"Dr. Young, everyone who meets her feels the same and that's not a fraction of it. I've been with her for five years and I still can't get used to how cool she is. Plus, she's an incredible mother."

The word "mother" affected him. He asked quietly, "To Anna?" and I said yes. "Judi said you're like a second mother to her," he said.

"I can only wish!"

When we got to the lounge we went to work. He wanted permission to do a test called a pneumoencephalogram that would give "his team" a better (X-ray) picture of what was in Judi's head but I needed to understand it carried serious risks, sometimes debilitating to the patient. It involved draining fluid out of her spinal column and replacing it with air and that's what made it dangerous. Then he reluctantly said, "We need to get a clearer picture in order to determine *if* we can help her." This sounded beyond ominous.

I touched his arm and said, "I understand what you're telling me, Dr. Young." Then I told him what my family had recently gone through with

Dave, and that I understood the nature of the beast because, dear God, he had said "*if* we can help her."

"If it was your wife, Dr. Young, what would you do?"

He grinned as if to say "I'll be damned" and then said, "Judi told me you'd ask me that. If it was my wife I'd say yes!"

"Then I say yes too!"

Judi had already signed a consent form, so I did too. Then we walked to her room and when she saw me she said, "Finally." We held each other like there was no tomorrow. Dr. Young explained that they'd do the test the following morning and that she'd be sedated for the rest of the day so it might be better if I stayed home and took care of the little one. Someone would call as soon as the test was over to let me know how it went and we said "Okay." Before he left Judy asked him about the steroid drip and he said it was to get the swelling down around the "abnormality." He added it was necessary for the test and also "the best tool at this time to relieve pain."

"Are there side effects?" she asked.

He replied, "The immediate one is water retention, which means possible bloating, but let's see what's going on in your head before we worry about that."

After he left, Judi, I, and her IV stand walked down the hall to a little sitting room on the eleventh floor with a view of the city and part of the Charles River. We tried to digest what was going on. "How's Anna doing with me here?" she asked.

"Better than me!" I suggested we call her when we got back to her room. Then she said, "Look, sweetheart, I know this is freaking you out, especially with what happened to Dave. With him they couldn't take out the 'bad stuff' but with me if there's anything there they probably can, and besides, we don't know if it's what Dave had. But no matter, I'm in the best place in the world so let's see what the test says."

"Do you have to be so frickin' rational about this?" I asked.

"Yeah, but I don't mind!"

I said that while she was having the test I'd tell our families what was going on and that we'd give them info as we got it. Back in her room she called Anna and I watched in awe at the way she took care of her daughter over the phone. "Are you taking care of Daddy?" she asked, and I heard, "Uh-ha. Daddy plays songs." After supper I left to put the little one to bed and was up all night thinking, *this can't be happening!*

The next morning Anna asked, "Daddy, where's Momma?" I told her Momma might have a boo-boo in her head and she was in a place where they would make it better. Then we went to Judi's mom's and they were stunned. I told them the truth that we just didn't have enough information to determine how serious it might be. Then we went to my parents and told them the same. "Momma has a boo-boo!" They were equally stunned and had the same *I can't believe this* feeling I did. Anna was so good about it all and didn't whine a single time about being stuck with me. In every respect, except those that don't matter, she was taking care of me more than I was her. She truly is the daughter of a woman who floated the earth.

Later that day the hospital called saying Momma survived the test without complications and I could see her the next day, so I arranged for Anna to stay with my mom. When I arrived Judi was sleeping, loosely tied to her bed with a medieval-looking device holding her head still. Because of the test she had to stay like that for most of the day. If she moved, it could cause tremendous pain. A nurse got on the phone and said, "Dr. Young, Mr. Foster is here." She led me to a room where he had a series of X-rays up on screens and I could see by the silhouette of the face they were of Judi.

He said, "I thought it would be better to show you instead of tell you what we've found." He said the problem was in the worst possible area for there to be one; the "pons" section of the brainstem, which was the grand central station of where all signals pass back and forth from the brain to the body, and it was a very narrow terminal. He pointed to a dark mass the size of a dime and said, "That's the culprit!" I couldn't believe how small it was. He said if it wasn't in such a difficult location it wouldn't be so dangerous but because it was, it was!

I *had* to ask the question I dreaded more than anything. "Can you get it out?"

"No, it's too far in. If we tried it could kill her and if she survived she'd most likely be paralyzed."

"Can you get some of it?" I asked.

"That poses the same risk."

"What can we do, then?"

He took a deep breath because I think my direct questions, which were only a defense mechanism, took him aback. I was a "damn the torpedoes" veteran now because of Dave. And I know I'm a fool for explaining it like this, but because of the strange way my mind processes information in musical and historical contexts his explanation for the "culprit" reminded me of Lincoln's letter to Horace Greeley that he'd do whatever it took to save the nation, whether it involved removing all the cancer or some of it or leaving it the hell alone because he knew far better than abolitionists like Lloyd Garrison that if the *Last Best Hope Of Earth* was to perish, the cause of slavery would be strengthened a thousand fold the world over. This was how Dr. Young became my "good doctor," just as Lincoln did for the nation. Both used "cold unimpassioned reasoning" because this was the only way to truly help my best friend. Prayer and wishful thinking couldn't hurt but in the case of cancer/slavery Dr. Young and Lincoln knew that caution and reason must rule until an opportunity to strike arrived, if it would at all. Dr. Young said, "We'll continue treating her symptoms with steroids and when the time comes we'll use radiation on the *tumor* to try to slow its *spread*." So there they were, two of my favorite words meaning flesh against flesh, just as slavery did to our nation.

"What kind of tumor do you think it is?" I asked.

"It's hard to be certain, but because of its shape and density we're treating it as if it's the severest kind of *malignancy*." Another of my favorite words because, as I learned with Dave, it meant "likely to cause death." Dr. Young went on, "The steroids will *temporarily* keep the tumor from causing too much more damage by keeping the swelling down, but *eventually* they'll lose their effectiveness and we'll try radiation because that *sometimes* works on cells that are growing faster than healthy cells *but* we can only use it sparingly because it must pass through healthy tissue to get to the bad."

"So let me get this straight, you suspect the tumor is cancer?" I asked.

"Yes."

Dear Lord God; this truly was The Civil War. "Are you saying there's no cure?" I asked.

He said, "Only *complete removal,*" which sounded like The Thirteenth Amendment. Dear God in heaven, the selfish coward I truly am instantly became a believer and I prayed a silent prayer; "Please hear me God. My wife, my best friend, my confidant, my baby's momma, my every inspiration and comfort is going to die, and there's nothing mortal man can do." To the doctor I said, "Doctor, I'm interpreting these pictures as revealing a death sentence. I don't want to put you on the spot but how long will it take for nature to take its course?"

"Usually, less than two years," he said and added, "Our job is to make her as comfortable as we can."

I asked if I could look at the X-rays for a few minutes and he said I could look as long as I liked. After several minutes I said, "Dr. Young, this dark mass in my wife's brain reminds me of why Abraham Lincoln called slavery and cancer the same thing, because when it's allowed to spread, it kills!"

He said, "That's true. The problem with cancer is it can't survive without spreading and it devours *everything* healthy around it!"

And I thought, *My God, no wonder the Confederacy fought so hard for the privilege of spreading cancer to the free-soil territories of the nation. They knew if they didn't their way of life was doomed; how very sad for all of us!*

The technical term for Judi's tumor was a pontine glioma, but to me forever after it became slavery. And her brainstem, so vital to her life, became the South because a healthy South was vital for the nation and democracy the world over,

343

but it was infected with the disease of slavery/cancer and was so screwed up it thought it was healthy and so formed a Confederacy of "sister slave states" as she proudly boasted, to protect a disease they called sacred. But the South was not the only place infected by carcinogens; the North was infected with racism, bigotry, and ignorance too and that's the cause of slavery everywhere. The only difference was people like Lincoln were trying to get rid of it while Jeff Davis and Alexander Stephens, president and vice president of the Confederacy, respectively, were trying to protect and spread it. Dr. Young, like Dr. Lincoln, would treat it as gently as he could in order not to harm my wife. But unlike Lincoln, Dr. Young wouldn't get the chance to remove it.

I couldn't stop thinking within my odd historical and musical parameters because there were no words I could find to describe the sadness, fear, and utter panic in my heart. I was dumbfounded with grief and desperation, trying to come to grips in the only way I knew how. A very dear friend, a great historian and lawyer recently came back from the national archives in Washington after doing research. He brought me a copy of the map plainly visible under the table depicted in Francis Carpenter's famous painting of Lincoln called, *The First Reading Of The Emancipation Proclamation Before The Cabinet* that hangs in the capitol. Lincoln was fascinated by it and studied it like no other map because it was the 1860 census map and dark masses, like the one in Judi's head, illustrated the extent of cancer in the American South. Lincoln used it to plan military movements through less infected areas just as Dr. Young would've if he could've. And because there was always a political aspect to the cancer Lincoln dealt with, the map helped him determine what his emancipation policies would and could be. He performed surgery only when he felt it was safe to, not before!

Not too long after Lincoln was killed by a lover of cancer, two of his harshest northern critics, Greeley and Garrison, came to admit they were wrong to have said he didn't "cut out" slavery as quickly as he could because the map made it crystal clear The Good Doctor moved against it as quickly as military victory allowed him to. Unlike Greeley and Garrison, he was unwilling to let the Union, his patient, dissolve in order to separate from the cancer. The United States had to live, and when the chance to strike a blow against the disease came, he struck boldly and swiftly *against* the advice of his cabinet and did so in a methodical, medical, military, legal way that no one could argue with. He told a friend this was why he'd been born. It was the right thing to do at the precise time the nation was ready to accept it, though not everyone was. He said if he'd done it six months earlier it would've been too soon, and six months later, it would've been too late. Dr. Young explained radiation to me in the same way, making me think of Frederick Douglass saying that blacks knew Lincoln's proclamation was the end of slavery, even if it was only effective on paper, because it put rifles into the hands of upward of 200,000 black Union soldiers willing to give their lives so America could be what it was supposed to be.

When I look at the map today I see Judi's X-rays and think of what Lincoln said before the war, when he was asked why he didn't speak out about getting rid of slavery where it existed. He gave the analogy of children sleeping in bed with a poisonous snake and their parents not knowing what to do about it because striking the snake might harm the kids. But if their kids were sleeping without a snake and one was found slithering toward them from a dark corner the parents would most certainly strike it dead. That's how he explained why he didn't know how to get rid of slavery where it was. Also, as he unfortunately yet correctly explained, the government had no legal recourse to do so, and even if it did he didn't see how it could be done without unimaginable suffering and bloodshed, and the massive war regrettably proved him correct! But, as he also said a hundred times in the 1850s, the best way to get rid of the damn thing, "sending it to ultimate extinction" was to stop its spread. For us, steroids and radiation, like all the gut-numbing compromises from the founding of our nation, were only a temporary trick.

Lincoln's friend, Alexander H. Stephens, as vice president of the Confederacy said in an interview printed in *Harper's Weekly* on March 1, 1862, a month before the brutal battle of Shiloh that, "The Revolution of 1776 established the right and the capacity of white men to govern themselves; the Revolution of 1861 is to establish for all future time, the inequality of the white and black races, and the inalienable right of the former to the service of the latter. Slavery is, in a word, the cause, the end and the aim of the present rebellion. It was begun to prevent the restricting of slavery within its limits. It is carried on to secure, protect and extend it. Every leader of the Rebellion has placed himself on record *in favor of perpetual slavery* of the negro race, as their natural and normal condition, upon which the white race can live side-by-side with the black. To believe that the South would surrender slavery for any consideration whatever is to suppose the South unnecessarily giving up *the only thing it is fighting for,* and yielding gratuitously, the whole point at issue." This statement by Stephens was not an isolated one. Every Confederate state put out ordinances and resolutions explaining exactly the same thing to their citizens about why their state was seceding, or attempting to. No southerner who could read was in the dark about why they were fighting.

This is what slavery/cancer knows; it cannot survive without spreading. Lincoln thinking it evil and Stephens thinking it sacred knew this explicitly. Davis and Stephens said the Founding Fathers were right in all things except one, slavery. That their generation was far wiser and more advanced than that of Washington, Jefferson, Franklin, and Adams that said slavery was evil and should not be allowed to grow. The Confederacy was going to correct that fatal flaw in the Founders' thinking because their generation's updated science proved, along with their religious high ground, that God put blacks on the earth for the benefit of white men. They truly were diseased by this insanity and their minds too far metastasized by an aristocratic, bigoted culture to ask or ponder the issue. All while many northern, conservative textile industrialists with their greedy, disingenuous view of the southern system of labor made millions off it. As Lincoln said, over and over, "We're all guilty!" The 1860 census map revealed to him that South Carolina had a population of 57.2 percent slave followed by Mississippi with 55.1 percent slave, *not* coincidently the first two states to secede, descending on down showed cancer in the South was far larger than the cancer in Judi's head. If it grew, Dr. Young knew it would kill her just as Lincoln knew slavery would kill the nation.

Ministers, priests, and rabbis of the South religiously defended slavery preaching, as did Reverend Dr. Thornwell, who taught young seminarians at the Presbyterian Seminary in Columbia, South Carolina, that, "Our slaves are our solemn trust; and while we have a right to use and direct their labors, we are bound to feed, clothe, and protect them; to give them the comfort of this life; and to introduce them to the hope of blessed immortality. They are moral beings, and it will be found that in the culture of their moral nature, we reap the largest reward from their services. The relation of slaves to master, itself, is moral; and in the tender affections and endearing sympathies it evokes, it gives scope for the most attractive graces of human character. Strange as it may seem to those in the North who are not familiar with our system, slavery is a school of virtue, and no class of men have furnished sublimer instances of heroic devotion than slaves, in their loyalty and love to their masters. We have seen them rejoice at the cradle of the infant and weep at the bier of the dead; and there are few among us who have not drawn their nourishment from their generous breast. Slavery is the cornerstone and foundation of our Confederacy. It is the most sacred institution of our Southern society." This reveals how utterly insidious in sheer audacity and condescension slavery/cancer was and always will be. It's the lifeblood attitude of every aristocrat ever to walk the earth; that "slavery is a school of virtue."

When I went back to Judi's room I gazed at her and *felt* a powerful hatred for cancer. I thought she was asleep when she said, "It's okay hon, I know they can't operate."

"How do you know that?" I asked.

"I've been awake and your breathing tells me what you're thinking. Your grandmother could tell what your grandfather Abe was thinking and you breathe like him. Please understand sweetheart, I don't want you to be sad.

I've smelled more roses than a lot of people and we'll smell more yet! This is going to be harder on you than me, so you need to concentrate on taking care of Anna, otherwise *I won't be able to do this* and you won't survive, and Anna needs you to and I do too."

I couldn't talk. I felt like I did when Dave told me he'd make a good kamikaze and I cried.

She said, "Don't cry, sweetheart, you'll make me cry and I have to stay still. We'll have a good one later if you want. I'm going to sleep. Go home and tell Anna Momma loves her so much, and that I love her daddy too!"

She fell into a deep sleep so I left, because I needed to be with the little one in order to keep from jumping out the eleventh-floor window. I asked the nurse when Judi could go home and she said in a few days, then I asked when I could bring the little one to see her momma. She said, "You can visit twenty-four/seven." I hadn't known that. Going over the Tobin Bridge back to Lynn I was a wreck and reached for my lifeline. I turned on the radio as loud as it could go before distorting to hear the opening notes of Jimi Hendrix's "Little Wing." I couldn't believe it came on at that exact moment. If I wasn't so numb it would've freaked me out because it was always *the* song of all songs in the universe that made me think of Judi. It's about a woman whose inner beauty is only surpassed by her generosity. I began to violently weep and the highway was not the best place for that, especially with a little girl depending on me to make it home in one piece. When Jimi sang, *"Take anything you want from me, anything!"* it was Judi singing to me and my world shattered into a million pieces, for she sang it as if God and I were one.

Before going home I made a quick stop at the Lynn library and the same librarian who helped me learn about Dave's cancer and chemo saw my face and said, "Don't tell me . . . what now?" She helped me find articles on brain tumors, steroids, and radiation. Once again, I sat in the same chair I had when I read about Dave. I trusted everything Dr. Young told me but my curious, pain-in-the-ass mind had to learn more so I could better discuss things with him. Knowledge is *always* good in a time of war and equally so in a time of peace. It confirmed everything I feared; Judi had been sold into slavery and her suffering would be of a nature no one should endure. As death approached it would attempt her "ultimate extinction" by robbing her of her dignity, by separating her and her baby, and no mother or baby should go through that.

Well, man, oh man, and holy moly combined, did the nurses on the eleventh floor of Mass General ever go crazy over the little one when I brought her to visit her momma the next day. Like her mom, she had, and still does have, an aura that makes you feel good to be alive. And these are not the words of a proud sentimental father because I can't emphasize how many times I was told how "unusually pleasant" it was to be around this little human. Eyes sparkled wet in the sockets of these hard-core battle-seasoned nurse veterans, because damn, after being blown away by her momma's never complaining understanding, to meet her daughter with the same disposition was tough, even for those who believed they were immune to the music of the human heartstring.

Anna sat on her momma's bed most of the day while they played games and read stories. When I took Momma for a ride in her wheelchair Anna sat in her lap. Within a few days Judi's balance and pain were stabilized, and Dr. Young introduced Judi, Anna, and me to a nurse named Jan Corbett, a member of his brain tumor team. We instantly fell in love with her. She'd become my *technical* security blanket and advisor. She gave me a schedule of appointments every other week for the next three months and prescriptions for steroids and pain killers, along with her phone number. She said to call any time, day or night. "If anything, even if it seems insignificant, comes up. Don't hesitate!" Here was a real deal Clara Barton, who during the Civil War said that as long as *her soldiers* fought, she'd stand, feed, and nurse them, "anywhere between the bullet and the battlefield."

The next day we brought Momma home and she couldn't button the "civilian" pants I brought for her. She thought it was odd because she hadn't been eating and said, "I guess Dr. Young wasn't kidding about water weight."

From what I'd learned at the library I knew our nightmare with steroids had begun. But to have my girls home with me was magical despite the circumstances, because my instincts to protect and care for them could be satisfied to a degree. Seeing them together tore me up though, because Dr. Young's words, "usually within two years," kept ringing in my ears. I experienced anguish no words and very little music can describe. I was sad for myself but the sadness for my girls was unbearable. After Judi asked me not to cry in the hospital I became an expert at hiding my tears, but the little one caught me a few times, and still does. I couldn't help it because everyday I could see the second hand of her momma's clock ticking off her time left on earth and her sun sinking slowly to oblivion. It's the goal of slavery/cancer, and doesn't stop till the deed is done. And even then it's never satisfied, so after the good suffer their last, it turns on itself.

We lived as normally as we could in this nightmare, and I think we did better than the vast majority would have in our situation, which was purely due to Judi's attitude. She never complained once, never asked "why me?" I'd start my day with a half hour meditation and let the little one sit in my lap for the last five minutes so she could feel the peace. I'd been doing that since she was born. I was very lucky that my boss at my day job let me work double shifts twice a week, which gave me just enough hours to keep our health insurance. I'll forever be grateful for this because the medical bills were already into many thousands of dollars. With my crazy work schedule I would've been lost without our families helping to keep an eye on my girls.

At night I'd gig a little, but never far from home, and this provided extra cash so we never went without. The only thing growing faster than our little one was the slavery in her momma's head. I tried to protect our daughter by deciding early on to be totally honest with her about what was going on. I didn't know if it was a wise choice but it turned out to be. She needed to understand why her momma couldn't play with her like she used to, that it wasn't because her momma didn't want to, but because she wasn't able to. Even before her momma got a "boo-boo" in her head people said talking to Anna was like talking to a little adult. Now she helped me with house chores without being asked. When her momma dropped something she usually got to it before me.

Judi couldn't drive or work anymore, but could do quite a bit because the steroids stabilized her balance to a degree, but not enough to pick up Anna. Not only did Judi not want to fall with her daughter in her arms, but the act of bending over could give her a headache that a migraine would've been a relief from. I watched her struggle with this, and it made me so sad because nothing's more powerful than the instinct of a mother to pick up her child. It killed me because every little kid wants to be picked up and Anna was no exception. I had to have an adult conversation with her to explain that when she wanted to be picked up to come to me and when she saw her momma sitting that she should crawl into her lap. She understood and said, "Okay Daddy." Because of this my left bicep grew huge and her momma's lap became the place to be.

During the day, if Judi felt up to it, the three of us would go for drives along the North Shore coast or through the beautiful farm areas of Topsfield, Georgetown, and Boxford. Judi and I did this a lot before we had the little one, and we'd fantasize that after I made it big in music we'd live in one of these beautiful places when we were in the States and when we were in England we'd have a thatched cottage in the boonies, both with piano rooms. When she felt strong we'd go for walks up Pine Grove Cemetery, a truly beautiful place, just around the corner. She'd be on my arm with the little one alternating from my shoulders to walking.

Our plans of returning to England were gone and were the least of my worries, but it bothered Judi and she told me so. But somehow, despite my being depressed or distracted or whatever word someone who understands these things has for it, as always happened in my life, I began meeting and becoming friends with some of the crème de la crème of musicians north of Boston. This made Judi feel a little better about us not going back to England because, God help me, she believed her illness was somehow responsible for that.

When these new musicians met her they fell in love with her just like my sweet English Confederates had. But what she didn't know, because by some miracle I was able to hide the extent, was that I was slipping into the fog, autopilot, distracted, zombie-like stage of my life that I'd be in for well over twenty-five years, that I've never completely come out of.

The most influential musician was a dear friend of my duo partner Dennis. He was the great keyboard player Brian Maes who'd go on to great heights as a much sought-after session player for the likes of Peter Wolf, Aerosmith, Robert Plant, June Carter, and too many others to mention, as well as writing a Top 40 hit in the '80s, "When Your Love Comes Back Around" with a band called RTZ, which included former members of the band Boston. Today he's the lead singer and keyboard player for Ernie and The Automatics and their debut album is absolutely fantastic. For me, what separated him from others, more than his incredible musicianship, was his songwriting ability. Den invited him to see us in a cool little club up near Salem State University. Over the course of the night we mixed in a dozen or so songs I'd written, and when Den introduced us it was like the time I'd met Colin because he asked if I wrote the songs. When I said yes, he said, "We should go in the studio sometime."

Through him, I was introduced to other incredible Boston musicians and producers who'd become my lifelong friends. And I know it's arrogant to say, but these great musicians became attracted to me for my songwriting ability just like Jonathan and my old English mates had. And if there was any musician within a hundred miles of Boston to have in my corner, I couldn't have found a better one than Brian Maes. The problem was, I no longer had the energy, insight, or desire to let him or anyone help me the way they were offering to. I was exhausted, miserable, and defeated because my inspiration for doing anything was a dying slave. My "get up and go" had gotten up and went, or at best, was stuck in neutral. Thankfully though, Den, Brian, and others never gave up on me.

Somehow I kept writing because, along with meditation, history, and exercise, it was how I coped with the civil war raging in my soul. As for professionally recording or promoting what I wrote, I couldn't have cared less, but Judi nudged me out of my nest of gloom just enough to put my ideas on tape. I wrote with her and the little one by my side. Writing is as personal to me as prayer is to others, and Dave, Judi, and Anna were the only people I ever felt comfortable having around while I searched for seeds to grow things. Somehow these new musicians wanted to play these seeds even if I was only with them in body and not mentally, emotionally, or spiritually enough to fully participate. They were so kind and knew my heart and mind were with Judi and Anna. And once again I heard, "She looks like your sister! Is she always that friendly?" and "You're so lucky," and "The little one looks just like you." At first Judi's personality made it impossible for anyone to believe she was in trouble but like the ocean tide that always comes, the disease soon made everyone see, and feel *nah . . . this ain't right.*

For awhile she had the strength to come to my gigs but gradually it became impossible. The steroids dealt with her symptoms, but not the slavery relentlessly invading the "free soil" section of her brain. Her emotional state, cognition, and decision-making weren't affected but motor skills, like walking, tasting, seeing, feeling, and swallowing were wasting away. Not being able to see me play was a huge, sad insult added to injury because, "It's how we met!" Without her, gigs became a boring, passionless chore when they were once a sacred sacrament. I still played and prowled the stage in an aggressive Pete Townshend–like fashion because I could never abandon a song, but no one knew how disenchanted I was with it all.

One night Brian dropped in to the smoky little club where Den and I played a lot in Salem because his band was working in a larger club down the street. There was an old upright piano I could bang on that we hung a microphone down just enough to pick up the sound of termites munching but not enough to cause feedback. Brian and his band walked in just as we began to play two new piano songs, "Let Your Love Shine" and "Mystery Time," which I'd written that week. When we did the place went nuts. After the set Brian suggested we go into a studio right away to record them. His band was made up of Berklee grads and like my Hartismere mates, were a well-oiled machine so all we needed was a day or two of rehearsal. We booked a cool studio in Haverhill and recorded the songs live with only a few takes for each. Brian played my piano parts and did to them what Jonathan had done in England, which was mind-blowing. I played acoustic and sang backup with Brian while Den sang lead. When we heard the playback we felt we'd captured something really special. The producer said it was catchiest thing he'd ever recorded.

Den was working in a little sandwich shop in Boston during the day that a lot of musicians frequented. Frank Zappa was in town (around the time of his "Peaches in Regalia" period) touring with one of the most unbelievable bands ever, and the bassist and a couple other guys from his band came into the shop for lunch. Den didn't know them from Adam but had our song "Let Your Love Shine" playing over the shop stereo and the bass player asked Den if he knew whose music it was. Den said it was his and the bass player asked him to play it again. After it was over he told Den he thought it was a hit and that he should do something with it. He gave Den two tickets for the Zappa show that night and he went with his girlfriend. I had consciously challenged myself to write "Let Your Love Shine" as a danceable song flavored with a not-too-blatant disco feel, (kick drum anyway) without any ridiculous "oogie boogie on downs" or "get it on with me all night babys," as this was 1978. I wanted to try to write something good and catchy that anyone could dance to that also rocked. So what Zappa's bass player said to Den was music to my ears because I couldn't tolerate disco almost as much as I can't 99.9 percent of today's rap, so much of which I find to be crude and so awfully embarrassing.

When we recorded it Brian didn't know I played bass because he'd only seen me play acoustic and piano, so he enlisted an incredible bass player, Craig Spinney, who made the groove come alive. My strange vision came out a little light compared to what I was writing at the time, but it sounded very professional and catchy. People said they couldn't get it out of their heads and nothing sounds better to a songwriter than that. We were constantly asked to play it and no one thought it disco-ish, and I kept the inspiration for it to myself. We made a few hundred cassette copies and whenever someone came into Den's shop and asked what they were listening to, he'd say, "It's me and some friends," and hand them a tape. We passed them out at gigs too. There was no picture or bio; it was just a rinky-dink cassette with our phone numbers written in Den's hand, which even he could barely read.

We never learned how, but somehow a cassette got into the hands of a guy named John O'Toole who had worked with or for Aerosmith in some capacity at one time, and he gave it to a man named Frank Welling, who was an agent for the world-famous William Morris Agency. When Welling heard the song he invited me and Den to his home in Framingham, Massachusetts. It was a beautiful place with a grand piano, and he asked us to play the song and several others. I would've brought my acoustic had I known we'd be playing. Then he brought us to his office, which had gold records on the walls with pictures of him with Frank Sinatra, Engelbert Humperdinck, and stars of that genre, and it was so ironic that Den and I were there in torn dungarees, holes in our sneakers (and our heads), trying not to mess up his rug or knock things over. He was in his mid '70s and we made him laugh. He said he wanted "to manage a young, hungry act before he retired."

I wasn't sure we'd be a good fit, but he asked if we could play a full set of original material with the band so we casually mentioned it to Brian who casually said, "Let's do it!" Somehow Brian found the time for us and his band to learn a whole set of my songs, including "Blue Is Just A Word." Within a month we booked The Soundstage at the Cambridge Music Complex, which was used by bands to do live showcases for record companies interested in them. It was a cozy little room that felt like a glove when you walked into it. So we put on a show for Mr. Welling and his two young associates. A hundred of our friends showed up even though the place could only hold fifty comfortably. They screamed and yelled and would've done the same had we only been burping over our microphones. When it was over Mr. Welling asked if we'd do another showcase in New York if he paid the expenses and, because this was Brian's band, we ran it by him and Brian said yes. Everyone was ecstatic except me.

I raced out right after talking to Brian. I needed to get home! Judi hadn't gone to a gig for awhile, but insisted on going to this one so she'd been taking extra doses of painkillers that day because they were starting to lose their effect. Her pain had been intensifying because slavery was spreading. I had earmuffs to put over her ear-plugged ears if she needed them. Just as we were leaving for the show she said, "Oh my God . . ." If I hadn't been holding her she would've tumbled down the stairs. I sat her down and she couldn't speak. Her pain was so severe her body shook. She clutched my arm and held up a finger signifying, "I have to stay still and can't say anything." I asked if she wanted water so she could take more Percodan, her pain medication, and she held up a finger that indicated yes. Luckily I had her leaning against the railing so I got the water and pill in seconds. Then she held up two fingers—I'd never seen her take more than one at a time—and when I came out with the second she motioned that I had to put them in her mouth and tilt the glass so she could swallow them. This was a major task and her frown revealed terrible pain. She got the pills down and I started to get up to call Cambridge to tell them to cancel the gig or play without me but she grabbed my sleeve and I crumbled down in a heap of misery. After several minutes of silence the pills began to work and she said, "Honey, I think I can talk now, please don't be scared. Give me another pill." So I gave her a third and after a short while she was able to turn her head a little and I brought her to bed. She sat and reached for the phone. I thought she was calling our case nurse, Jan Corbett, but she said, "Mimi"—Anna called Maureen Mimi—"could you please come down?" Before I knew it Judi was asking our eleven-year-old upstairs neighbor if she'd stay with her till I got home from the gig and she said she would.

When Mimi left to tell her mom, Judi said, "Don't say anything, sweetheart. Go blow the doors off the place or I'll never speak to you again. I'll just be sleeping anyway. Jan told me to start taking as many pills as I need to so from now on I will. I'm okay now, and all I want to do is sleep. Don't argue!" She was slurring her words like a drunken sailor about to get seasick on dry land and it made me so sad. When Mimi came back I had Judi undressed and tucked in. She was in a deep sleep and I explained to Mimi this wasn't a usual gig; that I'd be home before 11 because we were only playing a fifty-minute set starting at 9. I left right away and cried the whole way. I arrived late and when Den saw my face all I needed to say was "Judi" and he hugged me. He loved her so very much and said, "I'm going to sing my ass off for her tonight!" And he did! When we went on stage I was so emotional I had to turn my back to the crowd several times because I couldn't keep from crying. Judi was on my mind every second, and even though I knew she was safe I couldn't wait to get the hell out of there. Having someone from the William Morris Agency seeing you play would've been a dream come true for anyone but within a minute of the last song and after talking to Brian I said to Mr. Welling, "I've got to go! My wife's very sick!"

There were no cell phones in those days so when I got home and saw Mimi doing her homework it was an enormous relief. She said Judi never made a sound so I checked on her and she seemed okay, but as I gazed at her I had my first inkling of "if you want to slip away my friend, you can." It was way, way, way too soon to think a thing like that, but I thought it anyway. I couldn't bear to see her suffer and, because of Dave, I knew well the elephant that was coming.

After Mimi left I made my first of several late-night calls to Jan. I apologized for the late hour and she said, "This is my job. There's no bad time for me, just for you guys!" It's strange how you remember things because I distinctly felt that when she said the words "just for you guys," it was an afterthought or slip because she, like everyone else who met Judi, was deeply affected by her. I told her what was happening and she said to start giving Judi pain pills on a regular basis even if she didn't have a headache. She added, "When the pills lose their effectiveness we'll find something stronger." Then she said something I didn't want to hear. "I know you won't like this but starting tomorrow, *you'll need* to double her dose of steroids."

I said okay but hated the prospect. They were already making her bones weak and she'd put on close to forty pounds of water weight, which wasn't the same as normal weight on a healthy bone structure. This was a bloated, liquid weight that was very uncomfortable for her. It was slowly changing her appearance in such a sad way, making everything soft, round, squishy, and pillowy. It gave her an unnatural cartoonish look, and although she didn't know what pride was, she said she wanted to look good for me. I told her that if she could look like that for the next sixty years I'd be the happiest man alive. And damn it, she giggled and said, "Then I'll try!"

After I hung up with Jan I thought, *I can't believe this is happening.* Then Den called to ask about Judi and tell me how happy Welling was with the show. I said New York was too far to be away from Judi and he said, "Frig New York, take care of her!" After I hung up I sat in silence for a long time. Finally the little one, who was at my mom's, popped into my head and I realized I'd better go to bed. Before I did I gently lifted Judi's head to get some water into her to help a Percodan slide down her throat. It was 3 a.m. and I set the alarm for 5 to slide another. If I was going to manage her pain I was going to be good at it, because talking with Jan made a light go off in my head. If Judi was going to be with us for any length of time it was up to me to make her comfortable in order that her time be worth living. With our little one now in the picture as much if not more than me, if there was a way I could keep her momma alive long enough for her to form some lasting memories of her, I was responsible for that too. As I tried to sleep I heard Mick sing, *"Time waits for no one and it won't wait for me."* I rolled on my side and held my dear friend. No one was taking her tonight!

CAN'T LOOK AWAY

All along our beloved English Confederates had been writing us. Colin and Stephen said everyone couldn't wait to see us, but when Judi got sick I didn't have the heart to tell them. I stopped writing back and eventually their letters stopped coming; the last batch I didn't even open. I hate lying in any form but didn't know how to tell them the truth. It reminded me again of Lincoln saying, "God cannot be for and against the same thing at the same time." Today, I think not telling them was a colossal mistake, and wonder how many of them still walk the earth. I abandoned Dave to find them and by not writing back I abandoned them. I also couldn't help wondering what happened to the band, and I found out in a roundabout way when Judi was sleeping in the car on our way home from Mass General.

An advertisement came over the radio that the English band The Troggs—they had that huge hit in the '60s with their iconic anthem "Wild Thing"—were playing for two nights at a club in Worcester, Massachusetts, called The Cave. The radio DJ who was at the first show said that, even if you weren't a Troggs fan, they had a hot new left-handed guitarist who played a black Les Paul and he was well worth seeing. Somehow I could feel it was Colin. I wanted to get in my car, drive to him, throw my arms around him, and tell him how much I missed, loved, and admired him. But if I did, his first question would be about Judi and I couldn't lay that on anyone. As the day wore on I began doubting my instincts, and that possibly it wasn't Colin. By early evening my curiosity got the best of me so I called The Cave to ask if the guitarist was about five-foot-nine, slim, with brown thinning hair, a Roman nose (as Colin described it), soft-spoken, and did he smoke little thin cigars? The guy on the other end of the phone said yes to everything. Then I asked if he knew the guitarist's name and he said, "Yeah, it's Colin something or other." I asked, "Is it Colin Fletcher?" and the guy said, "Yes, do you want to talk to him? He's somewhere behind the stage, I'll get him for you?"

This stunned me! I was confused because I now knew the band had broken up or got dumped by Charisma, and I believed it was my fault and still do. And not to knock The Troggs, but their music wasn't the kind of music that would've interested or challenged Colin. When I say my Hartismere Confederates could've played with the *Johnny Carson Tonight Show* band, I'm not kidding. That's how good they were. Colin, Andy, Julian, and Jim never played for money. Yet playing with The Troggs would certainly help someone shackled with bills if they were being sued by a record company that had invested huge sums into them, but because they were unable to deliver thanks to their bass player *abandoning them* at the worst possible moment to attend to a family matter in America, thereby creating a breach of contract because said bass player said he'd return soon but didn't; that could haunt the music career of anyone left behind in the mess. Maybe it was just my paranoid mind "paranoiding" as usual. But when I heard those clicking heels that always clicked on the English shoes he wore coming closer to the phone I thought, even if all I thought was wrong, there was no way in hell I could lie to him about Judi so maybe I wouldn't. But when I heard the sweet soft voice of my best man at my wedding say, "Hello," I gently pushed the button ending the call. Only cowards hang up on people, especially ones they love. I'd never hung up on anyone before and haven't since but still, I'm a coward.

This sent me into a tailspin of despair and I couldn't tell Judi about it because she had enough on her plate to worry about. It hit me that of all the things dying before me, the one that made me the saddest besides seeing a little girl losing her momma was that I could no longer empty my cup of woe for Judi to sort out and fix because she simply didn't have the strength for my nonsense anymore. Musicians, family members, and friends began to worry about me, asking if I was okay but, like *"the tears of a clown when no one's around,"* I became more expert at hiding my anguish from everyone, even myself. I was losing my mind and I allowed the Achilles' heel of my life to infiltrate my being and take root, which was believing *everything wrong in the world was somehow my fault.* This has never completely left me and I wish to God it would. Thankfully my continued practice of meditation told me this couldn't possibly be true, but it was so hard to know that amid my civil war battle. Still *I knew* meditation whispered truth.

It would serve no purpose in telling the daily episodes of heartache and beat-downs that came our way in the first half of our war with slavery. And even if it did, I'm not strong enough to. Suffice it to say it was simply awful, and if not for the little one, I don't think I'd be here. But, because the truth Dave and Judi taught me *to know* demands it, I must tell a little!

After a year on steroids Judi put on so much water weight she couldn't move and I had to take her everywhere in a wheelchair. At my insistence, she was taking increasing amounts of pain pills that made her sleep. When she'd awake, pain was always waiting. So, during one of our visits to Mass General, Dr. Young suggested this might be the time to try radiation. He said in some cases it had tremendous results and not to be surprised if it did on Judi. But it sounded like Sherman's March to the Sea because a lot of innocent, healthy cells would be destroyed in the process. He didn't have to tell us the results, if positive, were only temporary because as young soldiers of war know; life itself *is* temporary.

After Jan explained the procedure for the "zapping," Judi floored us by asking, "Dr. Young, what's the most common way I'll die? If you don't have an exact answer a guess is okay." Her question brought silence, but from her, not an awkward, uncomfortable silence, but instead somehow peaceful. Dr. Young, Jan, and I were one now; awed by this remarkable person asking the question. He said she'd most likely slip into a coma and go that way, but sometimes tumors ruptured and she'd slip away immediately. He got emotional so Judi reached for his arm and said, "I'm sorry I asked, I've just been wondering, that's all. Please don't be sad, it's okay!"

I don't know why, considering everything, but watching Judi having the sides of her head shaved and bull's-eyes drawn on her with red markers to direct the radiation affected me deeply. This was the best modern medicine had to offer but it felt like some cheap science-fiction movie with ray guns. It made me realize in so many ways that modern medicine still used utterly primitive, brutal, yet sometimes effective weapons in its war with cancer/slavery. It truly was like Sherman's March through Georgia; where good got destroyed in order to get to the bad. Someday, in the not-too-distant future (we hope), radiation will seem barbaric and someone will say, "I can't believe they did that back then." But as barbaric as it might be, the results were astounding. Judi's headaches eased and even her balance got better than it'd been for a long time. She was able to cut back on pain pills so she wasn't as groggy. Best of all, she, Anna, and I were able to get out for some country drives in the New England fall—nothing's more beautiful—of 1978 and we saw such miraculous colors. Momma was like a leaf because it's when a leaf is dying that it becomes the most beautiful.

Radiation made Christmas possible. The little one was a month and a week shy of three years old and Judi was determined she'd have a good one. Judi was excellent with arts and crafts, so my girls made little knickknacks like toy soldiers out of wooden clothespins and many other creative things we hung on the tree. Anna and I still hang them. On Christmas morning Anna got up early and came quietly to me so we could let momma sleep and, although we had plans to wait until Judi got up to open presents, Santa brought so much stuff I told her she could open one. Just as I took a picture of her doing it, Judi opened the bedroom door and I unintentionally captured her on film struggling to come out to see her little girl on Christmas morning. How she got up that early I'll never know. I didn't realize until I had the film developed that I'd taken a picture of her courageous effort. It's an extremely gut-wrenching picture to look at, but makes clear why the word "valiant" was invented. She was moving without assistance and it would be one of the last times she would. We stayed home that day in our warm, cozy little apartment and people dropped by to say hello. The little one, like her mom, was welcoming to everyone; not like her stick-in-the-mud dad. But it was exhausting to Judi. She'd cut way back on her usual dose of medicine so she wouldn't fall asleep on anyone, and I could see her losing the battle with pain as the day wore on. When the Prince of Peace's birthday neared its end I loaded her up with drugs and tucked my precious angels into bed. I stayed up to clean up and it felt so lonely and quiet. Nothing stirred, not even a mouse, and I thought, *This, this is what it's going to be like.*

Soon the cold winter faded and the warmth of spring enticed her cancer to heat up and come out of hibernation for its final act. This time the beast would be ravenous, all-consuming, and the curtain would rise with a sudden jerk, revealing a vengeance nothing could satisfy. She needed more pain medication than ever but it was never enough, so Dr. Young suggested a new powerful concoction of morphine to kill pain mixed with cocaine to keep her awake. It was called Brompton cocktail. It wreaked havoc on her dying system and didn't get rid of all her pain but kept a lot at bay. She said, "At least I get to stay awake with you guys but I *hate* this stuff!" It was as close to a complaint as I'd ever hear from her.

I said, "Jude, I've never heard you use the word 'hate' before."

"That's because I never have. It's such a hateful word!" she said and we had a little laugh. But soon the contradictory mixture of this primitive medicine at war with itself began to lose its effectiveness, so in the early summer of '79

I called Jan to ask if there was any chance of Judi having more radiation. She said she and Dr. Young had discussed that very thing that morning but weren't sure "if it's worth the risk, even in a small dose." She added, "If it worked at all, it wouldn't have the dramatic effects it had the first time, but might help a little."

I remember like it was yesterday saying, "I understand Jan, but to us a little means a lot."

And like a great drummer is to a bass player, she didn't miss a beat. "Good point, I'll call you within an hour." The next day Judi got another Mohawk and red targets on her head.

The gamble paid off. She felt some relief, but the shaved areas of her head were burnt. Dr. Young told me to enjoy the summer "with your ladies" as best I could. He didn't have to say it'd be our last. I then called my Uncle John, my mom's brother, to accept his kind offer of letting Judi, Anna, and I escape to his cottage on Cape Cod. He knew what we were going through. He'd recently lost his wife, my beautiful Aunt Trudy, to cancer. Just before leaving, we had an appointment with Dr. Young and Jan. They were always happy to see us but this time seemed tense and they hit us with a bombshell: Judi was pregnant! We couldn't believe it. How could it happen? I loved Judi more than words can say but as for physical intimacy, it was far, far down the list of priorities. To put it bluntly, slavery/cancer destroys everything good, healthy and right between humans, and it's especially cruel to those who love each other with a passion.

I looked at Judi and asked, "How the hell did that happen?"

"Don't look at me," she said.

And we both looked at Dr. Young and he said, "Don't look at me; I had nothing to do with it." This brought what I can only describe as the nervous laughs of conspirators about to be hanged. But this was a grave, sad, serious situation. Dr. Young said Judi most likely had been pregnant for quite awhile but because of her extreme water weight, along with the effects of medications, they missed it. And then he did something he didn't have to, he apologized "for not catching it earlier."

This made me lose it. I broke down and cried, "It's my fault!"

Jan said, "It's no one's fault." But I couldn't believe her. *Nah . . . this ain't right!*

Dr. Young said that, because of Judi's condition, it was imperative to terminate the pregnancy immediately because she couldn't survive the trauma of giving birth. And damn it, Judi asked, "Can I try?"

Dr. Young said, "Even if you survived, the radiation and meds have made having a healthy baby impossible. We're strongly advising you to terminate today, and we've made the arrangements." Then they left us alone to decide.

I said, "Jude, we have to do this!"

She started crying and said, "I know, but I don't want to."

"Me neither."

Before we knew, we were in a room and I was holding her while the "procedure" (a devious word if there ever was) was done. We cried the whole time and a nurse and female doctor doing it became sad too. It was surprisingly quick and we somehow got through it, but you never *really* do. The nurse said, "I'm so sorry you had to have this done." It would've been better if she just said it to Judi.

On our way home I asked if she was all right as she was dozing off and she said, "No, sweetheart, I'm not, but Anna needs you to be. And Beau, I can't cry *anymore*. It makes my head hurt."

All I could say was, "Okay." As she slept I thought of Dave telling me how cancer/slavery made it impossible for him to laugh and now it made it impossible for Judi to cry. Truly they were slaves and I was a milder version of one. And now there was a new twist: a tone of defeat in Judi's voice that was completely foreign to me.

Our civil war (like America's) was relentless and about to get worse as we pulled into our driveway. I was about to learn exactly what Abraham Lincoln meant when he said, "If there's a worse place than hell, I am in it!" Judi was sleeping so I unlocked the house door as usual before bringing her in and was met by a ringing phone. It was Pat, Judi's sister. Her voice not only had the tone of defeat, but death. I thought something might've happened to her mother but the news was the worst possible because it was of a young person. Judi's brother Norman (named after his dad), who was less than a year older than Judi, had that very morning been killed in a car accident. Pat, my sister-in-law, confidant, and good friend to this very day, didn't have details and, God forgive me, I didn't want them. She relayed the important one: Her brother was dead. Norman was a wiry, chiseled little guy who always had a smile and helping hand extended for you with *never* a bad thing to say about anyone. He was as humble, honest, and kind a person as God puts on the earth. He and Judi were very, very close.

I didn't tell Pat or anyone—only Anna years later—what Judi had just gone through. When I hung up I wanted to scream at God, "What the hell are you doing?" But I didn't because the honest part of me knew God had nothing to do with the misery we were in. My relationship with God, especially then, was such that no matter if he or she existed, I *knew God was always on my side.* But dear Lord, how was I going to tell Judi about her brother after having a "procedure" permanently terminating her last biological (adoption would've been equally beautiful) chance to give her daughter a brother or sister? I decided not to tell her till morning because it was getting late, and I needed to get a crapload of pills down her throat so she could sleep without slavery's jackhammer slamming the back of her skull. I also had to bring the little one down from upstairs. Somehow I was able to get Judi to bed after giving her medication out in the car. She never fully woke. When I went upstairs to get Anna I asked Mimi if she'd watch her for a bit the next morning. As always, Mimi was there for me and still is today in more ways than one!

The next morning I waited till Judi stirred before taking Anna upstairs. I had it down to a science by now. It was never a good night's sleep that woke her, it was the low rumble of a distant, fast approaching locomotive carrying a cargo of the most excruciating pain. Within a second of its arrival her eyes would pop open from the onslaught of pressure and I'd have my hand under the back of her head, tilting it forward so a strong shot of Brompton cocktail could carry a Percodan past her vocal cords before she could say, "Good morning." Then I'd gently lay her back to let the poisons do their thing. It took a few minutes before she'd say her usual, "Thank you sweetheart," and I'd ask, "Do you need more," to which she'd reply, "Let's see if I can go without for awhile." When she said, "I'm ready," that meant, if it was a bad day, I'd put her in the wheelchair, and if a good day, I'd help her shuffle to the bathroom.

This was a wheelchair day so I had to help her on and off the toilet and, as crazy as it sounds, it was always an honor. When she was done I had the chair secured, the wheels ready to unlock, with the motor purring for our four-foot journey back to the kitchen where she'd have tea with a Brompton chaser. Usually we'd plan our day, but I told her Anna was upstairs because I had some bad news to tell her.

She said, "Hon, you look terrible. Don't worry, you can tell me anything."

I said, "Sweetheart, listen, I wish to God I didn't have to tell you this. Last night Pat called and said Norman was killed in a car accident yesterday morning. She didn't volunteer details and that's all I know."

If there were words invented to describe her expression I'd use them but there are not. She began to sob but pain reminded her she wasn't *free* to cry anymore. Plus, her ribs and lungs were too weak to. Her head began hurting so bad she *had* to stop crying! Watching this connected me to the eternal. I now understood that a person's need to grieve for a loved one is so fundamental to being human that to be deprived of that freedom of expression is to encounter despair beyond comprehension. I, too, had never been sadder. We were slaves, controlled by events that were nobody's fault.

In a few days I was wheeling her down the aisle of a church in Cliftondale for her brother's funeral. I didn't want to bring her because I didn't know if she'd survive, but she insisted. I would've wheeled her to the top of Mt. Washington if the funeral had been there. As we went to the front pew, friends, neighbors, and relatives who hadn't seen her in awhile gasped in horror at her appearance. Involuntary groans, cries of "oh my God," and weeping went on like a switch.

I couldn't get upset with a single person who reacted that way because that's how I reacted every day. They'd seen this once incredible, vibrant, athletic person floating in their midst and now this watery ball of helpless skin. It was too much to handle and many looked away, just as many in our nation look away from slavery to this very day. The truth is, to know what slavery is, *you can't look away!*

Like a southern preacher telling his flock that an all-loving God shouldn't have "pesky questions" asked of him about the rationale of slavery, the priest at Norman's funeral was a neurotic. I could feel Judi listening. "Our faith provides us with comfort that God has his reasons for taking someone so young. And it is in our faith that we can look with confidence that the eternal soul of the departed"—*Say Norman's name for Christ's sake, you sick bastard,* I thought—"is forever at peace with Jesus." I wanted to scream at him to shut the hell up because his words weren't bringing peace to Judi, just more torture. But he couldn't help himself as none of these guys really can. He was addicted to an ancient dogma of nonsense and Jesus was not about to walk onto the altar to whisper in his ear, "Please sit down. I never taught you any of the stuff you're saying to my sad brothers and sisters." The Lord was nowhere to be found and all I could hope for was someone, anyone, to come along with a giant butterfly net to take the little peddler of blowhard away, but no one came.

Judi cried profusely. Thank God she had worked out a system where she could cry without shaking too much, which was okay as long as I was there to wipe the river of tears flowing down the copious, about-to-explode cheeks of her moon-shaped face. She couldn't wipe them herself for slavery had invaded the free-soil section of her brainstem, rendering her arms useless. Soon she'd be completely paralyzed. Finally the service that felt like a *disservice* came to an end, and I was prepared to defy her for the first time by not bringing her to the cemetery to see her brother's body lowered into the earth. But as I turned for home she didn't protest, she'd had enough and was sleeping.

All that night the sad look of her mom imprinted itself on my soul. It's how I know what Civil War mothers looked like when they listened to words that didn't bring their boys home. And that their sorrow was only surpassed by slave moms whose loss had no rhyme or reason, no matter how many lunatics in pulpits said, "God has his reasons."

The Last Time
I Saw Judi

A few days after burying Norman, Judi, Anna, and I drove to my uncle's on the Cape. Everyone thought we were crazy but Judi said, "It'll be good for Anna!" With suitcases of drugs, food, and beach toys, off went a floating saint, her angel daughter, and a maniac who should've been locked up. Judi was going to die, but I thought I could postpone the unpostponable if we kept doing things healthy people did. How I got her across the sand dunes in her wheelchair to the gorgeous beaches of Brewster I'll never know, but I did. I slathered up my girls up with massive amounts of sunscreen (couldn't let them get skin cancer) and had a large umbrella and white sailor's hat for Judi. We stayed an entire week and when she said that watching Anna and I play in the water made it worthwhile, it almost did!

In late September I had to apply for emergency assistance, a fancy term for welfare. Judi was completely helpless now, and I had to be with her 24/7. I got a leave of absence from my day job and, thank God, was able to keep our health insurance as long as I paid for it. Jan wanted to set us up with a visiting nurse but I couldn't stand being away from Judi for a single moment.

And besides, nobody could take care of her better than I. Whether that was true or not was another matter, but my instincts to protect were in overdrive. We *knew* we were losing each other and every second meant the world to us. And in a strange twist of fate, the social worker who came to our home to see if what I'd written on the welfare application was true was a good friend of mine. He'd been one of the best high school hockey players in the city and I once gave him guitar lessons (for free, of course). When he walked in I thought of the last lesson I gave him, when, without a care, he said of Jimi Hendrix, "Who would've thought a nigger could play like that?" It stunned me and I didn't know what to say.

A week after he said that, my team was playing his at the old Lynn hockey arena and as he came up the ice with the puck I hit him so hard he had to be carried away on a stretcher. It wasn't a cheap shot so neither coach scolded me. Mine actually said it was good to "send a message" every once in awhile, which I found ridiculous because we were just kids. Coincidently, my coach was also my history teacher who didn't understand the difference between Jeff Davis and Abraham Lincoln, so he was just a big macho dope. I wasn't penalized for the hit but felt ashamed, because I was *never* a tough guy or fighter. Now, my friend was in our home about to decide our financial fate. Once he laid his eyes on Judi he said we'd receive a check right away. As he was leaving he asked, "Hey Bob, why did you check me so hard that time?"

And I said, "I'm so sorry. I was mad at you for calling Jimi a nigger!"

"Jimi who?" he asked.

"Hendrix."

"Oh, yeah."

After he left, Judi, who was propped up on the old couch with her eyes closed said, "Hon, that's why I married you, you know!"

I said, "I thought you were sleeping."

"Yeah, but I'm always listening."

The next day we received a check, hand delivered by my friend.

In the second week of October, an overpowering desire to make a Thanksgiving dinner somehow possessed me. I loved to cook but had never made one so when I mentioned it to Judi she said, "Well, why don't you make one? I'll teach you!" So Mimi came down to sit with Judi while the little one and I went to the store to get the "victuals," which again, is what a young hill Reb often called his food. When we got back Judi was sleeping in her wheelchair in the kitchen and the sound of grocery bags woke her. She smiled because the table was full of everything she told me to get. The prospect of the project perked her up. She was a fantastic cook and once made a pumpkin pie from scratch when we first met that was so damn good I could never let her go after that. And no offense to my mother or any mother for that matter, but Judi's turkey stuffing *is* second to none. I gave her a double dose of Brompton and we went to work. She'd doze off here and there but when the little one and I finished making the stuffing she said, "Mmmm, I can almost smell it." The truth was, along with her appetite, slavery also destroyed her ability to taste and smell. She told me we had to let the stuffing cool because it wasn't healthy to stuff a turkey when it was hot, so we had a cup of tea while Anna watched TV. She said, "You must think I'm going to die soon and you want to know how to make my stuffing so you guys can have it when I'm gone, right?"

I said, "I don't know when you're going to die sweetheart, but I'd like to know all your recipes *just in case.*"

She said, "Smart move, tomorrow I'll show you how to make spaghetti sauce," and she did. But on this day we made turkey, stuffing, gravy, turnip, squash, mashed potatoes, cranberry sauce, and peas. To this day, the little one, her family, and I have the best turkey dinners in town, courtesy of her momma.

Father Tom was coming by every week now. He was saddened deeply when he learned Judi had been diagnosed with cancer a month after he performed that beautiful, little church wedding for us. During the third week of October, he visited for the last time. We were having tea in our tiny living room while

Anna played with some kids on the porch when her momma surprised the hell out of us. "Father, do you believe in an afterlife?"

He began to say, "Our faith teaches us . . ." but she gently stopped him. "No Father, no. I'm asking you as my friend, not as a priest or what faith teaches!" I thought he was going to drop. He looked like a deer in the headlights and turned whiter than white and began to get emotional.

Judi said, "Please don't be sad, Father. I'm sorry if I've asked an improper question. I'll live on in the hearts of people who love me and that's more than enough!" I was never so proud or more in love with this person who happened to be my wife than I was at that moment.

Father Tom tried to compose himself and said, "I don't know how to respond, except to say you're closer to God than anyone I've ever known." As I walked him to his car he asked how long Dr. Young said she had to live and I said a couple of weeks or less. He said, "She's going to die on All Saints' Day. Judi is a saint!"

I said, "Father, you're not telling me anything I haven't known for a long time." He hugged me and as he drove away I thought it was good for the world that at least one priest knew that sometimes saints ask "pesky questions."

Later that week the sound of terrible moaning woke me. It was that of mangled kids, Blue and Gray, at Malvern Hill, Fredericksburg, Gettysburg, Chancellorsville, Vicksburg, Fort Wagner, Franklin, Cold Harbor, and ten thousand other places that slavery caused it. And it was coming from Judi. It was the moan that wishes for death, prays for it, and when it doesn't come asks God, "Why have you forsaken me?" I got a shot of Brompton down her throat with a Percodan but there was no relief, so I gave her another dose with another pill. A minute later she cried, "Dear God, the pain is unbelievable!" So I got a bowl of Cheerios together and brought it and our little one upstairs to Mimi. When I got back Judi was still moaning and said the pain hadn't gone away, so I gave her another shot and in desperation, God help me, another after that. Finally the morphine stabilized her and she passed out despite being loaded with cocaine too.

I then called my mom and asked her to come get the little one and she did. Then I sat with my friend and, although it's probably distasteful to always think in musical and historical terms, it's how I survive. Where others may reach for rosary beads or religion, I thought, *My God, how the kids, Blue and Gray, must have suffered without the medicine I have for Judi.* They must have suffered almost as much as people who were forced to live as slaves.

A few hours later she woke while a part of me—a big part—had been wishing she wouldn't because I couldn't stand to see her suffer. I got more crap down her throat and told her I thought it would be wise to take her to the hospital where they could treat her pain far better than I could and she looked directly through me and for the first time I saw fear in her eyes. "No Beau, I don't want to die in the hospital. I want to die here with you!" So we stayed, but as soon as she dozed off I called Jan and told her what was happening. She told me to keep giving Judi all the medicine she needed and when she woke to tell her that if she did go to Mass General, she could go home once her pain stabilized. I told Jan what Judi said about dying with me and it was the first time I heard silence from her. Clara Barton had to gather herself and after a few seconds said, "Tell Judi, I promise, there's no chance of her dying without you!" I said I'd tell her, but I had to wait till dark because she slept a long time.

Pain woke her. "Oh my God, help me Beau!" I gave her a double dose of pills and liquid and somehow it helped. She said, "Honey, when I pass out don't let me wake up."

I began to cry and she said, "I'm sorry!" For the first time ever she put me on the spot because the world was set up all wrong but not her, no, not her.

"I wish you could put a pillow over my face and end it. This is not worth it and I'm not afraid to die. I've been ready for a long time. Just remember how much I love you! Sweetheart, you've been *the truth of all things to me.*" As she drifted back to sleep I thought, dear Lord God, I'm not worthy to be the truth of all things to anyone, especially this person.

Years later a well-known historian would say to me in Gettysburg, "You see things others don't and you should write about it!" He didn't know who taught me to see these things.

Yogi Berra was right, it was, "déjà vu all over again." First Dave and now Judi had asked me to end their suffering, and I abandoned them because I didn't have the courage to do it. And I'm *not* advocating helping anyone die, but here were beautiful people pleading for relief from pain beyond comprehension that served no purpose whatsoever. Death was their *only* way out. They were asking to end their bondage, *not their lives,* just as the well-documented slave mother (who inspired Beecher Stowe), who escaped with her children yet killed them with her bare hands when they were about to be recaptured rather than let them go back to slavery/cancer. What a godforsaken nightmare the Confederacy was and we were in it!

Suddenly it was midnight and I stood over her with a pillow close at hand and before I knew it, it was 4 a.m. and I was soaking wet, standing and trembling. At 6 I got a triple dose down her throat and called my dad to help me lift her into the car because I decided to take her to the hospital against her wishes. It never dawned on me till years later that Judi was incapable of deciding what was best for her. All I thought about was honoring her wishes.

It wasn't easy but we got her into the car. She moaned but didn't wake. At Mass General I grabbed her around the rib cage to put her in her wheelchair, and when we got to the eleventh floor, Jan, my own sweet Clara Barton, was waiting. She looked at us and said, "My God," and directed two nurses to take Judi. One said, "Don't worry, Mr. Foster; we'll take good care of her!" Jan grabbed my arm and led me to a small room near where they took Judi and told me to lie down. She asked if I'd eaten, which seemed strange, and when I said I couldn't remember she returned with a glass of OJ and a tuna sandwich. I asked if it had onions because no one who has consideration for anyone should put onions in a sandwich without asking. She smiled sadly and said, "I don't think so. Eat and try to rest."

When I woke in the afternoon Jan was tugging my sleeve and explained that Judi's pain had stabilized. They were injecting her with massive amounts of morphine and recommended they put her on a continuous morphine drip the following day, but warned if we did, I'd never be able to speak to her again because she'd be so out of it. I said, "Let's do it!" Then Jan asked if I knew how Judi recently broke two ribs and I said I must've done it by the stupid way I lifted her out of the car. I began crying and she said Judi's bones were so weak from the steroids that sneezing could break them, but her words didn't comfort me.

Then I went and sat with Judi. When she opened her eyes she looked straight at me but didn't see me and I thought she'd already gone to yonder regions. A little later she opened them again and said, "You'll have to find a good woman to care for you" and "Anna is lucky to have you!" and nonsense like that. When it was late I passed out in the chair next to her and woke to hear her asking where she was. When I told her she said, "Beau, please don't let me die here. I want to be home with you. Oh God, my head is killing me!"

I said, "Don't worry darling, you'll be with me!"

Jan and Dr. Young had gone home, so I told the attending nurse that Judi needed a shot of morphine and she said, "Certainly," but came back agitated a minute later. She told me the doctor on call had said, "The last shot should be enough for now." Well, I lost it. I got up and found the close-to-my-age doctor sitting at the nurses' station and politely told him my wife needed help *now* and he said he'd order a shot within the next half hour. When he said that, I literally picked him up by the collar and brought him to Judi's room, handed him the phone, and said, "Does she look like she can wait? Call for a shot right now or I'll throw you out the goddamn window!" So he did while Judi watched the whole thing. When the little aristocrat slithered away she smiled and said, "That was a good one, hon. Anna will be safe with you. I love you so much!" When the nurse gave her the shot she looked into my eyes and as she drifted away she said, "I love you, Beau!"

"I love you too, sweetheart!" My music name was the last word she spoke on earth.

I could've stayed with her all night but I needed to be with the little one so I left around 4 a.m. The next morning I had breakfast with Anna at my parents' where I explained, "Momma might not be coming home this time."

She said, "Okay daddy." Her trust in me was unfathomable. It still is and it blows me away.

When I got to Mass General, Judi was in another room hooked up to a morphine drip. Dr. Young came in and said he heard about the commotion with the doctor the night before. When I said I wanted to apologize he said, "It's us who should apologize to you. I would've done the same thing!" He said Judi was in a coma and finally *pain free*. Those last two words felt like a two-ton boulder lifted from my chest. I told him I wanted to bring her home which he had anticipated. He said it might be better if they transferred her to Union Hospital in Lynn, which was right down the street from our home. I asked if this would benefit her and he said, "No, but it will you and your daughter. You've done all you can. They'll let you sleep in her room whenever you want." I asked if he could make the arrangements and he said he already had.

Then he said, "Robert, watching you and your wife has been one of the great honors of my life. It's why I became a doctor. It's been a privilege to know you both, and I've learned so much about how to do this. If there's anything I can ever do for you, don't hesitate. It was because I could be honest with you from the beginning that you've helped me more than I can say. I don't know exactly when Judi will die but it'll be soon, less than a week."

Somehow I had learned he was a Catholic so I said, "Dr. Young, she's going to die November 1, All Saints' Day."

He welled up and said, "I'm sure it must be so."

I loved this man and knew he was truly a great and compassionate doctor who must've been even a better husband and father. He was my personal Lincoln in a civil war to save my world, my nation, my all, my best friend. I'll never forget him or Jan, my Clara Barton. When they came to Judi's funeral I told them I didn't realize they went to funerals of patients and Jan said, "We don't, but we do to those of our friends!"

All during the last days of October people came to Union Hospital to say good-bye to Judi. I was overcome by the intense sadness of everyone. I knew every person had the little one on their mind because hardly anyone asked about her because it was too hard to get the words out. I knew that for some who came from afar, who hadn't seen Judi for a long time, she was unrecognizable and I made sure to stand behind them with a chair in case it was too much. I told them the important thing was Judi wasn't suffering anymore.

On October 30, Judi's sister, my parents, brother, and future sister-in-law, Mary, came for the last time. Mary is and has always been one of my closest confidants. She loves me very much and I her, but how I wished she'd had a chance to better know the person I married because they would have been the best of friends. October 31, Halloween, "Grammy" (Judi's mom) was the only one there besides a nurse taking Judi's vitals. Judi had said eight years earlier that if I gave her mom a chance I'd grow to love her, and she was right. I not only loved her but we became the closest of friends and remained so for the rest of her life, which lasted long after Judi left this world. When I entered the room I said, "Hello Grammy," and the nurse said Judi's heart rate went up. The same thing happened earlier in the day when I came.

Grammy said, "Some things never change." I felt like I was somehow getting in on a secret I wasn't supposed to know. The nurse said, "Your wife knows when you're here." From somewhere deep my friend could *feel* me.

After Grammy left I stayed till it started getting dark and said to Judi, "Sweetheart, I'll be back soon, I'm taking the little one trick-or-treating. I'll bring a Reese's Peanut Butter Cup for you." (She loved them.)

Anna was the cutest little ghost, and when she got tired she asked to ride on my shoulders. The cool New England air felt clean on my face and we had a good time. I didn't get back to Union till 8:30 because Anna and I had to sort the goods, and she let me have a Reese's Cup to give her momma. There was no hurry because All Saints' Day wasn't arriving for a few hours and I wanted to tuck the little one in bed. I knew, because soldiers of war are very good at sensing these things, that the next time I'd tuck her in bed she'd be a motherless little girl. When I got to the hospital I told the nurse I was going to lie down on the cot next to Judi's bed but to please wake me before midnight if I fell asleep. Then I gave Judi a kiss from her daughter and said, "I'll be right here sweetheart, and your Reese's is too!"

I didn't sleep, but instead listened to her breathing. Toward midnight it got slower and more sporadic. I thought, *Man, oh man, the Lady and God are timing this perfectly.* When Halloween said good-bye to All Saints' Day I crawled into her bed and put my left arm under her pillow to cradle her head. For the next two hours I caressed her face, and every time her breathing slowed a little more I told her she was doing great, and there was nothing to worry about, and how amazingly proud of her I was. At 2:11 a.m. I thought she'd taken her last breath and said, "It's okay baby, it's all over now. You've done great. You've made this crazy old world a better place and you don't have to suffer anymore. I love you so much, and I'll see you soon. Don't hang around another second. I love you forever!"

But at 2:12, she surprised me with one last *nah . . . this ain't right* feeling by taking a deep, final breath, to make it a good one. Then the most remarkable thing happened. When she let it out, tears flowed down her swollen cheeks and from somewhere down a long echo cave women were weeping. Nurses who knew by the monitor at the nurses' station that Judi's heart was shutting down had come to the doorway and heard me say good-bye to my best friend. One put her hand on my shoulder, "Your wife heard you in the last moment of her life." The other, older veteran, feeling no pulse, said, "It was a beautiful death. Are you all right, Mr. Foster?"

Somehow, hearing "Mr. Foster" and thinking that might be me awakened me from a place where names mean nothing. I got out of Judi's bed and asked the nurses if I could stay with her for awhile and they said in unison, "You can stay as long as you like. We're right down the hall." Before the older nurse left I asked if death was always this peaceful and I'll never forget what she said. "No, every one is different! Generally, a person who lives a selfish life will die a lonely, selfish death, and they and those around them, if there are any, are usually the most miserable. But in a case like your wife's, a person who lives a life with love and goodwill toward others will die a peaceful death because they've lived *within the love of God*. But your wife's death *can be* the saddest for those left behind because it's of someone so young. And even though I'm guessing she never complained about fulfillment, you'll always know what's been lost. If you're someone who needs to find purpose in this, give it time!"

"Thank you," I said, then crawled back in bed to feel the last remnant of warmth leave her broken body. When it was gone I got up and wiped the tears on her swollen cheeks with my finger and moistened my lips with them. Then I kissed her forehead three times with that holy water on my lips and then a fourth. "Sweetheart, give that one to Dave."

I brushed her hair and folded her hands across her upper abdomen and pulled the blankets to her elbows. I loved tucking my girls into bed. She looked so innocent, like a picture I have of her when she was eight years old in her Easter best with hands folded just so. Her suffering was over. No longer was she a slave to cancer or the madness of the world created by the "meanness within man's heart." *She belongs to the ages!*

The Eyes Have It

When I got to my parents' house they were finishing breakfast with their granddaughter. I didn't have to say a word. I took Anna down to the pond where her dolphin uncle once flew and said, "Sweetheart, I have something to tell you."

"Okay"

"Do you remember I told you your momma might not be coming home?"

"Uh ha."

"Well, last night she died, so we won't be seeing her anymore."

With her mother's expression of compassion she searched my face to rescue the same lost sheep her mother had eight years earlier. "Don't be sad, Daddy. I'll take care of you!" she said and then crawled into my arms. I wasn't strong enough not to cry. "It's okay, Daddy. Momma doesn't have a boo-boo anymore."

After the funeral I must've fallen asleep on that first dawn, because little lips on my face woke me. "Daddy, it's time to get up." The first thing I saw was Dave's message from the Temple of Delphi—*Know Thyself*—right where it had been when I drifted off, and there she stood with her hand on my shoulder.

I said, "Hi, baby girl. Did you and Nana already go shopping?"

"Uh ha. Can you get up and play with me Daddy?"

"Sure I can, go upstairs and I'll be up in a few minutes."

"Okay," she so matter-of-factly said.

Everything in Dave's room, The Beatles, The Stones, Dylan, and Jimi, seemed okay. Even Billy Yank and Johnnie Reb were behaving. Maybe this was what life was like for normal people. If the little one wanted to play, it might mean she'd been spared the nightmare because she'd been somewhere safe on the home front while the elephant trampled the life out of her mother, as he had her uncle nine months before she was born. *Thank you, God,* I thought for letting saint and soldier blood run thick in her veins. Then a miracle happened! I sat up.

Somehow I felt compelled to sit in the chair of Jonah's whale before leaving Dave's room. The old conglomeration of wood, springs, and polyester fuzz hadn't woken yet so I didn't sink as far as someone foolish enough to trust the old beast would later in the day. I only had a few minutes because I had a playdate, so I grabbed the book quickly. *Wait; would this being a single parent thing mean I'd always be in a hurry?* I thought. If I only knew a tenth of it, but God would she be worth it! Jonah knew there were three pairs of eyes I needed to look into because, now, *I knew them intimately!*

The first pair led a Blue army and looked at me from a wicker chair during the Wilderness Campaign of 1864. They were about to lose more men than his Gray army opponent had alive. He didn't know that, but accepted it when it happened and kept on pounding because, like his commander in chief, he understood the numbers. His eyes so very sad; not defiant, angry, or in possession of any remote ability to gloat; eyes humble, resigned, wounded, about to weep, sadder in victory than defeat. In defeat there's a determination to "lick 'em in the morning" even if he has to "smash his head through a cement wall." It's why the man who put him in charge of it all stood by him no matter what the papers said of his aversion to "Adam's Ale." And what kind of man is it who appears sadder after victory? It can only be an American who understands that all the suffering he's seen and inflicted was caused by the impetus of aristocrats, his fellow citizens and friends, some, not too long ago, even in his wedding party. His eyes tell us why he called their cause the worst ever fought for in the history of the world. His eyes say *this is not what we want!*

Then, another pair of eyes, as dark as they are sad, emotions held in aristocratic check; bondaged within a controlled look of shock, bewilderment, and still-breathing defiance the photo of the first man doesn't have. It's clear; there's *self-evident* contempt that even he, the greatest of all Confederates, cannot hide. No one who looks into these eyes with honest eyes can miss it. The problem was that nobody I knew at the time bothered to look that deeply, except my history teacher mother. These eyes would slowly turn inward toward the end of their time on earth and would mellow, but here his "fighting blood" is still "up." Their surrender to the first pair of eyes is only a few days old in this image, so the mellowing hasn't begun. Not long before he dies, he'll tell a friend that being in the military was a waste of his life. My God, Marse Robert *said it all* in that statement! And why aren't kids in history classes across America taught about that? It says nothing about his career but everything about *his cause.* One pair of eyes has tasted victory, the other defeat, but both, equally American, say *this is not what we want!*

I put the book back and pushed aside a small mirror reflecting eyes I had no desire to see. Eyes I'd never let anyone see, even my daughter. When asked, to this day, "What's wrong, Dad?" I automatically tell the lie of "Nothing, Ann, I'm okay!" and will for the rest of my days. Where my eyes say *this is not what I want,* mine are more like Grant's than Lee's for there's no hint of failed nobility, just everlasting, hidden melancholy lurking under the surface of clown skin. If I have a saving grace, it's knowing to my core that the eyes of God toward our nation from 1861 to 1865 were more like Grant's than Lee's, which meant the nation could live. And this is not to say I blame Lee, because even in these times of digital technology, no one has yet been able to choose where they're born. It's why the wisest of men, who felt it all, said of the millions of eyes of his fellow Americans, "If they were born where we were, they'd be like us, and if we were born where they were, we'd be like them." For no race of man, black, white, red, yellow, or brown, has a monopoly on compassion or brutality. If the idea of America is just, how can it be otherwise and how could I blame anyone?

I had tasted and digested the sadness of both Blue and Gray eyes and that was enough education for any life. Blame was the last thing I wanted. It was the opposite of everything Dave and Judi lived for. The desire to understand and the love of a little girl were miracles that made me get up from Dave's bed to sit in Jonah's chair. I now *knew* what war, slavery, and cancer were and would try to live with it because an innocent child needed me to. But I needed to know the logistics *of how,* because I was not a righteous saint or brave kamikaze and no longer had the time or talent to become a philosopher, historian, or musician, because being both a mother and father would speed up the world so damn fast. But still, there'd be time to be a skeptic.

And if skepticism made me read and investigate with all my remaining might so I could explain to her with some tiny shred of *reason* why it's sacred to ask pesky questions, then maybe that's why music, history, meditation, Dave, and Judi made me understand that the eyes of Grant and God were of humble servants, singing like Jimi sang, *"Take anything you want from me,"* but only if it makes the world a better place.

I reached for another book with eyes I needed to see more than all the others; eyes belonging to *the* American face. When I looked into them, they were looking straight into mine this first morning after my world was buried. They said, "Everything good in life is worth fighting and dying for. And to you personally, *I understand!*" These eyes had seen the elephant's destruction and felt the agony of the widow and widower alike, along with the fatherless daughter and motherless son. These eyes had seen such sadness and know they'll see more and will look at it directly, *without malice.* These eyes had seen the deaths of two precious sons and hundreds of thousands of sons and daughters equally as precious, of his fellow citizens. These eyes saw his sister and mother die when they were young, and they've seen his wife and nation drift toward and then go over the brink of madness. But he knew that what was true was meant to be true for all, and was determined to prove it no matter how much blood it took.

It's why he said to people like Joe Medill, editor of the *Chicago Tribune,* when a person like Joe, coincidently from Illinois, told these eyes that his state couldn't possibly send another young man to the meat-grinder slaughterhouse of war when these eyes made yet another request for troops, "Damn you, Medill, you will send me more men! It was people like you that cried for this godforsaken war just as much as the slaveholders did. And now that I've given you what you've asked for, which was something I never wanted to give, you say the game is up. Well, it's not up as long as I'm alive, or until every drop of blood drawn by the lash is paid for by an equal amount drawn by the sword. We will see it to the end, so help me God. There's no turning back! This nation shall live or we'll die trying to save it."

These gazing, piercing, deep gray eyes are Abraham Lincoln's; looking directly into the lens as directly as anybody has ever looked at anything. He *knows* this is how America has to look at the world if the world is to survive, and he does it by trusting, hoping and expecting that, as Americans, we'll look back and never run from the truth. He wants us to *feel* what war is, particularly this one. He knows we *need* to understand that when America runs from the truth it cannot win and the entire world suffers, but when it embraces truth, "we cannot lose," because this is what rational thought tells him of a universe that might be ruled by "a just God." But even that pales to the *conviction* in his soul that truth is what his countrymen, Blue and Gray, deserve.

The picture was taken around the time he was contemplating "a few chosen remarks" to make on a blood-soaked field in Gettysburg. It's his judgment, now, above all others he must trust, for he's listened to advice from the nation's top military, political, religious, and social advisors and soaked it all in, yet the war goes on. Now he'll take the good and discard the rest, as he took from the Bible what made sense and discarded the nonsense.

His eyes are not unlike Grant's and Lee's, where theirs say *this is not what we want,* but his eyes are unlike theirs in that theirs appear to begin and end there. His say, "This is not what we want but is what we have and we've brought it upon ourselves. The evil in this world, all of it, is manmade and the agony of this war is self inflicted; an attempted death by suicide. The solution, the only solution, is to believe in the goodness of man even when he's our enemy, and believe it so assuredly that we live it protected by 'the better angels of our nature'." His are the eyes of a man true to himself. When that happens, they're eyes of one true to mankind. It's why, toward the end of his life, knowing no matter what anybody said of him then or in the future, he could die in peace because in the deepest region of his soul, "my tired spot" he called it, he knew he'd done the best he knew how for his country and world. Dave and Judi could say that too!

His expression says to us, "You don't have to go through what we've gone through. You can learn from us so the innocent will not suffer needlessly." By doing so we can know right from wrong, good from evil, freedom from bondage, liberty from tyranny, human reason from deadly superstition (a lot of it religiously based, as it was to him), compassion from jealousy, and forgiveness from revenge. His eyes said to me in this private sitting on the morning after putting my wife's war-torn body into American soil just feet away from where my brother's body lay and yards from Union Civil War soldiers, that, "I have done my best for you and even though you've lost so much, there is much goodness and work yet to live for. I have seen the worst of it, and you a little too, yet we can share the best of it as we are equal, too." As I looked into Lincoln's eyes the words "Thank you!" whispered from my mouth. In the depths of my soul I heard a reply: "The honor was mine, now do the same for your nation and fellow man."

Here, on the morning of November 5, 1979, it was not the words and prayers of a well-meaning priest or relatives and friends who comforted me, but the words of a three-year-nine-month-old little girl who said, "I'll take care of you, Daddy. Momma doesn't have a boo-boo anymore," along with the sadness in the eyes of Ulysses S. Grant and Robert E. Lee, in a room full of musical geniuses, court jesters, and scoundrels, combined with the wisdom, compassion, forgiveness, and most humble serenity of Abraham Lincoln.

My little one expected me, so I climbed the stairs to open a door to a foreign universe that I'd never feel kosher in, that I'd never quite fit in, but that somehow, like the old one, was filled with beauty and intrigue nonetheless. Never an extrovert, despite being on stages playing music, when I walked through the door and said hello to my mother I was well on my way to being the strange introvert I am today.

FATHER FOSTER'S
CONFESSIONAL

Anna and I played hide-and-seek in my parents' backyard, and then went home. I wanted to collect her momma's clothes and donate them to the poor. I had to do it right away or I'd never do it. Thank God the little one was with me; she helped me fold everything. Her matter-of-fact conversation was therapy and her little voice was music to my weary spirit. I'd never been sentimental about material things like I am about memories and ideas, but we saved a lot of things I couldn't part with. One, a brown leather American Indian shawl, with strands around the bottom and on the chest, which only looks good on someone who was a pure, true blue flower child of the American 1960s. Roger Daltrey looked good in a similar kind of vest, but Judi brought it to another level. She looked sacred in it. I saved a dress I loved, and all the letters we exchanged when there was an ocean between us. Also, all her arts and crafts, and a sand dollar she saved from Lynch Park Beach in Beverly with a date she inscribed on the back: October 4, 1971. The day she let a lunatic kiss her for the first time.

Within a week my dad offered to get me "a real job" at General Electric. This would be good for his granddaughter because it'd be a factory job and not a temporary summer job like mowing lawns that he'd gotten for me in the past. I'd only been inside the factories a few times and it was always loud, dirty, smoky, hectic, and intimidating. Back then, machinists were pieceworkers so the harder they worked the more money they made, which seemed like a pretty fair system. It kept the place hopping.

I started with an entry-level job (hourly, not piecework) driving a fork truck, where I'd retrieve and return machine parts repaired in a building centrally located in this industrial complex as large as a small city. I quickly learned the layout of the plant and was surprised at how many of the younger workers, of the 12,000 that worked there, knew me. Guys I didn't recognize would see me driving by and would play air guitar or flash me the old '60s and '70s peace sign or yell, "Fuckin' rock 'n' roll, baby!" and "Kick out the jams, motherfucker!" and stuff like that. Some would stop me and ask, "What the hell are you doing here?" and I never had a good answer. Some though, touched my soul, "Hey man, that sucks about your wife!"

I fell in love with so many of them but hated (perhaps too strong a word) the job at first, because I never in a million years envisioned I'd be doing something like that for a living. I didn't think it was beneath me or anything, because it truly was an excellent job with tremendous opportunities to rise to a better position, which I did. I just never thought it'd be something I'd ever do. But the plant was unionized, so the work was as safe as humanly possible and the pay far superior to what I'd ever made before, and that helped me and Anna in ways I couldn't imagine. Our health insurance was terrific. Jobs and plants like that don't exist anymore because even though GE made record profits year after year, it was never enough for the aristocrats who ran the place from somewhere in the clouds. I could understand shipping jobs to foreign countries if GE was losing money, but they were making record profits and because we made jet engines for the U.S. military, these jobs were funded by the American taxpayer, so the public was getting ripped off too. Time and again I watched GE tell the union if they agreed to certain changes in the work rules jobs wouldn't get shipped overseas, and every time the union agreed, within a year, they got shipped anyway. Over time I watched a workforce of 12,000 disintegrate to 2,000 while buildings were turned into parking lots.

But I am forever grateful to have had a chance to see the last historic remnants of one of the greatest job-creating and manufacturing industries the world has ever known. I got in at the tail end of its U.S. glory days, paid for by the blood of American patriots of WWI, WWII, Korea, and Vietnam. To my everlasting joy, the place was loaded with so many good Americans who only wanted to provide for their families. Many are close friends today.

Somehow I got along as well with management as I did with the workers. As I rose through the ranks by promotion I was offered management positions three times but said no because I didn't want to make that kind of commitment, plus my heart wasn't in it. I *always* wanted to be with my fellow Confederates on the shop floor where I felt safe. I never whined about anything to management because my dad, who was a company guy and his father, Abe, who was a union guy, both gave me the same advice, which was, whatever my boss told me to do, "no matter how stupid it may seem," just say okay. So I tried it and it made my day go smoothly. I made suggestions if I thought there was a better way and my bosses were almost always open-minded because I wasn't a complainer, so I made out very well.

What kept me from quitting that first week (besides Anna) was that the guy training me, Billy, always had a book (a Louis L'Amour cowboy adventure) on the fork truck because when we'd go to a building to bring a broken machine part back to ours for repair, it sometimes wouldn't be ready for transport for twenty minutes or longer. Billy said that as long as we were where the boss wanted us to be we'd never get in trouble for reading while waiting for a part. He said, "It beats twiddling your thumbs." The idea of being able to read a minute or two here and there and always during lunch made me think, *thank you, God.* It meant I could continue my self-education, which made being there not only bearable but worthwhile.

My first week I put *Atlas Shrugged* by Ayn Rand *The Source* by James Michener, and several Civil War books by Bruce Catton and Douglas S. Freeman in my locker. Every morning that little stack of thought, history, philosophy, opposing political perspective, and entertainment gave me a reason for showing up. As I finished one stack I'd bring in another, then another, and another. For every American or European classic, I'd read two or three Civil War books.

On days there wasn't time enough to read an exit sign I could still read on my lunch hour. I became known as a 'reading geek,' a term I was immensely proud of. And because there were other Confederate readers there too, from the highest bosses to floor sweepers, they'd see what I was reading and by osmosis (not reality) I became known as the Civil War, American history, and Eastern philosophy expert in the plant. These wonderful, curious people would converse with me and bring me more books. I never dreamed the questions, conversations, and challenges they laid at my feet would help me one day answer questions—my favorite thing—in front of audiences about what the Civil War was actually about. Through my fellow Confederates I discovered that as long as I could back up my answers with historical facts, without holding any back, I'd be listened to and trusted.

On the home front, because Anna and I were considered a "hardship case," she bypassed a long waiting list to get into Christ Child, perhaps the best day care and kindergarten in the city of Lynn. The school contacted us after some kind soul (I never found out who) told them of our plight. I only learned we skipped the waiting list *after* Anna got in and felt bad about it, but the place was a godsend for us. All were lay teachers and they really loved kids. "Your daughter is *unusually* sweet and mature. She shares with everyone." It wasn't far from GE so I'd drop her off at 6:40 a.m. and, God, was she adorable waving to me till I drove out of sight. I'd pick her up when my shift ended and for the rest of the day and night we'd be peas in a pod.

After a while my old musical partner Den and other musicians began inviting me out to play a little. They, especially Den, were worried about me. Slowly but surely I began gigging a few nights a week. My mom, Judi's mom, my grand-mother, and Mimi would alternate watching Anna. Sometimes, if I gigged in a small local club, I'd bring my grandmother and daughter with me for the first set. They'd be so damn cute, with the little one dancing around their table. Then I'd bring them home and get back just in time to start the next set. Between my forty-minute sets I'd sneak off to read behind a stage or bar just like I had when Judi saw me do it before we met. Den called me "The Professor," but knew better than anyone that I was just an old busted-up, broken-hearted songwriter.

Between work, acting as a mom *and* dad, gigging, and any free time I had, I managed to read at least a little every day. I was addicted, and still am, and somehow life appeared normal. Some days I almost felt glad to be alive, until one day, a year after Judi died, I was driving my fork truck through a building thinking of ideas for songs, oblivious to everything around me. I was humming one that excited me so I pulled over to a pay phone, put a quarter in and started dialing my home phone number to ask Judi to put the phone near my cassette player so she could record what I sang before I forgot it. We did that all the time. After the first ring, the second, third, and fourth, I thought "Where the hell is she?" and then, *wham!* "What am I doing? She's dead!"

I was stunned and went to the building's locker room, sat on a bench, and cried like a baby. The last recess of my spirit finally admitted her death. She *wasn't* coming back and nobody ever does. This death thing was permanent. It had taken me a year to grasp the concept that she wasn't going to answer the phone no matter what kind of long distance I used. For the past year I'd been living in some sad, sick, happy-go-lucky fantasy that everyone, even me, thought was a semi healthy adjustment to life without her. But it was a ruse!

Now I understood how people could fool others and most of all themselves into believing the trauma of slavery/cancer didn't cause permanent, psycholog-ical damage to those left behind, a trauma that has long-lasting, devastating, residual effects. All I wanted was to go home to curl up in the back of my closet where no one could find me. Physically, mentally, and spiritually this was the death of my desire to be, to love, to challenge, to sing, to even ask a damned pesky question. I wanted to be left alone. Later that day, I had a new fork truck license picture taken and when I looked at it I saw the saddest person I'd ever seen. That night, after I tucked my little one in bed, I went to the couch to officially enter my quiet, zombie like, go-through-the-motions part of my life that would last for decades. Everyone asked what was wrong and all I could say was "Nothing!" I wouldn't find out for sixteen years that I was clinically depressed, shell-shocked by slavery, guilt, and maybe something I was born with or all of the above.

The '80s were an anxiety-filled decade. Meditating, exercise, writing music, reading history, and being with the little one were my security blankets, but I still had to interact with the world, which I avoided "at all hazards" if I could. Watching the little one become a young lady with so many traits of her mother was a privilege of the highest order. I could look at her and think that if her momma was watching she was proud. I kept up my charade of a somewhat normal outward appearance by doing the things I usually did because I didn't know what else to do. I learned many powerful, useful, and wonderful philosophical and historical things in my readings, but learning them was not the same as having them register where it counted so they could help me. But one did. Bestowed on me by my favorite ex-Confederate soldier Mark Twain was the notion that the best way to cheer myself up was to do a good deed for another. Although when you're depressed it's hard to know you are. Somehow this registered, so I tested it and it worked a little. Along with my security blankets I understood that if I was kind to everyone it would override my desire to kill myself because I *knew* how someone would want to do that.

Gradually, and I never knew why, people at work and elsewhere began to confide their deepest, darkest secrets, problems, and dilemmas to me. Maybe because I was someone who could keep a secret or they were under some illusion I could help figure a way out of their misery. All I really knew was how to listen. The guys at GE even made a sign and put it over my work station that read, "Father Foster's Confessional." Now if that wasn't ironic? I'd tell my fellow sinners that I was the biggest sinner of all but no one believed me. My quiet demeanor, as well as my always having a book in my hand, must've made people think I had some kind of inner wisdom.

Somehow I kept writing songs and Den made sure hot local musicians heard them. Occasionally they'd back us to record some and when a song or two got played on the radio, like on WBCN, despite us not being signed to a label, I never gave a crap. Part of the death of my desire was that my "mojo" for pushing my music was gone but Den, Brian, Craig Spinney, Steve Muriello, George Croteau, and later my indispensable Joe DeLeo, Eric Brown, and Kelli Consoli, all outstanding stage and studio musicians, never forgot me or my songs. I wrote as a sick duck swims or drowns, but I no longer cared about seeking a recording contract, a music career, or playing live. I had all the opportunities in the world with wonderful people willing to help. Every time I was offered something good I'd say no and had the ready-made excuse of having to stay close to home to raise the little one. It sounded sweet and honorable but it was phony, because many musicians raise kids and the lifestyle, although hectic, if done right, and it would've been with Judi, can be rewarding and healthy for all concerned. Still, I got a little kick writing songs that attracted musicians, but it always faded quickly and I'd crawl back into my pity pot hole of doom and gloom. No one ever said it to me, but I knew people thought I was blowing it. If Dave and Judi had been alive they would've given me a huge kick in the butt.

I did get drawn in a few times though. Once with Den, who was the perfect partner for someone with my erratic mood swings. We somehow formed a five-piece, loud, kick-ass hard rock band with three incredible musicians. Perhaps arrogantly, we called ourselves, The Foster and Tully Band because we were already popular around Boston and the North Shore as an acoustic duo. I wrote the music and Den contributed lyrics. The musicians seemed to really get off on the songs. We auditioned a good half dozen keyboard players that I'd show the parts to, but after each audition the guys would say I should play the keyboards. So in another irony, a weird kid who almost got his ear ripped off in grammar school for playing the piano, played the keys for songs I wrote on piano and played acoustic guitar for songs I wrote on that. Mostly we played in Boston and the North Shore but got out of state occasionally too. None of the guys were married or had kids, so only Den knew how hard it was for me to maintain my day job, rehearse during the week, gig, and be a mom and dad to my little girl. Anna became part of the crew and many times I brought her to rehearsals, putting earplugs in her ears as she sat under my keyboards doing her homework. Sometimes when I looked she'd be curled up sleeping.

By the mid '80s we were playing the best clubs in town and music people and producers were checking us out as we got more popular. One sweaty summer Friday night we were booked into The Channel, a large club down by the old Boston waterfront, that's now buried under the Big Dig, I believe. The venue held a couple thousand people, where big names and up-and-comers played original material, so it was a good gig. Just as I was about to get picked up at home, the person who was supposed to baby-sit Anna canceled so I got her sleeping bag and earplugs and brought her with me. During the show she sat off stage with our guitarist's girlfriend. She was so cute. I could see her mouthing words between yawns. She'd known the songs since their infancy when her dad discovered them. We played well that night and during our encore I looked over to see her sleeping. After the show the club offered us opening-act slots for some big names coming to town. Everyone was excited, but I had to take my little one home.

Like an idiot, I decided to take her in the equipment truck because the band and their girlfriends were going out to celebrate. There was just enough room for us to sleep between Marshall stacks. As I held her on the way home I was glad we didn't get offers to go "on the road" to be an opening act, but I saw that event coming and it made me queasy. I knew I wouldn't go because every time I abandoned someone I loved, bad things happened. It's how my depressed, paranoid mind was working while my little angel slept in my arms. But I felt serene, too, because I knew at the very least I'd never abandon anyone for any reason, ever again, especially her, so I tried to sleep. As I dozed, my civil war of conflicting emotions was violently interrupted by the truck slamming hard into the side of the Tobin Bridge. Our much overworked roadie (John G., who's still a dear friend) had passed out at the wheel for a split second. The crash woke him so he kept going, but the impact sent equipment flying everywhere. A Marshall stack tipped over, putting Anna and me in a triangle of speaker cabinets while Steve's guitar smashed hard an inch from her head. Maybe because she still had earplugs in she never woke to learn what her moronic father almost let happen to her. Somehow, no one got a scratch.

When John pulled off at the next exit we became white as ghosts as we looked at the whole side of the truck caved in. He was in tears and I couldn't get mad. He's such a good person who only wanted to get closer to the music, much like a brother I once had. But I was so mad and disgusted with myself that I decided my gigging days, in a band anyway, were over. If there was "a just God ruling the universe" maybe she was trying to tell me something.

All I wanted was to secede from myself. I was so, so, bloody tired and felt no hope, for living the kind of musical life Dave, Judi, and I had planned. Without hope my "get up and go" got up and went. I now understood that the motto of the world-renowned Memorial Sloan-Kettering Cancer Center was true: *"HOPE. Of all the forces that make for a better world, none is so powerful as hope. With hope, one can think, one can work, one can dream. If you have hope, you have everything."* Slavery is hopelessness, and to think that four million people, many of whom could've been farmers, teachers, doctors, engineers, preachers, politicians, historians, poets, musicians, or philosophers, all had hope sucked out of them by a Confederacy formed to protect the sucking, is simply too bizarre and sad to believe, but believe it we must! So much of the flower of the North and South died on the battlefield, but it pales in comparison to the flowers smothered in slavery before they had a chance to bloom.

The next day I told the band I was done. They'd heard about the accident, but I explained my leaving was for reasons that had nothing to do with that.

They were deeply disappointed but not bitter. *Thank God,* I thought, this would be the last abandonment of people I loved that I'd ever perform.

Den and I continued our acoustic thing because it required no manager or other musicians so there was no one for me to abandon. Still, the band and new musicians kept dropping in to see us. They'd always ask to hear any new songs we might have and one night in the early '90s I sang one about Judi that I hadn't shown to Den yet. It was called "When Was The Last Time." As soon as I started it one of those weird things happened in the loud (still smoky at the time) club; everything became quiet. That can happen if there's magic in a note. It went over so well that I forever after got requests for it. The musicians insisted we go into a studio to record it and I said okay. Den thought it was one of the few songs we did that suited my voice so although he was a far better singer than me; I sang it. At the last minute someone suggested I sing it as a duet with a female so I asked my friend Kelli to join me and she nailed it.

Then a musical cousin of mine, coincidently named Dave, who was forming an independent record label out of Londonderry, New Hampshire, heard it and asked if he could enter it in a *Billboard* magazine nationwide songwriting contest and I said okay. It came in the top ten out of several thousand and *Billboard* sent me a beautiful mahogany plaque with the song title on it. Everyone connected was excited, but all I wanted was to take a nap. One cool thing, though, was a couple who always came to our gigs asked if they could use it as their wedding song and I said of course. The song's about being together forever, and the last I heard they're still married. I never followed up on it, and my cousin thought I was nuts for saying no to offers to tour and play festivals.

In the mid '90s I found myself in my forties with my little one away at the University of New Hampshire, getting her degree in child psychology. Today she's an Occupational Therapist in the Lynn school system and I'm so very proud of her. Her being away was the first time since my first year in England that I was totally on my own. My family—mostly my mom, daughter, and sister-in-laws—and friends said this was a good time for me to think of myself, get out, socialize, date, and have a good time, but I became more of a hermit than ever. It wasn't that I didn't want to rejoin the human race. I tried hard a few times in the '80s to have a healthy relationship with someone, but every attempt ended in more of a disaster for the woman than for me. It was no fun for anyone who wanted to get close to me to be repeatedly called the name of a dead person, and realize that for all intents and purposes I'd always be in love with a ghost. Who could compete with that and who should have to? I was trying to recapture something I'd never captured in the first place. Every time I found *almost* love I thought might lead to the real deal, I'd get claustrophobic and bow out. Deep inside I knew the problem was me, so I vowed to never make another woman unhappy. The bitter irony was I knew Judi wouldn't approve of this.

But I knew then and know better now that even if I'm never able to accept or be comfortable in love again I've been blessed far more than the average person. For I know beyond dispute that Lord Alfred Tennyson was right, *"It is far better to have loved and lost than never to have loved at all."* I'm one of the lucky ones, for I've experienced what true love is, and there's no lyric by Tennyson, Bob Dylan, or Shakespeare that can capture it.

When I'm analytically honest with myself (if I ever am), I can become sad because I know being with someone, holding them, caring for them, and they you, laughing, conversing, along with sharing everything from holding hands to trapeze sex, are all healthy and sacred things for humans who think rationally. But for me, if it's not in the cards, it's comforting to know "I'll never be" anybody's "Beast of Burden."

Meditation (there's no doubt) kept me from completely losing my mind. And as my reading went through the stratosphere I began to wonder if I ever really had the kind of innate organic songwriting ability that Dave and Judi believed in so strongly. I wanted to test it without being asked to join a band, go on the road, or make a commitment. My dreams of a musical career were over, but I still wrote songs because I'm always curious to see what my mind might conjure or discover. Now I *had* to know if I had the ability my two heroes believed in, and one night an event of horror inspired me to find out.

I was watching the news when the story of an innocent little girl killed by a stray bullet came on. She was only ten years old and the shot was meant for a gang member, a "misguided brethren" at war with himself just like America was in the Civil War. She was sitting in front of her home and got *"stranded, caught in the crossfire,"* as Stevie Ray Vaughan once sang. When they interviewed the mother her grief was unbearable to me. She had the same sad eyes I hid from everyone, and I became mad and my old desire to protect woke from its slumber. It was the first real shred of genuine emotion, although a negative one, I had had since Judi died. It awakened a dormant, enslaved part of my spirit, and I reached for my acoustic with angry goose bumps and wrote a song called "Gangs."

For years and years and years I'd envisioned a band that was something like a cross between Zeppelin and the Dave Mathews Band, but this was long before there even was a Dave Mathews Band, and there'd be brass too. I immediately felt the Latin percussion flavor of the song and within a few hours I had it on tape with words for the bridges, choruses, and midsection. The next day I played it for a brilliant lyric writer friend, L. J. Walsh, who'd seen the story too. I asked him to write the verses because he'd do a better job than I ever could. Then I brought the song to a friend, Eric Brown, an incredible drummer and all-around musician and arranger, who owned a small digital studio that had "sound modules" (bells and whistles) for every conceivable noise I heard in my head. When I played it for him he got it instantly. In the end his contribution to the song was as much, if not more, than mine!

I then took the groundwork disk of the rhythm section (drums, bass, percussions, and brass) that we recorded and programmed in Eric's studio to Newbury Sound in Boston, because they were the hottest studio in town with even more bells and whistles, including 64 tracks where we could separate everything with room left to spare for my acoustics, vocals, and Joe DeLeo's electric guitars. I knew the studio owner, Ken K., and assumed he'd do the beast with me but he'd just hired a monster engineer, Jeff D., whom everyone wanted to work with. He'd recently worked with members of The Cars on solo projects, and although I was never a big Cars fan I thought that was cool. When Jeff heard the tracks he got excited and, as we added the electric, acoustic guitars, and vocals, he kept giving me a "What the hell?" look. I wrote the song to fit my voice so after I sang the lead and 6 tracks of backup vocals we did a rough mix before calling it a night. As we listened I'll never forget what he asked.

"Who are you, and how come I never heard of you before?"

I said, "I'm nobody, I just like combining styles and sounds in my head and wanted to get this on tape. It's just an experiment. I kind of wish we had a female singer here because I can hear one singing on top of the choruses and some verses."

He said, "I can hear it too. Fuck it, I just broke up with my girlfriend and she hates my guts but she's the best female singer in Boston and she'd love to sing on this. I'll call her."—it was 2:30 a.m.—"She's probably just getting in from a gig. She won't believe this!" He picked up the phone next to the mixing board. "Tracy, please don't hang up, you have to sing on this track. Trust me, it's fuckin' hot!"

Within half an hour a tiny woman with long straight jet-black hair and an appealing take-no-prisoners hyper energy (reminding me of Maggie Bell) had head phones on, listening and learning the track while holding a lyric sheet with lines I'd underlined for her to sing. "This is an incredible song . . . I'm ready!" She sang her parts like she'd known them a long time. We got everything in a few takes to borrow from each to combine in the mix. When I tried to pay her she said, "No way, this was a pleasure. Call me anytime. People have to hear this!" Then she left.

Jeff and I mixed it the next day and he asked what I was going to do with it and I said, "Nothing!" He laughed, thinking I was joking.

A month later I was in a Barnes and Noble, getting a new stack of Civil War books, when I saw a familiar face on a magazine cover. It was Tracy, the girl who'd sung on "Gangs." Tracy Bonham's debut album, *The Burdens of Being Upright,* was becoming a monster hit and moving up the charts. Her picture and posters were everywhere. She was about to be nominated at the Grammys for best new female artist and a host of other things. Soon I'd read her interviews in *Rolling Stone* and *People* magazine and I'd think of how she'd sound doing them. She was such a kind, generous lady to me. The fact someone of her stature liked what I wrote, let alone sang on it, was definitely cool, but what impressed me more was finding out later that she was an accomplished, classically trained violinist and pianist. Today she most likely wouldn't remember me from Adam but if she heard "Gangs," with her voice blending with the strange introvert's who wrote it, she might. A year or so later I got a big kick seeing her in *Rolling Stone* with Robert Plant's arm around her as part of Zeppelin's Robert Plant & Jimmy Page Orchestra.

"Gangs" temporarily proved what I wanted it to, and for a brief moment I was happy, but as in all things, except my daughter, in the end it made me sad. I was in my mid forties, suffering from clinical depression and not knowing it, but the song made me feel that maybe my half-assed efforts of the past chasing music weren't a mistake; that events of slavery/cancer, which couldn't be helped, somehow derailed me. But I was honest enough to admit that a bigger probability was that I just blew it!

My last little hurrah, probably, was that my cousin Dave had taken "When Was The Last Time" and a few other songs—not "Gangs" because I never showed it to him—I wrote and put them on CDs and sent them to radio stations around the country. There was no real band; I just had people come in and out for whatever a song needed. He promoted the music as being by a band called Foster Child and he got it played on several stations, including in Nashua and Portsmouth, New Hampshire. One of those stations asked him if we'd be a feature act for an outdoor music festival they were sponsoring which was promoting "future stars of rock" or something silly like that. When I said, "Nah, that's okay Dave, I'm too old for that!" he replied, "Maybe so, but your music's not." He was so disappointed when I turned it down, and I didn't blame him a bit. We parted ways on friendly terms. He finally realized I was as total a screw up as I'd been telling him all along. Beyond a doubt though, he truly tried to help me. He put my phone number on the back of the CDs along with his and a station from Indiana called me one time when they were playing "When Was The Last Time" and asked when we'd be touring in that direction. I said, "I'll let you know." Slowly I stopped gigging with Den, too, and drifted deeper into the lonely abyss of depression.

Like an old soldier, *I let myself* fade away. To this day I've never really figured out if I was just lucky all those times, brushing up against the elbows of musical greats because of my warm and fuzzy personality, or if it was actually because people liked my songs. There were so many people who tried to help and love me that I disappointed by not reaching for the golden ring they were extending. If there is ever a way to tell them how sorry I am for pushing away their kind, helping hands, I'd do it in a second.

LINCOLN'S
WISEST WORD

In 1997, at that point a full-fledged recluse except for work and monthly drives to see Anna at UNH, two life-changing things happened that were lifelines out of my despair. The first came by way of an article in our local paper stating that on the second Friday of every month the North Shore's General Lander Civil War Roundtable met in the historic Grand Army of the Republic Museum, one of the jewels of our city of Lynn, at 58 Andrew St. to have historians and authors speak about their latest books. They also hosted local speakers who specialized in certain aspects of the war to give talks for anyone who wanted to learn. I had to rub my eyes. Never in my wildest dreams did I think a club like that existed. I knew about historical societies but a club that talked about the war and *I assumed* the political and social issues leading to it was something else altogether. My passion may have been in a coma but, thank God, never my interest.

Seeing the article poked my dormant passion awake for a second, and I decided to go to the next meeting. There I heard a marvelous talk about the battle of Gettysburg and "Where the hell was 'Jeb' Stuart (the main eyes and ears of Lee's army)?" I couldn't believe it. All ages attended and they seemed like the nicest people. Finally, something besides work and Anna got me out of the house. From this group I learned of several dozen roundtables around New England and of Civil War symposiums at various colleges. For the next three years there wasn't a week I wasn't attending something in Massachusetts, New Hampshire, Vermont, Maine, Rhode Island, or Connecticut. I even went to Virginia and Maryland several times and once to Indiana to the Fort Wayne Lincoln Museum. If I could go to England to sing a song, traveling in my own country for history was a no-brainer. At every event I'd sit in back and slip out as quietly as I'd slipped in. I never said a peep even in the question-and-answer periods, despite my new fellow reading and historical traveling companion from GE, Jim Tilden, along with attendees and the occasional history professor who heard me make a comment during a break, saying my slant was insightful and that I should bring it up or God forbid get up on stage and speak about it sometime. But that was never going to happen.

The second momentous thing of '97 happened during a visit to UNH. Anna was learning about depression in her psych class and said I might be a classic case and that "It wouldn't hurt" if I saw a therapist to find out. I felt another twinge poking my comatose passion, and it came with a great sense of pride in this remarkable young lady reaching out to help a lost sheep like someone once had before she was born. I *knew* something was wrong with me and she knew it too. But now, if there were reasons for the way I felt, knowing them could only help. For years I'd been waking up at night in cold sweats, finding it hard to breathe, feeling lost, like Satchel Page was right; that something was "gaining on me," all in addition to my not wanting to socialize or go anywhere. I really didn't even want to go to my new Civil War activities but they had something I wanted—*information*—so I went for selfish reasons.

All her life Anna had caught me crying at the stupidest things, like if the Skipper yelled at Gilligan too harshly or Robin and Baba Louie didn't get enough credit or Pugsley and Cousin It or Herman and Lilly or McHale and Parker or Bert and Ernie or SpongeBob and Patrick got into a fight or if Hail Bop and Jim Jones (lunatics) seduced poor "misguided brethren" into committing mass suicide or when priests *I knew* got caught raping little kids while their bosses looked the other way or when friends and classmates (Nam vets) drank themselves to death or blew their brains out because no one gave a damn. It didn't matter, the serious, silly, or mundane, it all made me sad. She said she couldn't remember a time I wasn't sad. And because she had no recollection of her mom she couldn't remember that I was once happy. I quietly listened because when you know someone truly loves you and has your best interest at heart, you have to listen.

When she was done she asked if what she'd said had upset me.

I said, "No sweetheart, the opposite is true. I think you're right and I'm very curious to find out. I'll call my doctor tomorrow and ask him to recommend a therapist. I know I'm not right."

She said, "Yeah, Dad, but you're still fun to be with!" which made us laugh.

On my way home I had an epiphany of deep proportions. I remembered asking her when she was ten if why she hadn't asked me about her mother in a long time was because it made her sad, and she said, "No Dad, it's because it makes you sad!" It brought me pause to the depths of my being, that my mental state had deprived my daughter of better knowing her mother.

She gave me several articles from *Psychology Today* and magazines of that genre, and when I got home I took a peek. It was like someone who knew me had written what I needed to hear. I read them all and each description of the pain, guilt, and helplessness experienced by those who are depressed gave me relief, because information helps me understand and understanding is the root of compassion essential to forgive one's self. This was a huge, positive, life-changing revelation. I recognized that knowing these things; even if I didn't know what to do about them, would help me see that a lot of my personal pot holes of misery could be somewhat avoided by simply acknowledging them. They might never go away, but knowing they'd *always* be coming, they'd no longer take me by surprise, causing me to swerve into a ditch of despair. I felt powerful sympathy for people suffering silently, not knowing *some* of those holes in the road could be avoided. I thought, "You poor sick bastard, maybe this is why you feel like you do."

Reading the term, "destructive behavior," made me think of history because there was nothing more destructive than slavery/cancer. It hit me hard that the harmful things people perpetrated on each other and ultimately themselves were usually the result of suffering they didn't understand or weren't aware of; a civil war inside them. Meditation had taught me to see this in a deep, organic way. And I'd always remember as a teenager hearing Jimi Hendrix say that suffering came from believing untrue things that caused internal violence, which often led to violence on others. Now, having lived with the experience of slavery/cancer and reading all of this years later from psychiatrists made it connect in a round way. If what psychologists, psychiatrists, Jimi, history, and meditation were saying to me was true, and it was, then maybe the Confederacy was a collective of mentally ill people, with a good dose of illness in the North too. For how could anyone who said slavery/cancer was a good and sacred thing be otherwise? It was a harsh, "radical" idea I never heard from anyone that might be worth considering.

My God, I thought in my strange, historical way, even Hitler must have been mentally ill instead of only evil. I knew and will always know what victims of slavery/cancer suffered, and it made it impossible to argue that the architects of their suffering weren't ill or evil and many times both. But I knew too, that for the rest of my days I'd always pull back from calling the Rebs evil because those "misguided brethren" were ours, and as American as any of us. They were ill, brainwashed from birth by being born in a mentally ill society whose political, economic, educational, social, and above all religious foundation was based on the righteousness of one human owning another. Of course slavery was an evil system, but obvious too is that only an ill person can say it wasn't; as the antebellum preacher from South Carolina so eloquently put it, "Slavery is a school of virtue!" If that was so, why did it turn good people into pawns of brutality and despotism?

Lincoln knew the disease held the nation hostage and told the story of a highway crook who blamed a person he robbed for killing them because they wouldn't hand over their money; then asked a judge what alternative he had. The crook was not only the ultimate aristocrat, meaning a slave to greed, but ill in believing his logic made sense. So, if demanding the "bread earned by the sweat of another" and killing them when it's not handed over, regardless if they have any or not, isn't ill, what is? Ex-Confederates later formed the Ku Klux Klan and insanely (I wish there was an easier word) blamed the war and devastation of the South on ex-slaves. How I wish to God I was making that up! They shared the same twisted logic of the highway crook; that if slaves had only remained content being slaves instead of wanting things like voting rights and legally being able to own their children, everything would have stayed as God intended.

For the first three years of my Civil War meetings and adventures I heard wonderful speeches about battle strategy and military maneuver that were more than satisfying. I assumed naturally that eventually someone would give a speech about the cause and meaning of the war, and thought how very much knowing that could help us understand the greed of aristocrats in the world today, but no one ever did. I found that to be very peculiar and a sad waste of enormous potential for roundtables to do some good for this tired old planet. Speakers only talking about battles made the meetings feel like walking into the last five minutes of a Who concert, when the boys were destroying their instruments. You didn't hear the music leading to the smash up.

No "Pictures Of Lily," "My Generation," "I Can See For Miles," or songs about the First Continental Congress in 1776, with Thomas Jefferson saying if they didn't put a provision in the Declaration of Independence to get rid of slavery there'd be a huge bloody smash-up of states in the not-too-distant future. No slavery Compromises of 1787 and 1820 or Denmark Vesey's Slave

Revolt (he was a free black man, a hero) of 1822, or Nat Turner's Slave Rebellion of 1831 or 1832's Nullification Crisis (that in reality was a trumped up fiasco because shortly after, John C. Calhoun said it had really been a smokescreen to test how the South would stand up to the federal government on the issue of slavery—*his logic,* not mine). No 1847 (Mexican War and what it was about, or The Wilmot Proviso) or Congressional Debates of 1850 (the most important in U.S. history) or 1852 and 1853's *Uncle Tom's Cabin* and how Harriet Beecher Stowe received the severed ear of a slave in the mail from his owner to let her know what he thought of her book, or Kansas/Nebraska or *Popular Sovereignty,* or Lincoln's 1854 reemergence into politics, or 1855 and Bleeding Kansas or the 1856 presidential election or Charles Sumner's caning, or the 1857 dreaded Dred Scott Decision; no 1858 Lincoln/Douglas debates, no 1859 John Brown debacle, no 1860 presidential election with the Republican platform saying no more spread of cancer, no rendition of "Pinball Wizard" and most troubling of all, no "We Won't Get Fooled Again."

If the six or so other Massachusetts Roundtables I'd been going to were unwilling to discuss why the smash-up happened, that was perfectly okay with me, but during breaks or after speeches I'd hear some whisper the war was about taxes, states' rights, and even something more sad and ridiculous, that the South was a cavalier society that believed in chivalry, honor, the principles of (the) Magna Carta and that slavery had nothing to do with it, that the South was injured and insulted by a devious, money-grabbing, honorless, tyrannical North, and if we didn't understand that we were mistaken big time! But those who sang that tune always did so off-key, flat or sharp, and always in hushed tones from an *ill*-informed larynx and not the diaphragm, where love and the heart live, where you're supposed to sing from. It was never sung out loud on stage for all to hear but off stage, during breaks, by a strong, influential minority of leaders of these clubs who preached it to innocent newcomers, though not by my hometown roundtable leaders, who were only interested in the truth. And sadly, they never whispered that Lincoln shouted as loud as he could, that when a southerner talked of states' rights he meant he wanted to live in a state where the right to buy, the freedom to own, and the liberty to do with another person was unhindered by a tyrannical central government as 99 percent of southern governors, senators, and congressmen had shouted for many decades before the war; that, "Without slavery, we have no freedom."

This twisted, mentally ill logic *was a historical fact* and to say it wasn't or worse, to ignore it in whispers, troubled me deeply. And to add further insult, once the war began no one but no one argued more strenuously for the need of a strong central government than Robert E. Lee and Jefferson Davis. It's one of many great ironies and hypocrisies surrounding the Confederacy that caused so many to suffer and die needlessly.

It was well and fine if people didn't want to hear the music, but to my everlasting joy I slowly discovered that the vast majority of these wonderful, truth-seeking people wanted to discuss why the smash-up happened, but somehow the subject was off limits and there was no one to play the song. I just thought it might be healthy to know how 730,000 kids (the figure is rising much higher with recent research) ended up dead over something not in the creed of our nation. Hadn't the Blue and Gray earned the right for *all* the truth to be told? Wasn't it more than just a war over honor so we could have clubs that only talked about the smashup 150 years later while we ate pastries? A war like ours, in a country like ours, has to be about something!

Lincoln said the war was about the "eternal struggle since the beginning of time between right and wrong," that we could all learn from to do something good with our American lives; that we had the ability to teach the world by example what freedom really was because we'd spent our first "four score and seven" teaching the world what it wasn't. Also, the word "honor" was tossed around an awful lot by the whisperers and although I knew beyond doubt, if I'd been born in the South, I would've been a Reb, because I would've been brainwashed the way slave societies brainwash those they send off to defend it, but my God, here, now, today? Where's the honor in saying it was honorable fighting for the right to buy and own another person even if you didn't have the money to do it?

My history teacher mother taught me that to be valid, history has to include why the downtrodden were trodden down. That, combined with Dave and Judi's battles with slavery/cancer and my love for meditation (that helps you to see things without prejudice if you let it), made me come to the Civil War community knowing something I'd never read in any history book; not even in a tip-toe way! And that was, the South was a place where someone, if they were white, could legally murder a black person, i.e. their property. Have we as Americans (especially white ones) ever really thought that through? That America was a place where one human could murder another with immunity while the United States Supreme Court said in the Dred Scott decision that three-fifths of that human, considered human for disingenuous political reasons (all the more pathetic when knowing the argument) in the Constitution (but with no rights whatsoever) had no recourse *and never would* be able to protest.

God forgive me, but where is the honor in murdering someone without repercussions, where the highway crook was the only one who had rights. Nobody talked about that or the easy to understand cause of the war. But for those who insisted "the cause" be kept confusing in order to keep the Confederacy from being exposed for what it truly was, and for those who want to shine a light *on everything,* like that the North wasn't innocent either in its complicity to keep cancer/slavery alive, Lincoln gave both persuasions a vehicle to come together, for his time and for all time. It was *the wisest word ever spoken* by an American: "Somehow." He gave it the way a parent gives it to a child he can trust will eventually get it right *if* guided by "the better angels of our nature." Education and honesty turns that *if* to *when.*

"*Somehow* slavery caused the war," he said on that drizzly day of March 4, 1865, and I found it deeply troubling that no one gave a speech about it. I slowly began to understand why Pulitzer Prize–winning historian/author Bruce Catton said shortly before he died in 1978 that his biggest and only regret in his lifelong love affair with teaching the world about the war was that the American people wouldn't be willing to accept the full truth of it for perhaps another hundred years. Well, my life was more than half over and I couldn't wait till 2078. None of us should have to. I knew to the core of my being that if there was anything in our family history we needed to know, it was *how* the American Civil War happened, because if we had that right we could get just about anything right. But, if we had it wrong, we could be wrong about everything.

I began seeing many elephants in the room that could speed up the process Catton feared would take too long. And a very painful one that I never heard any historian talk about (like this anyway) was how the South insisted that a slave be counted as three-fifths human for census purposes to increase the amount of congressmen each slave state could have, resulting in the United States having "The Three-Fifths Clause" in the Constitution. So, did that mean there was some two-fifth's states' rights clause "not implicitly implied in the Constitution reserved to the states?" Dear Lord, I was serious because the South looked guys like John Q. Adams in the eye when he questioned them in the halls of Congress and they justified their way of ruling their roost with this type of logic: "Hell, we only kill the two-fifths part of our slaves that aren't human; it's unavoidable if the three-fifths we consider human gets drawn into it. It's not our fault this is causing turmoil in the nation. It's the fault of the damned northern abolitionists and nigger lovers who want to add two-fifths to three-fifths to make a slave a whole person."

Lincoln and his army ultimately ended up fighting a war against the sick dogma of these enslaving aristocrats. Many were his friends and relatives (in-laws) that were saying American democracy and the fair and square electoral process that had worked so well in the past were no longer "adequate for the present." Repeatedly, he said the arguments of the South only had validity if "a slave was not a human being," or if "you could convince yourself there was nothing wrong with one man owning another." He hated the South's reasonless passion while in all likelihood he was suffering from unbearable depression and "melancholy" of his own. Yet somehow, thankfully, he was wise enough to admit his suffering to himself, and again, to friends like Joshua Speed who suffered from it too. They called it their "nervous dispositions." This gave me hope that if I could find a way to help Catton's prediction come a little sooner; then maybe I could feel a little better in spirit for having contributed something good to the world.

A great many historians and psychologists say Lincoln's honesty with his suffering substantially contributed to his empathy for others. If so, I wondered if my personal history could make me more empathetic in a useful way. I'd understood for a long time that southern and many northern aristocrats never had an iota of empathy for slaves and it made the old hippie-dippie liberal that I am so very proud to be realize, for the sake of the innocent (slaves), that maybe *some wars* like the war thrown in Lincoln's lap, are actually necessary. Did this mean I was becoming, God forbid, practical or just getting older, losing naivety and innocence I never had? I knew from long ago that Lincoln once asked why it was no one asked a slave's opinion whether they wanted to be a slave but now I had a new understanding of why he thought in that compassionate way. Maybe his suffering helped him, and maybe that's why he knew the voice of a slave was *the only voice that mattered.*

Within a month of a floating mother's daughter telling me I was depressed, I was sitting with a therapist who helped me discover a myriad of issues I was dealing with and how to understand them. After hearing of my experience with slavery/cancer and seeing what it had done to the two people I loved most in the world, she said that, in addition to my being, "probably prone to depression," that my personal history contributed to my having a condition similar to post traumatic stress disorder. She said that so many people who suffered from mental illness ended up self-medicating themselves with drugs and alcohol to numb their pain. I told her I'd tried that but it only made things worse and I despised the after-effects so much it wasn't worth it. And besides, I'd learned long ago that those things affected the quality of my meditations and nothing but nothing was worth messing with the precious peace that gave me. She said my dedication to physical fitness, meditation, and curiosity to understand were most likely the reasons I didn't slip into deeper mental distress and that I was truly blessed to have those things.

She prescribed an antidepressant I hated the thought of taking because I don't like taking an aspirin if I can avoid it, but said I didn't have to take it forever and it might give me a chance to "catch my breath." So I took it for almost a year and it helped tremendously with sleep and my overall dealings with life and society in general. It gave me a breather until I felt the time was right to stop taking it. I never went back to it but would have no qualms if I felt the need. I was getting older and life was flying by, and I wanted to fight again, to contribute, to show thanks for the life and country I had by somehow helping to speed up Catton's woeful prediction. I was rediscovering purpose and feeling inklings of my two favorite emotions: *gratitude* and *conviction*. I wanted to give back what Dave and Judi had given to me, but I didn't know how.

Rising From
The Ashes

In late 1999, at my local North Shore Roundtable meeting, a speaker called in sick at the last minute so an officer from the Boston Civil War Roundtable volunteered to give an impromptu talk about why the South went to war. I was so excited that finally the cause of the war would be discussed. This officer, a dear friend now, who still wears Rebel flag pajamas that I didn't know about at the time, talked about states' rights being the reason the war was fought and that slavery had absolutely nothing to do with it. I couldn't believe it! I heard the music of the old *Twilight Zone* with Rod Serling as he spoke. When he said Lincoln didn't care one way or another about slaves, I immediately thought of Frederick Douglass saying that Lincoln was the first white man who ever treated him as an equal, and about how Lincoln asked Douglass to go on a secret covert mission in 1864 to get as many slaves out of the Confederacy as possible, because he thought he might lose the next election and wouldn't be able to help any escape after that. I also thought about Mary Lincoln coming home from the "freedman's camps" that'd been set up in Washington for ex-slaves who'd escaped bondage, and telling her husband that half the new

414

babies there were named Abraham. These newly free people trusted Lincoln and no one wept harder than they when a lover of slavery/cancer killed him, and that had to count for something, I thought. So did the fact that when Mary's ex-slave seamstress Elizabeth Keckley, who knew Lincoln personally, wrote of his death, she wrote the South, "murdered the Moses of my people." Enough things to fill an encyclopedia were going through my mind, and my friend Jimmy nudged me, "You can't let this go. You have to say something!"

When the talk ended my hand shot up like it was pushed and pulled at the same time, maybe by Dave and Judi. I was shaking like a leaf but somehow I asked, "If the war was about states' rights, could the speaker please give three or four examples of rights the Lincoln administration was threatening to take away from the South?" When there was no response, I asked for two and then one and still no response. The truth was and always has been that there are none to give, yet to this day those who wear Reb pajamas insist there are, but can't tell what they are. The ultimate irony is that, when you read the letters of Jeff Davis to his slave state governors and Robert E. Lee, it's crystal clear that nobody argued more *against* states' rights and more *for* the need of a strong central government than Davis and Lee. Lee even made an example of some North Carolina officers by having them executed when they used the excuse of state's rights to justify their refusal to cross into Maryland in 1862. He told his army that anyone else who tried using this argument would suffer the same fate. The bottom line is when the speaker said Lincoln didn't care about "the one thing" (Lincoln's words) causing all the suffering in his nation, he was so very wrong. I couldn't help but think of a letter Lincoln wrote to Joshua Speed in 1855, where he said that the thought of people in chains "is a constant torment to me!"

I had more questions. I asked the speaker, if the war wasn't about slavery, then why did every southern governor, senator, and congressman say over and over that it was the only reason they were fighting, and explain that fact to their citizens in resolutions and ordinances so there'd be no confusion? Isn't that why Lincoln said, *"All knew slavery 'somehow' caused the war."*? Was the speaker's speech an example of the denial of reality Bruce Catton was talking about? I had no doubt! My questions made the room quiet except for some nervous shuffling of feet and people smiling at me with the "go for it" look, which surprised the hell out of me. Suddenly the gavel cracked, thereby ending the meeting. Somehow I opened a can of worms I never knew existed. Before Jim and I left some wise seventy- and eighty-year-old owls, who were caretakers of the Civil War museum where we have our meetings, who always sat silently observing in the back, told me that every time the subject of slavery came up in the past it caused certain people to argue but no one was arguing now. One owl asked, "Hey kid, can you give us a speech sometime?" I couldn't believe it. I told the president, a great guy and seeker of truth, that someone suggested I give a speech, and he said, "It's a good idea."

On my way home the task of writing a speech seemed possible, but speaking it to an audience terrified me. So I reached for my lifeline and cranked the radio and Dear Lord God thank you, the opening notes of Jimi's "Voodoo Child"—I hope someone plays it loud enough for Dave and Judi to hear at my funeral—came on and reminded me of when I was little and of my mother saying that if the South had won, Jackie Robinson and Willie Mays wouldn't have been able to play baseball. Now I realized Jimi wouldn't have been able to be Jimi and that made me angry, not a good emotion but an honest one. Another part of my spirit that'd been dead for the twenty years since Judi died began rising from the ashes when Jimi sang, *"chopping down mountains"* with *"the edge of my hand, turning them into islands"* and *"raising grains of sand."* His metaphors were Dave telling me to turn mountains of dangerous, unhealthy rhetoric into grains of truth with the edge of historical fact because *when the powerful lie, everyone suffers.*

Somehow in 2000 I found myself giving my first speech, titled "How To Understand The American Civil War," to a packed house in the Leominster Civil War museum, because bombing out there wouldn't be like bombing in front of my hometown. I worked on it night and day for many months and was shaking in my boots until I got in front of the crowd. Out of the blue I felt like I was playing music so I knew if I played it honestly, staying within my range, that I might do all right. I touched on as many political issues of slavery that I could in less than an hour, from 1776 through 1865. When I was done people applauded more than I thought I deserved and more than half, including all the old owls of their roundtable, stood. It blew me away. People asked for business cards I didn't have and where I was speaking next and if I could speak to their group. I couldn't believe it. A ninety-year-old guy, whom I'd grow to admire very much, said he'd been waiting his whole life for someone to tell the truth about the war. It made me think of Dave and Judi because truth was what they were all about.

I got very emotional in an overwhelmingly grateful way when a person in his thirties, in a gray Reb coat, approached and said, "That was a speech an abolitionist would like."

I said, "Thank you very much. I consider that a great honor."

"It wasn't a goddamned compliment. I consider your speech an insult," and he stormed off.

An owl heard the exchange and said of the insulted aristocrat, "He thinks he wishes the South won the war. There's Rebel wannabes in all these clubs and the farther south you go, the thicker they get. Please speak to us again and don't let guys like that bother you."

On the way home I thought about the Reb wannabe and realized the reason these clubs had such a large, yet still minority, percentage of them was because where else were they going to go? I never had issues with the real Rebs because, again, I would've been one had I grown up in the antebellum South. And then I thought of Virginia's famous history professor and author, James "Bud" Robertson, who was deeply sympathetic to the South, and who'd recently spoken at the annual Oliver Wendell Holmes dinner for all the roundtables of Massachusetts. He said, "Knowing what we know today, you'd have to be a lunatic to defend what the South was fighting for." I couldn't have agreed more, but the critical point he left out was that that was precisely Lincoln's, Grant's, Douglass's, Sumner's, Garrison's, and millions of others' sentiments back then. It's so bizarre how Robertson's words and even the words of Davis, Lee, Stonewall, and Stuart can't persuade today's Reb wannabes to change their opinions. Maybe they're just addicted to nonsense?

Soon, our roundtable hosted a wannabe Reb to give a speech. He happened to be a high school history teacher. I saw him in the parking lot outside the museum and he had a Reb flag on his front license plate. *Here we go,* I thought. He boasted of being a lifelong Civil War buff, then proceeded to buff the reality of the war to make it soft, smooth, and pleasant to look at, to take down from a mantel to emphasize one's superior intellect. He glossed over the nightmare dimensions of the war to make the rough, ugly, bloody hide skinned from a still-breathing bull into something velvety and clean. The South, in his mind, was pure, without fault, and slavery had nothing to do with it.

Here was my favorite kind of wannabe Reb because all you have to do is give 'em a podium. There's tens of thousands just like him in the Civil War community. The only problem, besides them procreating, is this one was a history teacher. The can of worms I'd opened a few months prior made our members (even little old ladies) ask him pesky questions that'd once been forbidden. They registered strong objections to his cherry picking of his partial facts ideology.

Every time I heard a speech like his, blaming the North for the mess, saying slavery was "dying out," I'd think of Dr. Young showing me X-rays with a growing cancer in Judi's head. Dear Lord, the reality was that in the slave states with a population of 5,000,000 free whites and 4,000,000 slaves, the 1850 U.S. census recorded 347,525 families owning slaves, and by 1860 that number grew to 385,000; a huge increase of 37,475 new families becoming the proud owners of people in just ten years. So slavery wasn't "dying out," but was growing stronger while the laws to protect it more brutal and sadistic. It was taught in every southern school and preached from every pulpit as the all-American dream, like the two-car garage and a chicken in every pot. One hundred percent of whites in the South and a minute number of free blacks and Indians could legally buy black people, but no one, regardless of color, could buy a white one.

When wannabe Rebs say the South was only fighting for the right to secede, I think of the Confederate constitution being written and South Carolina Senator James Chesnut (Mary's husband) suggesting that, if they really believed in secession, they should put it in their new constitution for the world to see. Remarkably, but not surprisingly, they voted down his proposal 11 to 1, with only James voting for it. This astonishing hypocrisy reveals that the United States and the Confederacy *were both against secession.* The South never fought for the right to secede; it fought to secede so it could grow a slave nation two-thirds larger than the one they thought they had; where the right to own people would remain sacred.

My speeches were making it apparent to people that I admired Abraham Lincoln very much, warts and all. Somehow I became the go-to guy when we were contacted by a local high school, college, or cable show that wanted to do a program on him. I never felt remotely qualified, and still don't, but I didn't mind sharing what I knew to be true; that simply, he did what he thought was right for the country. One of the basic things I asked Reb wannabes who criticized him was, "Knowing what Lincoln knew when he knew it, without our 150 years of hindsight, what would you have done differently than he did to save the nation he was sworn to protect?" I can't think of a single time a reply wasn't something like, "Well, I can't think of anything I'd do differently," which is the right answer if there is such a thing for a question like that. Then I'd tell them something that might be valuable for everyone who loves America.

In my humble opinion, if there's anyone in world history who has earned the benefit of doubt, it's Lincoln. When you give him that, you can safely go into the issues people criticized him for then and now and see that what he did and said, even if it rubs our modern sensibilities the wrong way, which is a good thing, that he nearly always had a rational reason designed to move the modern sensibilities of *his* time forward. Beyond a doubt, in the cause of freedom, he moved too slowly for some and too fast for others, but unlike many of the slow or fast, he *never, ever* took a step backward once he'd taken one forward. How many of us can say that? I can't!

As my reawakening passion for living was taking small steps forward it was about to take a giant one backward, but my mother's indomitable spirit wouldn't permit it.

My brother John and I had just pulled off a surprise fiftieth wedding anniversary party for our parents. As we watched them walk up the stairs of a rented hall they didn't know was filled with relatives, long-lost army buddies, teachers, and friends from the old neighborhood we noticed our mom looked very tired. Within a month she'd be dead; a victim of a brutally fast pancreatic cancer. She'd been my everything, my go-to guy since Judi died and if I was ever confused about anything she helped me figure it out. We talked daily. She'd been getting the biggest kick out of me speaking to history clubs and societies. I'd recently said to her, "Ma, when I get good at this you have to come see me!" but it was too late. Thankfully my dad would see me.

Just before I gave my very first speech I asked her if she had any advice. She said, "Don't bullshit anybody and if you don't know the answer to a question, say 'I don't know'!" A week before she died I asked if she could remember when I first became interested in the Civil War and she said, "I can't remember a time when you weren't and you always had a soft spot for the South. You understood their cause was wrong but that good and bad people were on both sides."

The hospital Chaplain, a Catholic priest and really good guy, had long conversations with her in her last days. I met him in the hall after one of these conversations and he told me he'd never met anyone so interesting. The next day I walked in as he was giving her the last rites and she winked at me as if to say, "I'm letting him do this for his sake, not mine."

After he left she whispered, "I think the poor bastard is more upset about this than I am."

"Well what do you think of all this, Ma?"

She said, "It's too incredible to describe!"

When she died I had the honor of holding her hand as she took her last breath. My love for music and history came from her. And she gave me a sense of fairness with a desire to never take advantage of anyone. She's how I *know* all are created equal.

Between 2000 and 2003 my speaking engagements were numerous. The intense preparation and rehearsal, like music, seemed to keep my depression at bay but still it crept up on me. It's such an overpowering, awful feeling I wouldn't wish on anyone. Those who think you can simply snap out of it have never experienced it. Sometimes you just sit on the couch and stare at a piece of dust for hours because that's all you have the strength to do. People who don't know what I mean are lucky. But somehow each speech was like a gig I did in England and the States where I only played songs I wrote, so I had to get off the couch. Historical societies outside the Civil War community began offering me money to speak but I'd never accept it. I'd always donate it back with the stipulation that, if they found an iota of value in what they heard, they should "spread the word!" And somehow I was elected vice president of Massachusetts' North Shore General Lander Civil War Roundtable, where I still am. It's an incredible honor.

The themes of my speeches then got a huge infusion of knowledge at one of my clubs frequent dollar raffles. I won *The Complete Works of Abraham Lincoln*. They contain his speeches, letters, state papers, and miscellaneous writings edited by his secretaries John G. Nicolay and John Hay in 1894. Of course a tremendous amount has been discovered since then, but to me, it all reinforces what's in *The Works*. Before I read them I tried my best to put aside everything I knew about Lincoln and the war and to learn about him and the war from his perspective. I wouldn't be relying on a historian's interpretation but could make my own. I spent the next two years doing it. All through the process I'd laugh, remembering my old ex-Reb friend Mark Twain saying that after you gather all the facts you can, you can distort them however you want.

But, what I found in "the long and short of it"—how Lincoln introduced himself at six-foot-four and his wife at five-foot-four, which got on Mary's nerves—was that so many historians had it right. I felt that for my whole life it'd been fascinating and sacred to learn about him through the war and his times, and now I could learn about the war and his world through him. It made my understanding feel balanced, like how I first understood music, at the feet of my Uncle Joe, to where I was now in the studio seeing how a master statesman became one.

Thousands of books describe Lincoln far better than I ever could but if I could say one thing, it'd be that somehow I'd been right all along to trust him. For here was a politician the people of the United States could trust like I trusted Dave and Judi.

In the Lincoln/Douglas debates he not only asked free men of Illinois and Sangamon County but "free men everywhere" to judge him by what he said, did, and how he voted "upon this issue," that of slavery. And said, the *only* way he could be "misunderstood" was if he was "misrepresented." It made a powerful impact on me. That he'd forever be tickling my funny bone was an added bonus. This reasonable man from the most unreasonable of times would lead me to something that *never,* in a million years, would I ever imagine: that I'd soon be rubbing elbows with America's greatest Lincoln historians and scholars by becoming a lifetime member of two clubs that studied him and his times.

A fellow Lincoln admirer and officer from the Boston Roundtable invited me to a dinner meeting of the Lincoln Group of Boston. This is a club of mostly New England–based college history professors, a few English professors, high school teachers, both current and retired, and a smattering of amateurs like me. When I walked in I was one of the youngest there. Men wore suits and ties and the ladies wore professional outfits. I had on sneakers, dungarees, and a flannel shirt so I felt like a jerk but somehow, strangely, not totally uncomfortable like I always do in social settings. They looked at me in a curious, friendly way. Dressed like a slob I found a corner in back to be as obscure as I could while I listened to these wonderful people telling Lincoln jokes and stories over dinner. They were excited about newly discovered Lincoln documents just like new records by The Beatles, The Stones, and Jimi had excited me and Dave all those years ago. I thought that maybe I'd died and gone to heaven.

Somehow I related to everything I heard from these professional truth seekers who made careers of sharing what they found, but no one was paying them today. They were like musicians playing music they play for themselves after the club closes. After dinner and a marvelous talk by an author on a book tour promoting his latest on the Emancipation Proclamation, a question, answer, and comment period followed, where pesky questions *were encouraged.* Every answer was backed up by reason, which left freedom for welcome debate and opinion. These weren't wannabes but real deals. I felt like I was back in England in the corner listening to my honest-to-their-souls Hartismere Confederates, paying homage to American music the way it was meant to be paid with the same rules applying. Historical facts were supported by others like instruments in tune with each other so they could play against or go with the flow to reach back to Beethoven's 5th through Abraham Lincoln's "House Divided" to Robert Johnson's "Crossroads." When things are right you can feel them, Judi had taught me. Could I once again jump in on bass?

My heart was pounding because I'll never truly know if I'm just a wanker but my hand got pulled up by that unknown force. I asked if I could comment on the subject matter and when the speaker said, "Of course," I went for it. When I thought I'd said too much I said, "I'm sorry if I've said too much," and a professor turned around and said, "Please keep going, young man." I wasn't a young man but I did, and when I finished I apologized for the clothes I had on and another professor turned around and said, "If you join our club we'll dress like that at out next meeting," and they laughed. I've been a more properly dressed member ever since and I still feel like a crude self-educated rock musician who somehow gets to play with the maestros every once in awhile, even though over the years, the professors have assured me, "Don't be afraid to make a point, you know your stuff!"

They have more historical knowledge in one finger than I do in my whole body but every now and then I'd play a melody they'd never heard before and I'd hear, "You should consider writing about your perspective," which seemed ludicrous because I thought I did nothing more than state the obvious. Somehow though, despite my depression or whatever the heck is wrong with me, that always makes me feel like an imposter, I loved going to Brown, Roger Williams, Harvard, Bridgewater, and a host of other places with them. It felt and still feels so right being among friends of Lincoln.

When the professors suggested I check out a collection of historians and authors from around the globe, who met every November for a three- or four-day symposium in Pennsylvania called The Lincoln Forum of Gettysburg, I got tickets for Jim and me because the keynote address was to be given by one of my all-time favorites, James McPherson, the Pulitzer Prize–winning author of 1988's *Battle Cry of Freedom*. It is the single best book about the cause and course of the war ever written, in my opinion. My mom read it and said McPherson had it just right.

Entering The Forum in the main function room of Gettysburg's Holiday Inn felt like walking into London's Marquee Club for the first time. I wasn't among musicians who made records I admired, but was among historians who explained *how* the world became the way it is. My admiration for each was exactly the same because their passion for their art *is* the same. *Dear Lord,* I thought, *there's something in this world for everyone to be passionate about and once again I am among the passionate.*

On their roster from past and present were Michael Beschloss, Gabor Borrit, Ken Burns, Mario Cuomo, Jean Edward Smith, Richard Nelson Current, William C. Davis, David Herbert Donald, Eric Foner, Gary Gallagher, William Gienapp, Doris Kearns Goodwin, James McPherson, Edna Greene Medford, John Marsalek, Mark Neely Jr., Stephen Oates, John Y. Simon, Edward Steers Jr.,

Craig Symonds, Tom Turner, Michael Kaufman, Tom Horrocks, Joe Fornieri, and several hundred others who over the next few years I'd either meet and have dinner with or spill gravy on their shoes. And God forbid, those who heard my perspective told me to write about it. The president, Frank Williams, and vice president, Harold Holzer, both great authors and historians, are the crème de la crème of graciousness. Somehow I was in a sacred place where facts mattered!

THE MOTHER
OF ALL OF US

I walked the battlefields and streets of Gettysburg between lectures and was drawn into the cutest little book shop. It felt peculiar seeing authors I'd been listening to on the shelves. In the children's section was a Civil War coloring book with a sparkling clean Yank and Reb on the cover shaking hands as if they'd just finished a game of croquet. Civil War chess, checkers, and card games were there and I wondered if they had a monopoly game with a "get out of bondage" card in it. The adult section had books about *The Gray Fox* (Lee) and *The Gray Ghost* (Mosby) and I wondered if there was a cookbook about *Gray Brisket*. I bought a book about Willie Pegram, the young, brilliant artillery officer in Lee's army who was killed as the war was winding down. I'd enjoy learning more about that brave, near-sighted little Reb. He epitomized everything good, bad, and ugly about the Confederacy. Then, just before I left a miracle happened, and a book purchased me.

It was *Hidden Witness* by author Jackie Napoleon Wilson, a grandson of an ex-slave. It was a collection of daguerreotype images of slaves passed down through the ages. I had a hard time looking at the cover because it was the most real image I'd ever seen. It was of a mother holding her baby during the war, entitled "Madonna." Her eyes, more than anyone from the lunatic wannabe fringe to all the seasoned professors and authors who are serious about this stuff, said more about slavery than any book or speech ever written. She knew the South was wrong, not from any education or because she was a slave, but because she was a mother. Dear Lord, I knew this look intimately through the privilege of being raised by a musician, history teacher mother and having an honest, courageous beyond measure, soldier brother, and to have been the husband of a woman who floated the earth, who only touched ground to do good. For Judi had had the same look in her eyes, knowing cancer was separating her from her baby. So this "Madonna" deserved more than a casual look and to then be put back on the shelf. She deserved the common courtesy to be looked at because, God help me; *she is the mother of all of us.*

The more I looked, the more beautiful she became. Her face, her neck, hair, skin, sadness, her longing for freedom, her baby, clothes, demeanor, bearing, composure, kindness, understanding, generosity, strength, forgiveness, her humanness cloaked in femininity and motherhood made me want to know who could find it in their heart to look at her and say the Confederacy was justified in any way whatsoever. My old desire to protect kicked in because I knew men had looked upon her in not so honorable a fashion. Hers was the look of Judi knowing cancer/slavery was taking away all she loved. So Lincoln was right: The war wasn't about "dollars and cents." It was about decency, fairness, and dignity.

In a perfect world where everyone would have the courage and love my brother David had, people would look and she'd be able to tell them the truth, that "This thing slavery, that they call 'a school of virtue,' murdered my baby's father because he wanted to love her. They did so under a red flag with thirteen stars that say, 'I have and you don't, I can read and you can't, I own my children and I own yours, I can marry and if I allow you to I can do with your spouse as I please, I can sit at the altar and you must sit in back if I let you come to church, I can rape you, sell you and your baby and you can do nothing about it. I can pursue life, liberty, and happiness, you can't. I can hang, disembowel, and set your men on fire in front of your children. You have no rights I am bound to respect; our sacred Confederate constitution guarantees it. Your fate is instituted by God. If you were my equal you'd understand but you're only my property." But the world isn't perfect so Madonna will say to me:

"Here I am. This isn't right and somehow, you know it. The people who own me and my baby don't see it that way so there's nothing you can do. But we have seen each other and I can see you've experienced something that makes you *feel* the world we live in. It has inspired you to look and that is more than most, who pass us by or steal a glance as they push us out of the way. But you've brought us to the window to take a closer look. Thank you, the sunlight feels good. To most we're a distraction and that's the sadness of your generation, but you're different so let me ask, can you see this baby is all that is precious to me? All I ever wanted was to hold her, to watch her grow as your mother watched you, but my expression tells you I'm not encouraged to hope for that. Somehow you understand that I love as any mother loves, and I mourn as any mother mourns. I want my baby to see the beauty in this world and not the sadness *mine eyes have seen* every second of every day. My only wish is for my child to live free. And if freedom means living without me, *'Let It Be!'* Show her this image and tell her I was not a slave who was her mother but I was her mother who was enslaved. And somehow, with the grace of God, teach her to have 'malice toward none,' not even to her oppressors."

I returned to my room with Madonna close to my breast and looked out a window located between where Lincoln spoke of "a new birth of freedom" and a battlefield where innocent, brainwashed kids in Gray gave their lives saying, "We don't want that!" It was Remembrance Day weekend so I watched as thousands of Blue and Gray reenactors from around the nation arrived to march in the annual parade. I laughed, thinking how ironic it was seeing an overly plump family of Rebs emerge from a Lincoln . . . Continental. I wondered if the Confederate mother and father told their round little belles how real Rebs were so starving they sometimes picked out pieces of undigested vegetables from piles of horse, mule, and donkey shit in order to kill those yellow-bellied Yankees trying to steal "everything worth living for." These were Lee's words. And I thought of the time a wannabe Reb lady said to me after I spoke to her club that we shouldn't take the war so personally because times were different back then; that, "Slavery was an accepted thing and not as big a deal or as painful as it would be today."

Gently I asked, "Why is that? Do you think it hurt a slave mother any less than it would you to have her child taken away forever for no reason except the benefit of someone else? Doesn't it say in Ecclesiastes there's truly nothing new under the sun? So how was slavery different than it would be today?" Her statement wasn't so much her fault because maybe she hadn't *experienced* slavery or had been taught a lie about it. Then I asked, "If we shouldn't take the lessons of our Civil War seriously, in a personal, teaching way"—*which is fun and liberating for crying out loud,* I thought—"what part of our history should we take seriously? For what we say about the war says very little about the war but everything about us!"

Lincoln knew the war and its cause could teach us everything we needed to know to keep America strong. But what could a person like me contribute to help people who still didn't understand, despite historians having explained the gory forensics so well? I felt like giving up when I felt Judi's spirit.

"Sweetheart, you can help fix this or die trying. It's why I married you!"

"How?" I asked.

"By helping *our* 'wayward brethren' *feel* what it's like to lose their hopes, dreams, and most of all the ones they love to slavery."

"But Jude, how can I do that? I'm no historian."

"But you have a story to sing!"

"Yeah, but that'd be an invasion of yours and Dave's privacy."

"Oh sweetheart, we're way beyond that. We just want you to know if you're going to persist in thinking you haven't contributed anything to the world, this is your second chance. Our grandchildren deserve to know their family's history is their country's."

"What grandchildren?"

"The ones we haven't had yet but are coming. Tell them there's never been slavery or bigotry in heaven and that the reason the *Our Father* has the line, 'On earth as it is in heaven' is because there's no place or time where slavery was ever right! Teach them to meditate toward 'the better angels' of their nature so they'll know the story of their ancestors can help someone who doesn't know it, to know it!

Tell them to ask all the pesky questions they need to, to find truth and their lives will be exciting, fun, and interesting. Tell them about your music and love of history and what you've lost and what the world loses every time slavery wins. Tell them how you *feel* about God and everything."

"But Jude, I don't know what God is!"

"Oh darling, that's the point. But you know what God isn't. *God isn't slavery!* And sweetheart, don't be afraid to offend older people in your old age. There's no fool like an old fool, but they're so few in number compared to the forever young in spirit, whatever their age. And there's no man or woman alive who's lost a wife, husband, sibling, or child to cancer or war who won't be on your side because slavery really *is* cancer and if you don't tell it the way you can, who will?"

"But Jude, what if I get it wrong?"

"You can't get it wrong because your intent is pure. And always know; I fell in love with you because no matter what you did I could *feel* that somewhere deep inside you it never mattered if there was a God ruling the universe because somehow you knew if God exists; God is just . . ."

AFTERWORD

In 2001, Anna married a great guy who is now my mountain biking partner. With the house to myself I built a small digital recording studio to record songs with personal, biographical themes. By 2002, I had ten recorded and was also giving a steady stream of speeches inside and outside the Civil War community, where I kept hearing I should write a book about my ideas. In no way, shape, or form was I a writer, but I put pen to paper anyway because somewhere deep, I needed to. Immediately I realized it had to be a full-time job if I was ever to get anything done so I told the musicians I was recording with that I'd be taking a year off to write a book, never dreaming it would take ten.

I went at it with all my strength, reliving long forgotten joys and sorrows while uncovering memories I'd never been able to face before. Writing about Dave and Judi gave me the courage to persevere until I hit a roadblock of emotions that made me feel like I couldn't go on. But then, a "teacher" arrived on Nov 23, 2004, when Anna and her husband put Judi's granddaughter in my arms. I fell so deeply in love with this new little friend and became both her grandfather and grandmother because she deserved a piece of Judi that only I could give.

Everyone said they'd never seen me so happy. Maybe the comfort of knowing I'd leave the planet long before her let me love her without reservation, or maybe it's simply because she's the granddaughter of a woman who floated the earth. Maybe I wanted her to understand how her grandmother felt the world meant nothing could stop my writing. Her parents entrusted me to care for her as much as I could while they worked so I literally rocked her with my foot as I wrote.

In 2008, GE was offering early retirements and I jumped on it. I never had, wanted, nor needed much money to live on and had plans on going to college to get my degree in history. But, the thought of taking care of my little friend almost full time was too powerful to resist. It was my wisest decision since asking Judi to marry me, and the rewards have been beyond description. When her little sister came in 2010 to ice the cake I was the happiest I've ever been and that would please Dave and Judi more than anyone. I'd been writing and rewriting for seven years without a day off and finally had a much too long, far too detailed manuscript. I then taught myself to type and had thirty copies of the 667-page beast printed to share with family, friends from Mass Civil War Roundtables, the Lincoln Group of Boston and Lincoln Forum of Gettysburg, most notably Tom Turner and Tom Horrocks, incredible historian/ authors, and others too. They, along with supporters like Jim Tilden, Nadine Mironchuk, Richard Briggs, Dave Provanzano, Dexter Bishop, Jeff Fioravanti, Al and Dave Smith, Joyce Kelly, Dick and Joan Swanson, Harv and Winnie Robinson, DeLane Anderson, Larry Cambell, Rich Cultrera, Liam Brady, Dr. Alan Smolinski, George Patrikas, Debra Johnson, Virginia Troisi, Jeff Wignall, Bob Matthias, Ed Gerard, Herb Comeau (three trustees of the Civil War museum in Lynn), and librarians where I'd given speeches, encouraged me to pursue this with all my might. All gave the same advice, that my voice deserved a place at the table and the right editor could help me find what I needed to say as opposed to what I wanted to say.

My cousin Adrianne, Uncle Joe's niece, a professional writer who'd read the manuscript, told me about the Grub St. Writer's Association of Boston, which could help me find a compatible editor. There were a dozen on their website, and I read things they either wrote or edited. All were excellent but when Stuart Horwitz agreed to work with me I was overjoyed. When he heard my music on a visit to my home he told me to think of words like notes on a piano and to use the musical part of my mind as we worked on the story.

By 2010 we were tossing the manuscript back and forth. Slowly his suggestions and guidance made my overly ambitious, cob-webbed bundle of passion and history evolve into a breathing spiderweb of clarity in three dimensions, making it human. I learned he was the senior editor at Book Architecture and the author of a book called *Blueprint Your Best Seller,* which explains how to organize and revise a manuscript using the Book Architecture method. So I had lucked out. I became the bull to his red cape and that's what I wanted. When we brought the story as far as we could he introduced me to copyeditor, Linda Feldman, who breathed additional life into it with her insightful, delicate touch and then to editor and publication coordinator, Chloe Marsala to ice the cake. Passion had always brought creative people my way; now it brought editors and friends. Any professionalism found in the telling of this story is due entirely to them.

Today, in 2015, I'm pleased that someone who's trying to slow the decimation of the middle class and lift the downtrodden is into his second term as our president. It troubled me deeply that in the last months of his re-election campaign, his opponent, who didn't seem to care if children were listening, kept accusing him of spreading a message of hate. It reminded me of the aristocratic nonsense Confederates said of Lincoln. It wasn't true then and it's not true today!

I hope to live a couple more decades on this beautiful speck of dirt floating through the universe and do so with my girls, where I've never been so happy. So much amazes me in the fountain of youth fields of music, history and science that continue to reveal there's so much more to things than we know. History tells it's always been so and always will be. For me, meditation is the key to perspective.

Lincoln said every generation has its wise and foolish among it and where I fit in that equation doesn't matter, but I've had my say. And somehow, it's brought Dave and Judi back into my life in ways that take my breath away.

Now, if someone should see two little blond sisters at the Shawsheen playground in Wilmington, Massachusetts, and the older one is pointing to an old man (in decent shape though) and she's saying to her friends—true story—"That's our grandfather. He used to be in a band," it might be me. Otherwise we'll be at a little shop on Mass Avenue in Arlington called The Chilly Cow that has the best homemade ice cream in town. The girls will be eating flavors their grandmother loved! My only goal for the rest of my days is to be as present as I can be for all of it, and maybe find out what kind of music is left in these old bones.

AUTHOR'S NOTE

Some of the quotes in this story have been reproduced verbatim from the historical record. Others, however, have been constructed from the record, historical tradition, lore, popular accepted anecdotes and supposition. The liberty to paraphrase has also been taken to bring into focus, in contemporary terms, the way in which human sentiment is the perpetual binding of the ages. Nothing has been exaggerated or taken out of the political or social context of the times the original words were spoken. Please refer to the bibliography for the origins of the individual quotes.

BIBLIOGRAPHY

Angle, Paul M. & Miers, Earl S. (editors). *The Living Lincoln*. Barnes & Noble, Inc. 1992

Austin, James C. *Bill Arp*. New York: Twayne Publishers, Inc. 1903

Benjamin, Thomas P. *Abraham Lincoln*. New York: Alfred A. Knopf. 1952

Bohm, David & Krishnamurti, Jiddu. *The Limits Of Thought*. New York: Routledge. 1999

Boritt, Gabor S. (editor). *Why The Confederacy Lost*. (Essays by various historians) New York: Oxford University Press. 1992

Boritt, Gabor S. (editor). *Why The War Came*. (Essays by various historians) New York: Oxford University Press. 1996

Carmichael, Peter S. *Lee's Young Artillerist: William R. J. Pegram*. Virginia: University Press of Virginia. 1995

Catton, Bruce. *The Centennial History Of The Civil War*. (3-volume set) Garden City, N. Y.: Doubleday & Co. 1961–1965

Catton, Bruce. *Mr. Lincoln's Army*. Garden City, N. Y.: Doubleday & Co. 1951

Catton, Bruce. *Reflections On The Civil War.* Garden City, N. Y.: Doubleday & Co. 1981

Catton, Bruce. *A Stillness At Appomattox.* Garden City, N. Y.: Doubleday & Co. 1953

Coffin, Charles Carleton. *The Boys Of '61.* Boston: Estes & Lauriat. 1896

Cooper, J. William. *Jefferson Davis, American.* New York: Alfred A. Knopf. 2000

Current, Richard N. *The Lincoln Nobody Knows.* New York: Hill & Wang. 1958

Davis, Jefferson F. *The Rise and Fall of the Confederate Government.* New York: D Appleton & Co. 1881

Davis, William C. *"A Government Of Our Own": The Making Of The Confederacy.* New York: The Free Press. 1994

Donald, David Herbert. *Charles Sumner And The Coming Of The Civil War.* Illinois: Sourcebooks Inc. 1989

Donald, David Herbert. *Lincoln.* New York: Simon & Schuster. 1995

Douglass, Frederick. *An American Slave.* Boston: Published at the Anti-Slavery Office No. 25 Cornhill, 1845. Republished, Barnes & Noble 2003

Farewell, Bryon. *Stonewall.* New York: W. W. Norton & Company. 1993

Foner, Eric. *The Fiery Trial: Abraham Lincoln and American Slavery.* New York: W. W. Norton & Company, Inc. 2010

Foner, Eric. *Reconstruction: America's Unfinished Journey, 1863-1877.* New York: Harper & Row, 1988

Foote, Shelby. *The Civil War: A Narrative.* (3-volume set) New York: Random House. 1958, 1963 & 1974

Freeman, Douglas Southall. *Lee.* 1934. Republished by Collier Books. New York: 1993

Gallagher, Gary (editor). *Fighting For The Confederacy: The Personal Recollections Of General Edward Porter Alexander.* Chapel Hill: The University of North Carolina Press. 1989

Glatthaar, Joseph T. *Forged In Battle: The Civil War Alliance of Black Soldiers and White Officers.* New York: The Free Press. 1990

Goldstein, Joseph. *Insight Meditation.* Boston: Shambhala. 1993

Goodwin, Doris Kearns. *Team Of Rivals: The Political Genius Of Abraham Lincoln*. New York: Simon & Schuster. 2005

Grant, Ulysses S. *The Personal Memoirs Of Ulysses S. Grant*. 1885. Republished, New York: Konecky & Konecky. 1980

Hesse, Hermann. *Siddhartha*. Germany: 1922. New York: New Directions (U. S.) 1951

Holzer, Harold. *Lincoln At Cooper Union: The Speech That Made Abraham Lincoln President*. New York: Simon & Schuster. 2006

Horrocks, Thomas A. *President James Buchanan And The Crisis Of National Leadership*. New York: Nova Science Publications Inc. 2012

Jennison, Keith W. *The Humorous Mr. Lincoln*. New York: Bonanza Books. 1955

Jones, John B. *A Rebel War Clerk's Diary*. 1866: New York: edited by Earl S. Miers and republished, Sagamore Press, Inc. 1958

Kantor, MacKinlay. *Andersonville*. Cleveland and New York: The World Publishing Company. 1955

Krishnamurti, Jiddu. *As One Is: To Be Free From All Conditioning*. New York: Harper/Collins. 2007

Krishnamurti, Jiddu. *The Awakening Of Intelligence*. Boston: Shambhala. 1973

Krishnamurti, Jiddu. *The Book Of Life: Daily Meditations*. New York: HarperOne. 1995

Krishnamurti, Jiddu. *Freedom From The Known*. Boston: Shambhala. 1969

Krishnamurti, Jiddu. *To Be Human*. Boston: Shambhala. 2000

Krishnamurti, Jiddu. *The Light In Oneself*. New York: Harper/Collins. 1999

Krishnamurti, Jiddu. *Think On These Things*. New York: Harper & Row. 1964

Krishnamurti, Jiddu. *Total Freedom: The Essential Krishnamurti*. New York: Harper/Collins. 1996

Krishnamurti, Jiddu. *On Relationship*. New York: Harper/Collins. 1992

Long, A. L. *Memoirs of Robert E. Lee: His Military and Personal History*. 1887

McPherson, James. *Battle Cry Of Freedom*. New York: Oxford University Press. 1988

McPherson, James. *Crossroads Of Freedom: Antietam*. New York: Oxford University Press. 2002

McPherson, James. *Drawn With The Sword: Reflections On The American Civil War.*

McPherson, James. *Tried By War: Abraham Lincoln As Commander In Chief.* New York: The Penguin Press. 2008

McPherson, James. *What They Fought For 1861-1865*. New York: Anchor Books. 1995

McPherson, James (editor). *"We Cannot Escape History"*. University of Illinois Press. 1995

Michener, James. *The Source*. New York: Random House. 1965

Miller, William Lee. *Arguing About Slavery: John Quincy Adams And The Great Battle In The United States Congress*. New York: A. Knopf, Inc. 1996

Morgan, Edmund S. *American Slavery, American Freedom: The Ordeal Of Colonial Virginia*. New York: W.W. Norton & Company. 1975

Neely, E. Mark. *The Last Best Hope Of Earth*. Massachusetts: Harvard University Press. 1993

Nicolay, John & Hay, John (editors). *Complete Works Of Abraham Lincoln*. New York: The Century Co. 1894

Oates, Stephen B. *Abraham Lincoln: The Man Behind The Myth*. New York: Harper & Row. 1984

Oates, Stephen B. *Lincoln's Greatest Speech: The Second Inaugural*. New York: Simon & Schuster. 2006

Oates, Stephen B. *With Malice Toward None: The Life Of Abraham Lincoln*. New York: New American Library. 1978

Pollard, Edward A. *Southern History Of The War.* Virginia: The Fairfax Press. 1877

Rand, Ayn. *Atlas Shrugged*. New York: Random House. 1957

Rothschild, Alonzo. *Lincoln: Master Of Men*. Boston: Houghton Mifflin. 1906

Royster, Charles. *The Destructive War.* New York: Vintage Books. 1993

Sandburg, Carl. *Abraham Lincoln: The Prairie Years*. (2-volume set) New York: Harcourt Brace. 1926

Sandburg, Carl. *Abraham Lincoln: The War Years.* (4-volume set) New York: Harcourt Brace. 1939

Stampp, Kenneth. *The Causes Of The Civil War.* Englewood Cliffs, N. J.: Prentice Hall Press, 1974

Stowe, Harriet Beecher. *Uncle Tom's Cabin.* 1852: New York: Republished, Barnes & Noble Books. 2003

Truth, Sojourner. *Narrative Of Sojourner Truth.* 1850. Republished, New York: Dover Publications, Inc. 1997

Turner, Thomas R. *Beware The Public Weeping: Public Opinion And The Assassination Of Abraham Lincoln.* Louisiana State University Press. 1991

Twain, Mark. *Wit and Wisecracks.* New York: Peter Pauper Press. 1998

Watkins, Sam R. *"Co. Aytch"* (1882 memoir of a Rebel Soldier). Republished, New York: Collier Books. 1962

Watts, Alan. *Myth And Ritual In Christianity.* New York: Simon & Schuster. 1954

Watts, Alan. *The Taboo Against Knowing Who You Are.* New York: Simon & Schuster. 1969

Watts, Alan. *This Is It.* New York: Simon & Schuster. 1962

Watts Alan. *The Way Of Liberation.* New York: Simon & Schuster. 1972

Welles, Gideon. *Lincoln's Administration: Selected Essays.* New York: Twayne Publishers. 1876-1878

Wheeler, Richard. *Voices Of The Civil War.* New York: Penguin Books. 1990

Wilentz, Sean. *The Rise Of American Democracy: Jefferson To Lincoln.* New York: W. W. Norton & Company. 2005

Wiley, Bell I. *The Life Of Johnny Reb: The Common Soldier Of The Confederacy.* Indianapolis: Bobbs-Merrill. 1943

Wiley, Bell I. *The Life Of Billy Yank: The Common Soldier Of The Union.* Indianapolis: Bobbs-Merrill. 1952

Williams, J. Frank. *Judging Lincoln.* Southern Illinois University Press. 2002

Wilson, Douglas L. *Honor's Voice: The Transformation Of Abraham Lincoln.* New York: Alfred A. Knoph. 1998

Wilson, Jackie Napoleon. *Hidden Witness.* New York: St. Martin's Griffin. 1999

Woodward, C. Vann (editor). *Mary Chestnut's Civil War.* 1861-1865: New Haven: Yale University Press. Republished 1981

Zinn, Howard. *A People's History Of The United States.* New York: Harper/Collins. 1999

CPSIA information can be obtained
at www.ICGtesting.com
Printed in the USA
LVOW03s2302060617
537196LV00001B/147/P